Second Life, Media, and the Other Society

Digital Formations

Steve Jones
General Editor

Vol. 58

PETER LANG
New York • Washington, D.C./Baltimore • Bern
Frankfurt • Berlin • Brussels • Vienna • Oxford

Phylis Johnson

Second Life, Media, AND THE Other Society

PETER LANG
New York • Washington, D.C./Baltimore • Bern
Frankfurt • Berlin • Brussels • Vienna • Oxford

Library of Congress Cataloging-in-Publication Data

Johnson, Phylis.
Second Life, media, and the other society / Phylis Johnson.
p. cm. — (Digital formations; v. 58)
Includes bibliographical references and index.
1. Second Life (Game) 2. Shared virtual environments. I. Title.
GV1469.25.S425J64 794.8—dc22 2010013823
ISBN 978-1-4331-0617-0 (hardcover)
ISBN 978-1-4331-0616-3 (paperback)
ISSN 1526-3169

Bibliographic information published by **Die Deutsche Nationalbibliothek**.
Die Deutsche Nationalbibliothek lists this publication in the "Deutsche Nationalbibliografie"; detailed bibliographic data is available on the Internet at http://dnb.d-nb.de/.

Cover art by Lowe Runo

The paper in this book meets the guidelines for permanence and durability of the Committee on Production Guidelines for Book Longevity of the Council of Library Resources.

29 Broadway, 18th floor, New York, NY 10006
www.peterlang.com

Printed in the United States of America

"What has been revolutionary about SL from the beginning is not the act of building something from nothing...but being able to do it together...While we cannot predict the future, it is clear that we have to continue expanding the bandwidth between us."

–Philip Rosedale (Linden), founder of Second Life, Opening Keynote Address, Second Life 6th Anniversary Celebration

CONTENTS

ACKNOWLEDGMENTS

I would like to thank the so many people I have met along the way during my journey through the virtual world of Second Life. First, I thank Kara Trapdoor for her wonderful gift of gab. She is definitely an explorer of Second Life, and she has sent many people my way for this book. Many of her contacts have been useful in generating sources for this book. I would like to thank my real-life husband, who resides with me in Second Life as Shock Soderstrom, and my two daughters Jennifer R. and Julianna W. for their patience and comic relief during this project. Always thanks to my father, Dr. Philip T. West (and his wife Alma), for inspiration along the way! Congrats to Nicholas and Jennifer on their upcoming marriage in RL Hawaii, a real-life fantasy. Nicholas, my son, preceded me on SL to help me get started! But he decided real life was much more fun.

I would like to also acknowledge the wonderful friendships I have made along the way, including that of Mel Orfein, who has the opportunity to walk, run, fly and dance in SL despite her real-life challenges. She is a brilliant young woman and RL/SL artist. I would also like to note my friendship to Dante Kiergarten, who has been a wonderful springboard from which to bounce off ideas and interpret SL experiences. Of course, this is the short list of people who have touched my real and Second life; it would be impossible to mention everyone that has made an impact in my lives—yes, lives as plural is an appropriate use in this case. There is a person behind every avatar, but sometimes we only know them as they choose to express themselves in SL. In a sense, a certain part of their life is validated inside Second Life. We are fellow travelers, exploring ourselves in this new world.

I have been pleased to meet so many people along the way during the making of this book, some of whom I have interviewed. Those featured in this book include: Trinidad Anatine, Josie Anderton, Hamlet Au, Matthaios Aquacade, Pennelope Bellic, Landis Desidero, Robustus Hax, Faith Hema, Draghan Marksman, Journey McLaglen, Toxic Menges, Frolic Mills, Brody Muircastle, Lowe Runo, Sher Salmson, Alesia Schumann, Resting Thor, Indea Vaher and MyGosh Yakan. These are their avatar names. But to me, they are real people whom I have connected with inside of Second Life. They have dreams and aspirations in both real and Second Life and should be considered forerunners to a future that has yet to be defined.

Even after the manuscript was in press, I met other wonderful people like Breezie Noel, Persia Bravin, Umberto Giano, Steven Dean, Maeve Strom, 2408 Alekseev, Douglas Story, Stretch Mayo, and Lingual Markus, especially through *Best of Second Life Magazine* and BOSL radio, the latter of which began in April 2010. All have helped me to understand that friendships and creativity can be nurtured in virtual worlds.

On that note, I would like to acknowledge the many talented musicians that strengthened the connection between the real and virtual live music scene through Chicagoland SL, which evolved into a social portal for virtual media performers and their audiences. I would also like to acknowledge the moderators and members of the Second Life Machinima Artist Guild for their guidance and contributions to this book. Eternal Creations owner Sonic Rang deserves thanks as well for his consistent hospitality for many of my SL educational projects.

I thank Linda Gassel for her technical support on the preparation of this manuscript. She is a blessing! Special thanks to the Peter Lang staff for all their hard work on this book, especially Sophie Appel! Thank you to Lowe Runo for the front cover photography and design. Thank you to all my MCMA Virtual Community graduate students for coming into SL to learn, research and create, particularly Brandee G. Davis who co-presented with me at the SL Virtual Worlds Conference in November 2008, sponsored by East Carolina University, North Carolina, USA. Finally, I would like to thank chapter contributors, Dr. Nanci Burk and Wagner James Au, for their inclusion in this book. Dr. Nanci Burk, resident faculty member at Glendale Community College in Glendale, Arizona, authored the chapter *Flying to Learn* for this book. Wagner James Au, author of *The Making of Second Life: Notes from the New World* (HarperCollins, 2008), graciously allowed me to interview him for the epilogue.

As I conclude this section, I would like to point out that Second Life is a dynamic world, some of the people and places used as illustrations in this book may not be present in SL at its publication release; as often is the case, new people, places and ideas replace existing ones as the virtual world turns.

SECOND LIFE: AN INTRODUCTION

> "'*This is Major Tom to ground control, I'm stepping through the door.*' When I was little, I really wanted to adventure into space...I can still remember lying inside a wardrobe box in my basement, ready to lift off, surrounded by knobs and buttons I had drawn around me..."
>
> —Philip Linden (Rosedale)

Today, Philip Linden might tell you that you are less than a minute away from a rocket blast into space. That might be true, if you are a member of the virtual world Second Life, a gaming community that has more to do with exploration and experimentation than actually defeating an alien monster. In Second Life, you can create an alien, and you can even build that spaceship. Last night, I voyaged to Mars through the inner space of my computer. My avatar, Soni, was my representation, yet through my eyes and ears I traveled through space. When I arrived on Mars, and went inside the space station, the view reminded me of a scene from *Total Recall (1990)*, starring Arnold Schwarzenegger, a sci-fi movie that blurs the line between reality and implanted memories. Unlike a real voyage to Mars, it was a quick teleport home to my residence in Second Life. I arranged a few things in my house, and had a late night dance with my husband on top of our rooftop. Okay, sounds a bit corny, but I am among the hordes of residents living in two worlds—real life (RL) and Second Life (SL). I am a professor in reality and SL fashion designer with several stores virtually, and my husband loves to landscape between our three ocean-front properties and his skybox house. Near one of my houses, my neighbor is a prayer and worship leader, with weekly gatherings on her property. Sometimes, she arranges for live musicians to come and sing at her place. Typically about 20 avatars from Australia, England, Canada and the United States drop in to listen and dance. Among those I have met in SL include artists, fashion designers, film makers, nightclub deejays, musicians, television show hosts, pastors, and educators. Some have similar occupations in real life as they do in their second life. Others are computer programmers and engineers, waitresses, nurses, retirees, and housewives in actuality compared to their occupations outside of Second Life. A number of universities and colleges are represented within Second Life, and some students get their first taste of online communities through courses taught virtually. Perhaps that is why you are reading this book; maybe this is your introduction to Second Life. You might scoff at the idea of being an avatar, and strolling through virtual daisies. But whether you participate or not, know that Second Life and other virtual communities are impacting our lives, and changing the way we understand the role of media.

Second Life is a digital culture that competes increasingly with real-life media and society and challenges the way we participate in media making and all forms of mediated entertainment. For the most part, Second Life provides an alternate space of communication and interaction within a mediated environment, one that nearly mirrors the real world in almost every way. An interesting read is *Youth Online: Identity and Literacy in the Digital Age* (Thomas, 2007) that investigates how emotions are evoked through digital culture, and how the Internet shapes new media literacy. In this book, Angela Thomas (2007) shares the variety of ways that youth communicate and role-play across the Internet, and has been a regular participant and lecturer on Second Life. Thomas relates how Second Life, and games like it, have the potential to challenge our identity and social conventions.

A number of scholars have sought to identify the ills and benefits of the gaming world. T. L. Taylor (2006) provides an overview of the social issues that developed in the early online game culture, and Richard Bartle (2003) reviews how design has played a social and political role in virtual world development. The tendency, however, has to been to study the social impact of the Internet from a real-world perspective, rather than from the vantage point of participants immersed within the game culture. Authors such as Philip Howard & Steve Jones (2004) of *Society Online* indicate that the Internet is changing the way we communicate in our life in every way imaginable. In *The Internet in Everyday Life*, Caroline Haythornthwaite and Barry Wellman (2002) review the Web's social influence on daily life, as we have come to depend on it for home and business communication, with our computers always on, and email accounts always ready to be checked for new messages.

In a groundbreaking book, anthropologist Tom Boellstorff (2008) takes a look from inside the gaming world, writing an ethnographical account of his experiences in Second Life. In a great sense, Second Life offers members an opportunity to examine themselves in response to circumstances apart from their daily life routine. They can reinvent their identities within this mediated virtual space through their participation in the game. To many, Second Life, unlike World of Warcraft, is not a game, but a community of residents who work and play in this second space, which actually exists, but is accessed online through the computer. Second Life is a medium that provides immediate interaction among members. This book is the first to explore the breadth of Second Life and its social and technological implications on media viewing, listening, and creation. It begins with a historical overview of virtual communities, and positions Second Life within the genre of Massive Multiplayer Online Role Playing Games (MMORPG). More significantly, this book positions Second Life as a medium for entertainment, information, socialization, business, and life in general—not unlike the television and Internet.

Second Life has become the bridge between real and second life, perhaps offering a glimpse into the future of media and society. Given the number of participants (more than 14 million registered accounts worldwide) and the growing number of real-world businesses in Second Life, it has become more than a game for many participants—it is a lifestyle. It has found itself woven into the plots of American television, and it is quickly growing beyond its once cult status. As of 2009, among Second Life's biggest competitors were the now defunct *There* with only 500,000 users, the widely popular Asian platform China's *Soft-World* (2007 release), and New York City-based *Area/Code* (2005 release), which engaged residents citywide in the virtual game. *There.com's* user base skewed a bit younger, between 13 to 26 years old. Alycia de Mesa (2007), explains, There was "originally intended for a tech-friendly crowd in their late 20s to early 30s," but its younger demographic has more to do with its world relating to a younger generation who had "latched onto the social networking phenomenon. Second Life, on the other hand, is attracting users more interested in creating a persona that diverges greatly from their real-life one."

Within Second Life's short history (since 2003), it has moved from game status to that of a virtual community, and now is studied for its societal influence and its implications on our mediated future in America as well as internationally. Second Life does not replicate real life, although its members participate in activities that simulate real life: shopping, dancing, studying, worshipping, building, performing and creating relationships and families. It might be difficult to comprehend Second Life without first having become an avatar, flying through a virtual sunset, swimming in a magnificent blue ocean without getting wet, building the home of your dreams, walking through a Van Gogh painting or a Ray Bradbury book, attending a physics lecture as a troll, and making friends across the world. Second Life is real life, with a better graphics card and without some of the human physical limitations. Second Life is revolutionizing education, putting a new spin on online shopping, and creating new venues for live music and theater.

Paid members have land ownership and building rights, and can rent their properties to non-paid members. Second Life members might be classified as residents or explorers. As explorers, some avatars merely enjoy the scenery, educational opportunities, and the interaction with others. As residents, members build and design properties for personal or commercial purposes. For many residents, there is a desire to designate a particular place as home. As in real life, participants admit a sense of comfort by having a place to entertain company or return to before they sign off for the night. Some members have even tucked their avatars in bed for the night, and signed off from there.

As quirky as this sounds, Second Life triggers real-life emotions and connections for many residents, and that is partly the reason why so many avatars spend so much time customizing their appearances and their homes. New members, awkward in appearance, are called noobies *(newbies, noobs, etc.)*. Second Life mentors and orientation sites are set up to assist new members in their transition into the mainland.

The means of transportation is flying, although cars, airplanes, blimps, and air balloons offer alternative ways of traveling across regions fairly close by to each other. Teleporting from one location to another is the most popular means of crossing long distances, or moving up and down floors in a building, such as a shopping mall, business headquarters, or apartment complex. The Second Life grid, as one massive entity, is comparable to a large metropolitan area, although it is broken up into various terrains. At any one moment when 40,000 to 60,000 users of the total SL membership are signed into the game, Second Life might appear barely populated because not all residents are logged on at the same time. The SL world itself is quite physically expansive. Many dance clubs and malls may be vacant at that moment, while many of the other hundreds of sites have 20 to 40 avatars interacting with each other. On occasion, Second Life festivals and special activities, such as large concerts and art exhibitions, might accommodate between 60 to 100 people in one place without a major overload to a region (experienced as lag, a slowing down of movement by avatars and cutting out of a music stream, for example).

Second Life has a listing of top sites to explore while online, and these showplaces include museums, art exhibits, dance clubs, parks, educational sites, and so much more. Some of the best moments in Second Life are those where members communicate with each other in voice or text, simply finding a quiet spot to share thoughts regarding real (their first life) and second life. You might be on deck of a yacht, chilling, enjoying the blue sky and open ocean, sitting around with a few friends talking, laughing, and taking some time away from the hectic moments of real life.

In this second world, the Linden Lab staff adopts the surname of Linden. Similarly, when people choose to join Second Life, in a sense they become part of the Linden family. Members can choose from a series of last names with first names being theirs to create. The how and why of Second Life begins with Philip Linden, a.k.a. Philip Rosedale in RL, inventor of Linden Lab, of which Second Life is a major part. As a physics major in college, Rosedale toyed with the idea of virtual communities early on before his career began. In 1999, during an interview, he said he had dreamed of space travel as a child and of building rockets into his 30s. One day he figured out that he wanted to create space, and travel into the innermost world of virtuality: "Now, 5 years later, I am convinced that in a strong sense I have really achieved what I had dreamed of as a kid…The way we did this was by building the space, rather than the spaceship" (Linden, 2005). He continued, "Instead of trying to get out of orbit, we at Linden Lab instead built the place that such a ship would travel into." Adding, Linden explains, "I think that the most compelling aspects of space exploration—the things that drew us all to it as kids—are in Second Life, or even in some sense *are* Second Life" (Linden, 2005).

That would be his space exploration. Rosedale describes Second Life as a 3D interactive online world where people simply build things. In a Stanford University interview, he explained that "you can actually walk around in [it and it] has the unusual property that everything made in it can be changed by you and everybody else that lives there. That makes it very different from an online video game…that everything you encounter you can't change" (Wyndowe & Vasconcellos, 2006). In 2006, Rosedale stated that SL was expanding by 10% monthly; at that time it was 90 square miles, nearly twice the size of San Francisco, or nearly the size of Amsterdam, with the density of Tokyo—and to operate a virtual city of this size it takes approximately 4,000 server machines (2006). Linden Lab, although based in San Francisco, has approximately 250 employees around the world. It was founded in 1999, after Rosedale left RealNetworks as Chief Technology Officer (Linden, 2005). He was 27 years old, and was about to launch his dream company, Linden Lab, without much of a clue on what he really wanted to do at the time. With several ideas spinning around in his thoughts, Second Life emerged, and revolutionized the concept of virtual community. Rosedale has earned numerous honors and awards for his virtual work with Linden Lab, with much of the company's energy focused on the residential, commercial and educational aspects of Second Life.

The inspiration for Second Life as a "building community" came when Rosedale was concluding a presentation to his board of directors. A demo of the game on the projector screen in the board room had concluded (Wyndowe & Vasconcellos, 2006). The idea behind SL, at that point, was similar to many of the games of the era, a bit of action, chase and shooting, plus a mix of building. Rosedale decided to let the live cam stay on the workers behind the scenes, with staff playing around creating stuff in the other room; the board members looked on with fascination. Rosedale explained, "It was at that moment that we realized, no, no, no, the thing here, the thing about this Metaverse, is that you can make things there with other people. You can have this collaborative, creative experience that you just can't have in the real world…unless you're extraordinarily lucky…" (Wyndowe & Vasconcellos, 2006).

In 2008, the same year that Rosedale announced he would step down as Chief Executive Officer (CEO) to spend more time on design issues, Linden's founder was honored at the 59th Annual Technology & Engineering Emmy Awards. The announcement was made on March 14, 2008, the birth date of his avatar, Philip Linden (born in RL on September 1, 1968). Two years prior, he received *Wired*'s Rave Award for Innovation in Business, on behalf of Linden Lab. In *Wired*, he said, "I'm not building a game. I'm building a new continent." Significant to that process, he added, Linden Lab is creating a social and economic infrastructure so that it can sustain itself.

In 2007, he was listed among *Time* magazine's 100 Most Influential People in the World (Vega, 2007). Rosedale's love for science and art fuels Second Life and this generates a unique mix of residents and ideas, a dreamy twist of imagination, theory and reality. Wagner James Au (2008), noted columnist on Second Life and former Linden employee, wrote on the early days of Second Life; and in his book, *The Making of Second Life*, he describes Rosedale as a rare person grounded in science but open to the world before him, and all its possibilities. The book offers a number of anecdotal stories that provide a glimpse into SL culture. One of Second Life's well-received large-scale in-world exhibits was the *Burning Man* festival in 2008 inspired by the real world gathering in 1999 outside the Bay Area in Black Rock Desert that once impressed Rosedale long before Second Life was conceived (Au, 2008).

This book *Second Life, Media and the Other Society* provides an introduction to Second Life, and how it impacts society, with a particular focus on how it functions as a medium for residents and how SL media operates within this virtual community spilling over into the real world. As with every medium, how media function must be contextualized in the society of which they are apart.

Outline of the Book

Chapter 1 sets the stage for the entrance of Second Life as a virtual community in the world of online gaming and a progression from what is called *The Victorian Internet*, the idea that early technologies like the telegraph were predecessors to the wireless transmission of information. In the latter half of the twentieth century, these wireless technologies cut across borders and territories, not always to the preference of governmental leaders. Artists, educators, and laypeople would form the beginning of unique virtual communities beginning in the 1980s. Today, Second Life is a virtual social network platform that allows its residents to create alternate identities, drawing from real and idealized life. One might envision a public sphere, where individuals often form memberships within community groups of like interests, perhaps gathering in public forums at a virtual nightclub, café, office, or beach. The possibilities are endless when in avatar form. Howard Rheingold (1998) discusses the emergence of the virtual community, as created through the Internet, and Sherry Turkle's work (1997; 2005) has affirmed that these mediated spaces have created communities that span across real and virtual life.

Chapter 2 illustrates how Second Life serves to extend the notion of social networking within a virtual community of residents. In Taiwan, Internet cafés draw people away from their homes into social settings. In the USA, although Americans retreat to their computers in their individualized spaces, they have an opportunity to communicate to people beyond their neighborhoods and workplaces based on varied interests. Christine Rosen's "egocasting" (2004/2005, p. 51) refers to various ways individualism and personalities are displayed "in the multiple media around us." MySpace, Facebook, and a plethora of profile management sites allow users to define and extend their list of friends, and present themselves in unique ways. From these platforms, viewers can send instant messages to other members, keeping in contact with daily life happenings among their circle of friends. Second Life is the ultimate social network that allows members to interact through daily conversations within a variety of settings reality inspired or imagined. Educators, computer programmers, students, media specialists, journalists and others gather in-world via specialty groups. Other times, this mixed cast of characters arrive at the same in-world destination for a public concert or news event.

Chapter 3 explores how identity is constructed in Second Life, as part fantasy and part reality. For some, Second Life offers a complete escape from reality, while others create their avatars to resemble their real appearance and personality. Some members have more than one avatar, with each expressing a unique side of their perceived, imagined or real identity. Second Life allows members to play with their identity in a safe environment that provides for nondisclosure and experimentation, but in an altered state of reality. Many authors, artists and educators prefer not to remain anonymous. Second Life can become as socially real as an individual desires. The boundaries between real and second life are individually determined. Identity can be expressed in Second Life through one's avatar form, gender, skin color, and fashion choices, as well as by the groups they have joined in-world. Virtual spaces are constructed to support real and alternate identities. This chapter introduces how community has been maintained and extended in the virtual environment through individuals assuming roles, perceived or fabricated.

Chapter 4 is dedicated to The Linden Dollar—the currency exchanged in Second Life. One hundred Lindens approximate four dollars in U.S. currency. Reuters News Service (2007) reporting on trends in Second Life, revealed in

January 2007 that 85% of SL consumers (a mean of 33 years old RL) spend more than $250 Lindens per month on clothing. Status is driven by one's ability to afford the right skin, shape and clothes, and even the right house in Second Life. A number of corporations advertise and have building space in Second Life, from soft drink companies to perfume companies to car dealerships to record labels; even adult entertainment companies and sports teams are represented in-world. Second Life is not utopia; some might cynically describe it as a brave new space that encourages exploitation as well as experimentation. For those who desire to work in Second Life, a number of service jobs, from sweeping floors to greeting customers to fashion modeling, to dancing at adult clubs, help members earn precious Lindens. This chapter examines the consumer culture of Second Life.

Chapter 5 explores Second Life as a new frontier, where members can claim space within various territories or regions. A spin around SL will introduce the novice to regions based after movies, music, and nostalgia; it is a playground for tourists and adventurers, and a sandbox for new world developers. Land sales fuel the SL economy for the most part. Real estate is the number one industry in this second space. Many participants desire to own a home in Second Life, and to do so they must be a paid member. Others rent condos or apartment suites. Some without homes admit that they feel unsettled or restless without a space of their own. With a designated home base, you can be assured that you begin at a "safe" location the next time you launch a session. For others, Second Life is an adventure without any particular destination. This chapter examines the meaning of space and territory as it relates to establishing a sense of home and shared space in Second Life.

Chapter 6 investigates the social and technical side of in-world advertising, from billboards to broadcast commercials. This chapter examines how advertisers have targeted the needs and wants of an emerging digital consumer, and provides an overview of trends and technology that encourage consumer participation. The Internet is a place for people to experiment with products and media through virtual platforms. The Internet has facilitated viral marketing in virtual communities like YouTube, mainly through commercials that rely on good storytelling techniques and their delivery systems. Storytelling as a marketing consideration has been integral to drawing the consumer into the Internet, and particularly virtual communities. Plastered in shopping malls and nightclubs, and sometimes un-zoned residential neighborhoods, virtual billboards call attention to avatar products and services. Numerous advertising agencies and marketing services are available in Second Life; some of which are extensions from real firms. This chapter investigates the marketing realities and potential of Second Life.

Chapter 7 reconsiders the concept of learning virtually across the globe. One of the biggest industries in Second Life is education. Educational institutions are seeking new ways to teach and to attract students. This chapter takes a look at how learning is conducted in-world, and the impact from bringing students into a virtual classroom. A multitude of groups exist in Second Life that allow for educators to collaborate and discuss real issues in a second learning space. Moreover, museum exhibits and art galleries contribute to an atmosphere of life-long learning. This chapter was guest-authored by Nanci Burk, Ph.D., resident faculty member at Glendale Community College in Glendale, Arizona. She spent a year-long sabbatical within Second Life exploring its use among educators, including surveying and interviewing them. She teaches at Glendale, a campus that has taken the lead in exploring the potential of virtual worlds for enhancing learning and using technology to connect students to different cultures across the world.

Chapter 8 lets us listen into Second Life. A big part of this virtual community is the use of radio and streaming of music that is performed in Second Life. When Second Life hosted its 5th anniversary celebrations, it featured non-stop live music over a few days from musicians who regularly performed in the virtual world. Nearly every day, live music is performed in SL at a variety of venues, and many of these performers have developed their own fan bases. Representatives from RL and SL indie labels, as well as from major record labels, work from inside and organize events, anywhere from occasionally to routinely. SL Live Radio is one station devoted to the virtual indie musician. Some musicians double as nightclub disc jockeys; when they are not singing, they are spinning tunes. Nightclubs attract large crowds on weekends and certain weeknights on occasion. This chapter focuses on the world of music in Second Life, and its social and economic consequences.

Chapter 9 is a sneak preview into what avatars are watching on their virtual television sets. Treet-TV, formerly Second Life Cable Network (SLCN), broadcasts within Second Life a variety of topical shows, from fashion to music to architecture. Beyond that, network television is making the connection between real and virtual spaces, increasingly, as an effort to market their programs and expand their audience base. On Wednesday, October 24, 2007, CBS invited viewers into Second Life's *CSI*'s Crime Lab. The network episode "Down the Rabbit Hole" would end with a cliff-hanger, inviting its audience to figure "who did it?" by solving the crime in Second Life. Throughout the show, Second Life avatars (70–80% more females than males) engaged in the process of crime-solving while watching the show. This chapter also examines the making of machinima, which are films produced in and about Second Life, noting the 2008 Home Box Office release of *Molotov Alva and His Search for the Creator: A Second Life Odyssey* originally titled *My Second Life: The Video Diaries of Molotov Alva*.

Chapter 10 reports on the role of print media journalism in Second Life. Real-world news networks and newspapers are increasingly making their presence known within Second Life, and now compete with independent news organizations that reside within this digital landscape. In-world newspapers are often the first to report on how corporate media from the outside are experimenting within Second Life, and the success of those ventures. They even critique Linden Lab policies. News companies like Reuters, at one point, had reporters assigned as avatars in Second Life to report on the Linden economy and social barometer of virtual reality. A number of newspapers and magazines have surfaced in Second Life, from those covering RL politics to in-world lifestyle news. This chapter reviews what is being reported about avatars and their communities within Second Life.

Chapter 11 deals with the darker side of Second Life, looking at issues of sex, violence and crime within virtual communities. For some, violence and sex is a part of their role-play activities. Others take violence to the mainland or private regions, resulting in some residents reporting incidents related to griefers pointing guns at members, attempting to rob or harass them. The Linden Lab maintains a community police blotter listing criminal activity and sanctions on a regular basis. Some advertisements promoting the sale of weapons have depicted images of scantily clad women holding high-powered machine guns. Firing ranges are set up by members in designated private or public areas in Second Life. A number of public venues post signs warning "No drama" and "No weapons." Add to that, "drug stores" sell scripts to avatars to simulate the effects of illegal drugs. Residents can experiment with sex, violence and crime in this mediated space without the conventional consequences, meanwhile challenging certain social conventions within virtual media.

Chapter 12 considers diversity within virtual communities, with Second Life comprised of an international mix of residents. Residents construct homes, meeting spaces, and their own avatars (and often multiple avatars), while extending their self and community identities beyond limitations of race, ethnicity and gender. In this chapter, opportunities in-world for the disabled population are presented for consideration as well, for diversity is a concept that needs to be expanded in both real and virtual worlds. A growing transgendered community is apparent in Second Life, with groups established such as Transgender Denmark, Femme by Choice, Transchristianism Othersexed in SL, Omnisexual Beings and so forth. A number of scholars have discussed how television has shaped the image of the queer community (Fejes &

Petrich, 1993; Gross, 1983, for example). One would be hard pressed to find an equivalent literature base devoted to new media. At least 10% of the female avatars are actually male members. Certain looks tend to dominate the landscape. The sexualization of the female form is also examined, as well as questions of race and representation in this not so utopian society.

Chapter 13 examines the concept of spirituality in Second Life, particularly seeking out those engaged with in-world prayer, evangelism, and missions. Nearly every religion is represented in Second Life, from Mormons, to Wiccan, to Buddhists to Pentecostals. Certain regions have become designated as religious sites by residents, and draw members into activities and fellowship. Some members are hostile to the establishment of religious communities, and some worship regions have had to contend with griefers—avatars that intentionally disrupt a meeting for example through indecent language or actions and perhaps even cause damage to a region through scripting viruses. This chapter examines prayer and ceremony in Second Life, and their impact on the possibilities of interfaith activities and tolerance among groups. Second Life, as a medium, is considered a power evangelistic tool, more so than other media, to many who practice religion in-world.

Chapter 14 concludes the book with some speculation about the future of virtual worlds. Second Life increasingly dominates the virtual landscape, and has been able to cross international borders commercially, allowing global businesses to be developed and relationships to be formed. Based on Linden statistics, Second Life's economy is thriving. Add to that, there is an abundance of virtual worlds directed at children. How long before the distinction between virtual and real is nonexistent in education, commerce and daily life? This chapter attempts to provide a social snapshot of the future regarding virtual technology, with SL as a metaphor. Mark Deuze (2007) reminds us, "[B]ecause of the pervasiveness of media in everyday life and the multitasking way we engage with those media, more than half our media use 'disappears' when we are asked about it." He directs us toward the wisdom of futurist Alvin Toffler, with words written nearly 30 years ago: "This invisibility of making and using media simultaneously can be set against the increasing invisibility of media in everyday life." Understanding how Second Life is intersecting with our real lives, although crudely at this point, might give us a glimpse into social, political and economical dynamics of the mediated future.

An epilogue follows, that highlights an interview with notable author Wagner James Au of *The Making of Second Life: Notes from the New World* (HarperCollins, 2008). He was there when it all started—on Second Life. So, it seems fitting to allow him some final observations on the evolving virtual world dynamics, and offer us some predictions toward the future as well.

References

Au, W. J. (2009). *The making of second life: Notes from the new world*. New York: Harper Collins.

Bartle, R. (2003). *Designing virtual worlds*. New Riders Games.

Boellstorff , T. (2008). *The coming of age in Second Life: An anthropologist explores the virtual human*. Princeton, NJ: Princeton University Press.

de Mesa, A. (2007, March 12). Virtual world branding for real. BrandChannel.com. Accessed July 10, 2009, from http://www.brandchannel.com/features_effect.asp? pf_id=358/

Deuze, M. (2007). *Media work: Digital media & society*. Cambridge, England: Polity.

Down the Rabbit Hole. (2007). *CSI: NY*. CBS TV Network, Season 4, Episode 5.

Gross, L. (1993). *Contested closets: The politics and ethics of outing*. Minneapolis: University of Minnesota Press.

Fejes, R., & Petrich, K. (1993). Invisibility, homophobia and heterosexism: Lesbians, gays and the media. *Critical Studies in Mass Communication 10*(4), 395 (December).

Haythornthwaite, C., & Wellman, B. (2002). *The Internet in everyday life*. New York: Blackwell.

Howard, P. E. N., & Jones, S. (2004). *Society online: The Internet in context*. Thousands Oaks, CA: Sage Publications.

Linden, P. (2005, March 12). Space exploration. Secondlife.com. Accessed December 15, 2008, from http://blog.secondlife.com/2005/03/12/space-exploration/#more-32.

Molotov Alva and his search for the creator: A *Second Life odyssey* (2009). HBO documentary films. Accessed June 9, 2009, from http://www.hbo.com/docs/programs/molotovalva/index.html/

Reuters, R. (2007, May 28). The price of tying the virtual knot. *Reuters News Service*. Accessed November 21, 2007, from http://secondlife.reuters.com/stories/2007/ 05/28/the-price-of-tying-the-virtual-knot/

Rheingold, H. (1998). *The virtual community: Homesteading of the electronic frontier*, Addison-Wesley Publishing Company. Accessed December 15, 2008, from http://www.rheingold.com/vc/book/

Rosen, C. (2004/2005). The age of egocasting. *The New Atlantis: A journal of technology and society*, 7, Fall/Winter, pp. 51–72. Accessed June 12, 2009, from http://www.thenewatlantis.com/publications/the-age-of-egocasting.

Taylor, T. L. (2006) *Play between worlds: Exploring online game culture*. Cambridge, MA: The MIT Press.

Thomas, A. (2007). *Youth online: Identity and literacy in the digital age*. New York: Peter Lang Publishers.

Turkle, S. (2005). *The second self: Computers and the human spirit; twentieth anniversary edition*. Cambridge, MA: The MIT Press.

—(1997) *Life on the screen: Identity in the age of the internet*. New York: Simon & Schuster.

Vega, S. (2007). Philip Rosedale. Most Influential Top 100. Time.com http://www.time.com/time/specials/2007/time100/article/0,28804,1595326_1615737_1615877,00.html.

Wyndowe, M., & Vasconcellos, J. (2006, November 27). Featured Interview: *Podcast by students of Stanford University's Business and Design Schools*. Matt and Julio–Episode 9: Philip Rosedale, Founder of Linden Labs and Second Life. Accessed December 1, 2008, from http://iinnovate.blogspot.com/2006/11/philip-rosedale-founder-of-linden-labs_27.html.

SECTION 1

Introduction to Second Life & the Virtual Society

CHAPTER ONE

Second Life, Imagination, and Virtual Community

> "And in her ears the little Seashells, the thimble radios tamped tight, and an electronic ocean of sound, of music and talk and music and talk coming in, coming in on the shore of her unsleeping mind."
>
> —Ray Bradbury, *Fahrenheit 451*

Imagination was reawakened by the convergence of the literary, musical, artistic, and scientific genius of the late 19th century and early 20th century. A gate had opened—and America and Europe became intrigued by *Amazing Stories* (published by Hugo Gernsback) with its plots often set in the future. Science fiction writers were inspired by technologies and their possibilities, evidenced by their social prophecies of new world orders and detailed narratives of curious new sights, sounds, and security (i.e., big screen televisions, walls of sound, and sensory monitors).

Wild speculation ran rampant about forthcoming technologies, social orders, and a host of utopian/dystopian possibilities. The rush toward technologies paralleled the rise of artistic movements. The race to create a global system of communication, in the midst of social and technological change, had become overshadowed by a corporate and public push for a tangible product: radio. Scientist Nikola Tesla had conceptualized inventions beyond radio, one where images and sound could be transmitted through high-rise towers built in key cities around the world—yet his ideas would fall deaf to "corporate" ears: "The concept is at least as old as Nikola Tesla, the turn-of-the-20th-century icon who used to demonstrate the wonders of electricity by letting it course through his body as crowds gawked in wonder" (Grebb, 2005, p. 1). He became "so fascinated with electricity and wireless frequencies that he spent the early 1900s constructing the Wardenclyffe Tower on land near Long Island Sound, partly to demonstrate that he could beam energy from one point to another without any wires" (Grebb, 2005, p. 1).

Tesla ran out of finances before he achieved his vision of wireless communication, connecting the world. His investors could not see beyond their imaginations, blinded by short-run profits. Decades later, scientists have proven that "one can generate power, convert it to lasers or microwaves, beam it to another point and reconvert it into electricity. Such a system could beam power to hard-to-reach rural areas without running expensive power lines—or could even beam it down to Earth from power stations in space" (Grebb, 2005, p. 1). The ideas behind the microwave oven—radiation frequency and frequency transformers—were those of Tesla. It is only in reflection that we appreciate such genius.

In 1902, when Marconi transmitted an encoded consonant (the letter "s" in Morse code), the race was on to capture sound and confine it within little black boxes, a less than endearing term for radio by its critics. Mark Seifer, author of *Wizard: The Life and Times of Nikola Tesla: Biography of a Genius* (1998), contends that Tesla's vision for universal, wireless transmission—of sound and image—challenged the electrical, lighting and telephone monopolies of the era. What becomes strikingly apparent is that Tesla in 1904 had envisioned the Web as a means of information exchange and the invention of recording units such as I-pods, and it is equally significant to note that he had no interest in profiting from technological advances that might have resulted from his writings or experimentation: "...Tesla envisioned, to the disbelief of most of the world, 'A cheap and simple device, which might be carried in one's pocket, may then be set up anywhere on sea or land, and it will record the world's news or such special messages as may be intended for it" (McAdams, 1996). "Thus the earth will be converted into a huge brain," and according to Tesla, "the system will have a virtually infinite working capacity and immensely facilitate and cheapen the transmission of intelligence" (McAdams, 1996).

Wireless Communication: The Vision and the Visionaries

A series of discoveries, some of which garnered little attention, unfolded in the 19th century that would set the stage for later inventions. When philosopher Gian Domenico Romagnosi reported in an Italian newspaper in 1802 that he had discovered a profound relationship between electricity and magnetism, there was no fanfare from the scientific community. Years later in 1820, Danish scientist Hans Christian Orsted, then unaware of Romagnosi's earlier findings, "discovered" the same principle of electromagnetism unintentionally as he was preparing for one of his lectures. A compass needle jumped and sealed a fateful moment when he turned the battery current off and on during his preparation.

English scientist Michael Faraday experimented again with this concept in

1831. Samuel Morse, a Massachusetts native, relying on Orsted's prior work, invented the electrical telegraph in 1837. Charles Wheatstone also filed a similar patent that same year in Great Britain. Morse would continue to strengthen the signal of the telegraph with the assistance of a colleague at New York University, chemistry professor Leonard Gale. In the late 19th century, British, American, and Indian scientists, and inventors from around Europe, invested time and money into understanding the principles and practice of reception and transmission of radio waves. At the 1881 Paris Exposition International d'Electricite, opera was transmitted through several strategically placed microphones and listener headsets. This apparatus paved the way for long-distance transmission of entertainment and speeches.

As the 19th century came to a close, Marconi received accolades for his telegraph message sent in 1902 without wires; he had previously transmitted and received his first radio signal in 1895. Two years prior to Marconi's feat, Tesla had presented and published his blueprint for wireless radio across the U.S. The telegraph, radio, and the telephone all seemed like extraordinary inventions to the public, many of whom were fascinated with turn-of-the-century comic books with storylines set in the future.

Tesla understood the larger implications of his work toward global communications. He stated that his counterparts were easily satisfied with simplistic applications of wireless communication, whereas he sought the simultaneous transmission and convergence of sound and light as a means to defy the physics of time and space. His 45-page autobiography, *My Inventions* (Tesla, 1908), outlines his rationale and vision for his discoveries, of which he lists five: The Tesla Transformer, The Magnifying Transmitter, The Tesla Wireless System, The Art of Individualization, and the Terrestrial Stationary Waves. He organizes these inventions within what he refers to as "The World System, the wireless transmission of "...any kind of signals, messages or characters, to all parts of the world, but also the inter-connection of the existing telegraph, telephone, and other signal stations without any change in their present equipment" (Tesla, 1908, p. 32). He offers this example, "a telephone subscriber here may call up and talk to any other subscriber on the Earth. An inexpensive receiver, not bigger than a watch, will enable him to listen anywhere, on land or sea, to a speech delivered or music played in some other place, however distant" (Tesla, 1908, pp. 32–33).

Music distribution across the world was part of Tesla's visionary world system, and would allow for comparable means of sharing news, documents, or photographs. His motivation for his inventions, particularly the magnifying transmitter (light transmission), centered on his desire to prioritize "humanitarian consequences" over that of commercialization which he anticipated to be a natural outcome: "The greatest good will come from technological improvements tending to unification and harmony, and my wireless transmitter is preeminently such. By its means, the human voice and its likeness will be reproduced everywhere." He continued, "Its introduction for telegraphic, telephonic and other similar uses will automatically cut out the static and all other interferences which at present, impose narrow limits to the application of the wireless" (Tesla, 1908, pp. 36–37).

Tesla opposed legislative efforts to monopolize wireless communication: "It would be calamitous, indeed, if at the time when the art is in its infancy and the vast majority, not excepting even experts, have no conception of its ultimate possibilities, a measure would be rushed through the legislature making it a government monopoly" (Tesla, 1908, p. 38). He feared that the government might limit the potential of wireless radio and similar transmission within U.S. borders, when its greatest application was still to come—one in which communication would be possible to every village across the world (Tesla, 1908). His eccentric (yet charismatic) nature and his extraordinary height of 6'4" contributed to his mad-scientist personification. His finances came to end, long before his imagination. He envisioned radio, television, computers, faxes, death rays, and robotics long before his scientific counterparts.

Unfortunately, many of his theoretic conceptions and designs provided no more than amusement for comic books. During his life, industry and science rejected his vision of a wireless network in which light and sound could be transmitted across the world in a variety of ways via a number of technologies. This tall, lanky man, inundated with thoughts and visions of ways to remix science, art, social responsibility and imagination, might be likened to a Philip Rosedale of our day. Tesla was a visionary so far ahead of his scientific peers that his ideas were considered fodder for entertainment, rather than a step toward a radical way of communicating and living life in years to come. His ideas would be revisited years after his death by scientists and inventors, as they sought to connect the world through technology, with no strings attached.

The Galactic Network, as Art and Science

Hugo Gernsback, 20th-century publisher of science fiction and technical trade magazines, challenged scientists and writers to think big—and helped to magnify the social and technological significance of electromagnetism. A new spirituality emerged—one that began to play upon man as an extension of technology (McLuhan, 1994) and technology as the means to tap into the energy that flowed through and around us. McLuhan (1994) states, "Electricity is organic in character and confirms the organic social bond by its technological use in telegraph and telephone, radio, and other forms. The simultaneity of electric communication, also characteristic of our nervous system, makes each of us present and accessible to every other person in the world" (pp. 247–248). The electronic age continues unfolding before eyes and ears. "To a large degree our co-presence everywhere at once in the electronic age is a factor for passive, rather than active, experience" (pp. 247–249), he adds. The idea that we might immerse ourselves into our computer, and engage with each other instantaneously and simultaneously in a social network of various possibilities locally and globally sets the stage for a science fiction tale—or a virtual community based in reality.

Ray Bradbury's *Fahrenheit 451* made no mention of anything similar to the Internet, but the nature of media (flat screens and seashell radios) described in his book foreshadowed interactivity that would become increasingly available to the public. He wrote of a new world where imagination was scripted, audience members could participate in story lines, and print knowledge had become dangerous to civilized society. That same year, Arthur Clarke published *Childhood's End*, in which he wrote the tale of aliens making contact with earth through radio waves and that children's minds had developed a century later into a high level of consciousness. Their minds merged with one being, the Overmind, who communicates through telepathy and telekinesis. Clarke, in the early 1950s, also wrote a short story, *The Sentinel* (the basis for the motion picture *2001: A Space Odyssey*), in which he alluded to the perils of para-communicative technologies. Tesla toyed with the notion of thought photography and attempted to communicate with Mars during his lifetime. The social history of technology, from the vantage point of science fiction writers and visionary minds, can seem a bit extreme and hardly grounded in the hard sciences, and often presents us with speculation and engaging tales.

There are typically enough facts woven into such tales to make them plausible to the audience. A famous photo shows Mark Twain and Tesla as friends, and being so, each contributed postulations from their respective literary and scientific perspectives. Saying that, one can understand how technological advances have been based partly on science, fantasy, and personal pursuit. Upton Sinclair's *Mental Radio* (1930) details personal experiments in telepathic communication—the ultimate wireless communication. Imagination is the critical element that awakens possibilities—whether science and/or fiction forwards a technological notion is not relevant. It is not so surprising, then, that Mark Twain befriended Tesla, or that the writings of Clarke and Bradbury were heralded as inspiration within scientific communities.

In 1962, a series of memos were circulated among Massachusetts Institute of Technology (MIT) researchers that proposed a "Galactic Network"—a global network of computers. The content of these letters is said to be the "first recorded description of the social interactions that could be enabled through networking." The author, J. C. R. Licklider (Leiner et al. 2006), "envisioned a globally interconnected set of computers through which everyone could quickly access data and programs from any site. In spirit, the concept was very much like the Internet of today." Robert Kleinrock had already presented on the Packet-Switching (PS) theory in 1961, and his theory was the basis for Internet connectivity (Leiner et al. 2006). A few years later in 1965, Larry Roberts introduced connectivity through computers over dial-up phone lines (2006). The Internet's emergence was one that began as a vision among literary and scientific genius nearly a century earlier and likely as early as the dawn of civilization as people looked to the sky and past their personal horizons wondering about others across earth and the universe. The Internet offered the potential for a worldwide collective and community. The Internet, in its first and rough form, emerged in 1969. The first consumer applications would not surface until the mid-1970s.

Technology as Social Art

At the turn of the 20th century, an international arts movement was founded in 1909 by Italian futurists, with F. T. Marinetti at the helm. The movement focused on technology as the source of inspiration and imagination. Technological and artistic suppositions and speculations were espoused and debated among scientists, artists, and writers. The turn of the century—and the years preceding and following—was an amazing era of discovery and invention that provided little time for contemplation regarding social and physical impact of technologies on the world. Luigi Russolo (2005), a leading innovator of sound, and other futurists began to lay theoretic groundwork (which was at that point fairly devoid) to provide meaning to and consequence of rapid technological change and liberation. Their theories embraced change, speed and brute power, and their influence gave authenticity to industrialization as progress. In 1913, Russolo declared in his manifesto, *The Art of Noises*, that *noise-sounds* were invasive and simultaneously reflective of our increasingly mechanized human spaces (Russolo, 2005, p. 13). He called for the artistic community to appreciate how technology had expanded creative boundaries and how the machine should be considered as integral to the making of art and music that would be meaningful to citizens of an industrialized society.

Twentieth-century author and social critic Neil Postman (1985) posits, "A technology is merely a machine. A medium is the social and intellectual environment a machine creates." He continues, "It is possible for a technology to be used that its potentialities are prevented from developing and its social consequences kept to a minimum" (pp. 84–85). Technology is not concerned about its impact on society. Although it evolves and matures through human inspiration, it is passive in its motivations. Humanity, on the other hand, in its effort to simplify life often complicates it. Our motivation is perhaps driven by that one part curiosity and one part efficiency inherent within our human nature. It is the curiosity that likely inspires virtual worlds such as Second Life. The challenge of this book, in some ways, is to help the reader to understand the relationship between technology and humanity—art and science as they are woven into the context of human relationships. Virtual worlds, such as Second Life, might allow for observing humanity as it interacts with technology within a simulated sphere, a sort of social-techno laboratory.

To some, virtual worlds simulate life and permit participants to extend their social and physical opportunities. Second Life, for example, offers a meeting space for artists, scientists, and laypeople to share ideas with each other in a safe space of intellectual play and experimentation. For some, Second Life provides a second chance at recreating a better world. Inside SL, on any given week, a number of people raise money for real non-profit organizations or causes through art and music events held in virtual venues. On any given day, educators create immersive virtual spaces to demonstrate scientific principles, share with each other unique ways to learn and teach difficult concepts using technology, and allow students to create and exhibit work in Second Life. The cultural impact of virtual worlds is extended moreover when network television invites the public to participate in its programming online. The immersion of a network television audience into a virtual world demonstrates the possibilities of storytelling across media platforms, and moves the viewer into an interactive space.

Origin of Cyberculture: Socio-Techno Cultural Convergence

The collection of scientific and literary works that highlight and speculate on the cultural influences of technology upon society and the individual falls under the category of cyberstudies. Jonathan Sterne (2003) puts a spin on this genre, for the definition of cyberstudies has been transforming as quickly as technologies evolve. Through Sterne, we begin to hear and see a digital culture that began to take shape in the 1980s and 1990s within a convergence of ideas and tools that soon helped users experience technology and create an increasingly immersive, mediated society. Sterne makes a plea toward researchers to consider the impact of sound in this new virtual world order, pointing out that it has been a neglected area of cybercultural studies. For instance, synthesizers and sampling are concepts that have culturally shaped sound, particularly from the late 19th century to modern times, from Elisha Gray's first electric synthesizer to John Cage's computer-generated music to Brian Eno's generative ambient soundscapes. Composer and sound artist David Dunn (2006), who examined the invention of electronic music around the 1900s, notes how electricity and music converged to form new technologies which would subsequently become commercialized:

> ...Bell, Edison, and Tesla became culture heroes who ushered in an ideology of industrial progress founded upon the power of harnessed electricity. Amongst this assemblage of inventor industrialists was Sr. Thaddeus Cahill, inventor of the electric typewriter, designer and builder of the first music synthesizer and...originator of industrial muzak. (Dunn, 2006, p. 3)

Popular culture has allowed us to comprehend how new technologies define our social, political, and economic structures. The computer is not only an external force that assists in our daily functions. Its role becomes evident in the social construction and physical governance of human life, in our creation of music as well as in our depiction of life. The Internet is a product of the many technologies from which it evolved, as well as the social, political and economic influences that shaped it. A multitude of inventions have complemented and contributed toward our present cyberculture, and our techno cultural visions of the future provide roadmaps on where we might want to go with technology.

Pop conceptions of the computer's role in our society reflect a shift in how our culture is shaped by technology. Stanley Kubrick's 1968 film *2001: A Space Odyssey* personifies the computer as Hal and hints toward the evolution of emotions in artificial life. More than 30 years later, *The Matrix*'s debut in 1999 challenged us to consider how digital culture might evolve in 2199 to a state where the computer was in competition with humanity. The very definition of life had been mediated and redefined by technologies. The audience gets a glimpse into this futuristic view through the very use of technology in the crafting of the film. One begins to reflect on how life is increasingly mediated via computer and how technology progressively alters our concept of humanity. In fact, the production techniques used to illustrate human-computer interaction in *The Matrix* are demonstrated through a series of digital snapshots, or sampling. In this way, the audience begins to understand that critical point where human life has intersected with technology. This awakening is nonetheless a call for the audience to consider how our dependence on computers and digital culture has progressively redefined our concept of humanity. Indeed, much of what has been discussed in this chapter so far regarding technologies contributing to the development of the Internet might be described as the Victorian Internet (Slater, 2002). This term has increasingly appeared in literature, and embodies the idea that early technologies like the telegraph were predecessors to the wireless transmission of information. In John Picker's *Victorian Soundscapes* (2003), he reconstructs the social history of the emerging technology of the 1800s, a convergence of literary writing and scientific works that ushered in new spun creativity and innovative perspectives on morality, science and romance. Picker (2003) follows ideas and dialogues from notables such as perceptual theorist Hermann von Helmholtz and inventors Charles Babbage, Alexander Bell and Thomas Edison, to writers Charles Dickens, Alfred Tennyson, and Joseph Conrad; through all this exchange, we begin to realize the long and winding cultural path of the modern computer and technologies as they unfold through history.

Ada Lovelace's notes, while working with Babbage, contributed greatly to the world's first computer program, and she has been referred to as the world's first computer programmer. Lovelace had visions that exceeded most inventors of her era. Picker introduces his book with a story about Babbage, who has been publicly credited as the inventor of the first modern computer: "For Babbage, the air acts as a giant scroll or phonograph, permanently recording voices that, he concedes, only God possesses the knowledge to replay" (Picker, 2003, p. 16). His computers were not completed, but Lovelace and Babbage had launched a passage into a technological frenzy. Babbage's close friend was Charles Dickens, and you can imagine the amazing conversations between the two as they pondered the future ahead, in a world where literature and technology would evolve together. Babbage and Dickens—like Twain and Tesla—would envision a utopian view of technology, one that afforded greater creativity, no doubt, through converging perspectives on literature and science.

Slater (2002) traces the history of the Web to the Victorian era, pointing toward the invention of the telegraph in the 1840s as laying the conceptual groundwork for signal network and interface. During the American Civil War the government would send signals across the nation through Morse code. The point that Slater makes is that the Internet, rather than a singular invention, was a progression in technology, which advanced through notions of efficiency and connectivity in sending and receiving information. As technology became simplified, its base of users expanded toward public spheres; the telegraph became a means toward social networking after the wars. Messages could be sent to families across large distances more quickly than by letter carriers.

Unlike Aldous Huxley's 1932 *Brave New World*, Marshall McLuhan (1994) views technology as a beneficial and necessary extension of humanity. Looking past the social ills of American capitalism and industrialization, McLuhan implies a period of time and transition in which technologies remain in a state of experimentation, groomed and perfected by those in government, industry, or universities who serve as the initial and primary users. After which, the social side of technology begins to emerge as users interact and consider ways in which the technology might be expanded and refined for personal and social use. The relationship between technology and humanity is fluid and expansive, and offers challenges and opportunities to re-conceptualize what it means to be human—individually and collectively—and what is the purpose of technology in one's life.

At the very least, the Internet is a series of computer networks allowing for the delivery of information and data nearly immediately, from public spheres into private sectors and homes. Information can be processed, analyzed and presented electronically through email, bulletin boards, and interactive chat rooms, or remain as an archive on a server or hard drive. The Internet's story in America, as we understand it in modern terms, began at a time when major U.S. universities and military defense agencies sought ways to transfer data through research networking initiatives. The Internet as a comprehensive network was set in motion in 1962, with a blueprint of the possibilities drawing upon early theories and advances that preceded it from the 1940s to the 1960s (Slater, 2002).

By 1970, information was being sent and received as bits, inexpensively through silicon-laced digital circuits invented in 1958 and perfected subsequently; information transfer was accelerated through "hypertext" in 1965 (Slater, 2002). It would be two decades later that the Internet would be become a reality to the public, with government, universities, and businesses being the primary users initially. The World Wide Web was launched in 1989. However, imagination preceded technological advances, and the desire for social interactivity advanced the dream.

Emergence of Virtual Communities

In the latter half of the 20th century, wireless technologies began to serve beyond the transfer of information for science and military operations; information would cut across borders and territories not always to the preference of governmental leaders. Artists, educators, and laypeople would form unique communities beginning in the 1980s, and part of this story is illustrated by Howard Rheingold's recollection of The Well.

Rheingold's (1998) *The Virtual Community* tells the story of the formation of a cyber-public sphere, The Well, one of the first user nets connected visionaries, educators, parents, physicians, and nurses to each other 24/7. The Well created an informal computerized counterculture. In Rheingold's book (1998), he discusses "the accidental history" of the Internet and how it created a community of laypeople, scholars, and professionals. It was the emergence of online activism, primarily because it facilitated an information flow through its community of participants. The Well's base of operations was in the San Francisco Bay area—also the start for Second Life. Similar to Second Life, it drew users from across the world. Its beginnings were humble and for "only $3 an hour, people with computers and modems could have access to the kind of online groups that cost five or ten times that much on other public telecommunication systems" (Rheingold, 1998).

Rheingold (1998) explains, that when he registered for an account, he had "previously suffered the initiation of figuring out how to plug in a modem...and [how to] use it to connect to computer bulletin-board systems, or BBSs, and the Source (an early public information utility)." Rheingold (1998) was active in those early days of the Well during the fall of 1985. The Well became a major part of his life by 1986, and he "wasn't willing to do without. My wife was concerned, then jealous, then angry." Rheingold (1998) points out, "The inexpensive public online service was launched because...[those] from a previous cultural revolution noticed that the technology of computer conferencing had potential far beyond its origins in military, scientific, and government communications." The idea behind it, according to Rheingold (1998), "was that it would be free, self-governing, and an open-ended universe that allowed for individual experimentation and design, and it would serve this collective of participants within the online community, and leaning on business to fuel it economically."

Similar to what the Internet offers users today, the service would allow members to discuss and share literature, art, poetry, music, pets, gardening, outside recreation, among a host of topics. Participants were not anonymous. The counterculture movement that comprised The Well was known as The Whole Earth, whose membership comprised the "core population from the beginning:" "the granola-eating utopians, the solar-power enthusiasts, the space-station crowd, immortalists, futurists, gadgeteers, commune graduates, environmentalists, social activists..." Another subculture among The Well participants were the Deadheads, based on the fan culture that surrounded the Grateful Dead band. Not to be mistaken for a groupie forum, however, The Well offered its participants access to information and technology, and as a collective it had the potential to empower its membership politically, socially and economically outside of the online community. Rheingold (1998) explains, "The prospect of the technical capabilities of a near-ubiquitous high-bandwidth Net in the hands of a small number of commercial interests has dire political implications. Whoever gains the political edge on this technology will be able to use the technology to consolidate power" (p. xx).

Significantly, Rheingold defines virtual communities as "social aggregations that emerge from the Net when enough people carry on those public discussions long enough, with sufficient human feeling, to form webs of personal relationships in cyberspace" (Rheingold, 1998, p. xx). He contends that these online communities allow people to share thoughts as they would do in real life, but removing the distance between them through computer-mediated communication. Sherry Turkle (1997) in *Life on the Screen: Identity in the Age of the Internet* envisioned these communities spanning globally across the borders of virtual life into real life. Spaces such as Second Life provide opportunities for persons to reinvent themselves, while challenging others socially and personally with questions on who they are in reality, or perhaps who they thought they were, as they interact with others in an alternate world. In *The Second Self: Computers and the Human Spirit* (2005), Turkle pursues her understanding on the social construction of community, as well as identity, in virtual spaces. These second spaces allow gender, race, and culture to be experienced and reexamined within a virtual reality.

The Matrix as the Metaverse

Edward Castronova's (2007) *Exodus to the Virtual Word: How Online Fun Is Changing Reality* posits that games like Second Life and EverQuest instill within its participants a false sense of happiness and security, and encourage escapism from social and political ills. In his critique of virtual communities, Castronova warns, in a similar vein to what Postman expressed in the 1980s' *Amusing Ourselves to Death*, we are setting unrealistic social expectations for the real world. Many writers and social critics have predicted doom and gloom scenarios associated with new technologies and inventions (Postman, 1992).

Second Life is a product of the technologies and ideas that came before it. The technical history of the computer, and the various technologies which developed parallel to it, might be easily plotted on a time line, noting social consequences. Such an exercise might help one to understand how technology is inspired by popular science notions, and how dystopian societies, as illustrated in the Hollywood movie, *The Matrix*, merely represent our fears of the unknown. The imagination, when realized, can be overwhelming within a society, especially to those challenged by a new social-technological balance in their life. Virtual societies comprise those willing to reconsider the meaning of reality. Neal Stephenson's novel, published in 1992, *Snow Crash* coined the term Metaverse, defined in a sense as juxtaposition to the concept of universe. Suddenly, we no longer look solely outward to an expansion of humanity, the idea that we are not alone in the universe. Now we begin to look inward toward the depth of humanity; in essence we move toward examining the idea of the human soul in a virtual laboratory, or the Metaverse. We might anticipate a future where social and political promises and abuses of technology are present in virtual worlds, as they have been in the physical realm.

Stephenson's novel provided the social and technical blueprint for massively multiplayer online role-playing games (MMORPG). His world thrived on interactivity among users. The first multiplayer online game (MMOG), a flight combat simulation, made its debut in 1987, five years before his novel. In the late 1980s and 1990s, a number of online role-playing games became popular, with EverQuest taking a leadership position among the pack by the late 1990s. World of Warcraft (WOW) became the dominant MMORPG with up to 11 million worldwide subscribers per month in early 2009. Earlier versions of Warcraft began in 1994, with the most successful of the WOW series making a debut in 2001. The vivid graphics of medieval landscapes with unfolding storylines involving various quests and battles have been lauded by gaming advocates and criticized by social critics, warning against the addictive nature of those features prized among players.

Rheingold (1998) contends Active Worlds was the first "virtual community" amidst the gaming world. Stephenson's 1992 novel is set in the early 21st century, and has been speculated to have inspired Second Life and its predecessor Active Worlds. In contrast, Rosedale has stated publicly *Snow Crash* was not his inspiration for SL. He had thought about such a virtual world prior to and apart from the novel. Before Second Life arrived on the gaming scene, Active Worlds had provided a forum for its users to communicate with one another online and encouraged collaboration and creativity among players within a virtual platform. Active Worlds foreshadowed the coming of Second Life, with its launch in the summer of 1994, when Ron Britvich created the nearly 3D virtual game WebWorld, an interactive world where several thousand players had their first glimpse into Stephenson's vision of virtual community and landscapes. Other developers helped to rename and shape Britvich's virtual community in those initial years. Amidst many limitations, the game encouraged players to collaborate within a project-based world. Most virtual worlds that had developed in the 1990s contracted with companies, like Disney, to create well-designed tourist sites for members to explore, rather than allowing for users to generate content.

By mid-summer 1995, Britvich's moderately profitable virtual experiment would become known as Active Worlds. By late 1999, the company experienced some financial difficulties and Britvich went off to other ventures, while some of the original designers remained at the company. Through the years, the company has managed to remain viable, even as new competitors like Second Life made the virtual gaming arena far more competitive. In 2008, Active Worlds promised the launch of customizable avatars to compete with Second Life, as well as other virtual worlds coming on the scene. By late December approximately 65,000 members, some who had been inactive members, had renewed their subscription due to the company's enhanced features.

The premise behind Active Worlds is to connect people socially within virtual environments, with benefits afforded residents and major limitations for tourists. Residents build, communicate and socialize together in these spaces as avatars. You can build a home or a business, or you can simply kick back and enjoy the scenery and interaction. As a tourist, however, you cannot maintain a unique identity—something that Second Life has also facilitated since its inception. Since 1998, Active Worlds residents have met in real life for game reunions, which is obviously the point where one can no longer hide behind an avatar identity. Consequently, one's virtual life intersects into real life at that point of meeting.

Get a Second Life: Extending Humanity into Virtual Reality

SimCity was created in 1989, with the purpose of allowing participants to build cities inside the game, and sometimes these sites were based on historical accounts. As part of the game's challenge, the participants would be confronted by a series of in-world disasters or villainous attacks from intruders, and would be invited to respond to them accordingly, individually. The point of the game was simulating life events (albeit extreme at times), not about losing or winning as with other role-playing games such as Warcraft. Players are situated in the center of their universe, as each responds to circumstances changing around them. Various versions of the game have been successful through the years, and its latest edition was released in 2007.

Second Life is the culmination of the role-playing games that preceded it. It allows for online exchange around the world between people as unique avatars. In this way it serves as the ultimate social networking platform, the idea that we can all connect in virtual space as individuals. Like SimCity, Second Life allows its residents opportunities to create cities and communities. SL takes this experience one step further, encouraging people to create a second life in these communities and to share these spaces with others. There is no plot to Second Life, merely a way for people to engage in arts, music, literature, education, business and even romantic and deep relationships of their own making. There is no winning or losing in Second Life; rather the focus is on shared spaces among avatars—some own land, some rent, and some merely explore. Nearly everything you can do in real life, you can experience in Second Life—the limitations of course are somewhat restricted by the aural and visual sensory modes available within the game and one's computer. Residents of Second Life, particularly in the educational sector, extend their real-life relationships beyond the virtual confines of the game to network among one another, sometimes discussing various topics and occasionally meeting at professional conferences—on and off-line. What begins as a virtual acquaintance might develop into a real-life friendship, with contact occurring outside of the game platform. With a late Fall 2008 upgrade to its software, SL allows users can maintain contact with each other off -line as well.

Similar to Active Worlds, participants can attend annual reunions in the real world, extending upon their in-world relationships and associations. Universities have increasingly conducted classes in Second Life, with some institutions constructing in-world buildings that replicate their actual campus. Among the universities involved in learning activities in Second Life are Princeton University, Harvard University, Duke University, Stanford University, University of Southern California, University of Southern Denmark, Cambridge University, Oxford University, Vrije Universiteit Amsterdam, Brown University, University of Illinois at Urbana-Champaign, University College—Dublin, University of Tennessee at Chattanooga, University of the District of Columbia—Criminal Justice Program, and London College of Communication, and the list approaches at least 30 institutions on a modest count, with the numbers growing every day.

Other instructors prefer to teach their students around a campfire, while all are seated on cushions on a sandy beach. The mix of residents inside Second Life represents a fantastic socio-economic range, from high school educated, lower-middle-class participants to those with advanced degrees in science, literature, media and computer engineering and programming. The population of avatars slightly represents more women than men, but at least 10% of the female avatar population is in reality men. EPN, a non-profit foundation, released a report on the demographics of SL users, based on a survey of 246 residents in late 2006 (Reuters, 2006). Women tended to frequent SL more than men, and reportedly were better educated ("often at the university level") than male members. As a qualifier, 10% of all members had experimented with gender, and that percentage increased to 16% for men. Second Life has been called an innovative space for the "creative vanguard" (Reuters, 2006). SL residents spending more than 30 hours weekly in-world tended to "belong to the creative or IT professions" (Reuters, 2006). Interestingly, members who enjoyed "happiness" and "success" in RL were likely to experience the same satisfaction in SL; saying that, however, "a small group which feels less comfortable in the real world that has discovered fantastic social possibilities in Second Life [includes] retirees, the unemployed, housewives and 'those who are ill or physically challenged'" (Reuters, 2006).

At the Creating Second Lives Conference in Bangor, Wales, in October 2008, scholars representing virtual gaming communities, primarily Second Life and World of Warcraft, met to discuss their respective games' impact on education, science, the arts and social relationships. What became evident was that partakers of each game were uniquely motivated in their reasons for participation. Warcraft is a game of strategy, and it is the competition that leads to strong relationships among fellow players. Second Life is less a game of strategy, more of art imitating life. Second Life allows residents to thrive between mundane and magnificent places, activities and landscapes; participants seek knowledge and explore concepts virtually, meet others in mostly passive situations, and generally attempt to reinvent real life or perfect it. Two of the leading games represented at this conference offered two motivations for creating virtual communities—one that reflects Rheingold's version of the Well where people come together to share ideas and thoughts. The other creates communities that compete against each other, where players cooperate for survival and where strategy and aggression is central to the game. Second Life is a game about self and social exploration. For the artist, Second Life can represent a blank canvas, with possibilities limited to only the imagination and technology inherent in the game platform.

Gaming worlds, in which identities are drawn from fantasy, create a scenario that often counters authenticity, as one would likely be most familiar with in terms of real-world encounters. There is unwritten consensus among players in games like World of Warcraft in which players must establish a trust between each other for strategic purpose. Hardey (2004) suggests, "authenticity is finally 'tested' when people move from mediated communication to meeting in the flesh" (p. 208). Authentic relationships appear more likely to be developed in games such as Active Worlds and Second Life than those which are entirely based on game strategy and conquest. Second Life thrives in sharing time and creativity among participants, although some residents are perhaps more authentic than others (as in RL). Aaron Ben-Ze'ev (2004, p. 2) contemplates concepts of authenticity between players in virtual spaces when he considers the wider of scope of relationships made in-world: "Cyberspace is a part of reality; it is, therefore, incorrect to regard it as the direct opposite of real space. Cyberspace is part of real space, and online relationships are real relationships" (Ben-Ze'ev, 2004).

He adds, "What is new about cyberspace is its interactive nature and this interactivity has made it a psychological as well as social reality. It is a space where real people have actual interactions with other people, while being able to shape or even create their own and other people's personalities" (Ben-Ze'ev, 2004). This trend or "move from passive imaginary reality to the interactive reality of cyberspace is much more radical than the move from photographs to movies." Humanity is connected through technology, and the lines have blurred between reality, actuality, and virtuality through computer-mediated communication (CMC). Digital crafting of a news story or architectural design within virtual worlds, for instance, typically employs the same tools and technologies of their respective professions outside of virtual space.

Wildermuth & Vogl-Baur (2007) draw briefly upon the work of McLuhan, the medium being the message (McLuhan & Fiore, 1967), to underscore the potential of the Internet in guiding us to extend humanity's reach into personal and public spaces beyond our local communities and identities (Levinson, 1999; McLuhan, 1964; McLuhan & McLuhan, 1988). McLuhan (1964) envisioned technology as a means toward achieving the global village, as an extension of our humanity, social and physical. How might these communities be defined, engineered, and actualized to contribute toward understanding science and science fiction, either contextualized within visions of utopia or Huxley's dark portrayal of society. Second Life can draw attention to the physical and social elements of culture that we often ignore in real life; the intensity of concentrated immersion into this virtual world allows for a greater introspection behind who we are and who we would like to be in real and second life. We are offered a space to challenge our social and individual identity. Or, might Second Life be that idealistic global village, if we are particularly discussing the notion of how mediated communication connects us throughout the world, initially as avatars, encouraging us to learn about one another in real spaces.

Our traditional borders fall and territories become defined virtually through new-found common interests beyond national constructions. The automobile allowed us to experience a new freedom and mobility, as noted by McLuhan (1951). He envisioned television as a means to link households with the world. Virtual spaces offer similar extension, and perhaps are more in tune with our imagination and experience. The individual and social constructions that emerge from our thoughts inside virtual space create the means for dialogue among each other. These experiences are contextualized within visual and aural aesthetics. Second Life extends our communication across national borders and into the homes of strangers.

Parks & Floyd (1996) suggested online relationships need proximity, eye contact, voice communication, and physical appearance to mature into intimate, authentic experiences. Wildermuth & Vogl-Bauer (2007), however, suggest that perception has a much greater role than has been otherwise assumed. How do we perceive in virtual worlds—how do we discern what communications are real in virtual spaces? This question can be addressed in various ways, particularly by inviting contemplation on how media influences us on a daily basis in real and Second Life. As media changes, becoming more immersive, how might society transform and respond to technologies that shape our life and role in real and constructed space. The idea of a digital divide between virtual world users and those who prefer to stay exclusively in reality might not be too absurd to consider as virtual worlds are created and offer alternate views of reality at an increasingly rapid pace. In a sense, one might suggest that "Resistance is futile," or should be particularly among media makers. One should not resist the opportunity to understand the influence that these technologies are having on virtual world participants, how that is impacting larger society on a global level as well as shifting media makers toward converging media technologies and platforms beyond national borders. Science and art have shaped communicative media, and virtual worlds thrive on human expression within a social construct.

Conclusion

Virtual worlds are communities of real people, with real professions, who wish to extend their lives beyond physical borders, and what began historically within imagination is now reality. Second Life has engaged millions of people to at least put their avatar's foot into a 3D immersive virtual environment, as a complement or substitute to their off-line world. Media in virtual worlds facilitate information flow among communities, provide entertainment, and help to document life as it unfolds within these new spaces. Toxic Menges is a machinima producer in Second Life and resides in London, England, in her real life. She has been online for nearly 15 years. She helped in the organization of the Second Life 6th Anniversary celebrations for June 2009. Her Second Life journey began around 2006, but she settled with her current avatar in 2007. Like most Second Lifers, she never intended to become so engrossed in the game, which for some becomes a lifestyle. Second Life provides numerous creative outlets and career opportunities and connections for residents who are serious about extending their artistic visions to virtual spaces. For Menges, her real-life job as an online community manager since 1999 would inspire her eventually to take interest in virtual worlds:

> The main reason I joined was my life job as a community manager. I managed communities online. At the time, I was a community manager for a virtual world of teens. It was near 2006/2007 when virtual worlds were sort of hot, the next thing. I became thoroughly interested in virtual worlds and the different applications for them. In the

> day I was a community manager for a teen virtual world. By night I was a resident in Second Life. And I joined to see what it was all about, how it was different, from the place I was managing and also to see if there were any common elements, and if there were anything that I could inject into the place that was my real-life job. I went into it with the experience of community management and lots of years online and things like that, thinking I would just be an observer. I won't get too immersed and I'm fully in control and instead I got completely addicted and have been in here ever since. (Menges, 2009)

For Menges and others like her who are heavily invested in virtual worlds through their life and work experiences, it all comes down to people having opportunities to communicate and interact creatively to each other within the structure of communities:

> I have been online since about '95, and I have been doing community management since about '99 and I always explain communities to people as a very small microcosm of real life and that is so true of Second Life. I think it was created to be a little bit of utopia but unfortunately people came in and did exactly what they did to their first life to it. And that's actually fascinating. (Menges, 2009)

References

Ben-Ze'ev, A. (2004). *Love online: Emotions on the internet.* Cambridge: Cambridge University Press.

Bradbury, R. (2004). *Fahrenheit 451: 50th anniversary edition.* New York: HarperVoyager. First edition, 1953.

Castronova, E. (2007) Exodus to the virtual word: How online fun is changing reality. New York: Palgrave Macmillan.

Clarke, A. C. (1953). *Childhood's end.* New York: Ballantine Books.

—(1951). Sentinel of eternity (The Sentinel). *The Avon science fiction and fantasy reader* . New York: Avon Periodicals, Inc.

Creating Second Lives Conference. Bangor University. Bangor, Wales, October 2008.

Dunn, D. (2006). A history of electronic music pioneers. Unpublished paper. Accessed December 2, 2006, from http://www.davidddunn.com/~david/witings/pioneers.pdf

Grebb, M. (2005, October 20). Space geek seeks wireless power. *Wired News* (pp. 1–2). Accessed May 26, 2006, available at: http://www.wired.com/news/technology/technology/wireless_special/0,69038-0.html

Hardey, M. (2004). Mediated relationships: Authenticity and the possibility of romance. *Information Communication & Society* 7(2), 207–222.

Huxley, A. (2001). *Brave new world.* New York: Voyager Classics (original edition, 1932).

Leiner, B. M., Cerf, V. G., Clark D. D., Kahn, R. E., Kleinrock, L., Lynch, D. C., Postel, J., Roberts, L. G., & Wolff, S. (2006). A brief history of the Internet. Internet Society. Accessed May 17, 2006, from http://www.isoc.org/internet/history/brief.shtml#JCRL62

Levinson, P. (1999). *Digital McLuhan: A guide to the information millennium.* New York: Routledge.

The Matrix (1999). Warner Bros.

McAdams, M. (1996, March). Nikola Tesla and the one-hundredth anniversary of radio transmission. Accessed May 26, 2006, from http://home.earthlink.net/~drestinblack/ anniversary.htm

McLuhan, M., & McLuhan, E. (1988). *Laws of media: The new science*. Toronto: University of Toronto Press.

McLuhan, M. (1951). *The mechanical bride: Folklore of industrial man*. New York: Beacon Paperback.

—.(1967). *The mechanical bride: Folklore of industrial man*. Reprint 1951. New York: Beacon Paperback.

McLuhan, M. & Fiore, Q. (1967). *The medium is the massage: An Inventory of Effects*. New York: Bantam.

McLuhan, M. (1994). Understanding media. Cambridge, MA: MIT Press.

—.(1964). *Understanding media: The Extensions of* Man, Cambridge, MA: MIT Press.

Menges, T. (2009, July 15). Interview, personal communication with author. Second Life.

Parks, M. R., & Floyd, K. (1996). Making friends in cyberspace. *Journal of Communication, 45*, 80–97.

Picker, J. P. (2003). *Victorian soundscapes*. Oxford: Oxford University Press

Postman, N. (1985). Amusing ourselves to death. New York: Viking Press.

—.(1992). *Technopology: The surrender of culture to technology*. Toronto, ON: Random House of Canada.

Reuters, A. (2006, December 12). Study on SL and the pursuit of happiness. *Reuters Online*, SecondLife.com.

Rheingold, H. (1998). *The virtual community: Homesteading of the electronic frontier*, Addison-Wesley Publishing Company. Accessed December 15, 2008, from http://www.rheingold.com/vc/book/

Russolo, L. (2005). The art of noises: Futurist manifesto. In C. Cox & D. Warner (Eds.) *Audio Culture: Readings in Modern Music* (pp. 10–14). New York: Continuum.

—.(1967). *Art of noises* (1913), transl. R. Filliou, New York: Something Else Press. Accessed February 25, 2006, from http://www.ubu.com/historical/gb/russolo_noise.pdf.

Seifer, M. (1998). *Wizard: The life and times of Nikola Tesla: Biography of a genius*. New York: Citadel Press.

Sinclair, U. (1930). *Mental radio*. New York: Forgotten Books.

Slater, W. F. III. (2002, September). Internet history and growth. Presented at the Chicago Chapter of the Internet Society, Chicago, IL.

Stephenson, N. (1992.) Snow crash. New York: Bantam Spectra.

Sterne, J. (2003). *The audible past: Cultural origins of sound reproduction*. Durham: Duke University Press.

Tesla, N. (circa 1908). My inventions: An autobiography. Bayside, CA: Borderland Sciences Research Foundation. Retrieved December 2, 2006, from http://magickiansofsimpleology.info/myinventions.html

Turkle, S. (2005). *The Second self: Computers and the human spirit; 20th anniversary edition*. Cambridge, MA: The MIT Press.

—.(1997). *Life on the Screen: Identity in the age of the internet*. New York: Simon & Schuster.

2001: A Space Odyssey (1968). Metro-Goldwyn-Mayer.

Wildermuth, S. M., & Vogl-Baur, S. (2007). We met on the net: Exploring the perceptions of online romantic relationship participants. *Southern Communication Journal, 72*(3), 213–227.

CHAPTER TWO

Social Networking: Extending Your Circle of Friends, Virtually

> Today, you walk down the street, surrounded by people you don't know...Social capital leaks into the air, wasted, and nobody notices. Could mobile, networked, computationally powerful personal communication devices weave us into social networks that haven't existed before...?
>
> —Howard Rheingold, *On Collective Action, Social Networks, and Smart Mobs*

In a special *Forbes* report, America's top wired city was Seattle. The Internet is accessible through coffee shops, universities, businesses, homes and other hot spots throughout the metropolitan area. Others making top spots on *Forbes*' annual list of most broadband-connected cities in the U.S. based on access and wi-fi hot spots (Woyke, 2009) included Atlanta, Washington D.C., Orlando, and Boston. It is mainly larger cities that are connected and facilitate instantaneous electronic communication among residents. Numerous rural areas throughout the U.S., for example, still have difficulty finding wireless service.

In 2008, the Federal Communications Commission (FCC) announced that it would investigate the role of broadband access in the U.S., collecting data upon Senate approval of the Broadband Data Improvement Act, which was intended to increase availability and quality of wireless service throughout the nation, particularly under-served rural and urban areas. In 2009, the U.S. government acknowledged its commitment toward improving and investing in the nation's broadband infrastructure, seeking to provide economic stimulus to "e-commerce, education and health care" in those regions of the U.S. that have been falling behind nationally (Woyke, 2009).

The significance of social connectivity was demonstrated by the Presidential inauguration of Barack Obama in January 2009 when millions gathered on Facebook to watch the ceremony live, while responding to the events simultaneously in text. Facebook had joined with CNN to present live coverage online and to track feedback across the world among its international membership. Some for the Facebook comments included:

> "Ever heard a million people chant 'Obama'"
>
> "Has there been a 2 million people gathering for a President inauguration in other countries?"

> In response, someone replied, "+ several millions on facebook."

Others simply made brief comments such as "Obama's coming out now" and "a lot of obama-mania" within seconds of each other. The world watched the images unfold while it followed Facebook comments in the sidebar of the CNN site (Perez, 2009). American citizens engaged socially in a political transition of power online, as well as offline: "The integration of the status updates on CNN.com Live was powered by Facebook Connect, Facebook's relatively new platform for porting your online identity anywhere on the web" (Perez, 2009). This event also demonstrated Facebook's new authentication system; for instance, when "a web site uses Facebook Connect, visitors can easily authenticate on that site using their Facebook account information—no need for a separate username and password" (Perez, 2009). Members log on with their real names, "a trend that perhaps speaks to the beginning of the end of online anonymity" (Perez, 2009).

For some, the CNN-Facebook coverage presented numerous technical challenges, and they signed off and turned on the television. Nevertheless, this collaboration between a news service and a social network company made history during the inauguration. Facebook's Web site provided its members' "take" on a national event that connected the world online. Some observers commented, "If there was any doubt of the power this platform provides, we've just witnessed an incredible—if not historic—example of what it can do. President Obama's inauguration is sure to knock Facebook Connect ahead of its [competition] in the realm of portable social identities." As President Obama spoke, more than 8,000 people commented on the Facebook feed per minute, from 3,000 leading up to his speech: "CNN didn't do too badly either...[breaking its] total daily streaming record, set earlier on Election Day, and delivered 5.3 million streams" (ReadWriteWeb, 2009). Nearly 19 million live streams occurred on CNN between 6 AM and 1 PM ET on Inauguration Day (Schonfeld, 2009). Members commented when Obama flubbed the oath, and some communicated the reaction around their office, noting, "Everyone is crying and hugging. Everyone" (Schonfeld, 2009). Another comment emphasized the ability of users to connect while at work:

> Watching events like these with people you know is always better than watching alone, but since most of us are at work today, Facebook serves as a proxy for a virtual living room that can hold hundreds of people. (Schonfeld, 2009)

More than 21 million streams on CNN.com and 136 million Web site views were recorded by the conclusion of the ceremonies (Schonfeld, 2009).

Creating a Participatory Culture

The primary purpose of this chapter is to examine how Second Life serves to extend the notion of social networking within a virtual community of residents. Second Life, however, is merely one of many ways to connect people online. The Facebook/CNN Connect example demonstrates how the online community is improving its participatory culture. Viewers are no longer passive observers, but can share in history making immediately with instant blogging, so to speak. The interactivity speaks to where we are headed in media usage, possibly into a universal chat room.

In Asia, Internet cafés draw people away from their homes into social settings. These cafés become gathering spots throughout large cities or centers of activity in rural districts. In many countries, the Web is used as a tool for activism, as a way of distributing counter information. Political movements gain momentum online, with 10,000 protestors coming together for a candlelight vigil in Seoul Korea in 2008 to protest the importation of what was believed to be tainted beef into their country. The protest originated online, and developed into a massive street riot. The connectivity provided by the Web allows grassroots organizations to establish networks among members and facilitate information distribution.

Americans typically retreat to their computers in their individualized cubicles, although increasingly they have an opportunity to communicate to people beyond their neighborhoods and workplaces. Christine Rosen (2004/2005, p. 51) discusses how individualism and personalities are displayed "in the multiple media around us." MySpace, Facebook, and a plethora of profile management sites allow users to define and extend their list of friends, and present themselves in unique ways. From these platforms, viewers can communicate instant messages to other members in an effort to keep up with daily life happenings. Second Life is the ultimate social network that allows members to interact through daily conversations in a variety of settings—reality inspired or imagined. Educators, computer programmers, students, media specialists, journalists and others gather in-world via numerous specialty groups. Other times, this mixed lot of characters arrives at the same destination for a public concert or news event inside Second Life.

In Hong Kong, online games form the basis of communities among youth. One of the most popular games in Taiwan, China and Hong Kong is Online Jinyong, "a network odyssey based on the fictional epic and kung fu novels of Hong Kong writer Jinyong. Players role-play specific characters from the novels, wandering and combating in the 'lifeworld' (jianghu)" across virtual landscapes of an ancient world (Fung, 2006, p. 131). In this way, Jinyong is a "community game" (p. 131), where players "must learn to join communities, make friends, deal with other players, and cultivate a socially acceptable virtual character because there are informal tribal rules in the game...it is not a game that celebrates individuality but a game of community" (Fung, 2006, p. 134). In his critique, Anthony Fong states, "I am both supportive and skeptical about the cyberlife—real-life connection. The discovery of the connection reveals the pervasiveness of capitalist and competitive life and its ability to penetrate into the new promised land—the Internet." He continues, "...Were the connection between the real life and cyberlife suggestive of the impossibility of cyberlife's constructing an ideal humanistic and communicative environment, imagined communities would have long ago lost their appeal" (Fung, 2006, p. 138).

Rheingold (2002, 2003) sees commitment as key to community development: the idea that we must individually invest ourselves into the online community through dialogue and shared resources. New media author Steve Jones (1997, p. 18) posits that community begins with the crafting of our various identities in life, how we plug those identities into our online experiences, and how that impacts our relationships to others. Specifically, Jones asks, "Who do we think we are when we are online, and who do we want to be there?" (p. 18).

Internet Cafés

Yahoo released a report in 2004 that named the best cybercafés, and that list included a San Francisco Laundromat known as the Brain Wash. The Phlegmatic Dog in Moscow was given high marks for its style, comfort and technology. The most remote café was situated in Timbuktu, Mali. London's Cafe Cyberia was launched in 1994, and since then approximately 20,000 similar cafés have opened in 171 countries across the world (Reuters, 2004). In Europe, the café has long been the traditional watering hole for many who wish to chat about politics and happenings in their neighborhoods and the world. The coffee shop as a metaphor for democracy, in which the café serves as a public sphere for all to come together to participate in civil discussion, is typically credited to Jurgen Habermas. Other scholars such as Michael Dawson (1994) and Catherine Squires (2000) would argue that this metaphor fails to acknowledge an exclusion of those with differing opinions, perhaps due to socio-economical considerations and related factors. The "ideal" café does not exist, as we know. Both scholars contend that the public sphere precludes the reality of a multitude of spheres, running oppositional and counter to the mainstream public, contending individuals have unique social spheres consisting of friends, families, coworkers and business associates. Additionally, individuals typically gravitate toward groups that they feel will respect their perspectives and represent their interests.

Across the Web, there are countless social networking opportunities, from pet lovers to sci-fi enthusiasts to matchmaking. In a sense, Facebook and MySpace.com create a fairly universal space that draws a considerable amount of people of diverse ages and backgrounds online; social networking services splinter off based on the interest and intended use of the subscriber. Posting to these various sites, when allowed, gives members a means to contribute to discussion boards; in other words, it allows them to participate in the conversation thread. These postings can be removed at the will of the maker. Regardless, with blogs, bulletin boards, and social networking services everywhere online, individuals and groups splinter off to form their own groups (Boyd & Ellison, 2007).

Internet cafés, or even the local ice cream shop wired to the Web, have become meeting spaces for those seeking a quick online fix along with a shot of espresso in their coffee. The first Internet Café was set up in San Francisco around 1990 as the SF Coffee House Network: "In 1990 Intel introduced the 33-MHz 486 microprocessor (AT Technology)...SFnet was an attempt to use simple communications technology to bring together two very different social milieus." The rationale behind Coffee House Network was to provide "coin operated public access terminals" throughout the Bay Area, to encourage "social interaction" and "focused community energy to a public chat that used a fast moving text interface that allowed for no visual clues as to who was speaking" (SFnet, 2009). On August 18, 1991, the front page of the *San Francisco Examiner* headlined the emergence of the Bay city's network of cafés, and the opening paragraph reads, "It is a bustling Monday night and the usual coffee house bull session is in full swing, careening from the pros and cons of anarchy to the wit and wisdom of Bart Simpson" (Flinn, 1991, p. 1). The story continues, pointing out what has become so commonplace nearly two decades later, "These latter day William Saroyans aren't in the same café. They're sipping espresso in coffee houses scattered around San Francisco linked by a first-of-its-kind computer network that also one day may connect them to the cafés of Paris and Vienna" (Flinn, 1991, p. 1). Our ability to connect instantly to one another across town and globe has the potential to create dialogue nearly anywhere, anytime.

Not all the goals for connecting are so lofty, for some merely want to play games and keep in touch with friends and family. To many hooked on the Internet, from home, work, or en route, there is no excuse to not check your email. Some shops are designed for laptop users simply needing a wireless connection. For the price of a coffee or two, they can sit for hours surfing, networking, and even playing games with others in the same shop or across the world. Business deals are transacted, currency exchanged, in minutes. If not a sense of democracy, definitely the Web has created a sense of immediacy in nearly every aspect of our life, from shopping to education to romance. Might all this lead to a solving of global issues, anytime soon? Probably not, but many online users are letting down their guard as they communicate and play with each other internationally. The social distance between our national spheres is shrinking increasingly.

In a 2007 report, there were 5,000 Internet Cafés in capital cities, and numbers increasing in smaller towns and cities across Indonesia (Rusdiah, 2007). In South Korea, more than 20,000 cafés serve mostly young gamers. More than 100,000, mostly males, 18–34, go to these hot spots across China for game play. In Europe as more competing businesses go wireless, and as more residences are connected, the number of cafés are shrinking. However, for those who cannot afford private connections, some governments like the United Kingdom are providing wireless centers. Although many of these gamers are mingling within their national borders, increasingly players are communicating across the world. Laegran & Stewart (2003) investigated Internet Cafés as techno-social spaces, and how certain groups interact within such spaces, inviting the computer geek into the realm of alternative lifestyles, from health to trend-setting. The Internet has created a culture and lifestyle that now permeates society, and social and business relations demand immediate attention, not merely in North America, Europe and industrialized nations.

A casual look across Flickr.com reveals the diversity of Internet Cafés throughout the world. Images of small shacks selling Internet time in rural Africa and Asia particularly leave an impression of a human desire to be connected to the world, beyond one's immediate locality. Wahid, Furuholt, & Kristiansen (2003) studied customer use in Internet cafés in Indonesia, and found that older educated well-to-do patrons seek information and read news online more so than others. The Internet caters to individual needs, and becomes an instant resource for health information, politics, and daily news. Cultural traditions and practices, however, are becoming rapidly and increasingly challenged in these countries. Poor countries face unique challenges as the Internet offers them a glimpse into a life that has been out of their view previously.

Online Social Networking

For South Korea, Cyworld is the equivalent to Second Life. Ninety percent of the nation's population in their 20s comprise this virtual world/social forum.

Nearly 25% of its population (approximately 13 million people) are members or have visited Cyworld (Cameron, 2005). Gift buying for friends is big part of the game, as well music downloading and decorating one's room. Everyone receives a private room, and the idea is to give gifts to your circle of friends to achieve popularity. South Korea is the "world's most internet connected country": in fact, "the way that people live in South Korea has probably contributed to the phenomenal success of Cyworld. Identical and economical, but unlovely, blocks of flats that rise by the hectare in commuter suburbs have created the perfect environment...a dense and easily wired landscape for broadband companies" (Cameron, 2005). Cyworld members are encouraged to create home pages on the Web to display their personality and to indicate their popularity status among other members.

"Join the circle," "connect to your friends and family, "be part of the network"—those are just some of the phrases that you might hear on television, radio, or see across the Internet. Social networking has become a buzz concept for the public and corporations. Until recently, social networking was a theoretical way of understanding human relationships with one another on various levels. Our dreams, education, work, religion, music, and hobbies help to establish relationships among individuals. Sociologists have performed analyses on groups of people to determine their extended networks. Family members might comprise one set of relationships, but each person in that circle has their own set of relationships. In this way, we study and chart the community links between families, groups, organizations and corporations. In the 1950s, social scientists began to seek ways to indicate patterns that emerged beyond established family ties and gender and ethnicity (Freeman, 2006; Wasserman & Faust, 1994). Today, cellular phone companies advertise that individuals can connect with each other at special rates by extending their circle of friends.

Facebook and *MySpace* are popular examples of personal social networks, where people are connected through their hobbies and interests. Today, European countries connect through Facebook and MySpace, as well as European-based sites such as Bebo and Xing. Xing operates out of Germany, and is a network for small business professionals across the European Union. Bebo was recently purchased by AOL in March 2008 for more than 8 million dollars (Garfield, 2006). The trend for many services like Bebo is to be consumed by larger networking companies for insane profits based on their membership base. What began as a European regional site in 2005 has expanded beyond the United Kingdom to North America, Ireland, Australia, and New Zealand to serve as a place to keep up with friends, music, literature, and events. In 2005, Michael Birch created Bebo with his wife, and within one year 25 million people joined it and it was ranked the 6th "most popular site in the UK, bigger than AOL, Amazon and bbc.co.uk:"

> Like Yahoo and Google before it, Bebo is a word that has gone from meaningless to meaning everything to its users in a dramatically short period...there are so many of them that soon the computerised world may have no one between 11 and 18 who is not a fanatic. (Garfield, 2006, p. 7)

Services like Bebo have in many aspects usurped the old days of "networking" in real life. People who would spend hours on the phone, now spend it online: "In the real world, social networking often involves travelling, drinking, personal digital assistants and business cards, but the internet has simplified the process...MSN instant messaging—online written conversation—changed that" (Garfield, 2006, p. 7). Indeed, you might say that the Internet is coming full circle, and it is "beginning to join itself up. It is like a giant digital chain letter."

Cyber Schoolmates

When Facebook tapped into the college market and was no longer limited to North America, it became a social phenomenon worldwide which today continues to expand its membership. In certain countries, regional services remain popular due to language and cultural differences. Some small online business owners (and increasingly corporations) use these social networks as forums for expanding their clientele. Whether fashion, music or gadgets are being discussed or sold, social networks connect people to individuals and companies with similar interests. *MySpace* for example is geared for the musician who wants to promote his albums or upcoming venues; the average Joe or Jane can link to their favorite bands. The indie bands can build their member base through these social vehicles. For the most part, friends and family connect with each other to keep in touch and sport their latest photos. Members within these social circles communicate by leaving messages on each others' sites and by instant messaging one another.

Web companies like Yahoo (with 248 million registered members) have created similar message platforms, where members can choose between one of several avatar representations. Second Life is a fully interactive instant messaging social network that allows members to communicate among friends, families and acquaintances, while they are immersed in a virtual world. In September 2008, SL released a client service that allowed members to instant message to in-world contacts when offline. Residents have created their own social networks similar to MySpace and Facebook. One service is simply called Second Life Social Network, available through Ning, an online social network provider. Koinup is a Second Life take off of Flickr, where members can post their SL favorite photos or videos. Social networking in the 21st century is a given; social networking sites help individuals to connect to friends, as well as someone's friends' friends. These sites never were intended to serve only the social networking interests of young adults and teens. One of the first such sites was Classmates.com in 1995, and it received attention as a means to find and reacquaint former high school chums. For many residents, Second Life serves as an imaginative social networking forum in and of itself. Members have profiles, and chat and IM each other. They can post pictures in their profiles, including links to their personal Web sites, and connect to a host of other personal networking services from inside Second Life.

Perhaps because of the preponderance of educators who have joined Second Life, membership ages skew away from young adults. For this reason, Kaneva was created to provide a service geared to those in their 20s and early 30s. Such sites, while competing with Second Life, fill a niche for dating and chat among clientele. Kaneva members connect with each other as avatars in a cyber-world like Second Life. Kaneva's Virtual Word was launched in 2006, although the company had been involved in the gaming industry since 2004. "Facebook on steroids" is how SL has been described in jest within the Metaverse. Kaneva operates like a streamlined version of Second Life, but it attempts to tap into the interests of its somewhat younger membership, offering live music and entertainment consistent with participants' interests as much as that is possible. Market researchers have encouraged businesses to look at these sites to reach certain customers; one article from Forrester Research even recommended that companies should consider ways to "friend" people who are most likely to buy their product, by matching member profiles to product services (Li, 2007).

For companies like Cyworld, tapping into one's network of friends can mean financial windfalls: "Koreans often spend hours rearranging their avatars' moods, outfits, and rooms. Cyworld has cashed in on this addiction, selling digital accessories to users to the tune of $120 million in Korea alone last year" (*The Korean Upstart*, 2006). But its approach is a bit different; it is a service that prides itself on being cute and nice, and is in tune with American popular culture icons. Its concept of funky mini-me avatars is no doubt borrowed from the movie character *Austin Powers*. Cyworld has made a concerted effort to target the college market: "If MySpace is like a hip party, where users vie for popularity and attention, Cyworld USA is a relaxed hangout that stresses existing friendships and hosts 2,650 clubs, such as 'Interns Unite!' Cyworld gives social networking a twist, combining photo sharing and blogging with digital avatars" (*The Korean Upstart*, 2006). Cyworld is currently tapping into the young adult Asian college market in the United States, with its presence already established in China, Japan, Korea and Taiwan. In 2008, it announced goals of extending services into Europe, South America and India, and plans to compete directly with Facebook, MySpace and Second Life. The membership base of Cyworld USA is growing, but mainly among Asian populations. Notably company representations of avatar characters are diverse in race and ethnicity. Cyworld offers interactive messaging, personal profile and Web management, and an immersive cyberworld of avatars. Cyworld is building a worldwide membership that has caught the attention of other services, who are beginning to understand the universal appeal of social networking at a corporate level.

Second Life: The Ultimate Social Network

Linden Lab has positioned itself strategically within the market of a plethora of social networking services. Second Life offers its members the opportunity to link with each other via IM or Voice. Members can chat within groups privately or in public venues. SL photos can be captured, saved, and exported into other networking services. Real-life photos can be imported into Second Life. Member profiles link real and second life, and one's Web page, blog, or social network site can be uploaded within Second Life. Other sites, such as Second Life Network.com and SecondAvatar.com, are independent operations that offer residents a Facebook-like platform intended for SL residents. Membership on these sites is very limited; why should someone join another service when their MySpace or Facebook can be uploaded from inside Second Life. One interesting difference between Second Life and other social networking services is that SL users tend to spend hours in-world. Second Life allows residents the means to communicate instantly beyond their established circle of friends.

The U.S. Centers for Disease Control is an amazing example of how information can be dispersed through social media forums. The CDC has had a staff member inside SL since 2007 as a liaison between both worlds to facilitate health information dispersion, but in a creative way: "There's nothing very unusual about two red-headed women chatting in the headquarters of a Federal agency...unless one of the women is actually a man, and the headquarters actually exists on a server somewhere in Linden Lab" (Weinreich, 2007). SL Reporter Nedra Weinreich (2007) continues, "That man is John Anderton, who is responsible for bringing the U.S. Centers for Disease Control and Prevention (CDC) into Second Life." Weinreich met Anderton's avatar, Hygeia Philo, when he came across "an announcement of a CDC Health Fair listed in *New World Notes* and decided to find out more about what the CDC is up to in Second Life" (Weinreich, 2007).

Anderton made a plea to his workplace to explore SL as a best practice for social networking, and in terms of creative social media platforms it seemed to be the right fit for the CDC to participate in health fairs. Anderton initially investigated "YouTube as a means of disseminating CDC health content, and ran across a machinima presentation on Second Life in March, 2006" (Weinstein, 2006).

Increasingly, Second Life events and activities are appearing on YouTube, from weddings to fashion shows to live music and events with avatar rock stars. A number of how-to videos help SL members learn to build and navigate around Second Life. Second Life is positioning its service as a point of convergence in social media; all social paths lead to Second Life per se. With an updated splash page on its home site, Second Life is marketing itself as the place to dance, play, learn and connect to people around the world, from your neighborhood to distant lands. It has become the ultimate matchmaking service, although in-world romantic encounters sometimes go foul with real newspaper headlines capturing those sensational moments in this brave sometimes sensual new world. Couples fall in and out of love in Second Life, as they would offline. These relationships can be documented in photos, hours spent online dancing and conversing, and established through SL marriages and RL meetings. For those using social media platforms, the concept of networking online is one without borders; and the concern evolves into where does the virtual begin and end for online communication.

A Virtual Journey

Journey McLaglen is a top fashion designer in Second Life. She owns stores in fashion districts in Tampa Bay and along the Best of Second Life Boulevard. She has been a mentor to aspiring fashion designers and those wanting to enter the business of Second Life. McLaglen is part of a business community that grew out of her experiences with friends she had established in Second Life:

> I also write for *The Best of Second Life Magazine*. I have a column with them as a travel writer, writing about journeys, appropriately called, that you can take in Second Life. I write about whatever the feature story is—the emotional story of the month. This month it was "relay for life." I have really focused on *Best of SL Magazine*. First I met the people, and I liked what they were doing. Frolic Mills is really quite an entrepreneur in this virtual world. (McLaglen, 2009)

Mills is the owner of *Best of Second Life Magazine*, a leading fashion and lifestyle magazine in Second Life. He also owns the surrounding fashion district around his magazine offices: "He is full of ideas. He has the golden touch. Everything he does seems to work out so brilliantly" (McLaglen, 2009). Her real-life experiences and SL contacts have provided invaluable opportunities for her. In Second Life, she has learned from watching, in some case, from the sidelines. Frolic Mills has established one of the leading fashion districts and in the nearby auditorium, he held Fashion Week 2009, an amazing array of top work from leading designers in Second Life. McLaglen (2009) explains:

> He built the Fashion District. They kind of grew up together. He started the magazine and it made perfect sense for him to open a district for all designers who were advertising in the magazine. That has grown and grown, and he developed a partnership with Patch Thibaud, who is a brilliant designer. Patch is the one who built the auditorium that Frolic's group *Best of SL* uses for all of their events. The Patch Thibaud Auditorium is an amazing place that is built over four sims and that allows you to arrive in alternating locations. So there is never a traffic jam. And it allows a speaker to be in one sim so there's not a lot of lag so everybody can hear things well. When that was developed, it really wasn't something that was happening everywhere. It was ground-breaking. So much of what Frolic is involved in is ground-breaking. He's just an interesting person overall.

McLaglen (2009) adds, being around Frolic and the BOSL staff has been an "opportunity to learn about communicating in this new environment. So writing for the magazine has been a great experience. It's fun because what I really get to do is what I started out doing in real life, and I started out as a newspaper features reporter. I was an award-winning journalist and then an award-winning PR person." As a media person, having established a career in public relations and newspaper writing, as well as dabbling in television, Second Life has become an invaluable medium to extend McLaglen's creativity and contacts into the virtual fashion world. Her real-life work drew her into Second Life:

> I changed jobs mid life. I went into project management for a Web-based training firm. In doing that, Second Life had figured very prominently into a lot of the new training methods that were being featured. I went to Learning 2008 in Orlando, and they really drove the whole thing home. When I first joined the company 3 years ago, I was introduced to Second Life. They asked me to become familiar with it, in case it became a really good teaching tool. So I did, and I became very familiar with it. I really saw so many opportunities for so many different things here. It just amazed me so I stayed.

McLaglen understood immediately the significance of Second Life as a social tool, and her first year she spent much of her time establishing relationships in-world:

> Some people jump right into building and things like that, but it took me a year because my life was very busy in real life, and really busy in Second Life. I had a lot of friends and things like that. I guess I was fascinated with the whole prospect of having people all over the world as part of your social network. I learned so much.

Her network grew as she continued to make friends and contacts in Second Life; among them, she met designers, builders, filmmakers, club owners, and journalists. In what might be thought of as a personal virtual evolution, she began to develop a feel for the social and business climate of Second Life. Her networking transitioned into a career in fashion and led to her being acknowledged among her peers as a top designer in the SL fashion industry:

> Eventually, especially with hanging around with friends who had been on here from the very beginning, I started to think about making things, and I especially like fashion. So that is where I focused my attention. As a fashion designer, it's a lot of work. It's constant; every night I come on here with maybe 10 things I have to do, plus respond to requests from customers and things like that. It's a lot of work, but I have a good network of support. At the same time, it takes a lot of dedication. Everything I do is tied to designing. I have a great family network. I guess some people call it a clan. I have a great family in Second Life that is very supportive. And it's mostly women, and there must be 20 women that are either my daughters or my sisters. There's never a lack of someone being around. I'm usually teaching someone, or helping them to decide on a career in a virtual world or something along those lines.

The relationships that McLaglen has made in Second Life are meaningful to her. She brings her media savvy, business sense, and people skills into Second Life. But she has also made a huge emotional investment that others from the outside might not understand. The connections made in Second Life are emotionally real and cannot be understated, as she elaborates saying:

> For everyone, it is different. People come in here and sometimes they draw the boundaries and say this is a game. And I'm only going to let it be a game, and I'm not going to let it go beyond that. And some people are more successful at that approach but it tends to be people who would secure themselves in a real world environment. For others, Second Life allows them to step outside the comfort zone and totally try things they would never feel comfortable doing in real life: meeting new people, being outgoing. So often people thoroughly outgoing here will say to me I'm really shy in real life. And I'm thinking, how is that possible. But it is. There are people with which this is an extension of a talent they are not comfortable revealing in real life. So I guess in the distinction between real life and Second Life, what I would say is—it's an evolution for everyone. I think anyone who has been here for a while will tell you it is never a game. It's not been a game. It is hard to explain to anyone who hasn't been here a while that it's likely to strip away the exterior of things.

When someone first enters Second Life, they spend time acclimating to the environment, seeking and meeting friends, and experimenting with identities and the new world around them. Once they have established themselves among a family of friends, a social network within their virtual clan, it is often difficult for them not to become emotionally involved in their established friendships, particularly if these friendships have evolved into business and social partnerships. When someone leaves Second Life, or breaks off a relationship, the connections broken trigger real emotions. McLaglen shared some personal perspectives along this line, recalling the connections that she has made not only through her business ventures but through what has also become an emotional journey for her in Second Life:

> Then you go through the devastating loss of a friend when they leave the game or a lover which is a terrible thing to go through. For many, it is the end of their Second Life. I have met so many people who have just said "I can't do this anymore" because it is almost harder than real life in some ways, because you have nothing but emotion invested, you know what I mean. Then for an outside person to look at you, and say how could you really love someone you meet and you don't really know them in person. But it is who we are as human beings. We like to connect. When that connection actually goes away, you feel empty like you have been amputated for awhile. I know this is my third year and I have had three long-term relationships for SL. My first one lasted about 4 months. My second one lasted close to a year, and my third one close to a year. You grieve when you lose it, just like you grieve when you lose friends. Every now and then a long lost friend will pop in, and you will say "Hi, how's it been?" "What's going on in your life?" You connect again for that moment. I think it is impossible to treat SL like a game for very long.

As in real life, McLaglen is a career woman, supported by a circle of friends. She attends to their needs on a daily basis. She adds, "When I'm not designing and I'm not marketing, and I'm not putting together a new store, or moving things around (laughs), and all the daily upkeep of the business, then I'm helping my friends and people I know in real life come into Second Life." For McLaglen, she has extended her circle of friends internationally within Second Life, and has helped others make the transition into establishing virtual social networks. She has achieved success in the fashion world of Second Life, and is known as an astute business woman. Her story will be continued in a later chapter.

Teleporting to the Real World

You might say that the Second Life Community Convention has become the window to where avatars teleport into the real world. Members, having established relationships in-world, transcend through a virtual portal into the physical realm. The first member convention occurred in July 2005, when a handful of SL gamers headed off to invade Linden Lab in San Francisco; in reality, it was a way to meet and socialize away from their computers where they had become online friends. From that visit, these would-be organizers tossed some ideas out on SL forums, making initial inquiry about the possibility of an event that would bring SL residents together for some real-world fun and chat (SLCC, 2009). The first major convention occurred October 8, 2005 in New York, several months after the idea had been conceived sometime around July. More than 150 residents showed for the event, which continues to be organized completely by volunteers. One of the conference highlights was when Philip Linden addressed the attendees for a keynote dressed as his avatar. In 2006, the convention was held in San Francisco, and 500 members attended the event

The following year in Chicago more than 800 SL residents attended the conference (SLCC, 2009). In 2008, the convention was held in Tampa, Florida, and remained successful at bringing SL members together for socialization and entertainment, with sessions and events related to virtual life. In 2009, the convention returned to San Francisco, with the event becoming increasingly acknowledged as the ultimate social networking activity among SL game players. Members register for the conference online and connect to other members through Facebook, Flickr, Google Group, and Twitter. The online registration site purports, "The Second Life Community Convention is the largest virtual world convention combining art, business, community events, education, music, non-profit, and the technical aspects of Second Life, virtual worlds, and its related technologies in one location" (SLCC, 2009).

The reality behind the motivations of the convention organizers is that they have transcended virtual life into the real world, and created a means for members to authenticate their in-world relationships. In essence, SL members can teleport at least once a year into shared space outside their virtual home. Virtual groups formed through such similar reference points establish identity and connections among members at a real world event (Ahuja & Galvin, 2003; Jenkins, 1996). The convention reinforces a shared social identity, a sense of an institutionalization of a collective identity, while individual identities become infused within group norms. The annual conventions offer members a common social identity outside the gaming space. Their in-world identities are accepted as an extension of their real world lives.

Conclusion

Internet technology has provided the means to create social networking circles, with the most extreme exemplification being virtual words like Second Life. Dutta-Bergman (2005) notes how the Internet has been a significant factor in establishing communities within regions and beyond. A sense of localism can be established in smaller circles, and other groups come together on special interests. The key is access and participation among membership. A sense of collaboration among members is critical to retain communication, and that might mean sharing photos, videos, information, or merely conversing on a particular subject. Second Life allows members to build a community together from a blank canvas. For some members, this means creating their version of utopia. For others, they find ways to join an existing community and to work within that group vision.

Many members in SL attend the annual Second Life conventions, bringing their virtual relationships into a real space. Most certainly this might be what Hlebec et al. (2006) conveys as the potential of the Internet to allow for online relationships to move offline. Online communication becomes an authentic part of one's daily life. Rheingold (1998) would add that the emotional component—the human connection—is what makes these relationships portend to be authentic to the people engaged in cyberspace worlds. The relationships are valid, and members participate as members in every way, but the space is merely within a virtual environment. It is a matter of perspective which world is more real to many members; there is "shared understanding" among participants (Wood & Smith, 2001, p. 110), and social intimacy within such relationships may develop from that reference point.

References

Ahuja, M. K., & Galvin, J. E. (2003). Socialization in virtual groups. *Journal of Management 29* (2), 161–185.

Boyd, D. M., & Ellison, N. B. (2007). Social network sites: Definition, history, and scholarship. *Journal of Computer-Mediated Communication, 13*(1), article 11. Accessed December 14, 2009, from http://jcmc.indiana.edu/vol13/ issue1/boyd.ellison.html/

Cameron, D. (2005). Koreans cybertrip to a tailor-made world. TheAge.Com. Accessed March 20, 2009, from http://www.theage.com.au/articles/2005/05/06/1115092684512.html

Dawson, M. (1994). A black counterpublic? Economic earthquakes, racial agenda(s), and black politics. *Public Culture 7(1),* 195–224.

Dutta-Bergman, M. J. (2005). The antecedents of community-oriented Internet use: Community participation and community satisfaction. *Journal of Computer-Mediated Communication, 11*(1), article 5. Accessed June 4, 2009, from http://jcmc.indiana.edu/vol11/issue1/ dutta_bergman.html.

Flinn, J. (1991, August 18). High tech small talk offered at city's cafes. *San Francisco Examiner,* pp. 1, A14.

Freeman, L. (2006). *The Development of social network analysis.* Vancouver: Empirical Press.

Fung, A. (2006). Bridging cyberlife and real life: A study of online communities in Hong Kong. In D. Silver & A. Massanari (Eds.), *Critical CyberCulture* (pp. 129–139). New York: New York University Press.

Garfield, S. (2006, June 18). How to make 80 million friends and influence people. *The Observer.* Accessed March 20, 2009, from http://www.guardian.co.uk/media/2006/jun/18/ digitalmedia.observerreview

Habermas, J. (1989). The structural transformation of the public sphere: An inquiry into a category of bourgeois society. Cambridge, MA: MIT Press.

Hlebec, V., Manfreda, K. L., & Vehovar, V. (2006). The social support networks of Internet users. *New Media & Society, 8,* 9–32.

Jenkins, R. (1996). *Social identity.* London: Routledge.

Jones, S. (1997). The Internet and its social landscape. In S. Jones (Ed.), *Virtual culture: identity and communication in cybersociety* (pp. 7–35). New York: Sage Publications.

The Korean upstart in Myspace's face. Accessed March 22, 2009, from http://www.businessweek.com/magazine/content/06_46/b4009088.htm

Laegran, A. S., & Stewart J. (2003, September 1). Nerdy, trendy or healthy? Configuring the Internet cafe. *New Media Society 5*(3), 357-377.

Li, C. (2007, June 21). How consumers use social networks. Social Networking Series, Part 1 Forrester.com. Executive Summary. Accessed March 22, 2009, from http://www.forrester.com/Research/Document/Excerpt/0,7211,41626,00.html

McLaglen, J. (2009, August 5). Interview, personal communication with author. Second Life.

Perez, S. (2009) Facebook and CNN: The power of the social web revealed. Readwriteweb.com. Accessed January 20, 2009, from http://www.readwriteweb.com/archives/facebook_and_cnn_the_power_of_the_social_web_revealed.php/

Readwriteweb.com (2009) Accessed January 20, 2009, from http://www.readwriteweb.com/

Reuters. (2004, September 1). Yahoo awards world's best cybercafés. Accessed February 6, 2009, from http://www.abc.net.au/news/newsitems/200409/s1189662.htm

Rheingold, H. (2003, September 22). *On collective action, social networks, and smart mobs.* CIO. Accessed June 19, 2009, from http://www.cio.com/article/29804/ Howard_Rheingold_onCollective_Action_Social_Networks_and_Smart_Mobs?page=1.

—(2002). *Smart Mobs: The next social revolution.* Cambridge, MA: Perseus Publishing.

—.(1998). *The virtual community: Homesteading of the electronic frontier.* Addison-Wesley Publishing Company. Accessed December 15, 2008, from http://www.rheingold.com/vc/book/

Rosen, C. (2004/2005). The age of egocasting. *The New Atlantis: A journal of technology and society*, 7 (Fall/Winter), pp. 51–72. Accessed June 12, 2009, from http://www. thenewatlantis.com/publications/the-age-of-egocasting.

Rusdiah, R. (2007). Challenges in building netcommunity in urban developing countries. Telecenter Movement & Partnership in Asia: Road Ahead—eAsia2007. Telecenter Forum, February 6–8, 2007, Putrajaya, Malaysia.

SLCC: Second Life Community Convention. (2009). History. Web Site. Accessed June 12, 2009, from http://www. slconvention.org.

Schonfeld, E. (2009). Watching the inauguration with all my facebook friends. Access January 20, 2009, from http://www.techcrunch.com/2009/01/20/watching-the-inauguration-with-all-my-facebook-friends/

SFnet coffee house network. SFnet Archive. Accessed January 21, 2009, from http:// www.sfnet.org/

Squires, C. R. (2000). Black talk radio. *Harvard International Journal of Press/Politics 5*(2), 73–93.

Wahid, F., Furuholt, B., & Kristiansen, S. (2003). Internet for development? Patterns of use among Internet café customers in Indonesia. *New Media & Society*, *5*(3), 335–356.

Wasserman. S., & Faust, K. 1994. *Social network analysis: Methods and applications.* Cambridge: Cambridge University Press.

Weinreich, N. (2007, November 29). The CDC's second life: A best practice for social networking. Spare Change. Accessed April 14, 2009, from http://www.fundraising123.org/article/cdc%E2%80%99s-second-life-best-practice-social-networking.

Weinreich, N. (2006, November 1). The CDC's second life. Spare change. Accessed April 14, 2009, from http://www.social-marketing.com/blog/2006/11/cdcs-second-life.html

Wood, G. S. Jr., & Smith, M. J. (2001). *Online communication: Linking technology, identity, and culture.* Mahwah, NJ: Lawrence Erlbaum Associates.

Woyke, E. (2009). America's most wired cities. Forbes.com. Accessed January 23, 2009, from http://www.yahoo.com/

CHAPTER THREE

Identity In-World: Self and Fantasy in Second Life

> "Itself a product of the American Dream, Second Life produces hordes of Kens and Barbies we call avatars. Like vehicles driven through an online landscape, they float blank-eyed in their magic kingdom, each hoping to strike it rich, become a star, find a friend, or simply explore new possibilities..."
>
> —Mark Stephen Meadows *I, Avatar*

Mark Stephen Meadows (2008, p. 8) tells the story of an influx of people to virtual worlds wanting to escape or improve their real life as avatars: "The immigrants coming to Second Life...are armed with ambitions to sell temptations. Some are here to solve problems that can't be solved in their 'first life,' and some are here to make new lives." Second Life, he suggests, sells the American Dream to those struggling to find utopia in real life. Others see Second Life as an opportunity to role-play through situations and emotions that might be more difficult to work out in real life. In her book *Youth Online*, Angela Thomas (2007) provides numerous case studies of teens that have used online communication to experiment with their identity to the point of creating a stronger image of themselves through role-playing.

Thomas draws upon theorist Michel Foucault in her discussion on how identities are shaped through discourse, a process that is performed intellectually and politically as we interact with each other in various scenarios through various levels of engagement. The process of becoming (such as in self-actualization) might involve total immersion into virtual worlds. In the case of Thomas' work, she investigated how youth came to acknowledge this process as the means toward freedom in expressing themselves through alternate identities constructed from fiction and/or reality. It is through online social communication tools that these youth have come to understand themselves in virtual environments and subsequently project their identity into the real world, transforming and overcoming fears that once hindered their personality and emotional expression. Whether acting out in virtual worlds or merely communicating with others online across various social platforms, the potential for identity exploration becomes evident. This chapter explores how identity is constructed in Second Life, as part fantasy and part reality.

For some, Second Life offers a complete escape from reality, while others create their avatars to resemble their appearance and personality. Some members have more than one avatar, with each expressing a unique side of their perceived, imagined or real identity. Second Life allows members to play with identity in a relatively safe environment that provides for non disclosure and experimentation, but in an altered state of reality. Second Life can become as socially real as an individual desires. The boundaries between real and second life are individually determined. Identity can be expressed in Second Life through one's avatar form, gender, skin color, and fashion choices, as well as by the groups they have joined in-world. This chapter introduces how a sense of community, reflective of the real world, has been maintained and extended into a virtual environment when individuals assume roles, perceived or fabricated.

Identity Formation

Social identity is shaped by many factors, mainly by the people and the social settings that surround us. Personality is what we bring to a situation, based on individual traits and shaped by socialization. Sounds fairly basic, right? Yet, sometimes our circumstances bring us into contexts that are very unlike what we have experienced, and we begin to contemplate on our identity: Who am I, really? In a sense, we have many sides to our personality; for example, we certainly know that one might respond differently to questions from parents regarding concerns about our life than friends' proddings on how we are dealing with a situation. Gender, age, ethnicity, and socio-economics, among other factors, contribute to our social perspectives and our individual personalities. We might be fairly aware of our responses at given social settings, but what if we are drawn into a word so radically different, in which we are for the most part anonymous, how might we view ourselves? Sometimes a vacation or a business trip to another country helps us to rethink our identity; longer stays, of course, which remove us from friends and family, dramatically increase the likelihood that our individual and social views will alter as a consequence of the experience. What I suggest here is our response to an immersion into a parallel universe—the Metaverse, which has elements of familiarity to real life while allowing for complete physical transformation of appearance, residence, and expectations. You can build your own rocket and travel to Mars, or you can buy an estate for a fraction of the cost in RL. You can become a troll or a beauty queen. The possibilities are endless. You can also make yourself similar to your RL appearance. You can search for people and places alike or different from yourself in this second world; nonetheless the quest will likely challenge your identity.

Creating Social Spaces for Avatars

Second Life is a second space that consumes time and emotional resources and ultimately questions social and individual identities. One has the opportunity to be reborn, so to speak, as anything one wants to be, within the limits of scripting. The architecture in SL often reflects our desire for human comforts; we typically want a chair to be a chair for instance in RL and SL. These icons remain social cues in Second Life, so one can readily adapt to a situation within virtual spaces. In avatar form, human perspective is very different. Flying is easier than walking, and only a few roads exist on which to travel. Exercise is out of the question, for losing or gaining weight is simply an adjustment to appearance in the edit mode. The actual physical construction of SL buildings and settings requires some rethinking about our physical needs, so we might accommodate settings to avatar forms and abilities. The advantages are that one can walk or fly through buildings, for example when they are set to phantom.

Architect Matthaios Aquacade, as she is known in SL, presented a lecture at one of my graduate student seminars in Second Life on July 19, 2008, sharing some guidelines on how humans as avatars emotionally and physically interact within virtual spaces. Aquacade is a licensed architect who has worked on construction projects, from private residences to larger commercial ventures, across Europe. She has extended her professional outreach into Second Life. Her European-based company, Citrus Virtual Ltd, has been contracted by educational and non-profit groups and institutions to design buildings, landscapes, and settings that are avatar-friendly.

She creates spaces in which SL members, in avatar form, can learn, converse, and explore naturally, with little disruption to their senses. Aquacade has developed a business for assisting academic or non-profit organizations with spatial design. She explains, "I try to use the ideas and approaches I developed as an architect, but I have found that they have had to be tweaked and altered for building in a virtual world." She is rewriting the rules for living in virtual spaces, as she explains:

> Virtual architecture is not the same as real world architecture. Virtual spaces have socialising as their main function; they are a stage set to the activities of people co-present in a virtual world. (Aquacade, 2008)

Specifically, Aquacade (2008) notes, "Spaces and their contents are props, aesthetic design is the mood lighting; it is all a backdrop to our activities and virtual lives." She adds, "It is this that makes a three dimensional world out from the 2D internet" (Aquacade, 2008). She is a top in-world designer who understands the human need to seek out the familiar in the unknown: "Being present in mostly human form bodies, many people want familiar spaces in which to inhabit them" (Aquacade, 2008). She explains, "They want the reassurance of the familiar to give them cues on context, function and behavior" (Aquacade, 2008). In contrast, other residents perceive Second Life as a space of experimentation that allows for imaginative expression: "Others want to experience flights of fantasy and experimentation. They do not expect the virtual world to be limited by the real. These two attitudes collide and overlap as well to create hybrid spaces, such as skyboxes" (Aquacade, 2008). She continues,

> The uses of virtual spaces are very varied—meeting spaces, offices, clubs, theatres, homes, shops, parks and role-play settings are but a few. Function is limited only by imagination and finding others who share the same vision. (Aquacade, 2008)

The New Kid in SL

When Second Life was created, much of it was a blank canvas, awaiting members to create landscapes, soundscapes, buildings, places of exhibition and gatherings, or solitary retreats. Some places were open to the public, such as parks; other places were intended for private use with limited access by members outside a group. Today, when a new member joins SL, he or she will encounter a variety of places already designed, ranging from private residences, to parks, tourist beaches, nightclubs, museums, churches, elegant to funky malls, stadiums, university buildings, company offices, and so forth. Immediately, new members find themselves transported into this surreal world, and they begin to question how they look. They sometimes are referred to as "noobies" (or "newbies"—with skin, clothes, and overall appearance looking rather drab compared to other members who have been around for several months to three or four years. Some people welcome them, and others ignore or snub them. As ridiculous as it sounds, new members can find themselves isolated and feeling like social outcasts. To offset this harsh introduction to this second world, some SL members volunteer as mentors, and encourage them to join newbie groups. Certain builds, like 5 O'clock and Eternal Creations, were created to be gathering places to draw people together to talk and share life, and they were particularly hospitable to newbies just getting acclimated to Second Life. Members warmly embrace new SL members, and invite them to sit around and chat on the beach. In the case of Eternal Creations, new members can sit around the beach campfire in lawn chairs with other residents, sharing stories and getting to know each other in RL and SL. Eternal Creations, a non-denominational Christian island off the mainland, has a Newbie Welcome Center. The sim 5 O'clock Somewhere was established for the most part as a beach hangout with live music. Eternal Creations has a dance club, live music, residential homes, tiki stores, and a plethora of social activities designed to encourage fellowship among Christians (and non-Christians as well). In later chapters, Eternal Creations will be further investigated when taking a look at religion in Second Life, and a peek at 5 O'Clock Somewhere will provide some insights on the meaning of home and space in virtual worlds.

I Am Avatar

When a person joins Second Life, they will arrive on one of several Orientation Islands, avatar boot camps set in tropical paradises. Members typically complete a series of skill tests before they are permitted to move on to the main island. These tests are designed to help new members with basic skills in appearance, mobility, and communication with others. From Orientation Island, members move to one of several help centers, which provide a host of free items, such as building textures, clothing, and gadgets to facilitate an avatar's experience in Second Life.

On Orientation Island, an avatar can select among several types of looks, and then adjust accordingly gender, skin, hair, body shape, and other physical features. He or she will also learn to walk, fly, communicate, and explore using maps. This indoctrination is necessary to help new members acclimate successfully into Second Life, which is intended to be an enjoyable experience collaborating and socializing with others. Several SL mentors are visibly on hand, ready to assist a newbie as necessary when they note any sense of frustration that might intimidate them to poof back to RL. It is interesting to note the interaction between new members, who tend to gravitate to each other while engaging in the SL boot camp experience. Many newbies offer friendships to other new members during training, realizing perhaps it is easier to explore this brave new world together than alone—the idea of not being isolated when confronting challenges, be they real or constructed, is a virtual instinct as well as natural one.

A sense of fear and awe is evident among new members who begin to shape their physical image on Orientation Island. The struggle to craft bodies, to consider skin color and hair color, all within the reality of being in a public space, with others watching them, or so it seems, this process can be overwhelming to certain new members. In actuality, members hardly notice each other during this stage of creation. In a moment, members must decide whether they want to look punk, elegant, or be a furry creature. They begin to form their first identity—maybe they want to be radically different from RL, or maybe they want to look similar. In those first minutes, they begin to shape their SL identity, which will evolve several times as they mature in their virtual identities in the months or years to come. Some members prefer to create alternates for work or play; a professional avatar works well for those engaging in business and educational activities. But for others, they simply alter their clothes and appearance to fit the social situation, like one does in RL. Most of us have a business look in real life that we strip off when we get home, and redress to hang out with friends and family. There is no right or wrong, in one's approach to SL. However, it may be very telling of one's personality.

The Profile

Once residents begin to spend considerable time in Second Life, they create profiles representing SL, primarily, and their RL identity if they wish. Profile stalking is fairly typical, and that phrase is merely used in jest. The profile is a handy tool to find out why someone is in SL, and what they like in RL. Some members look and act radically different between the two worlds, and others prefer to remain anonymous, offering no hints on who they really are. Those more willing to share with each other are often artists, authors, and musicians who are attempting to use SL as another creative venue for their work, as perhaps an extension of real life—Second Life imitating Real Life. In other cases, artists create works that are quite unique from their RL activities, and they perceive SL as a space to experiment with new forms and ideas.

Groups Joined

SL members are allowed to join 25 groups. Once you have been on SL for awhile, it is easy to attain that number because everywhere you go, stores, dance clubs, exhibits, and other places, a notecard will appear on your screen inviting you to join that particular group. By joining a group, you can get notices on the latest fashions from a particular designer, or you might stay informed about the performances of certain SL musicians. Performers, DJs, and designers are often represented by one of several major SL public relations organizations that send out notices on their behalf. When one clicks on an avatar profile, the identity of the person behind the avatar emerges with some clues to marital status, age, interests, and groups joined. Of course, there is no telling if much of the profile is fiction. Second Life provides a space where pretend and reality can confound even the person behind the avatar after awhile. The groups joined by members are hints toward their interests; some have listings of only dance clubs, some list primarily artistic venues and groups, and others indicate that the person is only engaged in educational work online. Those who attend dance club events typically have a certain profile, contrasted to those who attend educational activities and meetings regularly in-world. The cultural interests of members might also be loosely interpreted from a profile. Some of the profiles can be telling of one's cultural identity, as being Latin American or Asian for instance, simply by the groups that members have joined. Religion, national identity, age, gender, personality, and other details of a person can be speculated upon, after looking at the profile.

Blurring the Identity Line

For some the distinction between real and second life is clearly stated in their profile:

> *I prefer to keep RL separate from SL*
> *RL, what's that?*

For others, they proudly include their RL photo, with or without family and friends in the picture. Under their profile, they might add they are married, happily, and mention their occupation in real life. Some members convey an identity in the profile that is completely different from their real life, and one may come to find out that this person is in reality parent to four teen children yet works as an escort in SL. Others might be employed as a store or dance club manager in Second Life, and their real occupation is an accountant or teacher. Second Life allows people to extend their personalities, work and personal, and to dabble with real identities. They can be in Second Life what they dreamed of being in real life; for many men and women, as superficial as it seems, it is a desire to be a model. Numerous people state in their SL profiles that they are models, regardless of their age or physical appearance in RL. I have observed models of any age, even up to 70 years old. The age range of SL membership is fairly broad, yet nearly 40% are ages 25 to 34 (*SL Age*, 2007). I have met as many middle-aged members in Second Life as I have those in their 20s and 30s during my 3-year membership. The oldest person I have met through Second Life was 80 (in RL years).

Partnerships

Part of the SL identity, and a category in one's profile, is the concept of partnership. People can partner together in Second Life, regardless of gender and species. The partnership is among two avatars who acknowledge being committed to one another in SL. It may or may not be the person to whom they are engaged or married to in real life, which has caused some negative press for Second Life and other role-playing games. The idea of marriage is implied when committing to an SL partnership, particularly among those who define marriage by traditional boundaries as being relationship exclusivity. Others change partners every month, and perceive it as a part of role-playing and having little meaning outside of Second Life. But for those who take the commitment seriously, the stakes for cheating on RL and SL partners can translate to breakups in both worlds.

Extending Self: The Romance Metaphor

The idea behind partnership in the game world affords trust to one person above all others, particularly for skill-based games that require players to rely on each other during battle and strategic maneuvers. In Second Life, without such concerns, the partner has become symbolic of marriage to many residents. As in RL, some take that commitment more seriously than others. Second Life, like many virtual worlds, is a place of fantasy. One might become captivated by one of the deeply romantic settings in Second Life that conjure up RL memories, smiles and tingles of people, places, colors, smells, sounds and even touch. A person might succumb to the situation, and begin to feel emotions as when one becomes engrossed in a scene from a movie. Or perhaps, one recalls a special moment in the midst of an SL romantic garden. It is possible to feel a spark of romance without someone to share it with at that moment. Romance is one of those concepts that we rarely understand, but it conveys a mood of meditation, surrender, and adventure. We contemplate our surroundings, captivated by the senses aroused within us. As we connect to our senses, this experience becomes coded into our memory. Romance can be simple, a sharing of looks over dinner or holding hands walking on a sidewalk lined with cafés and shops on a lazy Sunday. Romance becomes internalized into our very being, and perhaps with whom we share these encounters, coded often within particular settings that trigger these feelings when our senses are engaged.

Second life is a life game that taps into our sense of adventure. Romance is defined by personal encounters, romantic movies, romance novels, and stories we have heard since childhood. Indeed, many search for romance, although they may not have shared it with someone else. Romance is often personally experienced through social constructs. One of the classic dictionary definitions for romance is adventure. Second Life provides an adventure to the eyes and ears. The colors, music, and ambient sounds interact to create a setting that stimulates us toward that sense of engagement with our surroundings—with our avatar and sometimes others.

Shared Identity and Moments

The avatar as a romantic icon can be powerful to our emotions. We choose what our avatar will wear, depending on where we think we might have it go. We define the setting for our avatar, as an extension of our personality and often our concept of romance. Even when another avatar joins in the experience, we are still there downloading our schemata into the situation, as others are as well. We are never alone—we interact with our avatar as ourselves and as an extension of ourselves. We share moments with our created being that are a product of our experiences and imaginations and that of the creators of the various sims we visit. Our profiles begin to tell our emerging stories, as we act out our hesitations or fulfill our dreams. We become actors in our romantic adventure, yet we are no longer alone.

On September 18, 2007, a couple made headlines when they met online in a chat room, but they had no idea that they were already married—and to each other. They struck up a conversation that turned into a heated online romance, and ended in a bitter divorce when both realized that they had "cheated" on each other, well sort of, you might say. It would seem that they had more in common after all. You also might say, that by divorcing, what they did was to cheat themselves out of that common bond that drew them together first in RL and later in a virtual game. The BBC completed a 3-part series in January 2008 on *Virtual Adultery and Cyberspace Love* that directed considerable negative attention toward Second Life; it also emphasized how virtual spaces can convey strong emotional cues to participants.

Second Life can convey a sense of mystery to online relationships, and people become drawn into conversations and relationships through the medium's ability to "romance" players, by elevating aesthetics over authenticity. The very definition of romance is not clear, and debate ensues even today "about what is romantic?—for everyone views romance differently. The differences not only exist between men and women, but each woman and each man also has their own idea about what is romantic" (Kerce, 2000). Second Life can stimulate and maybe simulate the feeling of romance among people through chance encounters. The romantic stranger becomes an opportunity to pursue fantasy with an idealized partner apart from the dangers of real life, at least for some members.

When one begins to examine the notion of a stranger, an individual learns that the dictionary is only of marginal assistance. Let's see how *Houghton Mifflin's American Heritage Dictionary* (2000) defines stranger: "One who is neither a friend or an acquaintance, a foreigner, newcomer, or outsider…unaccustomed to or unacquainted with something specified…a visitor or guest." *Merriam Webster Online Dictionary* (2009) notes that it is rooted in 14th century Middle English, from Old French "from estrange." It adds to the Houghton Mifflin definition: "one who does not belong to or is kept from the activities of a group." One might suggest that SLers are defined by their membership or by the fact that they have a common interest in virtual reality, as one has an affinity for country-western clubs. In SL, participation is limited to those with computer access, basic computer skills, and a relatively powerful graphics card. Of course, that is more than is required for someone to interact with others in real public spaces such as parks. In SL, when you meet someone in a virtual park, you can click on the avatar profile, and perhaps learn more in 30 seconds about that person than in a chance meeting in an RL park. Voice in SL offers potential for discernment about one's character, to a point of course. Williams, Caplan, & Xiong (2007) found that the addition of voice to World of Warcraft was favorably received among game players, who were pleased to be able to more accurately determine authenticity in gender, intelligence, and character, and this, in turn, increased levels of trust among relationships compared to when text-based communication was relied on exclusively.

Beyond "Real" Limitations

The documentary *Second Skin* opened in 2008, and featured the world of Second Life and other virtual games, promoting its storyline as: "Couples who have fallen in love without meeting, disabled players whose lives have been given new purpose, those struggling with addiction, Chinese gold farming sweatshop workers, wealthy entrepreneurs and legendary guild leaders—all living within a world that doesn't quite exist" (*Second Skin press release*, 2008). Sometimes you have to remove yourself from an environment to understand yourself. Unique challenges bring benefits and anxieties. Second Life allows disabled populations to experience freedom in virtual spaces, to walk, run and experience life beyond their physical limitations. In a sense, we all have an opportunity to go beyond ourselves in SL, to soar to a new level of experience unbound by circumstances. I have had the opportunity to be friends with a number of people in avatar form who are physically challenged. Second Life has offered them the ability to date, love, explore and interact with a variety of people whom they would not have met otherwise. Second Life is a space that challenges one to redefine life beyond physical, social, and economic limitations. You can own a mansion in SL for a fraction of the cost in real life. You can travel the world in seconds. You can reinvent yourself, in an attempt to find yourself. Second Life provides a means to get to "know yourself" in a boldly new interactive space.

For a moment, consider what is more authentic to relationship building—a sharing of innermost feelings in an SL romantic setting while dancing, or sharing one's disgust with a partner over RL dinner about the idiot at the office. When one considers the many divorces in real life, it becomes evident that we may never completely know someone, particularly at the start of a relationship. The world is hungry for relationships, something beyond watching a Friday night video at home and something deeper than hanging out at a nightclub. Think about what Second Life can do—it can "get" people talking with each other, engaging them, in a completely different context that draws them together into a space—either through text or voice. What do we know about SLers? We know that they like to communicate? That is a start. We know that they are probably looking to connect with others. We can also find out about them through their profiles, and that might be easier than some awkward Q&A on the first meeting of someone in RL. You can find out their interests by noting in what circles they like to travel—the botanical club, the furry artists club, or the weapons club, for instance. If one noted that a particular avatar had joined the latter, it might be a hint to teleport away with a quick "Excuse me, I am experiencing lag. I must go now." That again is a PERSONAL choice. Moreover, Second Life members could lie about themselves, but that problem is not unique to in-world relationships.

The Wildermuth & Vogl-Baur Online Studies

Wildermuth & Vogl-Bauer's 2000 study, drawing from an undergraduate sample, indicated that 46% of the respondents reported involvement in online romances or they knew family members or friends who had been involved in one, now or in the past. In 1996, Parks & Roberts reported that more than 90% of Internet users engaged in relationships online, and of this number more than 25% were "romantic in nature" (Wildermuth & Vogl-Bauer, 2007, p. 211). The 2002 Nua Internet Survey also reports that relationship building, which includes friendships and romantic partnerships, comprises more than 70% of the average Internet users' time (Nua, 2002).

Wildermuth & Vogl-Baur (2007) address the scarcity of scholarly studies dealing with online romance, and concur with earlier research by McQuillen (2003) who indicated online relationships had been defined too broadly, running the gamut between romance, friendship and sex under the same category. Wildermuth & Vogl-Baur (2007) call for studies that provide greater depth into understanding the characteristics of such relationships, and those which might provide clarity among "paradoxical" findings. Wildermuth & Vogl-Bauer (2007) point out the problem, however, is that much research has focused on Internet use as the central variable, rather than meanings within the communication, citing the work of Whitty & Gavin (2001) and Riva (2002) which depicts users "as social actors who shape the online context for themselves" (p. 212).

In the Wildermuth & Vogl-Bauer study (2007), approximately 70% of the respondents were female, and the majority of participants were White, USA citizens, and had attended college. Most respondents had engaged in "common interest" chat rooms, and 92% resided one hour or more away from their online partner, and more than 30% had an international partner (p. 215). Approximately 30% of respondents stated that they were either married or involved in a relationship apart from the Internet. Sixteen percent reported having a "mutual online friend" (p. 215). Forty-seven percent reported a successful relationship online, and almost 40% stated that they had met at least one online partner face to face. Wildermuth & Vogl-Bauer (2007, p. 215) stated that respondents experienced emotional intensity (87%) and "strong linguistic connections" (43%). Furthermore, their study indicated that more than 40% percent approached their relationships with caution. They conclude that when an online environment provides minimal contextual information (i.e., relying on text messages), participants are more likely to hold on to their idealized version of the relationship (2007).

The Authenticity of Online Relationships

Aaron Ben-Ze'ev (2004) in his book, *Love Online: Emotions on the Internet*, points out the unique role that cyberspace affords our imagination: "Cyberspace is a psychological and social domain. It is not tangible and some of its dimensions, such as distance, and location, are not measured by physical parameters, but by psychological content." He adds, "This often imaginary reality is not limited to the private domain of a specific person; rather it is shared by many people. Such a novel psychological reality is supported by sophisticated technology, but it is not defined by this technology"; concluding, Ben-Ze'ev writes, "it is defined by the various psychological interactions occurring in it" (pp. 1–2).

A recent study by Anderson & Emmers-Sommer (2006) explored the predictors of relationship satisfaction in online romantic relationships. Those predictors, according to the researchers, are "intimacy, trust, and communication satisfaction" (p. 166). They continue, "as partners grow close and depth increases, trust develops and as trust increases, so do levels of intimacy" (p. 166). Wright (2004) noted online relationships tend to progress quickly through a sense of openness that leads to increased intimacy (Anderson & Emmers-Sommer, 2006, p. 166):

> ...the role of intimacy in predicting relationship satisfaction in this study is consistent with a wealth of personal relationship [research] that indicates intimacy is a key component of relationships and marital satisfaction (e.g., Feeney, Noller, & Ward, 1997; Hassebrauck & Fehr, 2002).

Anderson & Emmers-Sommer (2006) remind us that the "online relationship is the relationship," so it makes sense that one's contentment with one's relationships would be directly related to "communication satisfaction" (p. 166).

Relationship experts on talk shows tout books and seminars that offer to provide effective communication strategies to mend marriages and friendships.

In an earlier study conducted by Parks & Floyd (1996), it is suggested that online relationships need proximity, eye contact, voice communication, and physical appearance to mature into intimate, authentic experiences. Wildermuth & Vogl-Bauer (2007), in contrast, dismiss such variables as unnecessary qualifications, and suggest through their findings and conclusions that perception has a much greater role than has been otherwise assumed. With that in mind, might a virtual experience like SL lead to greater emotional investment and intensity for online romantic relationships than other social networking services? The perception of proximity could then be as much an indicator of successful contact as physical fulfillment in RL: "...eye contact, body language, facial expressions, vocalization, hugs, pats on the back, cries, embraces, kisses and giggles are fundamentals of our evolutionary social emotional well-being" (Nie, 2001, p. 432).

In part, a premise of Wildermuth & Vogl-Bauer's (2007) work speculates that authentic relationships need to be "tactile" to create "a lasting bond" (p. 224). Can a tactile bond be accomplished through a mediator such as an avatar, as one's fingers interact with the keyboard? That is also merely speculation at this point. Wildermuth & Vogl-Bauer (2007) call attention to the "irony here in that the technological and disembodied world of ICTs that has often been depicted in depersonalized terms may also provide a haven where authenticity, negotiation, and the development of trust may lead to romance" (p 220).

Hardey (2004) presents a historical account of courtship to dating, and tells us that "significant changes during the second half of the twentieth century" have redefined our understanding of relationships (p. 208). Hardey (2004) points out that modern dating has become centered on the individual, and authenticity and trust are considered worthy components to a successful relationship, with a big part of that trust determined by communication. Gaming virtual worlds, in which identities are drawn from fantasy, counter this notion. Hardey suggests, however, that "authenticity is finally 'tested' when people move from mediated communication to meeting in the flesh" (p. 208). Ben-Ze'ev (2004, p. 2) elaborates on the concept of authenticity in virtual space, by considering the wider of scope of relationships made in-world: "Cyberspace is a part of reality; it is, therefore, incorrect to regard it as the direct opposite of real space. Cyber space is part of real space, and online relationships are real relationships." Ben-Ze'ev (2004) explains that the interactivity of cyberspace is indeed its novelty: "interactivity has made it a psychological as well as social reality. It is a space where real people have actual interactions with other people, while being able to shape their own and other people's personalities" (p. 2). In this way, the interactive real space is a step beyond the "passive imaginary reality," a transition historically "more radical than the move from photographs to movies" (p. 2).

The Aesthetics of Virtual Relationships

Among the top 100 rules of Second Life, Prad Pravthivi (2008) humorously quipped is "68. Your SL wedding should at least last longer than the ceremony." Such wisdom would be best heeded in-world if for financial reasons alone; weddings in Second Life have become an incredibly profitable business and increasingly so. An average SL wedding is approximately 30,000 Lindens, roughly 100–120 U.S. dollars. Custom weddings can range upward toward 80,000 Lindens, depending on whether one wants a majestic ceremony or a theme wedding, ranging from pirate, gothic or anything you can imagine in a virtual world. Weddings can be as inexpensive as merely a few real dollars if one wants to keep it simple. There is a small processing fee to make your partnership official on Second Life. The idea of two players bonding has become ceremonial, and symbolic of the ability of virtual relationships to borrow from our real lives and to create new traditions in-world. Perhaps these ceremonies give authenticity to one's time spent inside virtual communities, or they are merely the outward expression of our human extension beyond our physical representation. As with any tradition, the exacting care to which ceremonial practice is exercised indicates its importance to those engaged in the ritual. This is true of weddings in Second Life as well: "A lot of planning goes into a virtual wedding. A scripter needs to come up with pose balls, which let avatars hold hands or kiss. Flowers need to be bought; chairs need to be arranged; invitations must be sent..."(Peralta, 2006).

The physical crafting of the SL experience lends itself to an elaboration of life, and the invisibility of technology allows us to connect nearly seamlessly to the virtual environment as well as to others. Our avatar immersion and conversion into technological spaces are provoked by powerful aesthetic decisions borrowed from real-life spaces, imagination, and perceptual experiences. Pett & Wilson (1996) inform us of the perceptual meaning inherent in color; so why would virtual hues not engage our attention within virtual space, directing us toward constructed landscapes, buildings, and smartly dressed avatars. The social landscape informs the physicality of the virtual environment, but it is also a consequence of the virtual creation, allowing people to interact in new forms—but nonetheless interaction occurs among people and between people and technology. They are not merely representative of life forms, or icons; they are real people in real places. Virtual spaces are not intangible to sight and sound.

The setting or context of our conversations and experiences is relevant to relationship building, be it at work, home or on the dance floor at an SL club. On Valentine's Day, we light a few candles on the dinner table, or better yet, head for a nice romantic restaurant. So why should setting or context be alien to other experiences, online or offline? Certain settings work better than others, depending on the goals to be achieved. You want to have a late-night intimate swim with a friend; well a public pool is not the appropriate setting. Image is important. Yet, a message delivered apart from an appropriate context risks being not validated by the receiver. We learn about romance through our experience, as well as from talk show experts and books. We learn what works, what doesn't. I make brief note of Albert Bandura's (1977, 1986) theory of social cognition to remind the reader that how individuals engage in context is an experience that draws upon personal, social, and environmental influences. We learn from others, and from watching others, but we respond uniquely based on past experiences and the situation at hand. Ben-Ze'ev (2004) informs us, "The greater and the more profound the interaction is, the greater the psychological reality we attached to it" (p. 3). The meaning of the experience is widened as we move beyond text to that of voice, images and actual body movements. These experiences contextualize the text, and provide the stimulus to connect our imaginations with our memory and sensors. "Cyberspace is similar to fictional space in the sense that in both cases the flight into virtual reality is not so much a denial of reality as a form of exploring and playing with it" (Ben-Ze'ev, 2004, p. 3).

In general, we can make some basic assumptions about human behavior. Romance is not merely a state of being; it is the end product of learned social behaviors. The Van Gogh Museum in Starry Starry Night inside Second Life conveys romantic ambience whether or not one has a partner with whom to share the experience of viewing the virtual art and interactive exhibits. Romance novels stimulate our imagination, and reading is a solo activity for the most part. Some of the popular SL spots are Jade's Jazz Lounge, Sweethearts Ballroom, and Midsomer Isle, and these sites encourage interaction because the majority of dance and pose balls are created for couples. Second Life allows us to encounter romance in various settings, with various people. A partner or in-world friend often helps us to validate our perception of romance as adventuresome, reflective and interactive (among others and/or virtual places).

Wildermuth & Vogl-Baur (2007) draw briefly on Marshall McLuhan's idea that the Internet allows one to extend relationship reach (Levinson, 1999;

McLuhan, 1964; McLuhan & McLuhan, 1988). McLuhan (1964) envisioned technology as an extension of our humanity. Second Life allows us to reconceptualize commitment in relationships. Second Life not only offers access to others, but access to the imagination of others in a multitude of settings. We go beyond simple interests to those untapped feelings and expressions not readily communicated on a first date or encounter. There is perhaps what might be referred to as too much reality in a relationship that draws couples apart—bills, chores, office talk. Granted many SL couples want some sense of reality in their relationship (i.e., "in what country do you live?"; "you're not my brother right?"; "do you have an RL job?"), but there must be a willingness for both people to extend their communication beyond that which might limit their relationship to the mundane.

Science Daily reported on a relationship study by Catherine Mosher of Duke Medical Center and Sharon Danoff-Burg from the University of Albany (also, Mosher & Danoff-Burg, 2007). The researchers posited, "...men may be more willing than women to sacrifice achievement goals for a romantic relationship" (Springer, 2007). They asked more than 200 respondents a series of questions based on personality traits and life goals. "Overall both college men and women showed strong desires for individual achievement and relationship intimacy" (2007). Marriage is often considered the ultimate commitment in a relationship, and interactive worlds like Second Life have facilitated such extensions into virtual space.

For example, in the case of *Lucas Arts' Star Wars Galaxies* and other titles, it becomes obvious that partnership is fundamental to online gaming, especially in terms of trust and commitment in the game: "There are many husband and wives who play MMORGPS together...Although they are married in the RL they lead very separate lives in game play" (Torrone, 2004). This is also the case in SL, where an individual may have an SL partner who is different from his spouse in real life: "A curious offshoot of this is the husband and wife who play together, on the same server, many times in the same Player Association...and still choose to romance others...More expected, though, is the RL couple who also pairs off in the game" (Torrone, 2004). Often one in the real-life relationship persuades the other to play, avoiding any romantic snafus.

In Spohn's (2007) column on *Role Playing and Romance*, he points out how couple gaming is increasingly becoming a strategic consideration, and City of Heroes/Villains "allows them to make superhero characters that complement each other...Playing along with someone you know in real life can make a game quite a bit more interesting, especially if that person is your significant other." Spohn (2007) notes the old saying,

> couples who play together stay together, and this may turn out to apply to online games...Stories about wives that have been turned on to games by their husbands abound on game forums, and you'll even see a few cases where wives have lured their husbands into the hobby.

Virtual-world marriage is becoming increasingly common for such games, and EverQuest actually boasted of the first wedding simultaneously conducted in-world and in real life. The wedding was held at the 8th Annual Sony Online Entertainment Fan Faire, and the event became a major headliner (Gaudiosi, 2007). The event drew more than 2,000 people eager for a "sneak peak at upcoming games" and to watch history in the making (Gaudiosi, 2007). There had been "thousands" of weddings held in *EverQuest* and *EverQuest II*..."as well as many married couples who first met in the virtual massively multiplayer online (MMO) game world; this marked the first time two people were married in both the real and virtual world in one ceremony" (Gaudiosi, 2007). After the ceremony, the couple moved to "the side of the stage where two PCs sat and each took control of their in-game characters—Lady Quaddra and Lord Garthan" (Gaudiosi, 2007).

YouTube has become a unique archive for an increasing number of virtual marriages, with this one being no exception. YouTube broadcasts among its numerous virtual wedding videos one between avatars ScubaSteve and Polly that also took place in 2007, but within Second Life. The description online of the wedding begins: "They met each other in a pond building area in April 2007. Together they like to laugh, explore second life, find places to ride their horses and making a nice home at Vero Beach." It continues, "Alone Scuba likes to come up with surprises for Polly and Polly likes to find cozy spots for them to come back together to visit. Polly likes to call scuba Ghost and scuba likes to call Polly Muse."
It concludes...

> Their persistence and determination to not be overcome [by] the forces from within and outside SL that would otherwise stop them from seeing each other had made the relationship resilient and magical in every sense of the word.

The video runs about 8 minutes. Another wedding story of note was published in the *Second Life Daily Herald*. It would appear in this case, the couple as good friends had made a strong commitment to play together: "It's hard to say whether Bert and Alle are representative of the typical Second Life couple. Both are convinced that their marriage is no more than an enjoyable progression of their game playing in Second Life" (Eales, 2007). The bride described the ceremony as a commitment of friendship inside Second Life: "The easiest way to understand our relationship is that our avatars are in love and the real people in front of the screen just like to talk to each other and share SL experiences" (Eales, 2007). The duo proclaims love for each other, but only in-world for now. One thing that becomes strikingly clear is that for many in-world residents, being alone is not as much fun as sharing your experiences with someone. Reuters (2007) reported that some avatars have married several times, and the in-world bridal industry is profitable. Marriage announcements are routinely posted in the wedding section of SL newspapers.

In an article published in the *Houston Chronicle* recently, reporter Eyder Peralta went in-world to seek some answers on some of the social aspects of Second Life, including the desire to marry as avatars, and observed: "...in world' nobody calls Second Life a game. The emotional connections you make are real. If you offend someone, they'll remember" (Peralta, 2006). Peralta (2006) points out, "If you flirt or make a romantic gesture, it doesn't just disappear into a black hole; it's received by a human being on the other side." In essence, Peralta (2006) underscores how real SL is to its residents, "People spend millions of real dollars building their lives here because emotionally, it's more than a game."

Conclusion

Romance can be defined beyond conceptions of love to a desire for adventure across the virtual frontier. Romance is the exhilaration that beckons us toward adventure. The concept has been associated with the chivalrous medieval times dating back to the 12th century and the romantic literary period of the 18th century. *Wikipedia* states, "The story of the medieval romance focuses not upon love and sentiment, but upon adventure." Romanticism in the 18th century was a resistance to the growing industrialization, and a desire for liberation and exploration. Romance might also be thought of as an unfolding mystery. In the case of romantic fiction, the reader is taken captive for a few hours, and led astray into a fantasy. In Second Life, as in RL, the mask is often present, yet the emotional connection is real (good or bad).

References

American Heritage Dictionary of the English Language, Fourth Edition. (2000). Stranger. Definition. Boston, MA: Houghton Mifflin Company.

Anderson, T. L., & Emmers-Sommer, T. M. (2006, June). Predictors of relationship satisfaction in online romantic relationships. *Communication Studies* 57(2), 153–172.

Aquacade, M. (2008, July 19). *Second Life Lecture, in-world.* Southern Illinois University, Carbondale, IL.

Bandura, A. (1986). *Social foundations of thought and action: A social cognitive theory.* Englewood Cliffs, NJ: Prentice-Hall.

—(1977). *Social learning theory.* Englewood Cliffs, NJ: Prentice Hall.

Ben-Ze'ev, A. (2004). *Love online: Emotions on the internet.* Cambridge: Cambridge University Press.

Eales, K. (2007, September 9). Wedding stories in the metaverse. *The Second Life Herald.* Accessed November 26, 2007, from http://www.secondlifeherald.com/slh/2007/ 09/ wedding.html

Feeney, J. A., Nollen, P., & Ward, C. (1997). Marital satisfaction and spousal interaction. In R. J. Sternberg & M. Hojjat (Eds.), *Satisfaction in close relationships* (pp. 160–189). New York: Guilford.

Gaudiosi, J. (2007, August 13). Happily EverQuest after. Accessed November 23, 2007, from http://videogames.yahoo.com/feature/happily-everquest-after/525578.

Hardey, M. (2004). Mediated relationships: Authenticity and the possibility of romance. *Information Communication & Society* 7(2), 207–222.

Hassebrauck, M., & Fehr, B. (2002). Dimensions of relationship quality. *Personal Relationships,* 9, 253–270.

Kerce, R. D. (2000). *The psychology of romance.* Accessed October 15, 2008, from http://www.dateseeker.net/articles/psychology_romance.html.

Levinson, P. (1999). Digital McLuhan: A guide to the information millennium. New York: Routledge.

Meadows, S. M. (2008). *I, Avatar: The culture and consequence of having a second life.* Berkeley, CA: New Riders Press.

McLuhan, M. (1964). Understanding media: The extensions of Man. New York: McGraw Hill. Reissued by Gingko Press, 2003.

McLuhan, M., & McLuhan, E. (1988). Laws of media: The new science. Toronto: University of Toronto Press.

McQuillen, J. S. (2003). The influence of technology on the initiation of interpersonal Relationship. *Education, 123,* 616–623.

Merriam Webster Online Dictionary. (2009). Stranger. Definition. Accessed March 2, 2009, from http://www.merriam-webster.com.

Mosher C., & Danoff-Burg, S. (2007). College students' life priorities: The influence of gender and gender-linked personality traits. *Gender Issues, 24*(2).

Nie, N. J. (2001). Sociability, interpersonal relations, and the internet. *American Behavioural Scientist 45*(3), 420–435.

Nua Internet Survey. (2002). How many online. Accessed June 11, 2003, from http://www.nua.ie/survey/how_many_online/index.html

Parks, M. R., & Floyd, K. (1996). Making friends in cyberspace. *Journal of Communication, 45,* 80–97.

Peralta, E. (2006, May 26). In second life, the world is virtual. But the emotions are real. *Houston Chronicle.* Accessed November 23, 2007, from http://www.chron.com/disp/story.mpl/ ent/3899538.html.

Pett, D., & Wilson, T. (1996). Color research and its application to the design of instructional materials. *Educational Technology Research and Development, 44,* 19–35.

Pravthivi, P. (2008). 100 Rules of Second Life. Metaversally Speaking. Accessed January 17, 2009, from http://www.pradprathivi.com/

Reuters, R. (2007, May 28). The price of tying the virtual knot. *Reuters News Service.* Accessed November 21, 2007, from http://secondlife.reuters.com/ stories/2007/05/28/ the-price-of-tying-the-virtual-knot/

Riva. G. (2002). The sociocognitive psychology of computer-mediated communication. The present and future of technology-based interactions. *CyberPsychology & Behavior, 6*, 581-598.

Romance. Wikipedia. Accessed March 2, 2009, from http://en.wikipedia.org/ wiki/Romance.

Second skin award best documentary at NYC's ACE Fest. (2008). Press Release. Accessed October 15, 2008, from http://www.secondskinfilm.com.

SL Age Demographic. (2007). Second Life Update. Accessed January 17, 2009, from http://www.secondlifeupdate.com/uncategorized/sl-age-demographic/

Spohn, D. (2007). Roleplaying and romance. Accessed November 27, 2007, from http://internetgames.about.com/od/mmorpgs/a/romance.htm.

Springer News (2007, August 28). Men choose romance over success. *ScienceDaily*. Accessed November 25, 2007, from http://www.sciencedaily.com/releases/2007/08/070828 110650.htm.

Thomas, A. (2007). *Youth online: Identity and literacy in the digital age*. New York: Peter Lang Publishers.

Torrone, P. (2004). Love and romance in the world of massive multi online role playing games. Accessed November 25, 2007, from http://www.joystiq.com/2004/10/06/ love-and-romance-in-the-world-of-massive-multi-online-role/

Virtual adultery and cyberspace love. (2008, January). British Broadcasting Corporation, 1 of 3 part series.

Whitty, M., & Gavin, J. (2001). Age/sex/location: Uncovering the social cues in the development of online relationships. *CyberPsychology and Behavior, 4*, 623–630.

Wildermuth, S. M., & Vogl-Baur, S. (2000). The effects of stigmatizing discourse on the quality of online relationships. *CyberPsychology & Behavior*, 73–84.

—. (2007). We met on the net: Exploring the perceptions of online romantic relationship participants. *Southern Communication Journal* 72(3), 213–227.

Williams, D., Caplan, S, & Xiong, L. (2007). Can you hear me now? Voice and online community. *Human Communication Research, 33*, 427–448.

Wright, K. B. (2004). On-line relational maintenance strategies and perception of partners within exclusively internet-based and primarily internet-based relationships. *Communication Studies, 55*, 239–253.

CHAPTER FOUR

Extending Consumer Culture: Work and Economy in the Virtual World

> Houses look like tract homes, instead of, say, floating orbs. People run around in Abercrombie & Fitch knockoffs. Women are exaggeratedly curvy.
>
> —Kara Platoni, *Stanford Magazine*

Nick Yee, a researcher of online role-playing games, found that virtual life is similar to the real world, in that people tend to mimic social norms: "One thing that really frustrates me is that in a world where you can be anything and anyone you like, why does Second Life look so much like suburban America?...There's almost an overemphasis on looking stereotypically good" (Platoni, 2008). Quality fashion, houses, boats, and make-overs thrive on the Linden Dollar, the currency exchanged among SL consumers and business operators. Although basic membership is free, for one to be distinctive and virtually trendy demands some real cash. This second economy can complement or place a burden on one's real-life finances. One hundred Lindens approximate four dollars in U.S. currency.

Daniel Terdiman (2005) describes Second Life as "an open-ended virtual world whose players can create anything they can imagine and who can buy and sell land, vehicles, clothing and the like," adding that it "has also had its share of valuable terra firma." Other games with virtual economies have involved incredible real estate transactions, with one man, a film director, paying $100,000 for a virtual resort in the online game Project Entropia (Terdiman, 2005): "Jon Jacobs imagines he can bring in more than $1.6 million a year in revenue—all on a one-time $100,000 investment in something that exists only in the realm of ones and zeroes." That is because "a 'Project Entropia' island that famously sold for $26,500 last year has more than paid for itself" (Terdiman, 2005).

Reuters News Service (2007), reporting on trends in Second Life, revealed in January 2007 that 85% of SL consumers (a mean of 33 RL years old) spend more than 250 Lindens per month on clothing. The right skin, shape and clothes, and even the right house in Second Life are key ingredients to success in the game for materialistic members, or for those seeking a professional appearance for their SL/RL careers. It has become increasingly important to have a job in SL. Imagine coming home from your real-life job and then moonlighting as a nightclub owner or a land baron. For some, their only employment is in Second Life. That is true for some stay-at-home mothers and fathers, recently unemployed, and college students. With real companies moving into Second Life, it is easy to blur the economic lines between worlds. A number of corporations advertise and have building space in Second Life, from soft drink manufacturers to perfume companies to car dealerships to record labels; adult entertainment is represented in-world and contributes significantly to the virtual economy. Second Life is not the utopian answer to a happier life; at times it encourages exploitation while calling it experimentation. For those who desire to work in Second Life, a number of service jobs, from sweeping floors to greeting customers to fashion modeling, to dancing at adult clubs, helps members earn precious Lindens. This chapter investigates the consumer culture of Second Life.

The First Virtual Millionaire

The blog *Second Thoughts* tracks virtual culture in Second Life, particularly following the economics associated with it. Few realize how virtual economies work let alone how they extend into real life. Adventure capital includes everything from investments in companies like IBM to "[w]hoever spends money on a virtual world and in a virtual world for their own projects which they achieve through a virtual world" (*The Adventure*, 2009). For instance, in Second Life, "what people pay is not merely a rate, or a price for a piece of hardware, or a software license. They put significant development costs into the place, buying space, artists and designers services, etc. They are prosumers, sub-developers also extending out and developing the platform" (*The Adventure*, 2009).

Residents are engaged in the consumer culture of selling and buying virtual goods and services. Any day or night, members can shop for clothes, buy a nightclub, car or house. You can buy property around the world, and there is no need to work through a real estate agent or mortgage broker. The Second Life economy is based on Lindens, with members exchanging real money for game money. Members buy property to build businesses and private residences. Very few become wealthy in a virtual world, but some exceptions have made headlines. Buying virtual land has been perhaps the most profitable of ventures in-world. If you own land, you can build businesses on it. Some prefer to lease building space.

In Second Life, Anshe Chung, known as Ailin Graef in real life, became the first millionaire in Second Life, landing her on the cover of *Business Week* in May 2006. When converted to U.S. dollars, her virtual money was equivalent to $250,000 dollars (Hof, 2006a). She earned money through real estate purchases, having only made an initial $9.95 U.S. dollar investment. Her investments developed into "virtual shopping malls, store chains, and even virtual stock-market investments in Second Life businesses" (Hof, 2006a). By November 2006, a press release (*Anshe Chung*, 2006) posted that Chung, born and raised in China, had amassed millions from these digital assets. Hof (2006b), following up, stated that her virtual operation had developed into a real-life company which specializes in applications for corporate and education sectors interested in 3D immersive environments.

Playing with Real Money

In January 2008, approximately a dozen "pretend" banking institutions "funded with actual money" from SL users were shut down by Linden Lab, after "some of the virtual banks had failed to pay…'high returns on customer deposits'" as once promised: "The banks of Second Life were operated by other players, who enticed deposits by offering interest rates. While some banks paid interest as promised, others used depositors' money for unsuccessful Second Life land and gambling deals" (Sidel, 2008). Second Life implemented new policies stating chartered banks would be allowed to operate in-world, but exactly what that means will continue to be negotiated across the fuzzy financial global terrain of virtual worlds. Consequently, the situation led to "a real-life bank run" with many SL depositors discovering that they were no longer able to withdraw funds from virtual ATMs (Sidel, 2008).

The crisis was precipitated when Linden banned gambling due to widely inconsistent governmental regulations on gaming practices around the world (*Banking*, 2008; Sidel, 2008). Governments began to take keen interest in what had become major revenue inside the virtual world, as virtual money could be converted to real money. The playing field was a worldwide economy. A number of malls and venues had gambling operations as central revenue-making components of their operations, and many land investors pulled out of SL when Linden's new regulations came into practice. Subsequently, some virtual institutions shut down, and customer deposits had not exceeded the loss of revenue.

Ginko Financial went out of business having been a major investor in the virtual gambling industry in Second Life: "Linden essentially acknowledges that the financial services being offered in its virtual society have evolved to the point that they need to be regulated in the real world" (Sidel, 2008). When virtual economies crash, real money is lost, and in some cases up to hundreds of thousands of dollars—which impacts economies outside of SL. What becomes evident is that real money is behind every Linden dollar. Some financial experts and entrepreneurs, for that reason, have a keen interest in virtual economies. SL Beyers Sellers hosts a television show on virtual economies, and in real life he is Professor Robert Bloomfield at Cornell University's Johnson School of Management; he remarked that SL is the real deal: "there is not a whole lot that is fake about this" (Sidel, 2008).

The currency used within SL is virtual, but the economy is real. Some of the real brands featured in Second Life have included AOL, Reuters News, CNN, ABC-TV, CBS-TV, NBC-TV, Showtime, Sony BMG, Virgin records, American Apparel, Sears, Dell, IBM, and a number of car manufacturers. The UK, and Australian based company, Project Factory launched in Sydney in 2005 as a marketing ad agency specializing in digital services, and everything online from mobile devices to virtual worlds. In February 2009, it merged with Australian social media company Lean Forward, positioning itself to promote companies worldwide across digital platforms. Its campaigns featured exclusive digital content, complete with the development of fictional characters and narratives. Second Life, in a sense, might be conceptualized as a multi-layered interactive narrative comprised of ever-evolving subplots. The possibilities for content generation and marketing in a digital world are endless, given imagination is a key component:

> Imagine if you will that by some freak of undersea volcanic activity, a brand-new continent suddenly appeared in the middle of the ocean, and within a two-year period, 8 million people from 105 countries worldwide decided to make it a vacation destination, some on a daily basis. (Kenney, 2007)

Nearly 2 million dollars daily flow through this virtual vacation destination "putting its GDP in line with that of the Caribbean paradise of St. Lucia" (Kenney, 2007). The rate of U.S. currency exchange is approximately one dollar to 400 Lindens. An island costs approximately $1,700 with a $300 monthly maintenance fee. Many buy plots of land on these island retreats. Aside from residential neighborhoods, many of these islands are home to big brand stores representing companies from RL: "So what is it that brings American Apparel, Adidas, Coca Cola, Pontiac, Mercedes, BMW, Philips, Mazda, IBM and so many others to the game?" (Kenney, 2007). Cranial Tap CEO, Dave Levinson, who runs a full-service virtual world marketing and development company, understands how businesses seek innovative ways to achieve added value to their brand. Consumers can engage and interact with real products in-world. For example, in 2007, General Motors' Pontiac division invested in a "large patch of real estate in-world, and...erected a concert stage [serving] as a social meeting place for the avatar community. Does Pontiac make any revenue in either the traditional or virtual sense? No" (Kenney, 2007). These types of events help promote sponsors to their community of customers, "allowing for consumer trust and brand loyalty" (Kenney, 2007). The economic goals within role-playing games like World of Warcraft are completely different from those of Second Life, which relies on a unique consumer culture embraced by its residents who live, play and often work in a virtual environment on a daily basis.

Virtual Employment

> Welcome to Club Tokyo, We have what Your Mind Wants, and your Body Desires... Where dreams become real! Think you got what it takes to be a member of our family? Fill out the application form and drop it into the application box in our club! (Club Tokyo, 2009)

The job posting continues, asking for a few good "detailed" photos of the applicant's face and body, with preferably a nude shot in the mix. The applicant is then required to answer some questions, like why they should be hired, among other questions:

> Why would you want to work at club Tokyo? Do you have voice? Would you use it? A customer just tipped you REALLY generously (we're talking about a tip like, e.g., 1000L$). What would you do? Best of luck, we hope to get in touch with you soon! (Club Tokyo, 2009)

In the job posting above, Club Tokyo is seeking employees, although to perform what functions is not clearly specified. The application form gives the prospective employee some clues into what the job might entail at the club. Another business, LoveHolic, had the following job posting listed with an employment placement service inside Second Life. In its application form for hiring dancers and escorts, the owners were specific about the job qualifications:

> Hello, if you are new to SL and have a freebie skin and/or hair please don't apply. Before you fill out the application, please make sure you have the following things: Custom nice Skin, Prim Flexi Hair, Prim shoes, and Nice Sexy Outfits. (LoveHolic, 2009)

Then after a few basic questions, applicants were asked describe their avatar's personality, their dancing moves on stage, how they would greet a new or regular client, and how they feel about sex on SL. Finally the employer requested that the applicant submit a nude photo of her avatar.

With Second Life's economy fueled by Lindens, newcomers and old timers alike feel compelled to earn money to fit within the virtual consumer culture. Some of the easiest ways to make some quick income unfortunately involves becoming part of the sex industry that prospers within Second Life and other virtual economies. But to get a job in that trade, you need the appropriate look, which ultimately amounts to considerable Lindens; for instance one might pay into the hundreds or thousands of Lindens for realistic skins and shapes. Of course, there are free shops, but if you want quality hair, skin or shape, it costs money. Just to become employed, sometimes leads to a major investment in one's appearance.

Once someone invests in renting or buying a house (and paying the monthly mortgage or tier), the resident more often than not seeks employment to offset the property fees. Others earn their income by establishing businesses in-world. A number of occupations or trades exist in SL beyond the sensational jobs that typically attract news headlines and criticism from various groups concerned about sexual exploitation in virtual worlds. Everything from running a business to singing at live music venues can help members to earn income. Many businesses have set up automatic "campers" for members to earn currency. Campers generally earn about 1 to 3 Lindens an hour, by simply sitting or standing outside a store, lounging on a chair along a beach, dancing at clubs, sweeping floors at businesses, pretending to read books, or any one of a thousand jobs. Some businesses post help wanted signs outside their shops to advertise positions. Increasingly, SL employers use in-world job placement and recruiting agencies. Among them, PeoplePool is one of the larger and seemingly better-organized agencies, in that it is operated professionally. Employers post their job ads, and job seekers sort through the openings. Upon entering the agency, job seekers see the following sign:

> Welcome to PeoplePool. To apply for a job you must be at least two weeks old. Please prepare a resume written on a notecard. Then contact a recruiter to set up an interview. If no recruiter is present, please use the online recruiter board.

The agency presents an image of professionalism and credibility to prospective employees. PeoplePool positions itself as a company specializing in the "placement of temporary personnel," stating, "We have developed the tools to select, schedule, and monitor our temporary workers. If desired, we can train them to suit your needs." It also provides a Website, www.peoplepool.com. Some of the jobs posted include openings for shopkeepers, secretarial and financial clerical assistance, managers, and builders. For instance, one posting for Builder Paradise, a store that sells building tools, stated it was "looking for shopkeepers from the US or the AUS time zone." Qualifications included:

> You need to be at least 2 weeks old in SL, be kindly and helpful to customers. Experience in building is not required, but...helpful. You are dealing with customers who need some help at building :) No fixed times or schedules: 1–2 hours a day for 7 days a week.

Another position advertised was for a virtual journalist:

> AFKMagazine (www.afkmag.com) is a startup magazine with backing from a large secondlife company. We are looking to bring news about secondlife and other virtual worlds on the internet.

The posting specified that the journalist is required to possess "flawless English writing abilities; [an] interest in the journalistic side of secondlife, [and] photographic skills." The posting added, "Since the magazine is just starting up there are no revenues yet and so we cannot really provide a wage for the job. This will regularly be negotiated. In the start it will be 'tips for given work.'" Perhaps that is why there are more virtual dancers than journalists in Second Life.

Shake Your Money Maker

One of the most popular forms of entertainment in Second Life is dancing. Although dancing was not envisioned as a priority among the game creators, it certainly has become recognized by Linden Lab as a significant means toward recruiting members seeking ways to socialize online. Due to the popularity of SL nightlife, a dance economy has evolved among members. At the minimum, nearly every club seeks a hostess to greet patrons and a live deejay to handle music. A hostess might earn 200 Lindens per hour, but that money is supplemented by tips. Fees paid to DJs are variable depending on their skills, and the status of the club is another consideration that determines payment. PeoplePool also handles club and venue staffing. Other agencies seem to cater to owners looking to staff exotic dance clubs with strippers and escorts. Many employers ask that applications be filled out as part of the interview process. Applications for hostess jobs, for instance, inquire into how a job seeker would greet a customer or approach certain situations to maintain a professional environment. Lengthy applications are sometimes required for risqué positions such as escorts or exotic dancers. Some ask for RL birth dates to verify that applicants are least 18 years of age, as well as how much experience applicants have with the position they are applying for. In the case of Club Majestic, management asked several questions, among them:

> What can you bring to Majestic Island/Club Majestic that is unique?
> Can you come up with event ideas when asked?
> Can you do a 2 hour event?
> Are you able to dress accordingly to the theme of the event...?
> Why do you want to work with us...?

Many club employers make a good looking avatar a condition of work. The hair, eyes, skin, shape, and animation overdrive, as well as clothing must look attractive for many in-world jobs. Animation Overdrive (AO) is a scripting device that simulates realistic movement for an avatar. As a courtesy, some businesses supply a notecard on how to look good in SL for almost nothing. Other qualifications include a solid grasp of the game, several outfits, English as the primary language, being at least 18 years old, profile photo and bio, and ability to communicate effectively with customers.

In the virtual world, there are very few concerns regarding Equal Opportunity Employment or other anti-discrimination policies. Women are sometimes referred to as girls, English fluency is considered priority for most businesses and appearance is a huge factor in job placement and hiring. Positions for club promoters at dance and live music venues outline appearance requirements, plus other qualifications that include language proficiency. Many hostesses/managers are required to keep the club occupied throughout the day, and send out notices of events. Interaction with patrons is a significant component of their job, in the form of keeping up the level of chat and energy in the club.

Virtual worlds have been criticized for sexual exploitation, with concerns raised similarly to how women are presented in many action games available online and in stores. There is no real need for money in Second Life, and it would be difficult to make a case that someone is forced to work in these occupations. However, escort services and stripping are particularly lucrative jobs in-world. Venues like The Nice & Naughty Club that cater to the virtual sex industry in Second Life represent one business aspect of the game. Such places can be avoided, although many of these businesses advertise in event listings and classified sections quite extensively. Given the number of venues that cater to these services, the sex industry is difficult to overlook in SL. Add to that, once you consider the members who seek employment at these venues, particularly those not able to otherwise afford quality clothing or services in-world, there is unspoken pressure to work at these clubs, which often pay well. The rationale of those employed in the virtual sex industry is stated as "it is only a game." The question then becomes how does one's in-world occupation impact identity in both real and second life. Consider this job description as fairly typical of some of the more uncensored SL clubs, and know that these clubs draw applications from teachers to bored housewives:

> Wild! Uncensored! A nightclub that challenges all others! The Hottest party to ever hit Second Life has been unleashed. Do you dare to enter? The Nice & Naughty Club is THE top new exciting dance club in all of SL.

The Nice & Naughty club boasts a professional dj, occasional live music, and "Live dancers, Escorts ready to play to your every whim, Erotic, themed hotel rooms, Trivia, Games, Contests, Theme Nights, and much more" (Nice & Naughty Club, 2009).

Another posting gives an example of an SL club that has clear policies against escort services and conveys to prospective employees a certain sense of professionalism:

> We are looking for girls who know how to work a crowd and have a good time. Our staff remains classy always. You are to appear available to all but never be available to anyone. We do not run an escort service and freelance escorting is not allowed.

Of course, management refers to its women employees as girls, but dancing rather than sex appears the business in this help wanted notice. Some SL members engage in certain risqué occupations that they never would have applied for in real life. The freedom and anonymity provided in-world encourages experimentation beyond one's moral compass in their real life. School teachers by day might work as escorts by night in SL. Modeling agencies are set up in SL to recruit the best-looking avatars to showcase top designs during fashion shows, complete with runways and audiences eager to see the latest trends in-world. Appearance is big business in the virtual economy.

24/7 Consumer Culture: Understanding the Virtual Economy

Economist Edward Castronova has written two books on the virtual world economy over the past five years. His latest book, *Exodus to the Virtual World: How Online Fun Is Changing Reality*, came out in 2008, offering a glimpse into how immersive games like Second Life are changing how much time we spend in reality: "imagine what the world would look like if someone invented and marketed a holodeck not for starships, but for every home...A new technology has emerged, in just the last five years, that is shockingly close to a holodeck" (2008, pp. 4–5). He points out, "[C]omputer generated worlds are unquestionably the holodeck's predecessors. This technology will draw in millions and millions of people, and many of them will indeed dramatically reduce the amount of time they spend doing things in the real world" (pp. 4–5). Castronova (2006), in his highly acclaimed *Synthetic Worlds: The Business and Culture of Online Games*, explains that a significant part of making economy fun for consumers is to allow them to participate in the "joy of creation" (p. 178), in that such an economy permits "people to combine basic items into more complex items," with uniquely crafted items providing the most pleasure.

Castronova (2006) notes, "The rags-to-riches phenomenon seems to enchant many people; it is apparently very enjoyable to start with nothing and make yourself into a powerful wealthy person" (p. 178). He adds that the economy should have some risk in it as well. Meanwhile, amidst all this economic hoopla, the U.S. Joint Economic Committee has investigated possibilities of public policies and taxation surrounding profits made in-world and then converted into real monies. The complexities within the discussions involve how to interpret the value of virtual property ownership (Walsh, 2006). Hundreds of thousands of dollars are spent in-world on various games every month. The Real Money Trade (RMT) for the U.S. in 2004 was estimated at 780 million dollars, with the Korean in-world market valued at 830 million (Lehtiniemi, 2007).

Since then, virtual world economies have continued to expand within the USA, Asia, and Australia and across Europe. Second Life property as a land mass continues to expand, and has grown more than twice its size since inception. The land is filled with public and private spaces, and the uses are varied. The major economy in Second Life is based on property, shopping, dancing, and education. Education will be discussed in a later chapter, and the concept of "home" is the main subject of the next chapter, with home buying becoming a big business. For some, it is enough to build a small cottage on a small plot of land. For others, they long to buy or build a mansion on their estate, and it is a dream that is fairly easily accomplished in Second Life compared to real life. Residents take care to furnish their homes with chairs, sofas, beds, hot tubs, office desks, pools, and even kitchens. Of course in Second Life, one does not sleep or cook. Homes convey a sense of ownership and security for residents. Homes can serve as personal statements of virtual commitment or status. One might own a bungalow in real life, and a mansion in SL. The cost of homes in Second Life, although pricey for a game, is hardly anything in terms of the real estate market in real life.

Paintings, lamps, carpets, and laptops become accessories in this second space, representative of real spaces. Some paintings are of images drawn from real life; others are reflective of virtual culture. Artists sometimes forego home spaces to buy land to showcase their work or to curate the accomplishments of others. Exhibits and installations on occasion challenge portrayals of gender and culture inside Second Life. Some galleries merely serve as personal showplaces, whereas other spaces become major exhibition venues for real-world artists trying to expand their audiences. No matter, the purchase of art in Second Life has become part of consumer culture.

Live music entertainment is regularly provided freely throughout Second Life, and operates on tip contributions from patrons and talent fees paid by venue operators. Some musicians use these venues to create new online markets for their material. It would seem anything for sale in real life is available in Second Life, whether it has practical application or not in a virtual world. Cars, motorcycles, boats, submarines, blimps and balloons offer fun, but impractical, ways of transporting avatars from one place to another. Second Life affords some residents opportunities to experience the extremes of consumer culture unavailable to them in real life.

What You Wear

In Second Life, many of the club and live music venues are part of large mall complexes. With the idea that entertainment can bring in customers, many malls have performance spaces. Top designers are located in major traffic venues, near the biggest dance clubs. Many malls feature fashion shows in the performance region, with the intent of showcasing merchandise and increasing sales. In SL, you find discount warehouses too that offer merchandise at a fraction of retail value. Clothing can cost from 1L to 800L, with name-brand unique designs bringing in top dollar. Malls in Second Life are built and removed every day. People tend to seek out centers of activity, and malls create the perfect gathering space to allow shops to thrive together. Numerous clothing stores offer ballroom to casual wear, shoes to jewelry, and a host of accessories every avatar needs to fit in with the virtual social scene.

Some of the largest malls attract business throughout the day, across the world, virtually and in reality. The fashion scene in Second Life is full of extremes, perhaps more so than in real life. Walking through the malls, you might see someone dressed in a formal tuxedo; another adorned as a medieval princess, while one person is represented by a snake avatar slithering across the marble floor. All enter into the collective space of Second Life. Of course, some malls offer more specialty services than others, and that often determines the clientele. Music forums established within malls serve as public spaces to bring people together to enjoy the convergence of consumer culture in a digital world. Second Life has created its own popular culture, although much of it is reflective of the real world. Among some members, there is a sense of unique identity in clothes, hair, appearance, and attitude. New music and art—and unique avatars—are welcome to this new collision of cultures. That is not to say that for most members Second Life is no more than an extension of real life, allowing them to be a bit more experimental in their interests, personalities, and looks.

In such an environment, trying on a new identity is a simple matter. Many members seem to align their appearances to match real-life fantasy images of men and women. Women are often represented with fuller figures across in-world fashion billboards and advertising posters than in real-life magazines. Men are often portrayed muscular to the point of absurdity. In SL, the average height for women is about 6'3" and 7' for men. Of course, there are exceptions, with animal and character avatars coming in all sizes.

Body stores represent one of the most profitable businesses in Second

Life—the skin and shape industry. Other than gyms and cosmetic surgeons, there is nothing in comparison to them in real life. Once residents become accustomed to the plethora of skin and shape shops all over SL malls and venues, they routinely tweak their physical appearance. Members are challenged to rethink their appearance and hair style continuously, with perfection virtually possible. Housewives, retired teachers, and truck drivers in RL compete for modeling jobs in SL. In SL, you can look like a model without exercising, and the right script will provide you with the appropriate walk and moves. In SL, rock stars, mall managers, djs, fashion designers, and club owners are prestigious positions. Some of these SL jobs are held by real-life educators, housewives, physicians, and computer programmers. Qualifications prized with SL jobs include knowledge of streaming and graphic arts software, management and communication skills, and plenty of downtime to work in a virtual world. Scripting is always a plus in a game fueled by animations intended to simulate human emotion and activities. All in all, the virtual economy is an extension of the worst and best in Western (real world) consumer culture, depending on one's view of capitalism.

Second Life, although not intentionally, provokes residents to consider ways in which to fit within a virtual culture that at times seems similar to advertising propaganda in real life. When someone arrives into Second Life for the first time, they are confronted with culture shock, especially as they attempt to create an image of themselves that might or might not line up with their RL image. They have limited access to clothing upon entrance, and their choices for physical features are limited. As they become acclimated to SL, they begin to realize they can buy hair, skin, eyes, and shapes and other accessories to craft an image that suits the look they want to project—whether that be fictional or based on reality. The body is for sale in Second Life. Skin color, eyes and hair are all options. Tattoo shops thrive as well; while some members experiment with different designs on a daily basis, others incorporate tattoos as part of their identity. For educators, lawyers, musicians and others, tattoos become a fun way to express a virtual personality.

The Fashion Districts of Second Life

Journey McLaglen is a major player and designer in the Second Life fashion industry. She not only makes her own line of clothing, but she is involved in every aspect of the business, from creation to sales and marketing to running a staff of models and assistants. Her brand is called Prism, and her stores are located in the high- to mid-level fashion districts of Second Life, targeting a particular customer looking for stylish brands, adapted from the latest lines off the runway:

> I'm kind of mid-range in prices. So I'm more what I call the ready to wear market. So if you take the runway fashions, and you turn them into ready to wear, there's where I am. What I love about this market is people come here, and a lot of them don't want to look overly sexy; they want to look sexy but in a sophisticated way. So that is the customer I go after. I think that is really cool because what I noticed on my own sims since I started renting out my stores; I have all these different designers there now. When I see how unique their approach is—one of them is very 60s focused. And one of them is into things that would appeal more to people in college or the 18-to-25 age group. So it is really interesting to see the focus and realize there is an evolution. (McLaglen, 2009)

As in real life, owning and operating a business is nearly a full-time job or lifestyle. For business owners, Second Life becomes less game and more career, although most enjoy what they are creating virtually:

> It is never ending. You pay for the store in the expensive places. Then you have to go ahead and buy ads. And then on top of that, you've got to do a fashion show or two a month to keep your name out there. It just continues to add up. On top of all that, it does you no good to do a fashion show even once a quarter if you are not designing all the time. It is a cycle. I think it is fascinating. You really have to be a good marketer to be successful in SL. Those who are good marketers can be very successful. There are some very talented people out there that never go very far. I mean they become known, and then they just eventually give up or disappear because they don't become well known. What I have learned from that is that you have to learn to market in a virtual environment. There are a lot of very good marketers in Second Life. They come up with some brilliant ideas for driving traffic. (McLaglen, 2009)

Over the past several years, a number of business scripts and tools have improved attracting and tracking customers, explained McLaglen (2009):

> So there's just many tools that have been developed, and over the years it started out with simple things like lucky chairs, which really aren't simple but they are really brilliant. It moved on to many other tools and things and now we have the use of video as machinima. And we have the incredible art of photographing. If you look at the way that has evolved, we have so much that goes into making a business successful. So as a designer, you are looking at what are the things that are going to keep your business moving toward that top position that everyone wants. It's things like having a good staff of models on hand that can help your customers when you're not in the store, making yourself present in the store for events, doing one event a week, getting new materials into the stores at least once a week, which means carving out enough time to design which is time consuming. Not only that, but to do the photographs that need to go on the outside of the vendor [display], to get the vendors set up, to get them into your server, or whatever system that you are using. Then you need to get the bloggers blogging, and notifications sent out. Right now, there are 3,500 members in Prism's subscriber group and there are many stores that have many more than that. This is another brilliant tool developed. You can actually circulate information to people without having to occupy a group slot, which is great because you are not in-

> trusive. You're coming to them only when you have something special to say or offer. (McLaglen, 2009)

For SL business owners, such tools and scripts translate into major income, with some entrepreneurs making a living from Second Life. However, it is the collective energy of those on the leading edge of business—those creating tools, products and marketing strategies—in virtual worlds that will help shape online commerce in years to come:

> So there's just a limitless supply of tools being developed every day. But I guess the point is that it takes teams of people and ingenuity and brilliant minds to put together the things that have helped to develop commerce in Second Life. When you sit back and really think about it, it is astounding to think—and I work full-time and I don't have the time to focus the energy—but I know a lot of people who focus as if this is indeed their work day in Second Life. They bring in a salary of 80,000 dollars and above in real money. That to me is significant because what it says is that there is a tremendous opportunity in the future. Philip Linden spoke during the SL 6th Birthday ceremonies how Websites and such things will be changing, and how the [virtual world] model that we use now may soon become the model that we use to visit different Web sites. I think we are all very fortunate to be learning this and on the front end of this incredible new—I say new, it is several years old now but evolving every day, this incredible edge of knowledge and where it is leading business. That's it in a nutshell, a big nutshell. (McLaglen, 2009)

McLaglen (2009) admits she enjoys her moonlighting in Second Life, working as a fashion mogul in the evenings through the wee hours of the morning occasionally: "It's fun. I have to tell you. I look forward to coming home and just designing. That's my favorite thing to do. I have a life, I read, I swim, I like to get my exercise, and I go out with my friends. I went out to dinner tonight. But in the long run, my favorite thing to do is to relax and come back and design something. I get such a thrill, when people put it on and they really like how they look. It's just really exciting."

The Business of Romance: Valentine's Day, 2009

Logging into Second Life on the days leading up to Valentine's Day, the member home page flashed a reminder to not forget that special person. Second Life stores sold mock roses and candy and greeting cards, which were delivered personally or by in-world businesses. Members sought out special virtual gifts to demonstrate their commitment to loved ones in-world. Couples kindled their relationships in formal attire, sexy lingerie, or any number of ways—all bought from in-world stores. As in RL, holidays are big business for SL vendors. Classified ads announce special sales and gifts. That diamond ring or necklace costs a fraction of the price of jewelry in RL. You can dazzle him or her for about 500 to 1000 Lindens. For about 5 dollars in SL, you can present your loved one with diamonds and a night out at a premier club. Plus, avatars don't eat—so that makes the night even more affordable. Couples can visit Paris, Rome, exotic beaches, secluded resorts, or any one of a hundred places in Second Life that project an atmosphere of romance.

SL romance is a driving force behind the economy, whether that was an initial, intentional goal or not of Linden Lab management. The SL home page often showcases romantic images, and through its choice of images acknowledges the profound romantic connections made and nurtured by in-world settings catering to dance and romance—top attractions among SL members. Second Life offers an inexpensive option for those with limited funds or no place to go locally in real life. For example, small town residents might have few options in the way of dancing at a formal ballroom or even finding an urban club. All they need is an Internet connection, and they can dance at an elegant nightclub with people across the world. Second Life suddenly expands your options, globally.

On Valentine's Day 2009, couples came to romantic settings to converse, dance, and cuddle virtually. DreamLovers Gardens is a romantic space with a ballroom. Upon entrance into the site, one will receive a notecard in all caps boldly stating:

> DREAM LOVER'S BID YOU WELCOME TO OUR BEAUTIFUL DANCE GARDEN. HERE YOU CAN ENJOY THE BEAUTIFUL NATURE, CUDDLE UP WITH THAT SPECIAL SOMEONE IN ROMANTIC SURROUNDINGS, OR DANCE THE NIGHT AWAY TO YOUR FAVORITE LOVE SONGS...WE ALSO OFFER YOU A PRIVATE CUDDLE SPACEBOX, FOR THOSE VERY PRIVATE MOMENTS.

On Valentine's Day, nearly all the SL dance spots were decorated with banners, lights and flowers celebrating the day of romance. Some clubs celebrate love every day. The romantic club Sweethearts is a huge venue designed for couple dancing, and draws an international membership on any given day. Hundreds of avatars can be seen dressed formally in gowns and tuxedos, dancing the day away. At times, men and women stand or sit off on the sidelines, waiting for a dance partner. Other popular ballrooms include Frank's Place Jazz and Dance Club and Jade's Jazz Lounge. Jade's sometimes hires singers to croon ballads, performing live as couples spend an evening dancing together. Another unique video dance club projects classic rock music videos on all four walls to create a surreal yet intimate space for couples. Janis Joplin, Aretha Franklin, Bob Dylan, Bruce Springsteen, Joe Cocker and others are featured across video screens on walls and the floor. SL offers a romantic setting for any given moment at any season of the year; some gardens offer couples an opportunity to hold hands as they walk through pathways, simply by making available a special pose animation. Imagine walking hand in hand along an ocean shore or up a volcanic mountainside with the one you adore in SL.

Jewelry is a sign of commitment in SL, and engagement and wedding rings are part of the experience. Exactly how much money is spent on jewelry in-world is not known, but it is common to see avatars adorned in necklaces, earrings, rings, and a lot of bling. Certain venues ask members to turn off their bling (or particles) to avoid lag during live performances. Members have an opportunity to express themselves by decorating their bodies, and jewelry is one way to do so. Fine jewelry and formal wear are relatively expensive in Second Life, and a certain fashion status can be achieved in Second Life by dressing trendy among certain cliques. Good dance animations are expected at the top music venues. Dance pose balls are placed throughout SL at clubs and live music venues, and sometimes positioned near fiery volcanic mountain tops. Dance balls allow for couples to share interactive space and simulate contact. Dancing is big business. With individual pose balls going for 200 to 300 Lindens each, the cost of romance can become expensive fairly quickly. Couple balls that are well scripted can cost up to 10,000 Lindens, an equivalent of nearly 40 U.S. dollars.

Ballrooms draw together people from around the world. These formal dance halls offer a place for new people to meet others, and for all to meet potential romantic partners. Some members enjoy traditional formal ballrooms; at other venues like Tropicana, women dress up in elegant and flashy gowns to salsa and slow dance with men in tuxedos. Tropicana's atmosphere is festive, complete with hired dancers animated to orchestrated moves so as to cultivate a unique ethnic flavor. Top dance venues specialize in certain music genres: slow, rave, Hip-Hop, rock, trance, jazz, 80s, and country. Many venues are situated in malls that feature SL name-brand clothing suited to the interests of club patrons. Second Life has everything from biker to strip bars, and a plethora of gothic and vampire clubs. In terms of the seedier side of virtual life, it is possible to find any type of music, clothing, or entertainment. In contrast, for some a night of entertainment might be playing virtual bumper cars or enjoying carnival rides. Some regions feature theaters, and show DVD releases in-world. Drive-in theaters feature not only movies, but provide cars you can sit in to watch films. Most of these activities are free, and contributions are accepted in the way of tips, with special jars set up in certain areas that allow for donations by patrons.

Roads to Nowhere

The automobile is a strange concept in Second Life. There is no need to travel by car from one place to another, and it is certainly difficult to find highways upon which to drive down. Most roads end after several yards. As noted in earlier discussions, McLuhan understood the role of the automobile as an extension to humanity, specifically as an individual desire to travel beyond one's human capabilities. In SL, the car's main function might be to convey a certain image of its owner. The Second Life system of roadways is one that predated the ability to teleport to in-world destinations in a convenient and consistent manner, and was conceived as a possible means of travel within regions: "When Second Life first opened, there was no point-to-point personal teleportation. The only such travel available was through station-to-station 'telehubs.' Therefore, if you wanted to travel, there were really only three options: sailing the coast, personal flight, or utilising the mainland road system" (Ellis, 2007). Today you can still see roads intersect mainland areas owned by Linden Lab and some other regions here and there, but they are mostly untraveled now, "practically an archeological artifact" in Second Life:

> Empty: but still in place. And, in most areas, they're still fringed with buildings, some of which date back to the time where roadside location was still very much sought after...Three or four years ago, these were the important thoroughfares, the veins and arteries of commerce in Second Life. (Ellis, 2007)

Cars, motorcycles and boats are popular among residents—for show, if not practicality. The virtual car culture is symbolic of the world's fascination with automobile status. Fiat Latin America's headquarters has been an SL showcase, one of the recommended hot spots for virtual tourists; visitors can view its sporty designs in colorful and festive display. At this site, auto exhibits are centered along a circuit of roadways that appear somewhat like a racetrack. Very few roads exist in Second Life because flying and teleporting serve as the primary means of transportation. Cars, however, remain status symbols that look good parked in front of virtual houses or on a paved driveway or partial road. The St. Louis region is built around a model of the famous Arch, a landmark in the real city. In Second Life, visitors can see part of the highway and bridge with tall buildings lining the road as part of the St. Louis downtown cityscape. The highway just ends.

Automobiles are considered important symbols representing real life in virtual worlds like Second Life. They may not be practical in application, but they connect Second Life to real-life culture. On Orientation Island, newbies drive around a city to get acquainted with various vehicles. They may never drive a car inside Second Life. Pontiac had created Motorati Island as homage to car culture, and events and concerts were held on a regular basis in 2006. Toyota set up a brand office in Second Life to cater to its youth market when marketing its Scion models. When the Scion exhibit opened in November 2006, it sold about 200 virtual cars, with each vehicle being equivalent to one

U.S. dollar. During its exhibition, the company site created an image and character for each automobile displayed, with one car for example represented as a toaster (Valdes-Dapena, 2006a). Virtual cars are made with primitive objects, the building blocks of Second Life. Cars are sculpted into shape, and sometimes move through solid objects like walls and utility poles: "Someone posting on a blog for Electric Sheep, the company that created Nissan Island, mentioned his car was so fast it was able to drive over a bridge before the computer had time to finish making the bridge" (Valdes-Dapena, 2006a).

A search through SL Classified retrieves listings for a number of virtual car dealerships. Sculpted Cars, for example, features: "Cars inspired from Ferrari f430, Ferrari Daytona, Mclaren lamborgini Gallardo, BMW, Bugatti, Lamborghini, Ferrari, Porsche, Bentley Rolls Royce, Neons...Flying cars, vehicles, bikes, motors, Range, Rover..." The Dodge Viper GTS can be found at "Pro Street Cars, along with Acura NSX, Bentley Continental, Rolls Royce, Jaguar E-Type, Nissan 350Z, Audi R8, Subaru STI" and even police cars. Several dealerships exhibit a variety of real-life brands inside SL, and some sell helicopters, spaceships, blimps, and hot air balloons as well. A range of Harley Davidson motorcycles and related products are available in Second Life, and some cycle riding courses are set up exclusively for in-world riders. For many in SL, it is less about the thrill of taking to the open road than a satisfaction that they can afford the virtual version of a Harley or BMW.

Software Island

Sunbelt Software Island is featured as a Second Life Showplace; its tall corporate tower is in the midst of a winter wonderland that features live music on a regular basis. Winter Solstice, Blue Lagoon, Sunbelt Sandbox, and Boondock Live Music are some of its areas that draw traffic. This corporate sim is designed to provide helpful information on computer issues typical to Second Life, and it promotes Sunbelt's anti-virus (AV) software in-world. "Is your AV slowing down SL?" is one of the questions posed to visitors. Headquartered in Tampa, Florida, the company was launched in 1994. It describes itself as the "leading provider" of Windows security software. The company has SL listings for classes in building, streaming, and music events in Google Calendar.

Unlike at the IBM headquarters, which is also an impressive site, Sunbelt Software creates an interactive and playful landing for in-world customers to acquire assistance and information in a unique manner. In this way, customers learn about the product, as well as solutions for their gaming problems. The entertainment and gatherings provided at Sunbelt's special venues are comparable to customer service appreciation parties for virtual gamers. The beautiful surroundings attract visitors to come back just to dance as couples across the snow crystals. The music, ambience and visuals create a stunning experience for customers and visitors. This type of build demonstrates how corporations can tap into consumer culture facilitated within virtual worlds, and illustrates willingness among customers to participate and interact within these environments without being evidently offended by an obvious corporate mission to sell products or services. Other examples of how corporate investment into Second Life helps to sustain art, entertainment and education, from record label sponsorship of in-world concerts to educational firms underwriting university projects, is documented in this book.

Transforming Work Culture and Spaces

The main goal of this chapter was to show how virtual worlds are evolving as integral parts of the business world—in-world and off line, as well as how the concepts of work and consumer markets are becoming transformed by these new opportunities. Virtual worlds no longer are intended to solely complement business operations, but these web places provide interactive meeting sites to close communicative gaps between consumers and companies, bringing them into an interactive, intimate space that is user friendly. Candidates for real-world jobs complete much of their application process online, and increasingly job seekers attend Web career expos for job placement.

In the June/July 2008 edition of *Reveal Magazine*, a Second Life magazine covering lifestyle and social issues in-world, reporter Anjula Basevi investigates virtual employment services in the article "Vacancy—Real World Career—Click Here." Virtual worlds are transforming ways some companies are recruiting employees. Virtual job fairs are becoming more than fashionable, with companies awakening to the fact that these events are efficient ways to attract qualified and newly graduated applicants for informational technology, finance, business, and telecommunications positions. These potential employees are comfortable with new technologies, and most likely to assist companies as they attempt to position themselves toward future marketplaces. The article centered around Linden Lab's Second Career Fair on May 29, 2008, organized by Working Worlds Project. With thousands in attendance, the fair seemed to indicate companies were in line with future trends in hiring. Basevi (2008) notes, "Some of the biggest employers in Belgium, the Netherlands and Luxembourg were in world in Second Life interviewing eager candidates for real world jobs." She adds,

> This thoroughly modern approach...is intended to enable candidates from all over the world being able to participate. Some of the largest and more progressive organiza-

> tions from Western Europe's and global companies are taking part: Amazon, Bill, Lombard, Manpower, SS&C are just a few of the 'names' involved. (Basevi, 2008)

In the 2007 job fair, 300 interviews were conducted, after 1,500 applicants uploaded their resumes on the career website. One of the organizers, Cornelia Den Hartog, explains the simplicity of the process, "An interview with a long distance company is as easy as logging in and teleporting to the actual location…You can sit in the comfort of your own home and attend an actual interview…You can present yourself much more confidently and feel less intimidated by the interview process" (Basevi, 2008).

Many of the companies interested in this type of recruitment process are seeking innovative employees that might help them develop and extend virtual technologies within their businesses. The move toward VR (virtual reality) workplaces is an attempt to bring back an "in-person element to remote interactions" (Basevi, 2008). Although this notion seems a bit counterintuitive on how to increase intimacy among business and community sectors, consultant Dave Elchoness explains, "The 20th century saw the rise of the automobile, the airplane, the computer and the network…these remarkable inventions enabled long distance interaction e.g., commuting, business air travel, email…[W]hereas conventional electronic means of communication has allowed us to work with people long distances away, it has left us lacking interpersonal connection" (Basevi, 2008). Instead, he posits, what we have is a communications hangover; the glut of technologies has overwhelmed workers and consumers to the point that any sense of interconnection and communicative intimacy is disappearing.

In that same issue of *Reveal,* reporter Angelo Sydney (2008) followed up on research that indicated 90% of virtual world businesses fail, and her investigation indicated that was likely due to company approach to this new market (Sydney, 2008). Customers anticipate an interactive space where they can touch products and try them out, whereas much company effort is spent on creating beautiful landscapes and buildings (Sydney, 2008). Often these businesses are devoid of functional and interactive experiences that invite consumer participation and bring customers back to the store or company site. Part of the problem, no doubt, is that computer programmers who can script such environments are few and far between in these virtual worlds. Yet, virtual worlds are intended to allow residents to explore their imagination and defy physics, rather than serve as simply a means to simulate reality. Kimberly Winnington (Gianna Borgnine in Second Life), founder of Sandcastle Studios Inc, a virtual worlds marketing consultancy, explains, "So businesses need to stop thinking 'real life' and start thinking 'second life.' Physics prevents us from doing crazy stuff in the real world. But in SL you can have people walk through a lava flow in a volcano, star in a movie, jump out of an aero plane..." (Sydney, 2008). Based on a 2008 Forrester market research report, "Getting Real Work Done in Virtual Worlds," Virtual Reality Workplace CEO David Elchoness points out, workplaces "will be transformed when distance is no longer an obstacle—when you can work with people as if in person in the web" (Sydney, 2008). The future of the virtual world marketplace is best illustrated by thinking less about Web browsing and more about landing to actual Web places (Basevi, 2008).

Conclusion

Second Life is only one component of the growing virtual economy. As competing virtual worlds come online, companies will follow consumers in-world. At other times, some businesses will lead their customers in-world, by catering to them and by employing them. Virtual jobs have become real ways to earn incomes for some players. Physically challenged members can compete inside Second Life and other virtual worlds for jobs. Certain occupations might provide short-term incomes for some members, but the nature of the SL business might not be one from which someone can develop a real- life portfolio. Others, like photographers, journalists, and business owners, might find SL as a great way to jump start their career or to try a new direction with little risk. Increasingly, SL businesses lead to RL world income and notoriety. Real money is exchanged for Lindens in Second Life. The money is real. Real money is spent and earned. That is the bottom line.

References

Anshe Chung becomes first virtual world millionaire (2006, November 26). Press Release. Accessed June 21, 2009, from http://www.anshechung.com/include/ press/press_release251106.html.

Banking crisis (also) in second life. (2008), Second Life Research. Accessed February 1, 2009, from http://secondliferesearch.blogspot.com/ Reprint, *The Wall Street Journal*, January 23, 2008.

Basevi, A. (2008). Vacancy—real world career—click here. *Reveal Magazine*, June/July, pp. 15–16.

Castronova, E. (2006). *Synthetic worlds: The business and culture of online games*. Chicago: University of Chicago Press.

Club Tokyo. (2009). Job posting. Second Life.

DreamLovers Gardens. (2009). Notecard. Second Life.

Ellis, W. (2007, September 28). Second life sketches: Drive my car. Reuters.com. Accessed February 2, 2009, from http://secondlife.reuters.com/stories/2007 /09/28/second-life-sketches-drive-my-car/

Hof, R. (2006a, May 1). My virtual life. *Business Week*. Accessed June 23, 2009, from http://www.businessweek.com/magazine/content/06_18/b3982001.htm?chan=search

—. (2006b, November 26). Second Life's first millionaire. *Tech Beat*. Accessed

June 26, 2009, from http://www.businessweek.com/the_thread/techbeat/archives/2006/11/second_lifes_fi.html

Kenney, B. (2007, July 27). Second Life: What is it? (And why should manufacturers care?). *Industry Week*. Accessed February 23, 2009, from http://www.industryweek.com/articles/second_life_what_is_it_and_why_should_manufacturers_ care_14649.aspx?Page=4

Lehtiniemi, T. (2007, March 2). How big is the RMT market anyway? *The Virtual Economy Research*. Accessed February 23, 2009, from http://virtual-economy.org/blog/ how_big_is_the_rmt_market_anyw

LoveHolic. (2009). Job posting. Second Life.

McLaglen, J. (2009, August 5). Interview, personal communication with author. Second Life.

Nice & Naughty Club (2009). Job posting. Second Life.

Platoni, K. (2008, Jan/Feb). Seeing is believing. *Stanford Magazine*. Accessed June 12, 2009, from http://www.stanfordalumni.org/news/magazine/2008/janfeb/features/virtual.html.

Reuters, R. (2007, May 28). The price of tying the virtual knot. *Reuters News Service*. Accessed November 21, 2007, from http://secondlife.reuters.com/stories/ 2007/05/28/the-price-of-tying-the-virtual-knot/

Sidel, R. (2008, January 23). Cheer up, Ben: Your economy isn't as bad as this one in the make-believe world of "second life," banks are really collapsing. *Wall Street Journal Online*. Accessed February 1, 2009, fromhttp://online.wsj.com/ article/SB120104351064608025.html?mod=hpp_us_inside_today.

Sydney, A. (2008). 9 out of 10 virtual world businesses fail!—research. *Reveal Magazine*, June/July, pp. 4–6. Accessed June 21, 2009, from http://reveal-sl.com/resources/Reveal+Magazine+12.pdf

Terdiman, D. (2005, November 10). Man pays $100,000 for virtual resort. CNET.News. Accessed June 21, 2009, from http://news.cnet.com/Man-pays-100,000-for-virtual-resort/2100–1043_3-5945248.html.

The Adventure Capitalists. (2009, July 10). Second Thoughts. Blog. Accessed July 10, 2009, from http://secondthoughts.typepad.com/second_thoughts/2009/07/the-adventure-capitalists.html#more/

Valdes-Dapena, P. (2006a, November 18). Car companies open dealerships in virtual world. Extended warranties not needed, optional dragon heads available. Accessed March 12, 2009, from http://www.cnn.com/2006/AUTOS/11/17/ 2nd_life_cars/index.htmlReal cars drive into Second Life/

Walsh, T. (2006). U.S. govt eyes virtual–world economies. *Clickable Culture*. Accessed June 21, 2009, from http://www.secretlair.com/index.php?/clickableculture/ entry/us_govt_eyes_virtual_worlds/

CHAPTER FIVE

Safe Spaces: Home Sweet Home in Another World

> "The Web, virtual worlds, gaming are colliding and creating new opportunities for user engagement, interaction and participation past the virtual hype."
>
> —The Electric Sheep Company web site

Electric Sheep is one of many companies engaged in the creation and crafting of virtual worlds and their often surreal experiences. For average avatars, the journey begins when they first log onto a virtual world. For the newcomers to Second Life, the journey begins on Orientation Island. Mentors are eager to ease new members into their virtual life. Members are provided clothing, household items, cars, and a range of supplies that provide connection to the real world. Members enter into this new world without a home, and some do not feel compelled to buy a home. Most residents, at one point, want a space to call their own, or at the very least a space that makes them comfortable when they sign on and off the game. Some members rent spaces or stay with friends that they meet in SL or that they already know in real life. When residents become motivated to claim a space for their own, not only must they search for property, but they must contend with a booming real estate market in-world. Houses range from freebie cabins to mansions, to houseboats and skyboxes. Residents create gardens, exhibit their personal art work, and sometimes frame real-life photos of themselves and their family. Others simply rent spaces. Yet, the goal is the same: to find a space that makes them feel secure, offers them some sense of privacy, and allows them to express themselves in-world. Indeed, these are also the motivations for owning a home in real life as well.

Home as Sanctuary and Status

In our daily lives, we become accustomed to magazines and television shows that feature exotic homes from around the world, priced from the millions to the billions of dollars. Homes of the wealthy and famous fascinate people from around the world, for those houses are perhaps symbolic of a lifestyle that they may never know except voyeuristically. Imagine owning an island get-away in the sunny tropics. The possibility is achievable in Second Life for many members, more so than in reality. The comfort of home is one which rests deep within our dreams and memories. We retreat to that safe haven, where we can lock the windows and doors, draw the shades, and relax on a sofa with a friend. Residents have expressed the concept of home as a place of escape and security. For many, it is a fantasy that they can see and hear. My conversations with residents throughout Second Life reveal a strong desire to claim a space in the virtual world for their own and for various reasons.

The illusion is grounded in the wants of the dreamer. Beyond that, there is a feeling of displacement when one first arrives into the mainland of Second Life. One arrives in a land of strangers. Most often is the case that you know no one, and have no place to call your own. The world around you seems unfamiliar, although some regions have neighborhoods similar to the real world. When I first popped into Second Life, I teleported into a crazy medieval festival, and everyone was chatting with each other. They were dressed in armor, and I was wearing jeans and a t-shirt. Hurriedly, I sought any destination on my map to fly out of there, and to find some sense of solitude to where I might gather my bearings.

Years later, I owned a number of residences, although most had been non-traditional, such as space sky boxes and a castle. Residents seek spaces in which to retreat when they feel that they need a moment of solitude or privacy. It serves as a place to dress, to privately chat with friends, and to call their own. Only one of my houses has a security system, for that is the place that my husband and I call our personal space. Not much goes on there, but it is place where we can hang up family pictures and have some quiet time. If anyone comes near the house, they will be ejected from the premise, unless they are on our guest list. Others have security fences all around their properties to the point that it obstructs one's ability to fly over the landscape to simply cross the region. Many regions have covenants that dissuade land owners from using such systems. For those new to Second Life, it might seem silly to seek security and privacy in a virtual world. You might say, this is a game, right? Real-life conceptions of home spill over into virtual spaces. That is not to deny that some residents have specific reasons to maintain private and secure residences, which range from having in-world sex to having a private place to dress and work on one's appearance, or savoring a quiet place to shut the real and second world out for awhile.

Mediated Concepts of Home

Virtual homes might provide that philosophical bridge between reality and fantasy. By having a home in Second Life, residents have a reference point upon which to establish their new life. Security and shelter seem primary reasons for buying a house, but often as significant is residents' desire to transform their house into a home: "At this level, the house becomes a setting for meaning; it becomes not only a physical structure but a symbol" (Israel, 2003). Clare Cooper Marcus (2006), in *House as a Mirror of Self*, suggests that home reflects one's notion of self: "What is self? Why here? Why now? In trying to comprehend this most basic of archetypes—self—to give it concrete substance…I believe, man…frequently selects the house, the basic protector of his internal environment (beyond skin and clothing) to represent or symbolize what is tantalizingly unrepresentable" (Marcus, 2006). Home, according to Gaston Bachelard (1994), in *The Poetics of Space*, shares conceptions of home as our first space, our universe. Bachelard (1994, p. 5) states, "all really inhabited spaces bear the essence of the home," adding that they have the "illusion of protection" by which they can experience "the house in reality and its virtuality, by means of thoughts and dreams" (p. 5). The house becomes part of our personal narrative, as we shift in and out of memories, imagination and notions of home and physical space.

Winifred Gallagher's (2007) *The Power of Place: How Our Surroundings Shape Our Thoughts, Emotions, and Actions* enhances this discussion of home by considering the environmental context in which the house resides. Second Life allows residents to change their environmental settings to select times of the day, from sunset to midnight. Residents also choose the land on which they build. Moreover, environmental settings tap into the senses, and draw from our natural experience; indeed how light impacts activity levels of humans has been documented: "Our daily physiological and behavioral shifts are intimately connected to our seasonal ones because the brain, equipped with a light meter that gauges the day's illumination and a biological 'clock' that measures the day's length, uses information about light conditions to determine the time of the year" (Gallagher, 2007, pp. 2–30). Witold Rybczynski (1997) provides a condensed history of the home, by reviewing its cultural influences back to the middle ages, exploring concepts of privacy and intimacy as well as how light, air, and efficiency converge within homes. The point is, home is a significant symbol of our commitment to a virtual world. For some in Second Life, their store or studio becomes their virtual reference, and that is representative of their sense of meaning in-world. Many artists and media makers forego a traditional home for a studio, for they derive meaning in life from their work.

The idea that a virtual world can impact our emotions becomes more likely when you consider the work of psychologist Michael Terman. When he was director of the light therapy unit of the New York State Psychiatric Institute, he was involved in some experiments involving simulated environments.

To ensure a restful night's sleep, he turned on his "tropical dawn machine;" it is an "experimental computerized light device he invented to recreate Carribean-style dawns and sunsets in bedrooms around the globe. The electrical sun starts to sink as he gets into bed at 11 p.m., and by 11:25, he is fast asleep. Sunrise occurs promptly at 7 a.m., when he awakes refreshed and alert" (Gallagher, 2007). This machine tricks his body into sleeping: "The artificial twilight at night is like a hypnotic agent. Halfway through the sunset, one is calm and ready to sleep. Light can be a photic sleeping pill—a healthy one" (Gallagher, 2007, p. 31). In Second Life, there is a cycle of 3 hours of daylight and one hour of night that repeats itself throughout any 24-hour period. Imagine the havoc that might create on one's senses, but residents have the option to change the default setting to sunrise, midday, sunset or midnight. Residents can alter the mood of the day simply by changing the environmental setting. Many do alter settings for various experiences, such as dancing on a beach shore at sunset or watching a movie at a drive-in theater.

Home and Family

HDTV (Home Decorating Television Network) has capitalized on the fascination that Americans and Europeans have acquired for fashionable houses. The desire to fashion our homes in ways that reflect the personalities of our families and ourselves is one that is being increasingly marketed across television. On screen, homes are made to look cozy and lived-in and welcoming to guests. The concept of an emotionally healthy home, as it is projected across the media, is one that conveys a sense of acceptance and warmth. Think of the long-running show *The Cosbys* and how this family's home was open to friends that would drop in unexpectedly. It was a place where life issues were discussed, and joys were celebrated. The door was always open; the ideal of the nearly perfect family coincides with the nearly perfect image of a warm-hearted home. In real life, not all families are so inviting and welcoming to friends, neighbors and strangers. The image implanted in our minds, however, is this ideal of the perfect home and family. It is definitely a notion that is extended upon in virtual spaces, as people cast their dreams and fears toward these new frontiers. The same stereotypical views of home in real life are extended into virtual life.

In terms of reality shows focusing on real families, perhaps one of the first, if not the first, was *The American Family*, a 12-part PBS series, that debuted in 1973. It was a voyeuristic and emotional journey into the experiences of a family going through crisis. Some movies and television shows build plots around a dystopian view of families, which is done by showing the house as a place of division and confusion. In such cases, the house and its residents are characterized as distant and working against a common purpose. In the widely popular reality show, *Big Brother,* participants compete to be among the surviving contestants. The show has been syndicated, and adapted, across the world—with a modified version at one time being created for Second Life. In December 2006, Endemol Netherlands in Second Life made a call for contestants to participate in a virtual adaption of *Big Brother*. Fifteen contestants were selected across 3 time zones. They spent minimally 8 hours daily in a transparent house for a month, with in-world viewers able to watch them through the glass. There was even a Big Brother dance club. The contestants remained busy throughout most of the day, with the majority of their tasks involving building replicas of famous structures. Just as in the RL version, contestants would vote off members until the final winner was decided. Madlen Flint, the winner, received her own virtual island. The first avatar to be voted off was Gideon Television. In his journal, he wrote:

> ...five avatars with the lowest number of votes were announced...three would be evicted. Instructions for the final rites were given—if our names were called, we were to descend the tube to a place where the survivors could pick carrion from the corpses. (Television, 2007)

He continued, "A dramatic pause, and then Big Brother, his virtual breath reeking with a stench of pity, announced that "THE FIRST PERSON IN HISTORY EVER TO BE EVICTED FROM THE VIRTUAL BIG BROTHER IS...(Beat)...GIDEON TELEVISION" (Television, 2007).

Television shows like *Supernanny* and *Wife Swap* appear to capitalize off the notion of home as a place that should unify residents to create a family bond. The idea is to fix or remove the bad elements. Yet, such shows might be counterproductive in their efforts, intentionally or unintentionally. Family secrets and bad behavior are exposed on the various television episodes, and then discussed after the viewing online through related blogs and Web sites. Sides are taken among viewers on what family members should do or not do. The cliché home sweet home is reminiscent of classic television shows from the 1970s like *The Waltons*, where members strived to overcome pressures of life together against outside forces. Other shows, of course, have aired on television having a similar intent to portray the family as a positive, supporting entity.

In a space like Second Life, acting out "family" is part ideal and part reality as people attempt to duplicate or reinvent their concept of home. Some members get married, pregnant, and establish family units in Second Life. Children are role-played by members.

The Sims 3

The Sims series of games has been popular to players interested in role-play among various social settings and storylines. In response to competition from Second Life and other virtual worlds, its latest edition offers improved customization of avatars and personality types: "With the innovative and proprietary Realistic Personality System in The Sims 3, you can attribute each character with five distinct personality traits, helping shape your Sims behaviour and how they interact with others and their surroundings" (*The Sims*, 2009). The Sims series is geared toward role-playing with family and neighborhood characters: "Will you create the nosy, inappropriate, kleptomaniac grandmother who loves to meddle in other people's business? Or the commitment-phobic, hot-headed punk rocker whose rude nature and childish disposition keeps him from scoring a date?" (*The Sims*, 2009).

In Second Life, residents can create multiple avatars, and distinct personalities often arise from an enhancement of certain real-life traits. Each resident brings all or a bit of self into the game, and any sense of drama arises as members meet others in various contexts that occur spontaneously as in real life. The reason for an alternate avatar has more to do with providing anonymity to oneself in certain situations, for example when a celebrity SL dj wants some privacy. Some people misrepresent themselves, while others merely bring their real selves in-world. That is where the drama sometimes begins: the clash between those who see Second Life as a game and those who play it as an extension of real life. Real money, real love, real aspirations, and real drama propel the game. Relationships are a major part of Second Life, for some residents become friends, lovers, and business partners outside of the virtual realm. Others bring family members, spouses, adult children, and relatives into Second Life, and their relationships take on new dimensions in this second space. A house can be the point where friends and family gather together in-world. I know of a group of friends who would regularly meet late night in a hot tub at their apartment complex before exiting to the real world. It served as a debriefing of the day's events inside Second Life, and often concerns and issues from their real lives would be discussed and detangled. The emotional connections made among the members—friends—transcended space.

Traditional Home Values in Second Life

The plot behind *House Hunters* on HDTV is to follow a couple as they attempt to locate the appropriate sized house, in the right neighborhood, at a price within their budget. The situation is fairly the same in the virtual world of Second Life. One of the most popular creative outlets for SL residents is home construction and home design. For consumers who are not builders, it takes a few days, at least, to sort through all the available and affordable housing options. New residents typically seek houses to fit on small plots of land; these starter homes could range from a quaint cabin, a traditional home, or a skybox. Budget and property space are big factors to home buyers in Second Life, as in the real world.

In Susan Leigh Star's article "From Hestia to Home Page: Feminism and the Concept of Home in Cyberspace," she discusses how "large-scale electronic communications media are changing our working and leisure lives," in relation to concepts of home and women's roles (Star, 1996, p. 30). "The pace of work, its location and distribution, and the nature of play (what sort and with whom) are changing, from electronic banking to virtual sex" (p. 30). Star approaches this evolution by exploring the "physical and geographic boundaries around the question: Where is home; where do I live?" (p. 30). She explains, "Because I may communicate frequently over great geographical distances, and collaborate on work and continue friendships electronically, the question is complicated" (p. 30). For Starr, the question begins with Ancient Greek and Roman concepts of home, a round hut in which the fire never expired: "Hence the cult of the communal or sacred hearth was apparently universal" (p. 30) and not directly related to personification of a spiritual goddess. Home in Second Life is both individual and communal. It is a representation of one's personal ideas and experiences and the collective understanding within a space that allows bonds to be formed among friends and family.

Marcus (2006) states, "Some people have profound memories of a special childhood home and unconsciously reproduce aspects of its form or essence in a house of adulthood" (pp. 1–2). She continues, "A home fulfills many needs: a place of self-expression, a vessel of memories, a refuge from the outside world, a cocoon where we can feel nurtured and let down our guard" (p. 2). The home grows as we do psychologically, when such "development is punctuated not only by meaningful emotional relationships with people, but also by close, affective ties with a number of significant physical environments, beginning in childhood" (p. 2). Until recently, social sciences had not considered significantly the psychological, political and cultural meaning of home (Hart & Ben-Yoseph, 2005).

Home is place that gives social context to its artifacts. Inside one's dwelling may exist a variety of literature, paintings, and music that embodies the individual and the collective spirit of home. Colors, textures and designs give voice to the house. Akiko Busch (2003), in *Geography of Home*, points out, one can understand the symbolic transformation of the home by merely focusing on the social history of one of its artifacts: the door. Most people use the side door, off the garage, to enter their house: "[the] beautiful front door and center hall no longer serve the rite of arrival" (Busch, 2003, p. 30). Concepts associated with home have changed as the social functions of the house have evolved through history. Mica Nava (1991, p. 157) traces home identities to practices of consumerism in the 1950s and 1960s: "Highly visible, its imagery permeates the physical and cultural territories it occupies. Modern identities and imaginations are knotted inextricably to it." Nava (1991) continues, "Within the social sciences and cultural studies it has been a recurring concern, particularly since the consolidation of the consumer society in the aftermath of the Second World War, and investigations of it have spanned a range of disciplines and theoretical debates" (p. 157). Biddy Martin and Chandra Talpade Mohanty in their 1986 essay Feminist Politics: What's Home Got to Do with It? discuss "the configuration of home, identity, and community; more specifically, in the power and appeal of 'home' as a concept and a desire" and challenge us to consider the role of home through "social evolution" (p. 191).

Second Life serves as a metaphor to understanding home as a cultural repository. Here, memory and community might be transferred into collective space, as traditional space becomes reconceptualized in a new form that has evolved within virtually mediated and immersive contexts. The artifacts within these spaces can bring familiarity and trigger emotional connections to the real world. Houses are decorated with sofas, chairs, dining room tables, beds, dressers, stoves, refrigerators, toilets, showers, and so forth. These items are often purchased at furniture vendors in Second Life. Some of these items of course have no practical function for residents. Their purpose draws from traditional conceptions of home.

Readings in feminism and cultural studies have posited that the concept of home is rooted in consumerism and traditional female expectations and identities (Shiach, 1999). In a virtual world, there is no need for appliances. The kitchen stove warms creativity and conversation is stirred, for what is consumed is companionship. Although there are virtual chefs in SL, food is not edible in the traditional sense. Food is not consumed in Second Life, so there is no need for dishes, pans, and cups, nor any need to wash them. Yet, many residents in SL choose to have kitchens, complete with stoves, refrigerators, and sinks. No practical reason exists to have a stove or sink in Second Life. These appliances stand symbolic of home culture, in which traditional conceptions of gender come into play, particularly when couples decide to play out domestic partnerships in virtual worlds.

Living rooms seem appropriate to virtual houses as they define an area for socializing. One might consider the kitchen having a similar role to the living room; for many, both function as the center point of gathering in the home. Memories of family gatherings and birthday celebrations likely have contributed toward interior design considerations for many residents. In the virtual world, home becomes an intimate gathering space for family and friends. It is a place for SL couples to retreat for intimacy and reflection. Some of the most sophisticated animations in-world have been designed for sofas, chairs, and beds. Indeed, selling beds is big business in Second Life; at the minimum, beds are designed for cuddling and offer couples a chance to simulate a sense of closeness and shared space. One can buy art work at SL stores or in museums, and these works also contribute to a sense of self in one's home. During holidays, friends can celebrate by exchanging gifts and time together virtually in homes, no matter how far people live from each other in the real world.

Avatar Children

As an avatar, one's emotions and experiences from real life come into play. Concepts of families are carry-overs from real-life childhoods, good and not-so-good. Linden Lab has strong policies restricting the use of children avatars, mainly those that deal with any sort of pornography or sexual acts. One site, SOS Children's Villages, in Second Life was established to increase awareness of the importance of creating happy childhoods in real life. Adult visitors can build and interact through play, from riding a bike, building a tree house to playing in a sandbox. The non-profit group also collects donations to help provide assistance to needy children and those abandoned ("Moments," 2009).

Aside from non-profit groups such as SOS, some members in Second Life view being children, as avatars, as a way to relive their childhood. Catherine Neal (2007) reported on the role of children in virtual communities as a means toward creating "a sense of family." In one case, she observes a virtual family in a restaurant: "To my surprise three adults are role-playing a teenager girl, pre-teen boy and a three-year-old toddler." She muses on what she sees, and asks, "So what is the interest of playing a baby growing to a full adult in Second Life?" Adding, Neal (2007) states, "Any woman can wear a pregnancy prim that is scripted to move and kick in the virtual womb. When it is time to have a baby, the prim will notify by instant message that it is time to deliver and then the role-playing begins."

Therapists debate whether one can use SL to turn around negative childhood experiences using role-play. Hastings (2008) investigated children role-playing in SL, interviewing several child avatars, as well as their in-world parents: "To play a 4- or 5-year old is fun to some SL residents, but when virtual families break up the emotions can feel as intense as in real life." Is it a matter of some residents getting in touch with their "inner child?" (Hastings, 2008). For many, child avatars are alternates, and those members have adult avatars for much of their other SL experiences.

Many businesses inside Second Life restrict the presence of child avatars. Others catering to "family" needs supply children's playground equipment, toddler clothing, baby furniture, toys and games, DVDs, and pets. Alas somewhat reminiscent of a Crosby, Stills & Nash song "Our House," "with two cats in the yard," Second Life offers an emotional link to virtual objects symbolic of family, house, and childhood. Through assistance from family agencies, some residents simulate pregnancy, and they can experience parenthood through the raising of child avatars. Most residents, however, keep their virtual world, simple and child-free. For some, raising children in another life is far from how they would want to spend leisure time. It is more the case that members seek adult relationships, as couples, and try to build some semblance of home in a sometimes wild and wacky alternate life.

Group Communities

In another instance, I had the opportunity to interview a stay-at-home mother in real life who has been daily involved in Second Life since she joined in early 2009. Her avatar, named Faith Hema, is slender but athletic in build, has vivid green eyes, a gentle face with soft features, and mid-length brunette hair tipped with white at the bangs and ends. Tattoos run the length of her arms, and she has one tattoo just below her neck. On the day of our interview, she wore plaid jeans, with a white cut-up tank top. Other days, she might be seen with long wavy hair and a mini-skirt outfit, or her hair in a bun adorned as a princess in a ballroom gown. In Second Life, she can be who she wants to be at any moment. She has spent much of her real life helping sexual abuse victims, and has helped young women online over the years. Only two months into the game, she had purchased a sizeable amount of land, especially for being so new to this virtual world. At one point, she worked as a hostess at a popular dance club to accommodate the expenses of her SL lifestyle. She simply had to greet guests, and would often dress for work in formal gowns. She had a dream in Second Life to create a space for people to feel safe in both RL and SL. Here, they might socialize with each other, and at times help one another through personal issues in this anonymous environment. Her intentions were good, but the fact is, it is difficult to maintain the cost of land fees for many residents. As quickly as she had built her haven, she had to give it up for financial reasons. On her sandy beach, she had a mega-sized tiki hut that had plenty of hangout seating. Along the shore, she had rafts for people to kick back and enjoy the surf. She had a vision: "To me Safe Haven has been a part of my life for a long time. It was a dream when I was a child. But it just started coming into effect when I started going closer in my path with God. So about 4 years ago, I started reaching out to abuse victims, and it just kind of grew from there into a chat room on another site" (Hema, 2009).

Safe Haven, she explains, is about giving "people a place to go and feel welcome and [where they can] talk to people, and not have to worry about having the Linden [currency] of Second Life to be able to have a place to stay" (Hema, 2009). Safe Haven is not merely a home; it is a fellowship for new and old residents who need a place that "they can park…just somewhere to feel safe and not have to be put in the secular world or the other stuff that is out there in Second Life." She adds, "There are predators online; people, who can use you, manipulate you without realizing it, not only me as a mature adult but the younger crowd…Safe Haven is a place that can protect them and keep them from being affected in their real life" (Hema, 2009).

For a few weeks until her money ran out, Second Life helped her launch an idea to create a safe space for real people with real problems. Hema says, "why not" a virtual world:

> Second Life provides a lot more than the real life does. I don't get out in the community like most people would. I'm a stay-at-home mom. I'm not really out there to do things in the community. That's just who I am. I've been online for a long time, and I feel this is where there are a lot of people that need to be reached. Because the way things are going these days, people are online more than they are out in the real world. (Hema, 2009)

Safe Haven provided a space for "encouragement and support, being there for one another. Any community needs to have that togetherness, and to be able to be there for one another when something happens." Over time, she wanted to have "live events, singers, contests of one form or another, just things to bring people together." When she came onto Second Life, she pointed out, "I didn't have a home per se, but I had a community to come to with people that welcomed me and gave me chances at things and jobs or to hang out with them at their place. Eternal Creations was the first site that I went to when I came to Second Life." Eternal Creations is a Christian community, spanning five islands, that is welcoming to all regardless of religion or belief. The notion of community in virtual worlds is a foreign concept to many people. Others have made lifelong connections online, like this particular woman through various sites. She has plans to rebuild Safe Haven in the future—her first attempt perhaps being only a trial run and sees Second Life as providing a means toward that path over time, after she settles into the virtual world and lifestyle and reconsiders when and how to accomplish her goals.

Howard Rheingold (2000) in *The Virtual Community: Homesteading on the Electronic Frontier*, conceptualizes home as a community notion. The Well was the virtual gathering forum of the 1980s. It was the online neighborhood café, and provided for interaction among its users, who sought conversation to medical advice. Online live chat and role-playing, for example, contribute to meaningful connections among residents. Rheingold sheds light on how identity in an anonymous space develops into real relationships. Real connections, he states, can be made in virtual worlds. Such spaces of negotiation allow people to connect to others in conversation, social events, and romance, all within the senses of sight and sound in the virtual world. Second Life has a way of bonding members, and homes provide the perfect gathering sites to bring people together. One Fourth of July holiday, I invited friends and family to one of our SL mainland houses. It was a way for us to gather from across the country, and to share some time in a space that was private and personal to all of us.

A number of residents share land within groups. When land is deeded to the group, individual members can build houses or share the residence. The land helps to facilitate social gatherings and functions. For some residents, these groups provide emotional and technical support for them. Some groups bypass the conventional idea of home and build their groups based around entertainment centers or dance clubs. Wheelies is one example of a group of residents coming together to share activities. The group was designed to facilitate residents with disabilities. For some members, Second Life offers residents the potential to experience life without physical restrictions common to them in real spaces. It is an opportunity for them to work, play, and socialize in shared spaces, and discuss their desires and dreams with others who have experienced similar circumstances. They connect to the larger disabled population in-world and the real world, and can gain independence in SL through work, play and creating communities.

United Kingdom *Times Online* Reporter Laura Deely (2008) shares the story of Wilde Cunningham, who is "an avatar controlled by a group of nine adults with cerebral palsy (and their nurse) at the day-care programme they attend in Massachusetts. The group members are aged 30 to 70 and comprise four men and five women." In reality, most of them must rely on wheelchairs for mobility: "...in Second Life they have built their own houses, have pets, gardens, even a baseball field. They also have many close friends and a large social network" (Deely, 2008). Other communities bond together due to shared interests, everything from religion to music. Some people like a particular club or mall, and then decide they would like to live nearby. Some develop strong spiritual bonds with others, and seek dwellings where they can become part of a like-minded community.

A number of planned communities in SL are zoned strictly residential. Still for many in SL, finding a place to live is as random as it is in real life. You really don't know your neighbors until you live in an area for awhile. Some communities bring together bikers, fashion designers, pastors and club djs into one communal space. Other communities are designated as Gay, Lesbian, Bisexual and Transgender (GLBT) or Furry friendly. Such descriptors appear inviting to some residents and send caution to others who are less than tolerant of the diversity that comprises SL. The difference between Sims and SL has much to do with the people who engage in the games. For Second Lifers, the game is about having real and often random encounters with people in virtual spaces amidst a plethora of unpredictable circumstances. SL becomes an extension of real life, even if it is parallel or alternate to one's concept of home. In real life, you may own a 4-bedroom ranch home with a double-car garage. In SL, you might own a whole estate with cattle and horses. Others buy or build castles in SL while owning traditional homes in RL.

Nonetheless, your neighbors usually become the defining factors that determine your happiness in your community of residence. How secure people feel about their home is often determined by the activities and the people who make up their community. Those entering SL with a strong sense of experimentation and appreciation for diversity (particularly of a global nature) are those who find peace in many parts of Second Life. For it is nearly impossible to control your virtual world, similar to one's real-life experiences. A home affords a bit of isolation, but there would be no point to Second Life if one merely desired to seclude themselves into a virtual apartment or house. The more rewarding aspect of Second Life is the interaction that is possible among residents and that is what makes neighborhoods and communities thrive in virtual worlds. Virtual worlds that welcome strangers and practice inclusivity embrace the concept of community and the social potential of humanity.

Five O'clock Somewhere

One of the regions established to welcome newcomers to Second Life, building a sense of community as its membership increased was Five O'clock Somewhere. The region was established to foster a community of people who would gather to listen to music and discuss good times along the beach. My-Gosh Yakan and Shai Khalifa are the founders of 5 O'clock Somewhere, which grew to be one of the more popular beach hangouts in Second Life. Yakan (or MG as most people call him) joined Second Life on September 19,

2006, and Shai Khalifa (who took her name from her cat) joined soon after on October 19, 2006. Yakan is from the Southeastern region of the U.S. and Khalifa is from Australia. Shortly after she joined Second Life, Khalifa met Yakan at Laguna Beach, which at the time was one of the more famous regions of the virtual world.

As Yakan recalls, the first night they met, they spent considerable time chatting and listening to music at Laguna. As they talked, one of the things they discovered was a shared love for the music of Jimmy Buffett and that carefree Caribbean lifestyle associated with his music. They both liked the deck at Laguna where people hung out, listened to music, talked and danced. However, they both agreed that SL needed a really nice beach hangout that played music that was much more relaxing, fun, and more tropical than Laguna or other regions. A connection had been made that night at Laguna Beach from across the world. Yakan elaborates on the vision that began to emerge from that point forth:

> As we became friends, we continued to talk about the need for a beach hangout with a more relaxed atmosphere. Our vision continued to evolve to encompass not only the right place but also an atmosphere that was friendly to others like us that were new to Second Life. A place where people felt immediately at home and a part of a fun and friendly group. We continued to discuss our plans; we also began to search for just the right place to build our little hangout as we began to call it.

Over the course of several days they found the land they were looking for and between the two of them purchased what started out as about 1/8 of a sim and over time grew to an area of nearly a sim and a half. In addition to purchasing property, Yakan also leased a relay server so that 5 O'clock had complete control of the music played there. The server became home to a library of Jimmy Buffett music plus a few more songs fitting to the environment that the duo was trying to create. Yakan explained that the music was a big part of the ambience, and the playlist became a staple of 5 O'clock in the early days. The owners' focus shifted toward coming up with a name to suit their vision:

> The name of course, had to be something that tied back to Jimmy Buffett's music. But the name also had to be a name that was true to our vision of a friendly, laid back, tropical oasis from not only the ups and downs of real life but the hustle and bustle of life in SL. The ultimate way point to stop and relax, reflect, meet new friends and hang out with old ones. Initially, I had proposed "One Particular Harbor" as the name for the hangout. Not being satisfied that this was the perfect name yet, we continued to discuss alternatives as we began turning our little parcel of land into the tropical paradise we envisioned. As the transformation of the parcel of land to a tropical beach hangout began to take shape, we also settled on a new name. The name that became synonymous with the ultimate laid back and relaxed beach hangout in Second Life. (Yakan, 2009)

The name they finally settled on was based on a song made famous by Alan Jackson. It was also a duet with Alan Jackson and Jimmy Buffett and Buffett's only number one charted hit in his career. The name of the song and the name of the beach hangout became *5 O'clock Somewhere:* a name that represents a significant era in SL for Yahan and Khalifa and an important place for many residents since its inception. In order to build the perfect beach hangout that is associated with Buffett, explained Yakan, "the first thing you just have to have is a bar. Preferably, a Tiki Bar." Elaborating, he said:

> So, I went out and found the perfect bar for 5 O'clock Somewhere. And in the process also found a nice covered hot tub. In the meantime, Shai discovered a bamboo shack that also became one of the most recognizable buildings at 5 O'clock as the landing point for newcomers. With the bar and hot tub in place and the little bamboo shack set up, things began to take shape. Landscaping was being added, a stream was put in to meander through the property, and we began putting out tropical trees, plants throughout the parcel. We also began work on the party deck and pier.

In the midst of pulling things together, Khalifa and Yakan met two people that would soon become the first new 5 O'clock Somewhere group members:

> Gallia Plubeau and Randy Ventura. Two wonderful, friendly, fun people that helped spread the vision by helping new members get acquainted with SL, 5 O'clock and introduce them to other 5 O'clock members. Randy and Gallia started showing up on a regular basis and soon became staples on the beach. In addition, Gallia eventually contributed one of the signature items of 5 O'clock Somewhere, and still part of 5 O'clock—the Volcano with the waterfall and cave inside. (Yakan, 2009)

As the days moved along, Yakan finished his first original Second Life project, the dance deck. The pier was also completed. In addition, chairs were added on the beach and floats in the surf. So people now had a place to sit around and get to know each other. As it turns out, the addition of the chairs on the beach "became one of the driving forces and ultimately, the glue that held together the spirit of community that went with being a 5 O'clock Somewhere member. And that really is what 5 O'clock eventually transformed into: a community. A close knit group of people that enjoyed spending time together and making new friends and helping others," said Yakan.

By November, it became evident that 5 O'clock had been developing a strong membership. As 5 O'clock grew, Khalifa and Yakan began to formulate their vision for what this region meant to the new members. As Yakan recalls, "That vision of people helping people to learn the ropes of Second Life and to make sure everyone that ended up in 5 O'clock felt not only welcome, but part of the group."

This message was a message that kept people coming back over and over; and also, a message that the new members soon began to propagate to other new members. Continuing the cycle of "making anyone new to Second Life feel comfortable, welcome, part of a group, and also helping Second Life new members to find places to go for clothes, shoes, hair, skins and all the things that are sooo lacking when you first start in Second Life" (Yakan, 2009). This spirit of making others feel like they had a home, created the spirit that was to become the hallmark of 5 O'clock Somewhere.

Five O'clock became the hot spot for Second Life newcomers. When a new member arrives on the mainland grid, they typically have no friends and no place to go. This sense of disorientation into a strange land sometimes is the reason people decide not to return to Second Life. Five O'clock provided not only an atmosphere of "home" for newbies, but a place to socialize and just hang out—those relationship things that connect people to each other, as Yakan explains:

> As November moved along, 5 O'clock had its first party. Unlike many venues, 5 O'clock was not event driven. 5 O'clock didn't depend on live music day to day or DJs or parties or dancing to drive traffic. Events truly were special because they didn't happen often. When they did, they were planned, invitations sent, excitement created, and everyone would look forward to them. There wasn't anything really special about the events at 5 O'clock other than almost everyone knew everyone else. Any event was like a gathering of family. Most of the events were then driven in the early months of 5 O'clock, and generally done with a DJ and always extremely well attended, lots of pictures taken, and rarely was there an event that all the main group members did not attend.

Towards the end of the year, several key events occurred. Yakan and Khalifa acquired a low prim (now called homestead) sim that was previously just open water, which was in front of the 5 O'clock beach area and it had five small islands. One eventually became a home to Beej Barbarossa until 5 O'clock moved to its current location in 2008. Several other islands became hideaways, surfing islands and other purpose-driven islands. And, one became the site of the Volcano donated by Gallia Plubeau. This volcano became one of 5 O'clock's most popular features and one of the signature landmarks viewable from anywhere on 5 O'clock. This volcano had a waterfall with diving animations, and an amazing cave inside with pools and places for people to have private time together. Five O'clock also continued to tweak its image, adding logos:

> One other major benefit of adding the island sim as the open water sim came to be called, was meeting a very talented graphics artist named Beck Islander. Beck created the 5 O'clock Somewhere logo...Logos were used on the pier, the dance deck and even on clothing and became synonymous with 5 O'clock. (Yakan, 2009)

As 5 O'clock continued to grow, additional land was added, along with another beach area, another waterfall, bar area, and game room designed by

Khalifa. This beach area was named after a very popular beach in Australia called Byron Bay. Yakan also created an underwater club on the island sim that became a very popular site for parties. This underwater venue had all glass floors, and walls with fish, a sunken ship, and tropical plants underneath and around it. "The first party held at the underwater venue as well as several others maxed out the capacity of the sim and like most parties at 5 O'clock, the parties there were more like family reunions than open parties because everyone generally knew almost everyone else," explained Yakan.

Aside from the additional areas of land and island sim added to 5 O'clock, several other early members became the core of what was turning into a true Second Life family. Yakan describes the emergence of a core family, connecting newcomers to the islanders:

> Rekka Berchot, Moxy Barracuda, Tricky Bandit, and a few others were the heart and soul of 5 O'clock. In addition, like most successful ventures, there is that one person that keeps it all together and makes anything and everything possible. That person that always gives that extra effort whenever it is needed, and knows just what to say and how to say it to get everyone pulling the same direction and on the same page. For 5 O'clock, that person was Shai. Shai and the other primary group members had a constant presence on the beach. They were there day in and day out. Saying hi to anyone that showed up on the beach, welcoming everyone, introducing everyone, and creating the lively conversation that went on constantly and encouraging everyone to join in. Without this group, there would be no 5 O'clock.

Khalifi and Yakan worked hard at drawing people to 5 O'clock, inviting them to see what the "wonderful" place and "wonderful" group that had been created was all about:

> Shai spent many hours inviting people from the newbie home points to 5 O'clock. Shai also put in place the tools to capture the names of visitors and send them group invites as well as inviting them to events that took place at 5 O'clock. MG had a bad habit of wandering around some of the other beach areas and inviting those lost looking souls over to 5 O'clock to enjoy the people and not just the atmosphere of an incredible tropical environment. Together, they helped people to find 5 O'clock so they could experience what they were not experiencing elsewhere. (Yakan, 2009)

One of the secondary benefits of the family atmosphere that had been created was the long-term relationships that had developed between some of the 5 O'clock members: "There are quite a few couples from those early days that even after three years are still together. Such was the strength of the bond and sense of community that developed. Rekka and Moxy, Gallia and Tricky, and several other first-year members that met at 5 O'clock are still SL couples today" (Yakan, 2009). And, in Second Life, where a long relationship is three or four months, that is a testimony to the strength of the relationships that developed at 5 O'clock. In addition, many of the original group members are still friends in Second Life and in some cases RL after three years.

Eventually, some of the 5 O'clock group members became not only long-term Second Life residents, but contributed their talents to various aspects of the larger Second Life community. Some very talented builders, musicians, clothing designers, and so forth were early 5 O'clock members. Moxy Barracuda is still one of the most popular and entertaining performers in Second Life. Beck Islander helped his university establish an online presence; Khalifi developed an undersea fantasy world and game; Yakan created a scale model of the Las Vegas Mirage Resort. Other members have created islands that rent homes and various other ventures in Second Life. No doubt 5 O'clock cannot be given the credit for the many successes of its current and past members. However, that spirit of welcome given to each person that walked on the sim, the friendliness, and support for anyone that showed up certainly contributed to many in the group enjoying the Second Life experience and staying in-world long enough to learn how to showcase their talents.

As time has past, 5 O'clock has changed, moving to a new sim and the original group for the most part left for other adventures. Now there is a new group carrying on the traditions. Some of the Jimmy Buffett, kick back and enjoy the islands and each other atmosphere may have lost "some of the original new to SL feel of the early days" (Yakan, 2009). Five O'clock has also become more event driven and also retail driven in order to try to cover the cost of ownership and sim operation. Yakan points out, "It is still one of the nicest island atmospheres in SL, and a great place to go." But, 5 O'clock like many places has proven that it's very hard to keep that original excitement and motivation there as the founders and founding group members move on to other experiences.

The lessons learned have not been lost though. Just as SL is a constantly changing place, there are new ventures popping up every day. The owner of one such place, Bama Breeze, is working hard to try to recapture that early magic of 5 O'clock. "The tropical atmosphere is like no other in Second Life. The only motivation for the existence of Bama Breeze is a place for people to meet, relax, enjoy that island music and care-free atmosphere, and to welcome others that are looking for the same thing" (Yakan, 2009). It will be interesting to see if that same experience from 5 O'clock is "a repeatable process or a one-time thing. To see if that magical mix of place, people and time can converge again to create something that is an incredible memory for those that are part of it," notes Yakan.

Conclusion

It is interesting to note how home has become an important concept to members of Second Life. The very use of the term "residents" in place of members indicates that Second Life has the potential to lay claim on one's identity—individual and group, through certain community spaces and groups. People seek places in which they feel most comfortable spending time, preferably with others, while in-world. Perhaps it is part of the inescapable human condition of wanting to feel safe, being needed by others, that is as meaningful to many in Second Life as in real life. Artists, home builders, musicians, educators, priests, fashion designers, business owners and others come together to share virtual spaces in creative ways, as they seek ways to intersect with each other. Indeed, it is their intention to interact that is significant, made evident by their decision to join Second Life or an SL community; otherwise they could turn off the computer and sit alone. Second Life is a community of many communities that thrives when relationships are established. Islands, showplaces, businesses and even members come and go. But for those dedicated to establishing in-world relationships that nurture their creativity and understanding for others, Second Life can offer that but only when the people who reside there reach out their hand to the lost, wandering, or just arrived members.

References

Bachelard, G. (1994). *The poetics of space*. Boston, MA: Beacon Press.

Busch, A. (2003). *Geography of home*. Trenton, NJ: Princeton Architectural Press.

Deeley, L. (2008, March 24). Is this a real life, is this just fantasy? *The Times*. Accessed February 24, 2009, from http://women.timesonline.co.uk/tol/life _and_style/women/body_and_soul/article1557980.ece.

Gallagher, W. (2007). *The power of place: How our surroundings shape our thoughts, emotions, and actions*. NY, NY: Harper Perennial. 1994.

Hart, M., & Ben-Yoseph, M. (Eds.). (2005). *Psychological, political and cultural meanings of home*. New York: Haworth Press.

Hastings, H. (2008, September 1). A look at those who roleplay as children. *Metaverse Times*. Accessed June 1, 2009, from http://www.metaverse-tribune.com/

Hema, F. (2009, July 9). Interview, personal communication with author. Second Life.

Israel, T. (2003). *Some place like home: Using design psychology to create ideal places*. Washington, DC: Academy Press.

Marcus, C. C. (2006). *House as a mirror of self: Exploring the deep*. Lake Worth, FL: Nicholas-Hay. Reprint 1997.

Martin, B., & Mohanty, C. T. (1968). Feminist politics: What's home got to do with it? In T. de Lauretis (Ed.), *Feminist studies/Critical studies* (pp. 191–212). Bloomington, IN: Indiana University Press.

Moments of Happy Childhood on the island of SOS Children's Villages. SOS Children's Villages Web site. Accessed June 1, 2009, from http://www.sos-childrensvillages.org/Explore-

SOS/Second-Life/Pages/default.aspx/

Nava, M. (1991). Consumerism reconsidered: Buying and power. *Cultural Studies* 5(2), 157–173.

Neal, C. (2007, May 18). Children avatars in second life. *Associated Content*. Technology section. Accessed June 21, 2009, from http://www.associatedcontent.com/article/245698/children_avatars_in_second_life.html?cat=15.

Rheingold, H. (2000). *The virtual community: Homesteading on the electronic frontier*. Cambridge, MA: The MIT Press.

Rybczynski, W. (1987). *Home: A short history of an idea*. New York: Penguin.

Shiach, M. (1999). *Oxford readings in feminism: Feminism and cultural studies*. Oxford: Oxford University Press.

Star, S. L. (1996). From hestia to home page: Feminism and the concept of home in cyberspace. In Nina Lykke & Rosi Braidotti (Eds.), *Between monsters, goddesses and cyborgs: Feminist confrontations with science, medicine and cyberspace* (pp. 30–46). London, UK: Zed Books.

Television, G. (2006, December 1). Big brother second life diary: Day . Accessed December 3, 2008, from http://www.yesbutnobutyes.com/archives/ 2006/12/big_brother_sec.html.

The Electric Sheep Company. (2009). Web site. Accessed July 10, 2009, from http://www.electricsheepcompany.com/

The Sims. (2009). Accessed June 21, 2009, from http://videogames.yahoo.com/events/ the-sims/the-sims-3/1260473/

Yakan, M. G. (2009, July 30). Interview, personal communication with author. Second Life.

SECTION 2

Media Makers of a Virtual World

CHAPTER SIX

The Image Makers: Selling Fantasy and Reality in Second Life

> Escapism has always been an aspect of human life and culture, and in a way SL is the perfect escape....people I've met thus far seem to have a good grip on things and use SL as a place to hang out, have fun, and live dreams and fantasies.
>
> —Peter Stindberg, *Babel Translations* (Parker, 2008)

Imagine shopping in Second Life on Rodeo Drive, a part of the BeStyle Fashion District encompassing five sims, or perhaps stroll The Best of SL Boulevard: both homes to the burgeoning fashion empires of designers consolidated into upscale, high-rent districts. Second Life not only replicates the real-world fashion industry, sometimes you might say it does it even better. Second Life as a virtual world is good at image making; it is a media world composed of images. Those who succeed in Second Life understand the power of communicating through media, which is an awareness of how all media are converging into virtual-world platforms in unique ways that are rewriting business strategies and consumer culture. Debate, however, ensues on how to use virtual worlds and new media to market products and services to boost sales in the real world.

In October 26, 2006, the beef in the *Second Thoughts* blog was about hype on how businesses should market their products and services in virtual worlds. The column begins, with "Amen—and it's time that all the media hypesters grasp this basic fact of Second Life: there's no mass media inside the world..." (*Second Thoughts*, 2006). Adding to that, the blog continues, "even if you use the old-fangled old media like the *New York Times* or *Wired* magazine to hype the world itself," mass media as it exists in the real world is not a reality in virtual worlds (*Second Thoughts*, 2006). Meanwhile, corporate America attempts to follow customers into Second Life and other virtual worlds on the promise of reaching an ultimate target audience, a culmination of marketing fantasies to be realized by tapping into virtual culture.

But virtual culture is a part of the big mass media picture, still evolving. The irony of it all is "they already have their customers on the Internet, television, radio, magazines, and RL billboards [so] why do they need to follow them in THERE for?" (*Second Thoughts*, 2006). Second Life, like other virtual worlds, is one of many media that can be employed in an overall marketing campaign. It offers challenges as well as opportunities. This chapter contextualizes new media marketing within the larger scope of the Internet, and provides a means to understanding how virtual worlds play into Internet marketing specifically and mass media generally. A section of the chapter looks at how SL photography and the related fashion industry (and other industries) have larger implications for real-world business cross-over particularly among image makers.

Selling Image in a Second World

Throughout Second Life magazines, full-page glossy ads are placed strategically between articles. From skins to top fashion brands to nightclubs, virtual world magazines showcase businesses who appreciate the importance of advertising their goods toward resident avatars. Beautiful models perfect in every sense of the imagination draw the eye to products at malls and across the print media and on the billboards of Second Life. Second Life is about imagination. Yet, advertising in SL is real business. Top-ranked classified ads in the SL search engine start at 50 lindens and can go upward to the thousands, depending on how high a business wants its ad placed among its competitors and how much money it has to advertise. According to The Business Communicators of Second Life, nearly half of SL residents surveyed stated that having real-life brands in-world contributes to favorable company images, while a third of the residents asked did not care one way or another.

Guido Lang (2007), in his posting, cites research from *Real Life Brands in Second Life* indicating that the presence of brands might create a sort of credibility contributing toward a stronger in-world infrastructure although some members "harbor fears brands will harm small-content creators and put upward pressure on land prices." The Project Factory, a Second Life marketing agency, showcases clips of brands already with a presence in-world. The 30-minute video was edited for YouTube, and shows images on a mix of companies, from Apple's unofficial presence, to Reuters (before it left SL) to BMW, Sony BMG, Reebok, IBM, ABC TV, Showtime, Pontiac, American Apparel, Virgin, Dell, NBC, AOL, Sears, and Circuit City. Other companies include Toyota and Adidas.

Author of the *Brand Architect* Peter Collings took a shopping trip to one of the many malls of Second Life, trying to get a glimpse into customer preference. He began his outing in name-brand stores—first at the Adidas store...

> no one was there amid the perfect racks and in-store displays, I then headed over to the larger Reebok store. One person was there, but they were leaving. American Apparel had a nicely laid-out store with its merchandise well presented and unobscured,

thanks to the absence of shoppers. (Collings, 2007)

He observed that customers were shopping "in home-grown stores buying brands with names like VektorWear, Shiny Things, Cytranized Designs." Collings (2007) suggested that name brands were not successfully making their mark in Second Life. Over the past few years, the data has been actually inconsistent, depending on what the research company is asking, and whom they are asking. In general, real-world name brands in Second Life have mixed success in achieving in-world brand recognition and particularly recognition that extends into real-life benefits for the company.

It might not necessarily prove to be profitable for name-brand companies to sell avatar versions of their fashions in Second Life in the short run. Some real-world companies accept that reality, willing to consider that, at the least, it is about staking a presence online and investing in future economies. Company benefits in the short or long run are not guaranteed by merely being in Second Life or any virtual world. Collings says the problem is that Second Life to many residents is a role-playing environment fueled by fantasy. Brands that adapt to that environment can do well.

Residents who can be whoever they want to be at any particular moment transition from gothic and medieval attire to ballroom gowns and tuxedos to furry animals. How do you design fashions and goods for that type of environment? It is a world where many items are given out freely, from furniture, cars, sodas, to fashions. One survey of more than 1,000 avatars interviewed in March 2007 indicated that Adidas came out on top among brands in-world, with 69% awareness (*The perception*, 2007). Market Truths, a real-world research agency based in New Zealand, reported that The Weather Channel, Reuters, and Pepsi led among the top 24 brands mentioned in-world by residents of Second Life; IBM, Nike and Dell appeared to have the strongest positive impact for their activities within Second Life (Market Truths, 2007).

Electric Sheep Company creates virtual experiences for companies to reach out to customers, and among their branding advice to the virtual business world is to build a sense of community in Second Life. The idea is to "develop a strong community around a common interest, which may be a lifestyle or a brand's property" (Carella, 2007). Pontiac and Showtime are companies that have successfully embraced this concept in Second Life. Other companies rely on events to reach a broad base of residents. Examples range from NBC's Tree Lighting Ceremony, BBC Radio One live concerts and events, and a meet and greet with Bantam Dell's Dean Kootz (Carella, 2007).

CEO of Linden Lab Mark Kingdon, during an interview with Erica Naone in *Technology Review* in 2008, explained that Second Life is a growing force within the social media phenomenon, and businesses must realize that experimentation is a significant part of the process as virtual economies mature online: "If you look across all social media and social computing over the last two years, there's been a huge amount of experimentation by brands" (Naone, 2008). Kingdon points out, "None of the initiatives broke the bank when they failed...and the ones that were successful were wildly successful. So I think if you put it in context from a big-brand perspective, it's not like companies went into Second Life and built a presence and lost their shirts" (Naone, 2008). Kingdon sees this experimentation as "part of the natural evolution of social media and social computing" (Naone, 2008).

He stressed that companies "have to give the resident community something of value, something exciting, in order to get their positive attention...I don't think all of the experiments of brands in Second Life factored that in" (Naone, 2008). Kingdon added, "[W]e're in the midst of an incredible video revolution on the Web right now, as sound and motion become very central to the experience." Companies that begin to understand that the "the next natural wave" is for the digital shopping experience to be 3-D and immersive–basically encompassing "the attributes that we see today in Second Life" (Naone, 2008).

Test Drive Second Life

Sponsors have found creative ways to tap into virtual communities as well, everything from featuring brand-name cars for avatars to brand-name clothing. The idea is that if you like it in-world, you will want it in RL. Take a test drive! Try it on! Wallace (2007) reports on Calvin Klein's in-world experiment where its "virtual perfume bottles enable[d] SL users to spray each other with bubbles that 'initiate dialogue.'" The company's rationale for its campaign was that "ck IN2U" related to a new generation of customers called "technosexuals." This group is plugged into the language of technology, and is "the first generation to be defined more by their means of communication rather than fashion or music...the strongest force affecting the culture of the developed world at the moment" (Wallace, 2007).

Companies are looking beyond traditional forms of advertising toward virtual worlds. Considering that nearly 60% of national advertising budgets comprise integrated marketing and advertising (Lebkowsky, 2006), virtual worlds are only a small, but growing, slice of the financial pie. Businesses have already accepted the importance of presenting their corporate profiles online. Some companies have toyed with their corporate history as far as reconstructing a tale about their origins. Fun, corporate and sometimes fictitious profiles that fudge on the truth, for the sake of creativity, do not offend a new generation of consumers that seem comfortable moving between truth and fiction. Brands project images that represent lifestyles, and young consumers have accepted twisting the truth as part of the package. Sure, they want the product to be quality, but they also want that intangible element that can only be crafted by creative storytelling Companies that want to be trendy and relatable to younger consumers seek to connect through online portals, such Web sites, blogs, and virtual communities, among others. From personal communication devices to mock movies to company-sponsored independent record labels to music branding, online channels respond quickly to a fickle market.

The significant portion of the Second Life membership base comprises professionals who are more than willing to tap into the new media culture. Land and merchandise expenditures are some evidence of the people's acceptance of buying in-world and an increasing consumer culture within virtual worlds. Some companies have done extremely well connecting their virtual presence inside Second Life to their companies' real-world affairs. Some top fashion companies and modeling agencies experiment within virtual worlds to test their designs on consumers. The consumer base is mixed, with older audiences appreciating the nostalgic appeal provided within Second Life. Many members come aboard to see what all the fuss is about, and become captivated by the fantasy culture, particularly when it connects them to their past. In Second Life, they not only reinvent themselves, they are rejuvenated in appearance and physical form in a world that encourages them to explore, play, dance, and of course shop. Companies seek marketing strategies designed to engage consumers in an interactive environment, and one way to do this is to allow their customers to create their own "user" stories regarding products or services. But, before any real-world applications, consumers now have opportunities to experience products in-world. The experiences are based on emotional responses to a product. The image of the company is sold in-world, for many products cannot be tested in their physical form. An evening gown might look wonderful on a woman's shapely avatar in-world, and less attractive when worn in real life. What is sold, in reality, is the image of the product and the company through its corporate virtual presence. Software companies have a much easier time connecting their real products to in-world purchases: "If you want your game to run faster and more efficiently, then download this particular software." The growing 24/7 consumer culture in Second Life and other virtual worlds coincide with the already emerging online shopping experience across the Web. Consumer culture has been evolving and responding to changes in traditional and online media, and an overview of trends over the years provides a context upon which to understand virtual shopping culture.

Buying into Consumer Culture

In 1957, Vance Packard published his book *Hidden Persuaders*, an impressive book symbolic of the shift in consumer culture. The book served as a social commentary on the American consumer of that time. George Orwell's *Nineteen Eighty-Four* spoke of a big brother government that controlled society through propaganda. In the 1980s, Apple produced a Super Bowl commercial that introduced its "Macintosh" computer within an Orwellian world. That commercial at the turn of 21st century would become comedic fodder for the adult cartoon series *Futurama*: as a runner heads toward a huge wall screen, she thrusts a package into an image of "Mom" (rather than the Orwellian Big Brother). The TV is shattered. At which point, a man in the audience yells: "Hey, we were watching that."

All humor aside, advertising has a powerful influence on culture—making it, duplicating it, reshaping it, and distributing it in more efficient ways than ever before. It sounds simple, but the concept is powerful: advertising is a business in and of itself. It would be easy to dismiss the impact of advertising on our lives, if commercials had not become more relevant and entertaining than programs themselves at times. American culture is advertising culture, regardless of our position on its impact. Neil Postman's *Amusing Ourselves to Death* offers the reader a glimpse into how entertainment and technology have blurred the line between fact and fiction in news, religion, and politics. It was first published in 1985; consider how much closer we have come into that reality.

When we acknowledge that the advertiser's goal is persuasion, rather than to solely inform or entertain the viewer or listener, it becomes easier to understand how much power and control American consumers have turned over to marketers, even sacrificing their children to the advertising gods (Schor, 2004). Consider the work of Calvert (2001), DeGaetano (1998) and Elias (2004) as evidence to that influence. Their research has explored children's attentiveness to high stimuli and interactive media, and that trickles down to adult members of a household. As most parents eventually realize, children use word-of-mouth advertising. They prompt parents to buy things for them—and direct attention to traditional and online media. *Webkinz*, an online game for children, plays off the idea that children like pets, but cannot always own them for a variety of reasons. During this game, children can earn virtual dollars for time spent on the computer. When a parent buys a *Webkin* pet for a child, it comes complete with an online code. The child types in the code to unleash the virtual pet personality. The Web allows for children to re-conceptualize play and allows them to engage in interactive storytelling. Children growing up with virtual pets and game culture easily gravitate toward virtual worlds. Second Life's Teen World allows children 13 years and older into the game. Some of these children began playing online games since they were toddlers.

Power of Storytelling

In an editorial in the *Philadelphia Inquirer*, freelance writer Katie Haegele (2007) shared her thoughts on how storytelling transforms "the context of new forms of media." Online media exacerbate the power of storytelling through allowing consumers to interact within the plot. Professor Sue Thomas, who has developed online creative writing programs, explains the medium allows storytellers to change "their stories according to context and circumstance" and the Web provides "a fluid environment" for these ideas to stay "fresh" (Haegel, 2007). The "core of the narrative [is] intact," but a unique perspective is created by choice of the medium (2007).

Mark Deuze (2005) has concluded that consumers dramatically underestimate, albeit unintentionally, their media usage, after reviewing scholarly research nationally and internationally (e.g., Papper et al., 2004; BIGresearch, 2002; Huysmans & de Haan, 2003). It would appear that they lose track of time once engaged in a good story or activity. Companies rely on this hope, that viewers would become immersed into the storyline created around the product or service. Advertisements, as often is the case, blend into the fabric of life. Deuze (2005) states, "[B]ecause of the pervasiveness of media in everyday life and the multitasking way we engage with those media, more than half our media use 'disappears' when we are asked about it." Deuze (2005) continues, consumer "media making" is exhibited through blogging and podcasting, and by company solicitations for viewer feedback. Deuze (2005) describes the consumer evolution toward media making as merely "the phenomena of just doing our own highly individualized thing when immersing ourselves in the multiple media around us." Sonia Livingstone (2004) concurs that when consumers are engrossed in the media environment, not so surprisingly, the beginning and end of a message is lost. Instead, the feedback loop between the product, consumer and company image is continually evolving. The consumer participates in message design, production and delivery.

Credit card companies, like *Visa*, have intrigued us with commercials that take us on adventures through back roads, deep within jungles or high on mountainous cliffs, inside amazing James Bond plots. One commercial, themed *Visa–All It Takes*, begins with an American woman passenger traveling in a jeep accompanied by a guide on a jungle dirt road. The jeep stops when they spot a lifeless monkey ahead on the road in front of them. The woman leans over to check on the animal, which immediately sports a mischievous grin. She is suddenly aware that she has been "conned" by the chimp and its furry companions, now in the process of stealing her luggage. She eventually trades the luggage for bananas, and retrieves her *Visa* from them. All ends well with *Visa* is evidently the morale of the story. *Visa* commercials are among the many *YouTube* favorites, and the extra publicity is priceless.

You want to hook potential customers. Hook them on a good story. Let them help tell that story. Storytelling conferences draw thousands, who want to tell and listen to stories, annually across the U.S. and world. Is it then so surprising that audiences respond in similar ways to online invitations by sponsors to test products and give feedback? A plethora of digital storytelling workshops invite companies, universities, and lay people to learn how to tell their story. For several years, the *Wizard of Ads Academy* has been a leader in helping clients turn commercial announcements into emotional experiences for audiences and profits for businesses. The best advertising agencies, like *Dick Orkin's Radio Ranch*, know the secret to an audience's captivity is to entice it through a well-crafted story with a creative punch line. Storytelling is becoming a must for marketers, who relish the benefits of lifestyle marketing, relatable user stories, and a holistic strategic approach toward reaching consumers within a multi-mediated environment. Virtual worlds like Second Life can offer settings for corporations to share their stories with existing and potential customers in creative ways rather than driving them away with overt sales pitches.

Full-Circle Marketing

Second Life is open for business 24/7 around the world. Consumers living in the virtual world create their own drama and stories. Second Life is a real-life soap opera in a sense. Some members role-play inside SL more than others. Companies have looked for ways in the past to market their products and services in ways that extend beyond brick and mortar shops. As once featured on *60 Minutes*, the *Girls Intelligence Agency* (GIA) enlists young girls, 10 to 14, to host slumber parties where they and their friends test market products. Some of the GIA clients have included: Disney, Mattel, Procter & Gamble, Johnson & Johnson, Nestle, Lego, Sara Lee, Dreamworks, Sony, and Warner Brothers. Calls for user stories posted online facilitate 24-hour marketing campaigns that contribute toward a never-ending consumer lifestyle. *The Hollister Company*, an offshoot of *Abercrombie & Fitch*, appeals to teens with an interest in name-brand casuals (featuring a Californian surf look). The company presents a model example of lifestyle marketing directed toward 14- to 18-year-olds. *Hollister* launched its first store in 2000. Its corporate history is nothing more than a good tale, claiming early 20th century South Pacific Sailor John M. Hollister as its founder. As the story goes, he established the first store in California in 1922. Of course, none of this is true, and its target audience of young people is aware that the company is relatively new. They just consider the fictitious tale as a fun way to promote the company.

Image is part of the consumer culture in SL and RL. Clothing and everything count: from in-store atmosphere and a company's portal to the Web and virtual-world presence. Online, Hollister customers can relate to lifestyle video clips of teens hanging out, wearing Hollister clothing, in various beach scenarios. The company creates a culture around their product complete with video, music, and a strong online presence. Some real brands have crossed over into virtual worlds; some have been successful and others are merely sticking their toe in the virtual water. Some of the in-world clothing brands have included Reebok, American Apparel and the European label Bershka. When American Apparel entered SL, it had a difficult time attracting an in-world following; it was just another brand among the real and virtual labels already inside Second Life. Alycia de Mesa (2007) sees consumers of virtual worlds as "young people in love with these 3D Internet landscapes." She explains, "A cross between gaming and anime, virtual worlds such as There.com, Second Life, and Cyworld are emerging as places not only to create and hang out as an alter-ego avatar, but to engage in good old-fashioned commerce as well" (de Mesa, 2007). People join for free, and then get caught up in the consumer culture that encompasses it. That might mean an extension of real-world lifestyles; but in many cases, virtual brands compete successfully with real world brands. In any case, "just like in the real world—it costs money for clothes (to dress your avatar), for land (to build on), furnishings (to decorate your virtual pad), and even vehicles (to drive—while hopefully avoiding virtual traffic jams)" (de Mesa, 2007).

Advertising Age's 360 Media Guide (2006) is a compilation of articles and trade advertisements that boast of the never-ending sales ploys (omni marketing, 360 marketing, etc.) that have been successfully aimed toward consumers, especially the youth market. This omni environment is demonstrated through the wealth of media and marketing that intersects with daily life and purchases: Web sites, in-text messaging, ambient marketing, virtual communities, video games, media on demand, and so forth. Consumer culture is expanding beyond Web purchases and infomercials to interactive transactions within virtual communities, such as *Second Life*. *Reuters News Service* has followed consumer trends in *Second Life*, pointing toward a strong market of young adults, approximately around 33. One fourth of the in-world money is spent on name-brand fashions (Reuters, 2007). Shopping is a 24/7 experience, if one has the time and money—and avatar. The lines between media are quickly dissolving, and marketing to consumers should be designed to initiate multi-mediated experiences for them. No longer should they be conceptualized as single media events or in terms of linear programming. It's not a matter of choice between media as much as a way to reach consumers in all aspects of their daily lives.

Commercials have always been considered strategic elements in broadcast programming: "Some of the most creative thinking in television these days has nothing to do with comedy or drama. It's about the commercials. Fueled by a growing sense of desperation, networks are inserting games, quizzes and mini-dramas into commercial breaks" (Bauder, 2007). As companies bring their messages online and in-world, there is the risk of increasingly blurring the lines between establishing an authentic relationship with customers and simply attempting to extend their consumer reach. Ideally, companies should seek online venues through which to direct viewers to their products while making site content relevant to these users.

Viral Marketing

YouTube videos are probably the best example of viral marketing to date, with viewers tuning into funny commercials intentionally, and sending links to their friends (LaMonica, 2006; Leonard, 2006). To locate the youth of America, one simply heads toward *MySpace Video, Facebook, YouTube, Google*, and *Yahoo*, to name a few sites. David Verklin and Bernice Kanner (2007) reported on the army's latest marketing campaign toward recruitment: online reality video games. As the youth culture spends more time online, they have found new diversions there as well, apart from traditional media. *YouTube* and similar services provide hours of entertainment for viewers and media makers. Viral ads are often the funniest or weirdest TV commercials that scream for another look on the Web, or they are made intentionally for online viewing (with marketing hopes of creating a buzz across the Internet on *YouTube* and other video services). *CNN Money* published a series of articles in 2006 on viral advertising; one headline read, "Viral Ads: It's an epidemic. Hit videos reach millions." Another *CNN Money* headline exclaimed: "You create our Super Bowl commercial," in reference to Doritos' call for viewers to tape their own ads. Leonard (2006) explains,

> Madison Avenue has always tried to create infectious ads. Think of those beer commercials with catch phrases that some of your more tiresome coworkers repeat around the water cooler. But viral marketing truly came of age with the Internet.

He asks, "Can *YouTube* and *Google Video* figure out a way to make this a business? If so, could they become the web's equivalent of the broadcast networks?" (Leonard, 2006). Traditional expectations regarding advertising content and placement are being challenged by a growing consumer culture that feeds off television and the Web for information, entertainment and interaction—increasingly and often simultaneously.

Whether consumer culture is viewed as the outcome of product marketing and/or the force behind this 24/7 vision, industry trendsetters are calling for new approaches that fit within audience lifestyles as well as more opportunities for users to share testimonies. The synergy from user experiences—experiencing the product in various contexts—might be that added value that leads to buyer loyalty. Sometimes it is a matter of knowing your audience so well that you can have fun with them.

In the November 14, 2005 edition of *Chief Marketer*, New York advertising consultant Simon Williams, chairman of the Sterling Group, defines successful brands as those that influence culture (i.e., *Google*, *Nike*), have a point of view (*Fox News*), generate consumer creativity (for example, *Converse Gallery* where consumers are invited to create a 24-second film to stream online), encourage customization (i.e., *iTunes, Starbucks*), provide customers with "an experience" rather than a one-time purchase, make buying decisions simple for consumers, ferret out product weaknesses, accept social responsibility as a mantra (*GE's* Citizenship Report, *eBay's* Giving Works, *Target* Gives Back to the Community), respond quickly to trends and technology ("pulse, pace, and passion"), and push toward innovation: "Brands are inspired by *Apple* more than anyone else. They transformed the music business, and people are taking what they did seriously. *Procter & Gamble* and *GE* are driving this and have made innovation the core of their corporate strategy" (Williams, cited in Parry, 2005).

Real-World Connections from Second Life

Second Life is a platform that exists within the Web. It resides on the Web connecting real life to virtual life. Other media forms exist within Second Life and actually help to create and compose Second Life. The creation of media inside Second Life is an industry in and of itself. Take, for example, the fact that photography in Second Life is big business. Photography is used for wedding portraits, creating avatar profile pictures, and to capture life within Second Life, among other things. Photography has an essential role in the fashion industry, for crafting images in advertising and showcasing new designs. Off the SL runway to the in-world magazines, photographs connect people to the fashion industry. Full-page advertising spreads of fashion designs in some of the leading SL magazines such as the *Best of Second Life* are somewhat costly enterprises. For many photographers in Second Life, the virtual world is an extension of their real-life careers, or at the very least of their dreams. Trinidad

Anatine is a real-life photographer and model who made her debut in Second Life on June 19, 2007, after hearing about virtual worlds on television:

> Funny story how I found out about Second Life, I was actually watching Oprah Winfrey, and they were talking about it. There was a 30-minute segment on 3-D virtual worlds and it sparked my interest so I came in to check it out. I was hooked from that day forward. Basically the first few days, I just walked around and kind of got a feel for it. I ran across a photography studio and that for me was my inspiration and that set what I was going to do in Second Life. From that point forward, it took me I would say probably two months before I was fully in gear making money at photography in SL. In the beginning it was difficult because there are so many different aspects that you have to learn about the 3-D environment versus doing photography in real life. So there was a learning curve there for me. But, like I said, within 6 months, I had a pretty steady income for photography and within the first year it blossomed even further. It's been quite an experience. (Anatine, 2009)

Anatine's real-life experience includes professional photography, web design, graphic design, photo restoration, and she adds: "all of those elements I have used for photography in Second Life, especially a lot of the photo restoration, because so much of the imagery you see in Second Life involves Photoshop, so I'm constantly transitioning photos from Second Life into real life" (Anatine, 2009). Brody Muircastle, Anatine's Second Life partner, works alongside her in the photography profession within Second Life. In many ways, he sees her as his mentor. He arrived in Second Life in 2008, nearly one year after Anatine.

He heard about Second Life from a friend who himself had done some photography work in real life and was interested in exploring the possibilities inside the gaming world. Muircastle (2009) has no doubt that he professionally and creatively made the right decision to join Second Life:

> The interesting thing about Second Life is when I joined it, I knew nothing about it. The person who introduced me to it did some photography work as well. To get to a point where you are looking at it as a business, certainly working with Trin has been the best start for me. I did some other stuff in freebie studios and things like that, but really to try to develop it into some sort of business or some sort of platform where you can do this for people, it was because of Trin more than anything. She's a huge inspiration when looking at people who have incredible ability. When you see her work, at least to me, it was a big inspiration to really push forward and see what I could do.

Muircastle, like other media makers in SL, sees Second Life as offering a host of creative and business opportunities, and the skills learned have real-life applications and fulfillment:

> It's been a slow progression from the way a person looks at the game or Second Life. In some aspects, people play it as a game. In some aspects, people play it as an opportunity. I'm developing skills, for instance, working in photography, in Photoshop, and

> stuff like that. The interest I think really originates from real life, seeing the abilities in Second Life. Over a period of time you begin to see the abilities of Second Life and the people that are in Second Life. And for me it was just kind of a natural thing I wanted to do. There is a variety of things to do of course, but photography is certainly more of a personal interest from real life. This just seemed a good fit into Second Life. (Muircastle, 2009)

For some photographers, as Anatine (2009) explains, Second Life allows them a glimpse into the fashion industry of real life, a microcosm of the real-world industry, but very real at the same time when considering the business side of operations:

> Well you know I think that SL is quite comparable to what happens in real life. You have your drama and you do have your fashion empires in Second Life that are true money makers. Some of those empires have rolled over into real life. As a matter of fact there is one designer that I believe she is from England and she is a real-life designer and of course she has her business in SL. I've been a model in real life and I have done photography, so for me to see it in Second Life it's very much the same. The only difference of course is the amount the photographer gets paid in Second Life is not even comparable to what a photographer would get paid in real life. As far as the managing of a studio or a magazine or the fashion houses, it's very realistic.

Second Life is "an extension of a creativity that is already there" within the fashion industry or within those who want to become involved in the industry, states Anatine (2009): "A lot of the photographers have never been around the fashion scene in real life. So for them, this is a way to fulfill a dream that they may not be able to do in real life." Anatine's plan is transition out of the fashion industry eventually while continuing to develop her reputation in architectural and landscape photography.

Her work in architecture and art was featured in *Avenue Magazine–SLCC edition*. The magazine was published in the real world for the Second Life Community Convention that was held in San Francisco in 2009:

> I was selected to take some pictures for the magazine...My pictures are not fashion related, however some of the other photographers that are in the magazine are doing fashion. I handled the architectural and art. For example, I interviewed a real-life artist. She is selling her art in Second Life. Also, I did 3 or 4 segments on architecture in SL. So I thought that was pretty cool. This is the first time that I have heard of that anybody has crossed over a Second Life magazine to real-life [publication]. (Anatine, 2009)

In this sense, her work has transitioned into real life. Her photography work also includes portraits and profile pictures within Second Life. Anatine (2009) and Muircastle (2009), in the following interview segments, readily elaborate on opportunities for which Second Life professionals have had their work cross-over into real life, and cases where real-life businesses have shifted or expanded into Second Life.

> Anatine: With everything in life, you're going to have your good and your bad. SL is no stranger to that. I think it is important for people to know that SL is not just a virtual, 3-D world or a game. There are real lives here, people fulfilling their dreams that they could not fulfill in real life, as well as exploring different avenues in business that can cross over to real life. I have seen it happen quite a few times, especially in the fashion industry. With a couple of the modeling agencies here in Second Life, they have transitioned into real life and vice versa. I think it is important for people to understand that this isn't just a game. There are real businesses that survive here and succeed and it's a wonderful thing.
>
> Muircastle: And that's the amazing thing. The ability to create a business here—it's everywhere here. The ideas and talent—whether it be builders or designers or people writing scripts, I mean some of the people's abilities when it comes to photography work would blow you away. And not so much the ability to take the snapshot, but the ability to work with it afterwards. There's some incredible talent that is here.
>
> Anatine: And there's another thing too, on the photography level—there are photographers here in Second Life that are actually selling their work in real life. So it is transitioning, and I think it is going to get bigger the more that people become aware that Second Life exists and other 3-D worlds.

In a creative platform like Second Life, particularly in a world that remakes itself, as regions are continually being refashioned or repurposed, it is difficult for a professional media artist to retain rights to their work. Clients want to be able to modify and repurpose images; nothing seems to stay the same in Second Life. Media takes on an evolutionary life of its own. There is a cycle of constructing and deconstructing what is built and created through various media within Second Life, being among the larger media platforms that reside online.

In a sense, nothing is sacred in Second Life, or at least nothing is constant, and in this mix and mash-up culture, originality is part of a creative process. Works are shaped through various communities, business or artistic. Individuality and individual propriety are sometimes lost in the process and during such transitions, particularly when one is working with clients, as in real life:

> Muircastle: The interesting thing, and I'm learning this from Trin more than anything—the more you do photography work for people, for clients, we had this conversation the other day, there's this protection issue. If I do photography work in real life, it's mine.
>
> Anatine: Yeah.
>
> Muircastle: It's always mine. In Second Life, a photographer loses that ability to protect his work in some cases. Designers are looking for pictures of people in a beauty contest or a photo contest. They're wanting full mod (modification) rights. So as soon as you do that, you lose the ability to protect the things that you, as a photographer or as an artist, do. That's kind of an interesting problem.

> Anatine: It is definitely a huge issue and it's challenging.

Muircastle and Anatine, however, are convinced that Second Life offers incredible business opportunities for creative types within virtual worlds, with cross-over potential in Second Life.

> Muircastle: Second Life, real life, there is a tie. Anyone who doesn't say there is a tie to it I don't know what they're doing here. Ultimately, things you do in Second Life if it will benefit or change your real life it's hard to say. I met Trin, and that's an incredible thing in itself...And I mean you look at avatars and the way they have developed and people are creating skins and shapes and the things they can do with them.
>
> Anatine: Oh gosh, just in the two years, I've seen such a major difference in the skin designers. Everything is becoming more real. The textures are more realistic. So a lot of that creativity comes from real life and transitions the tools that people use.
>
> Muircastle: Look. They have the annual conference as a result of this in the real world. To go to it, there is that real life, second life, connection. Some people play it like there isn't one. But for the most part, if you're in some sort of business, then I think that people here can be very, very professional with what they do.

Virtual Strategies in Virtual Business

Jean Kilbourne (2007), renowned advertising critic and lecturer, has stated that Americans watch about three years of commercials in their lifetime. She notes that advertising is an industry of more than $200 billion annually, exposing consumers to more than 3,000 advertisements daily:

> Yet, remarkably, most of us believe we are not influenced by advertising. Ads sell a great deal more than products. They sell values, images, and concepts of success and worth, love and sexuality, popularity and normalcy. They tell us who we are and who we should be. (Kilbourne, 2007)

"Commercial culture is now inside our intimate relationships" is the cautionary message from Media Education Foundation's (MEF) *Advertising and the End of the World.* This documentary warns that Westernized nations are moving from "cognitive" to "emotional" consumer choices, a point to which advertising becomes unavoidable and truth and integrity are being conceptualized as opportunity and challenge. New media does not guarantee a more or less ethical experience for the consumer; it merely provides the interactivity to complete the marketing process. Advertising has become so influential to our culture; its viewers expect it to be evasive. The occurrence becomes another form of entertainment. *Futurama,* with its keen insight on the business world, satirized the concept of subliminal advertising in one of its episodes. Philip Fry, a relic from the 20th century, who was cryogenically frozen in the year 2000 only to wake up nearly 1,000 years later, is alarmed by an advertisement for Lightspeed Briefs broadcast during his dream in the middle of the night. The next morning at the office, he is still disturbed about the intrusive ad:

> Philip: ...you're telling me that they broadcast commercials in people's dreams.
>
> Turanga: Of course.
>
> Philip: How is it possible?
>
> Professor: Very simple, the ad gets into your brain like this liquid gets into this egg...in reality it's not liquid but gamma radiation.
>
> Philip: That's awful—it's like braining washing.

The punch line comes as no surprise, but it drives home the idea of where media might be headed (or fairly much its current state of practice):

> Turanga: Didn't you have ads in the 20th century?
>
> Philip: Well sure, but not in our dreams—on TV and radio, in magazines, in movies, and in ballgames, on buses, milk cartons, T-shirts, and bananas and written in the sky—but not in dreams—no siree.

Second Life, at times, provides residents a virtual vehicle, a medium, from which to experience products within a world of fantasy, a dream world per se, with hopes that connections will be made to real world purchases and lifestyles. At other times, Second Life is a microcosm of real life in nearly every way. How do you market escapism and fantasy? Well some might say that is exactly what propels marketing in real and second life. Second Life merely removes some of the real-life obstacles and barriers. What would cost zillions to build and implement can be employed for a fraction of the cost. What is being marketed in Second Life might be identified as possibilities. A business can soar beyond suggesting fantasy to the point where customers can experience it in a somewhat tangible way through a virtual world for minimal risk or investment. For marketers, the impractical becomes doable. Imaginative campaigns thus are not limited by real world physical and budgetary constraints, with interactivity becoming an integral component to campaigns.

In 2007, Coca Cola launched a contest to design a virtual Coke machine in Second Life. Subsequent to that promotion, a number of Coke vending machines could be seen throughout SL in malls, beaches, and hangouts. Touch the machine, and a can of coke would be sent to an avatar's inventory. Drag the can out of the inventory, and you could pretend you were drinking from a soda can all day long. Coca Cola solicited design submissions, and then asked contestants to submit them to YouTube. Nicole (2007) pointed out, that a "design can be implemented within Second Life, though real-life constraints would render it impossible. Not to mention, it would cost far less than creating a physical manifestation of a Coke machine, but still warrants all the branding and viral opportunities that marketing strategies aim for."

Looking toward the Future

Few know Second Life as well as Wagner James Au, author of *The Making of Second Life: Notes from the New World*. His exploration and documentation of Second Life as an avatar named Hamlet eventually grew into a book. He maintains his blog *New World Notes*, keeping his attention on tech culture in-world. He has covered the spectrum of topics, from fashion, media, politics and business. In his May 2008 column, Au reflected on virtual activity subsequent to Second Life making the cover of *Business Week*. Second Life generated some initial "interest from real-world companies looking to advertise in the user-created virtual world" (Au, 2008b). Au (2008b) points out, "Most of the early efforts were glorified 3D billboards that drew little reaction, and so the gold rush quickly died down....Despite downbeat reports in *Wired* magazine and elsewhere, more than a dozen metaverse agencies are still developing virtual ad campaigns for major real-world clients, often returning impressive results." Au has also recommended that successful companies visualize Second Life (2008a) "as a stage in which to create ads—both movies and stills—that can be pumped into the real world." Au (2008b) calls attention to "a tiny San Francisco agency called This Second Marketing [that] rolled out an avatar-driven promotional effort for the IMAX screening of the latest *Harry Potter* movie." In fact, a significant amount of opening ticket sales resulted from Second Life campaign efforts. Au (2008b) recommends that successful marketing campaigns "foster community:"

> To refer to the Second Life "community" generally means its most active users, currently about 550,000 people who go "in-world" an average of 40 hours a month. It comprises numerous smaller communities, formed primarily around personal interests and activities.

To Au (2008b), "the best entry point for outside companies is often through brands and products that already attract Second Life users. Au (2008b) notes, the "first relatively successful corporate-funded presence in Second Life was built for Showtime's popular series *The L Word*...[featuring] recreated locations from the show where fans can congregate and socialize...[in] a kind of virtual living room." Thousands of visits to such sites have provided beneficial publicity. Au (2008b) also suggests that beyond creating a sense of community, businesses "embracing the fantastic" are more likely to win at the virtual marketing game. Au (2008b) continues, "Some of the most successful grassroots locales play in the full spectrum of possibility: dystopian, *Blade Runner*-esque cities of the future, for example, or interactive art installations that seem like 3D dreamscapes. This is the essential eclecticism of the Second Life experience—what I call 'bebop reality.'"

Au (2008b) points out that for most companies, much of the marketing efforts in Second Life have produced "mediocre results." He reminds us to look toward the beginning of the Internet, when it "was initially dismissed as an irrelevant plaything of hobbyist geeks" (Au, 2008b). That all changed around the mid 1990s when corporations rushed to incorporate commercial Web browsers into their business strategies. Online company sites were hailed as cure-alls to marketing woes in a rapidly transforming marketplace until 2000:

> They had wasted hundreds of millions on Web sites that provided too little value for too few visitors. These sites were typically bland and noninteractive, or stylish but insubstantial. After the dot-com crash, however, those sites that had delivered sustained, substantial usefulness—the likes of Amazon.com, Yahoo! and eBay—dominated. (Au, 2008b)

Second Life does well within small social networking circles. Think about Second Life as a series of concentric circles, where circles of friends interact. Because of the social nature of Second Life, it facilitates a portal for businesses to tap into opinion leaders. In a 2009 Linden Lab panel, it was discussed how "huge events (more than 200 people) diminish the impact of social interaction both in RL and SL. Smaller groups are usually best for interaction" (SLDEV, 2009).

Since 2008, Mark Kingdon has concentrated much of his efforts on making Second Life an attractive option for corporations, everything from in-world conference meetings to marketing campaigns. Kingdon explained, "Enterprise is a really important growth vector for us because [Second Life is] a really compelling platform for learning and collaboration, especially today in large enterprises that are distributed [around the world]" (Hodge, 2009). Linden Lab has organized a team of 25 people to develop and market SL productions for businesses as well. It hired more than 300 employees around the world, and has several offices globally (Hodge, 2009). Linden Lab earns $40 to $50 million annually, with Hodge (2009) citing Au for those numbers. Moreover, "Well known as a virtual venue for games and activities ranging from university lectures to sex play, Second Life is increasingly being sold by San Francisco parent company Linden Lab as a powerful multimedia platform for sensitive corporate communications and teamwork" (Hodge, 2009).

Quoted in a CNBC (2009) news story on virtual business, Kingdon states, "You can sit on a beach; you can sit around a campfire...You can interact with people and have water cooler chat...like you do in the real world. So they saw some of the same benefits as the real world but a fraction of the cost and much less time." The report listed some of the major corporate players, among the hundreds, holding meetings and conducting business in SL, including IBM, Cisco, Xerox, Intel, and Unilever.

The report noted that IBM had a meeting for 250 employees on Feb. 27, 2009, indicating that $80,000 had been invested in the construction of a virtual conference center and firewall for its first in-world meeting in Fall 2008 (CNBC, 2009). By doing so, the company reported it had saved more than $300,000 dollars on travel and productivity. The report (CNBC, 2009) concluded by adding that SL's user transactions had increased 30% since September 2008.

The company that Au referred to as a successful one is This Second Marketing LLC (2009), which specializes in helping companies extend their brand into Second Life: "We are all residents of Second Life and have passion and respect for what it provides today and will become in the future. We understand what residents would like to see from brand marketers in Second Life because we live there and have studied this issue from the 'inside'..." Company president Joni West continues, "Equally important is our understanding of the brand marketers' side and what they would like to see happen as a result of their marketing efforts in this space. We help brands align their objectives...in ways that make real world sense" (*This Second*, 2009).

Some of her clients have had remarkable in-world success. Greg Foster, chairman and president of IMAX Filmed Entertainment, bragged, that his virtual campaign "was the highest one-on-one branded interaction known to date that ever took place on Second Life...Reaching 15,000 people in exactly the demographic" that he wanted to attract during the campaign (*This Second*, 2009). Joni Rich, as she is known in Second Life, took her more than 20 years of brand marketing into Second Life when she became a member in 2006: "At first, I thought it would be an interesting place to have an art gallery. It would be an entirely new way for people all around the world to be able to see my art and actually buy copies of it for their virtual homes!" (*This Second*, 2009). In a short time, after she started exploring, she became aware of Second Life's "greater" potential:

> ...in the not too distant future, when everyone who uses the internet will have an avatar and 3-dimensional environments [SL] will be standard online....This Second Marketing LLC is the agency born of my desire to explore, experience, experiment and share the metaverse called Second Life. (*This Second*, 2009)

Avarie Parker, reporter for *SL Entrepreneur Magazine*, profiled Peter Stindberg, who has built a successful translation business inside Second Life. His business is called Babel Translations. Although English is the base language in Second Life, less than 40% of the residents are native speakers: "There are whole regions in SL used exclusively by Japanese, German or French speaking residents. As a business owner in Second Life, you are suffering in those markets if you can't address them in their native language" (Parker, 2008). Fashion designers and real estate management comprise most of his clients. Stindberg predicts, beyond the virtual hype, corporate websites of today will be subsumed by Second Life or similar virtual worlds in the near future and considered business tools:

> ...(taking into account that companies have already realized a website is actually high maintenance too). There will be a fair deal of SL/RL business interactions...just as the web in the late 90s spawned a lot of purely web-focused companies, we will eventually see purely SL or VW content companies. (Parker, 2008)

He adds, "I see a massive impact on cultural and social interaction. SL is the logical step beyond YouTube and MySpace. Both allowed me to discover bands I never would had heard before (and consequently buy their CD's). SL may eventually give me the opportunity to actually 'see' them 'live'" (Parker, 2008).

Conclusion

Marketing agencies are realizing the opportunities from connecting various social media platforms and networking services, and allowing for multi-level campaigns that connect the Internet dots, you might say. Virtual marketing is still in its infancy, and Second Life provides a good place for fairly inexpensive experimentation. Although real money is spent in-world, much of the expense is far less than what a commercial campaign would cost on network television. On a smaller scale, some sims in Second Life are cluttered with billboards of various products from weapons and gadgets to exotic fashions to adult clubs.

For the average virtual business, the best means of increasing sales is through referrals (*In-World*, 2009). Having customers put your business name in their profile picks is one of the most effective ways to reach other potential buyers. People like to know what other people (or in this case avatars) are buying, doing, and experiencing in SL. Events are another way. Second Life functions much like a social network, and events are a good way to bring avatars together in a region. Some businesses hold live music events in stage areas near their shops. Some gain publicity though charity fashion shows, contests, or concerts.

Linden Lab plans to more effectively incorporate machinima (virtual filmmaking, to be discussed in a later chapter) into its marketing activities, and sees it as a way to "convey/demonstrate the power and potential of SL without the issue of firewalls and having to log into SL" (SLDEV, 2009). A search through YouTube will produce results of a growing list of companies who have held events in Second Life only to broadcast them as viral videos, allowing for real world exposure.

References

Anatine, T. (2009, July 15). Interview, personal communication with author. Second Life.

Au, W. J. (2008a, October 3). New world marketing: SL corporate site as no-SL soundstage. *New World Notes.* Accessed July 9, 2000, from http://nwn.blogs.com/ nwn/2008/10/second-life-cor.html/

—. (2008b, May 5). Second Life marketing: Still strong. Accessed July 9, 2009, from http://www.businessweek.com/technology/content/may2008/tc2008054_665274.htmSpecial Report/

Bauder, D., (2007, May 28), Networks try new ways to end ad skipping. Associated Press. Accessed May 29, 2007, from http://www.yahoo.com/

BIGresearch. (2002, November 21). BIGresearch study finds simultaneous media usage makes traditional planning passé. BIGresearch press release. Accessed September 15, 2007, from http://www.bigresearch.com/news/SIMM112102.htm/

Calvert, S. L. (2001, September). The children's digital media center: The role of identity and interactivity in children's learning. Keynote lecture presentation to the Association for German Speaking Developmental Psychologists, Potsdam, Germany. Accessed September 10, 2007, from http://cdmc.georgetown.edu/papers/Role_of_Interactivity_and_Identity.pdf/

Carella, C. (2007, May 14). Electric Sheep Company. Top 25 brands measured by traffic. Blog. Accessed July 11, 2009, fromhttp://blog.electricsheepcompany.com/?author=4/ ?feed=rss2&p=232/

CNBC News Report. (2009, February 27). Conferences go virtual. Accessed July 9, 2009, from http://www.cnbc.com/id/15840232?video=1047748741&play=1/

Collings, P. (2007). Brands in Second Life. *The Encyclopedia of Brands & Branding in South Africa.* Accessed July 10, 2009, from http://www.scribd.com/doc/7530041/ Brands-in-Second-Life-Patrick-Collings/

DeGaetano, G. (1998). Visual media and young children's attention spans. Accessed September 10, 2007, from http://users.stargate.net/~cokids/VisualMedia.html/

de Mesa, A. (2007, March 12). Virtual world branding for real. *BrandChannel.com.* Accessed July 10, 2009, from http://www.brandchannel. com/features_effect.asp? pf_id=358/

Deuze, M. (2005). Towards professional storytelling in journalism and advertising journal. *First Monday.* Accessed September 15, 2007, from http://www.firstmonday.org/issues/ issue10_7/deuze/index.html/

Elias, M. (2004, September 4). Short attention span linked to TV. *USA Today.* Accessed September 10, 2007, from http://www.usatoday.com/news/nation/2004-04-05-tv-bottomstrip_x.htm.

Future of advertising: Lightspeed briefs. *Futurama.* Accessed September 4, 2007, from http://www.youtube.com/watch?v=tmbBSiusMKs&mode=related&search=/

Girls Intelligence Agency. Web site. Accessed May 5, 2007, from http://www. girlsintelligenceagency.com/

Haegele, K. (2007, March 25). Does storytelling change in context of new forms of media? Opinion. *Philadelphia Inquirer.* Accessed March 25, 2007, from http://www.philly.com/ inquirer/opinion/20070325_Does_storytelling_change_in_context _of_new_forms_of_media_.html/

Hodge, P. (2009, June 1). Second Life's Linden Lab sells virtual realities to businesses. *San Fran-*

cisco Business Times. Accessed July 9, 2009, from http://sanfrancisco.bizjournals.com/ sanfrancisco/stories/2009/06/01/ story2.html?b=1243828800^1836431/

Huysmans, F., & de Haan, J. (2003). De langzame revolutie [the slow revolution]. In Henk Blanken & Mark Deuze (eds.), *De media revolutie* (pp. 168-192). Amsterdam: Boom.

In-world marketing. (2009). Accessed July 9, 2009, from http://wiki.secondlife.com /wiki/ Marketing_Your_Products_In_Second_Life

Kilbourne, J. (2007). Web site. Accessed September 14, 2007, from http://www.jeankilbourne.com/lectures.html.

La Monica, P. R. (2006, September 14). Doritos: You create our Super Bowl commercial. *CNN Money*. Accessed September 14, 2007, from http://money.cnn.com/2006/09/14/news/funny/doritos_superbowl/index.htm?postversion=2006091415/

Lang, G. (2007, May 24). Attitudes toward brands in Second Life. *Second Life Research*. Blog. Accessed July 12, 2009, from http://secondliferesearch.blogspot.com/2007/05/attitude-towards-brands-in-second-life.html/

Lebkowsky, J. (2006, February 25). *New media, blogs, & public relations*. Accessed May 25, 2007, from http://www.polycot.com/blog/archives/2006/02/25/new-media-blogs-and-public-relations/

Leonard, D. (2006, October 2). Viral Ads: It's an epidemic. *CNN Money*. Accessed September 14, 2007, from http://money.cnn.com/magazines/fortune/fortune _archive/2006/10/02/8387416/index.htm/

Livingstone, S. (2004). The challenge of changing audiences: Or, what is the audience researcher to do in the age of the Internet? *European Journal of Communication 19*(1), 75–86.

Market Truths study reveals 60% of Second Life users positive about corporate brand presences in the virtual world. (October 11, 2007). *PR Web*. Accessed July 10, 2009, from http://www.prweb.com/releases/2007/10/prweb560547.htm/

Muircastle, B. (2009, July 15). Interview, personal communication with author. Second Life.

Naone, E. (2008, April 25). A new vision for Second Life: Linden Lab's new CEO outlines his plans to help Second Life mature. *Technology Review*. Accessed July 12, 2009, from http://www.technologyreview.com/read_article.aspx?id=20678&pg=2/

Nicole, K. (2007, April 17). Coca Cola launches Second Life contest for new Coke Machine. *Mashable*. Accessed July 9, 2009, from http://mashable.com/ 2007/04/17/coca-cola/

Packard, V. (1957). *The hidden persuaders*. New York: Pocket.

Papper, R., Holmes, M., & Popovich, M. (2004). Middletown media studies. *International Digital Media & Digital Arts Association Journal 1*(1) (Spring), 1–56. Accessed July 1, 2007, from http://www.bsu.edu/icommunication/news/iDMAaJournal.pdf/

Parker, A. (2008, February 20). SLentrepreneur Profile: Peter Stindberg—SL is the logical step beyond YouTube and MySpace. *SL Entrepreneur Magazine*. Accessed July 9, 2009, from http://www.slentre.com/slentrepreneur-second-life-profile-peter-stinberg-sl-is-the-logical-step-beyond-youtube-and-myspace/

Parry, T. (2005, November 15). Simon Williams: The ten new rules of marketing. *Chief Marketer*. Accessed May 23, 2007, from http://chiefmarketer.com/

Postman, N. (1985). *Amusing ourselves to death*. New York: Penguin Books.

Reuters, A. (2007, January 18). Top women's apparel makers should raise prices: study. *Reuters*. Accessed September 14, 2007, from http://secondliferesearch.blogspot.com/2007/02/top-womens-apparel-makers-should-raise.html/

Schor, J. B. (2004). *Born to buy: The commercialized child and the new consumer culture*. New York: Simon & Schuster.

Second Thoughts. (2006, October 26) Accessed July 10, 2009, from http://secondthoughts.

typepad.com/second_thoughts/2006/10/index.html/

SLDEV. (2009, 3 March). Marketing forum transcript. SLDEV forum topic: Case studies, marketing and solution providers. Linden Lab. Second Life Wiki. Accessed June 29, 2009, from http://wiki.secondlife.com/wiki/ Marketing_Forum_Transcript/

The perception of the brands in Second Life. (2007, April 17). *Kzero*. Accessed July 12, 2009, from http://www.kzero.co.uk/blog/?p=454.

This Second Marketing LLC. (2009), Web site. Accessed July 10, 2009, from http://www.thissecondmarketing.com/

360 Advertising Media Guide. *Advertising Age*. Accessed May 26, 2007, from http://www.adage-360media.com/adage360/20061106/

Verklin, D., & Kanner, B. (2007, April 29). Why a killer video game is the army's best recruitment tool. *Chief Marketer*. Accessed September 14, 2007, from http://www.articlesbase.com/politics-articles/why-a-killer-video-game-is-the-us-armys-best-recruitment-tool-138054.html/

Wallace, M. (2007, March 21). Calvin Klein launches scents in Second Life. 3PointD.com. Accessed September 4, 2007, from http://www.3pointd.com/20070321/calvin-klein-launches-scents-in-second-life/

CHAPTER SEVEN

Flying to Learn: Exploring Real Life through the Virtual Campus

by DR. NANCI BURK

This chapter was guest authored by Nanci Burk, Ph.D., resident faculty member at Glendale Community College in Glendale, Arizona. She spent a year-long Sabbatical within Second Life exploring its use among educators, including surveying and interviewing them. Burke is a prominent member of a number of national and international educational and communication associations in real life and Second Life. Her Ph.D. study area was Human Development from Fielding Graduate University, Santa Barbara, CA. She teaches public speaking, interpersonal communication and introduction to human communication at Glendale, a campus that has taken the lead in exploring the potential of virtual worlds for enhancing learning and using technology to connect students to different cultures across the world.

Introduction

> I think it's safe to say now that nearly every college and university has some sort of project in Second Life.
>
> –Larry Johnson, CEO, The New Media Consortium

Twenty-first century students have grown up with rapidly advancing technologies and 24/7 Internet access that have been as much a part of their lives as energy drinks and cable TV. These *digital natives* (Prensky, 2001) have grown up expecting to instantly acquire information, create and share content, collaborate, share experiences, and initiate and maintain relationships via technological means. These types of expectations greatly affect one's academic experience. The technological revolution created a paradigm shift impacting all of us, but especially those born between 1981 and 1999, also known as Generation Y Millennials, (Twenge, 2006) unlike any other generation has been influenced. Living in an interconnected technological network, Gen Y relies on a mouse click or touch screen for immediate access to information and contact with others. The immediacy from which information is made available, gathered and reconstructed has led to a generation of interdependent, creative thinkers who are open to active, participatory, collaborative learning environments (Price, 2009).

Social networks like MySpace, Facebook, Twitter, Hi5, LinkedIn, etc. that provide public forums for sharing information and accessibility to large groups of networked friends capitalize on the surge in technology usage, and have grown dramatically since the turn of the century. These types of online, social networks demonstrate shifts in 21st century societal norms for seeking relational connectedness and information acquisition. Between 2007 and 2009, Facebook boasted the fastest growing numbers of unique members in the world of online social networks, with an astounding 1,085% growth in Latin American countries alone (Holahan, 2008). Rapidly expanding social networks, such as those listed above illustrate sociological shifts in the mediated means by which people communicate, stay in touch, and maintain relationships. Building community was a prime objective when Linden Lab launched Second Life.

While Second Life may be viewed by some people as a computer "game" this MUVE (multi-user virtual environment) is resident-created, unlike the majority of computer games. SL is an immersive, media-rich environment that provides a platform for what this author refers to as a compelling social network on steroids with game-like features. Although Facebook, Twitter, Hi5, and other online social networks provide forums for posting and responding to others in an individual's network, the presence of others at any given time is implicit. We cannot see or hear that another person is online simultaneously unless we exchange instant messages. There might be five others in my Facebook network online synchronously; however, the presence of others is not obvious. In Second Life, due to the use of digital, graphic representation of individuals, known as avatars, the real-time presence of others is explicit. The recognition that another person is present provides immediacy lacking in other mediated social platforms and contributes a positive aspect for facilitating discussions, including those about scholarly course content. The social presence of others evokes interaction and social connection. In SL, another avatar's presence impacts the space that my avatar inhabits. This does not occur in Facebook, Twitter, or MySpace.

The dramatically increased numbers of online social network users is one indication that people are motivated to learn about and acquire knowledge via technologies to stay connected and develop relationships. Although many students are online 12–17 hours a day, the halls of academe continually attempt to suppress the use of the tools that are crucial components of their identity, expand their worldview, and connect them to others and to the global community. Technologically savvy educators recognize that the tools that profoundly influence students' lives can be incorporated positively into course design without sacrificing pedagogical effectiveness. Second Life is a powerful instructional tool that many educators embrace to facilitate learning and to make course content relevant to students' lives. As Akintunde (2006) asserts, "technology is not a deterrent to the educational process, it enhances it" (p. 35).

Tradition vs. Vision

Since its launch in 2003, Second Life has provided unlimited opportunities for innovative educators to utilize this mediated platform for academic pursuits. Currently, SL is a bifurcated virtual environment, with 13-to-18 year-old users (requiring parental approval) confined to a Teen Grid, and not permitted access to the Main Grid. In the same manner, SL residents on the Main Grid, for users 18 and older, do not have access to the Teen Grid without having completed a rigorous background check. Discussions about merging the two grids have met with considerable debate within the academic community. Regardless of the outcome, K-12 and higher education educators continue to develop and utilize SL as an instructional tool to enhance teaching and learning.

For six years, educators and students have dreamed, built, collaborated, implemented and accessed learning and educational spaces throughout SL on both the Teen Grid and the Main Grid. One of the distinct advantages of using SL for educational purposes is the ability to manipulate movement, sound, color, and objects to provide visual and audio stimuli, as well as depth of understanding of complex models, activities, and ideas. The types of interactive opportunities for teaching and learning in Second Life are limited only by one's imagination. Where else can instructors show students the past, the future and a multitude of cultures, walk or fly around in that time and culture, and experience it together in real time? Traditional pedagogical strategies are not limited or abandoned by instructors using SL as an instructional tool. Rather, foundational pedagogical techniques are expanded, stretched, and adapted in ways never conceived of prior to the technological revolution and versatile virtual learning environments like SL.

Learning is inherent in SL and begins the moment one's avatar is created and rezzes (is visible) in world. The learning curve may not be as steep for experienced gamers, but everyone entering SL for the first time needs to learn the skills and tenets of the virtual environment and the SL culture in order to remain and function. Learning to communicate (in text, voice, group and instant messaging), walk, fly, sit down, alter appearance, teleport, offer friendship, manage inventories, use gestures and animations, use landmarks & translation devices, camera control, and understanding the metric system, and currency exchange are skills that will prove greatly advantageous to the new SL resident. However, more formalized learning takes place in SL in a variety of methods and locations, as well.

SL Educational Institutions

Hundreds of distinguished international educational institutions and school districts have established a presence in SL. Some colleges and universities have developed small plots (rented or owned), partial or whole sims, while others have developed whole campuses (sims, islands, virtual land) and/or replications of well-known landmarks and campus buildings for branding, academic courses, activities, and events. These virtually identical campuses may provide opportunities for marketing, virtual tours, and for housing learning spaces (i.e., classrooms, amphitheaters, labs, etc.). Flexible learning environments provide locations for students in distance, online, and hybrid courses to meet, explore, discuss, analyze, and experience places and cultures otherwise impossible for traditional classes to share due to budget and logistical constraints. "The virtual classroom (has) the potential to educate people and connect us in ways unimaginable just a decade ago" (Akintunde, 2006). In the past decade, online enrollments have increased dramatically in higher education and mark a paradigm shift in students' social and academic needs.

According to the 2008 Sloan Consortium Report, which reports online educational trends in the U.S., nearly 4 million students in higher education were enrolled in at least one online course in 2007, and over 20% of all students in higher education were taking at least one course online. While the overall growth in 2007 for students enrolling in higher education courses was a mere 1.2%, online course enrollments increased by 12.9%. Many universities capitalize on students' desire for online courses.

St. Leo University (Florida) is one educational institution that has taken full advantage of these online educational trends by creating programs that offer fully accredited bachelors and masters degrees attainable online from their creative and well-developed SL campus. Opened in 2008, St. Leo's three-sim virtual campus provides replicas of buildings that duplicate those found on the real-world campus at St. Leo's University in Florida. Some of these 3-D replicas are used for student social gatherings like the Student Community Center and the admissions and security building, for example. SLU's Second Life campus comes complete with residence halls for online students to decorate and personalize; Crawford Hall offers the latest technology for St. Leo's students and faculty; Lewis classroom building and Selby auditorium provide authenticity to the 3-D campus with recognizable duplicates of real-world buildings.

For many students and their families, having the option to take a virtual tour of a college or university campus without the expense of time and travel costs to the physical RL campus is economical and informative and creates interest. Several universities have developed identical replicas that serve this function well. For example, Princeton University established a presence in SL in 2007 replicating Nassau Hall, a university and national landmark, as well as Alexander Hall, a premier performance venue, Prospect Gardens, and Chancellor Green Library on its virtual campus.

Minnesota State University-Moorhead's SL campus also has a well-developed virtual campus and replicated many real campus buildings including Hagen Science Lab, Lommen Hall, Bridges/MacLean Bookstore, Center for the Arts, Livingston Lord Library, Comstock Memorial Union/Kise Commons, among other buildings. MSU-Moorhead's SL campus has also served as a location for faculty development.

An even greater number of colleges and universities are represented in Second Life by a singular library, research project, sandbox, or learning space. For instance, Harvard Law School provides students with a courtroom where they attend lectures and participate in mock trials. As part of the Dublin sims, Trinity College has a large orientation space to welcome new SL residents. As new SL users enter the virtual world, Trinity College offers a place for "newbies" to learn specific skills and functions that is less congested than Orientation Island. Like many universities and educational locations, this public space is available for all new SL residents where they can learn to communicate, walk, fly, and change their avatars' appearance in relative seclusion without the slow down or "lag" common in more crowded locations.

Still other educational institutions and instructors provide spaces for students to meet and learn in non-traditional spaces. Many instructors take advantage of the versatility of SL's virtual platform and expose students to learning outside the walls of a traditional classroom setting. For some instructors, the deck of a pirate ship, the courtyard of a castle, or meeting students beneath a canopy of trees in a rainforest provides an appealing environment in which to discuss course content from world languages or economics to psychology or literature. Others may choose to have students float in outer space at locations like Inspire Space, a cosmic encounter with spectacular meteors, plants, comets and stars while studying astronomy. Still others may choose to have students examine the Second Life-sized lunar module or space shuttle, or experience a space flight simulation at the International Spaceflight Museum while discussing physics or rocket science. Interactive simulations are well represented in SL as complementary pedagogical tools that enhance more traditional methods of scholarly discourse. Simulations provide opportunities to become immersed in an environment that otherwise could be dangerous, cost-prohibitive, or impossible to duplicate in the physical world.

SL Edu-Simulations

Simulations in SL are one method that educators employ to share immersive environments with students to facilitate learning, engage with the environment, and help them "experience" course content. Students tend to be motivated by course content that deals with real-world issues and problem-solving. According to Lombardi (2007), students prefer to take an active role rather than to listen passively (p. 2). Educators understand the importance of relating theoretical concepts to practical application. SL residents have many opportunities to visit 3-D locations and become engaged with the content rather than simply hear about it in a lecture or read about it in a textbook or 2-D environment (i.e., text-based web pages). This type of active, visual, "authentic learning" (Lombardi, 2007) cannot be duplicated in a textbook or typical classroom in the same ways: "Authentic learning typically focuses on real-world, complex problems and their solutions, using role-playing exercises, problem-based activities, case studies, and participation in virtual communities of practice (p. 2).

There are many locations in SL that provide these types of opportunities, some of which include role-play. It is possible, for example, for SL residents to visit Tranquility Base on the moon and walk in the footsteps of Armstrong and Aldrin; to explore the Galapagos Islands from the HMS Beagle as chronicled by Charles Darwin; to visit the home and era of Abraham Lincoln; to safely witness a toxic, industrial accident and practice evacuation procedures; and to sit through a tsunami and observe the devastation to a village. Copious academic disciplines are targeted in SL simulations. The following samples are a few of the many exceptional simulations featured on the SL main grid.

World Languages

One of the great strengths of the Second Life environment lies in its ability to transport users to worlds other than their own. While for some this might be a totally fictitious realm, for world language educators and their students, Second Life allows us to visit and participate in the very world that we target—without physically leaving our own. Many re-creations of real-life places already exist in SL and native speakers abound, fostering a rich environment for interaction. However, Second Life also provides another space for learning that compliments the learning styles of digital learners and traditional learners alike. Calisto Encinal (a.k.a. James Abraham, Glendale Community College, Glendale, AZ) has built *Mi casa es su casa*, a particularly innovative learning space for students of Spanish.

Mi casa es su casa began with the creation of a house, based on a colonial house like those found in San Miguel de Allende in Mexico, that gives students the 3-dimensional experience of walking through an actual Mexican house. Rather than relying on one of the traditional methods of demonstrating contextually rich information through two dimensions, *Mi casa* transports students into a virtual house with walls, doors and objects that closely resemble objects they would find if visiting or living in Mexico. Students must navigate the house by walking their avatar around, digitally touching doors and objects to trigger a response. This tactile experience leads to a more immediate and immersive learning experience.

This realistic backdrop sets the stage for role-playing activities, one type of learning activity that Second Life accommodates very well. Another type of learning activity embedded throughout the house leverages Second Life's native scripting language. Simple scripted objects can be made to speak or do just about anything when clicked. These "smart" objects can be linked together to form complex activities that excite learners and encourage the playful side of learning that draws students out of their desks and into an active learning mode. Working alone or with their instructor and classmates, students become part of the immersive environment, temporarily losing touch with their own, thus learning and participating in the target language.

After successful completion of Mi casa, it seemed only natural for Calisto Encinal to extend the model to incorporate an entire Mexican village. Using the knowledge gained from creating *Mi casa* and carrying over the strategies developed for it, this interactive village now engulfs the first house and includes a school, a pharmacy, a market, a restaurant, a flower shop, a hotel, a bakery, a newspaper stand, a laundromat/drycleaner and a cantina. Each of the spaces serves as an ideal location for role-playing where students and instructors assume roles and play out dialogs as if they were in Mexico. In addition, each building houses unique learning activities and games associated with the target language and the contextual vocabulary of the related course material. For example, in the pharmacy, students must engage in a dialog with a virtual pharmacist who asks them about their symptoms and possible remedies. In the market, visitors must match audio clues with fruits and vegetables by clicking on the appropriate stall when they hear them pronounced. These varied activities focus learning by adding a gaming element familiar to 21st century, Millennial students. The variety of village locations gives students a feeling of being in Mexico without ever having to travel. *Mi casa* and its village give educators one more tool to surround their students in the target language and its culture.

History

The Middle Passage Experience, created by Tamsin Barzane (a.k.a. Kathy Curnow, Associate Professor of African Art History at Cleveland State University) is a powerful and poignant simulation depicting a particularly horrific historic era. The designer and builder, Barzane, developed a small parcel of virtual land to represent a port on the African coast. The simulation is designed to have the visitor immersed in the experience of the slave passage. Visitors are invited to take free copies of biographies, clothing, images in the form of a PowerPoint presentation, and notes describing the passage for each participant. A notecard in the identity box (containing clothing and explanations of the passage) describes the detailed journey that the person endured. Participants are then instructed to remove their African clothing, wear only a loincloth and shackles and proceed to the slave ship where they are stripped of their African identity. Each visitor is given a new name, slave clothing and a notecard describing where the ship will take her/him, and describes the slave's life.

Participating in this type of immersive role-play in the 3-D recreation of the Middle Passage teaches about this specific historic era and evokes visceral responses in a way that books, lectures, and discussions cannot. Walking the virtual path in this realistic recreation is likely to enhance the visitor's awareness of the humiliating and demeaning treatment of those forced into slavery. Molka-Danielsen and Deutschmann (2009) discuss the effectiveness of role-play in Second Life: "It is argued that the believable environments give support to those taking on roles, that they can help the role-player to empathize with the role and can help all participants to become more greatly immersed in the content" (p. 18). In this way, the avatar becomes an agent of learning, and SL's efficacy as a powerful instructional tool is evident.

Health Professionals

A flourishing trend in SL simulations is the creation of medical facilities and sites utilizing SL's versatility for active, participatory engagement for health professionals, educators, and practitioners. Included in the list of distinguished medical education locations on the main grid are The Ann Myers Medical Center (AMMC), the Postgraduate Medical School, by the Imperial College in London, The Gene Pool, Virtual Neurological Education Centre, Centers for Disease Control and Prevention, and the University of Illinois, Chicago Initiative for Clinician Education (SLICE2). Each of these SL landmarks explores methods of training medical practitioners, bringing together educators, EMTs, nurses, medical students, physicians and medical technologists from all parts of the globe.

Fairly new to the SL medical landscape, SLICE2 was designed, developed and, managed by Jerod Bagley, (a.k.a. Gerald R. Stapleton, faculty and Director for Distance Education at the University of Illinois Department of Medical Education) in 2008. The clinic's goals are to facilitate communication, teaching, teamwork, life-long learning, practice management, and patient safety primarily for medical students and physicians. A modern, professional looking building, the clinic houses a lobby and theater, medical library, and a floor each with exam rooms for outpatients, family medicine, internal medicine, and emergency medicine. The lobby displays a large PowerPoint presentation, Developing Interpersonal and Communication Skills for Real Life Practitioners, which explains the clinic's objectives, theoretical foundations, program design, benefits and challenges.

In a 2009 interview with the creator, builder and administrator, Jerod Bagley affirmed the clinic is a first initiative to establish a training space for physicians to engage with persons role-playing as standardized patients (i.e., those trained to respond in scripted dialogues) to practice interpersonal communications skills in specific medical situations with physicians and practitioners. His hopes, once the clinic is fully developed and operational, are that it will have a network of standardized patients (perhaps coached medical students) who will learn from the physicians with whom they role-play. Secondly, Bagley visualizes a time when SLICE2 outgrows the space it now inhabits due to the demands of trainees wishing to use the space to practice patient/physician communication skills. Educating health professionals in interpersonal communication skills is a prime objective.

Like many educators in SL, Bagley values the support and cooperation of others in the SL academic community. Bagley (2009) expressed that he has been "nothing short of amazed at the collaboration of the educational community" in SL. Numerous educational groups in SL facilitate networking in-world as well as in RL for the dedicated academic community.

Educators Networking

A dynamic cohort of educators uses SL as a vibrant component in their teaching repertoire, and as a strategic method to connect with other scholars. The active academic community has established itself as a valuable resource for those who wish to network, research, share professional experience, and develop creative ideas in SL, as well as in their daily professions on- and off-line. Academic contacts, support, and networks developed in-world often extend to professional blogs, wikis, listservs, meetings and conferences outside of SL. Thousands of international faculty members, technologists, librarians, administrators, and students make up the members of over 600 educational groups in SL. Group membership is generally free for interested SL residents. Two of the largest academic groups are the New Media Consortium (NMC) and the International Society for Technology in Education (ISTE), each with over 5,000 SL residents as members. Both of these SL groups lend assistance to educators wishing to explore learning technologies that will enhance teaching and learning in SL.

The New Media Consortium established a formidable presence in Second Life in 2006. "The NMC was founded on a deep commitment to exploring and embracing new collaborations and learning technologies" (Linden Lab & NMC, 2009). NMC has approximately 300 member organizations (i.e., universities, colleges, museums, foundations and research centers) worldwide. The NMC's work in SL has focused on the organization's commitment to helping educators develop virtual, online, and face-to-face learning communities and to inspire innovation and creativity. NMC comprises a network of over 100 sims or regions in SL developed by NMC member organizations, including sims with libraries, museums, and various non-profit organizations as well as educational institutions such as Princeton University, Yale, the University of Southern California, Ball State, Penn State, and the University of Helsinki.

Ongoing scholarly research is inherent in a platform as rich in diversity, innovation, and opportunities as SL has proven to provide. Much of the research conducted in SL results in publications, symposiums, or conference presentations, several of which are sponsored by NMC. In-world and out, NMC offers many international conferencing options for educators who wish to share ideas and dialogue with others about the technology, pedagogy, and innovation that influence the teaching profession and ultimately impact students' lives. Professional development is a significant element in any career, and certainly essential for educators learning and using the latest technologies and innovative models of learning.

ISTE also offers impressive networking options as well as contributions for professional development in the virtual and physical dimensions. ISTE is well known in the SL academic community for its weekly social events that include a speaker series and a casual social gathering. Recently, ISTE added a talk show broadcast, the ISTE Eduverse Talks series to its repertoire of educational offerings. The talk show is filmed in front of a live SL audience and broadcast via the web from the SLCN (Second Life Cable Network) television station (now Treet-TV).

In addition to the NMC and ISTE educational projects, Linden Lab supports the extensive social and professional academic networks that benefit educators and students in SL. In fact, Linden Lab offers educational institutions, non-profit organizations, and academics discounted rates for purchasing land/sims on the grid. Monthly maintenance fees are nominal and land prices are typically 50% less than land sales for non-academic individuals or commercial ventures. Given the benefits of professional and social support, networking, and collaboration, SL is a remarkable platform for educators to explore for pedagogical opportunities unlike any other academic environment previously.

Conclusion

Although academic budgets continually experience fiscal tensions, one benefit to a recession or *economic downturn* is that it drives innovation. In economically challenging times, educational budgets are often strained or reduced in a way that inhibits development of classroom buildings, limits professional development, attendance at professional conferences, travel funding, etc. SL offers immediate access to opportunities for educators to collaborate with peers, share ideas and experiences, and network in ways that often defy real-world limitations and budgets. By using SL as an instructional tool, opportunities abound for faculty members and students to experience, participate in, and analyze dimensions, international locations, and cultures previously only imagined due to financial and logistical constraints.

Acknowledgments: The author wishes to thank James T. Abraham, Ph.D. for his valuable contributions to this manuscript, and for his continued support, collaboration, and collegiality.

Note: For this guest chapter, secondary sources are also included within the references.

References

Adams, D. C. (2008, November). Gaga for Google in the twenty-first century advanced placement language classroom. *Clearing House 82* (2), 96–100.

Akintunde, O. (2006). Diversity.com: Teaching an online course on white racism and multiculturalism. *Multicultural Perspectives 8*(2), 35–45.

Allen, I. E., & Seaman, J. (2008). Staying the course: Online education in the United States, 2008. Needham, MA: Sloan Consortium.

Bagley, J. (2009, July 24). Interview, personal communication with Nanci Burke. Second Life.

El Mansour, B., & Mupinga, D. M. (2007, March). Student's positive and negative experiences in hybrid and online classes. *College Student Journal 41*(1), 242–248.

Holahan, C. (2008, August 4). Facebook: No. 1 globally. *Business Week Online*, p.14.

Howe, N., & Strauss, W. (2007). *Millennials go to college*. Great Falls, VA: LifeCourse Associates.

Jones, J. G., Moreales, C., & Knezek, G. A. (2005, September). 3-Dimensional online learning environments: Examining attitudes toward information technology between students in internet based 3-dimensional and face-to-face classroom instruction. *Educational Media International*, *42*(3), 219–236.

Linden Lab & New Media Consortium. (2009). Developing new learning and collaboration environments for educators. Retrieved on July 28, 2009 from http://secondlifegrid.net.s3.amazonaws.com/docs/Second_Life_Case_NMC_EN.pdf/

Lombardi, M. (2007, May). Authentic learning for the 21st century: An overview, in Educause Learning Initiative. Retrieved July 30, 2009 from http://net.educause.edu /ir/library/pdf/ELI3009.pdf/

Molka-Danielsen, J., & Deutschmann, M. (Eds.). (2009). *Learning and teaching in the virtual world of Second Life*. Trondheim, Norway: Tapir Academic Press.

Prensky, M. (2001). Digital natives, digital immigrants. *On the Horizon*, 9(5), 1-2.

Ouzts, K. (2006). Sense of community in online courses. *The Quarterly Review of Distance Education* 7(3), 285–296.

Price, C. (2009). Why don't my students think I'm groovy? The new "Rs for engaging millennial learners. Retrieved July 12, 2009 from http://www.daltonstate.edu/ teachinglearning/pdf/cprice_millennials.pdf/

Twenge, J. M. (2006). *Generation me: Why today's young Americans are more confident, assertive, entitled–and more miserable than ever before*. New York: Free Press.

Welcome to SLU Virtual Campus. Retrieved on July 12, 2009, from http://info.saintleo.edu/COL/SL.cfm/

CHAPTER EIGHT

Tuned into Second Life: Avatar Groupies, Beer Gardens, and Soundscapes

> "I find it amazing, but I kinda knew about the potential to play to anyone, anywhere that had a computer and an internet connection. I love that I've made friends with people in so many different countries."
>
> —Maxmillion Kleene

AcousticEnergy Nitely, Mimi Carpenter, Tukso Okey, Digby Smalls, AMForte Clarity, Arimo Teixeira, Strum Diesel, and Maxmillion Kleene are among the most popular musicians inside Second Life. Kleene was featured in the July edition of *Rez Libris*. Reporter Vienna James (2009) asked him how it all started on Second Life: "I found out about SL from an article in *Rolling Stone Magazine*. It was about live music in SL, but I was more just interested in checking it out. After I stumbled upon my first live music event, I thought, 'hey, I think I can do this...'" Alternative rock/pop music bands like Follow are packing multiple sims during its performances, and it even had a well-publicized and well-attended, all-day, SL world tour across various time zones in March 2010. Other singers like United Kingdom's Josie Anderton are on their way toward establishing a strong fan base in Second Life. She will be featured later in this chapter.

Second Life radio stations often play the music of these performers on dedicated streams. The artists are represented by managers, who help to promote their CDs during performances. These musicians represent the rock stars of Second Life, and draw audiences so large that regions sometimes crash from too many people and too much computer streaming lag. Mimi Carpenter and Maxmillion Kleene performed July 2009 in Montreal to a Second Life audience. They invited their SL fans to travel from their virtual homes to hear them play in the real world. In Fall 2009, Kleene, Carpenter and a group of musicians met in Indiana to jam and share ideas on how to connect Second Life to real life on a larger scale. Two of those musicians included Anek Fuchs and Gina Stella, live musicians from Chicago, who play in Second Life on a regular basis, and have established strong followings. In October 2009, Fuchs and Stella began meeting with musicians, venue owners, recording engineers and technical personnel inside and outside of Second Life to create a large-scale 2010 summer jam in Chicago. This event would be a mix of real and second life musicians together performing outside the grid.

Second Life for musicians has the potential of being an incubator for new artists wanting to test out new music or to introduce themselves to a global audience. Other established musicians find it a spontaneous and creative space to meet and play with other musicians and to get to know audiences on a more intimate level. On any day, avatars wear t-shirts, sporting their favorite SL radio stations, venues, or performers. Radio stations—streamed and terrestrial—broadcast in SL. Some real-life stations sponsor remotes in-world, and much of these activities center around music events. National Public Radio hosts Science Friday inside Second Life, and has been successful at attracting a regular in-world audience. For the most part, music is one of the primary forms of entertainment in Second Life.

When Second Life hosted its sixth anniversary in 2009, it featured non-stop daily live music from in-world musicians who performed from their real homes and studios. Nearly every day, live music is performed in SL at a variety of venues, and many of these performers have their developed their own fan bases. Major record companies and indie labels are based in Second Life, and organize their own promotional and performance events. SL Live Radio is one streamed station devoted to the virtual indie musician. Other stations, SLive Radio and Radio Radio, have been programmed like real world stations, beginning from the early days of SL. This chapter takes a look at the use of sound in Second Life—as backdrop to daily life in-world and the use of sound in social settings. Moreover, Second Life serves as a metaphor to examine the social and economic consequences of online listening as it impacts traditional radio broadcasting and listening in general.

Toward a Definition of Sound Culture

Second Life calls attention to what we often ignore in our daily surroundings, and it permits us to contemplate on and interact with spaces not readily accessible to us. Second Life sound is borrowed from real spaces and crafted for a new world, as an audible import into simulated ambient and natural environments constructed within second spaces. What we under hear in the real becomes suddenly significant in these undefined, convergent points of human extension into a virtual space. How might we grasp the meaning of sound in our daily walk, when we cannot listen beyond our personal and mobile device playlists that serve as individual soundscapes? These personal soundtracks become overdubs to the living environment and mask the whisperings and bustle of real life.

Sound can provide keynote compositions to virtual soundscapes, or merely allow one to identify sound marks in a community, representing the real, imagined, or virtually experienced events in life. What we hear is encoded perceptually within the context of our experiences. In a sense, virtual worlds like Second Life can provide opportunities to understand those sounds that shape life—in all its settings, and bring significance to places and events. Certain natural sounds in our environment have become increasingly lost among a sea of noise, and are barely audible within the larger soundscapes of what we experience daily. Virtual spaces provide an interactive sonic space for past and present sounds, allowing one to recreate sound environments that once existed and archive sounds that surround us now across the world. Second Life can provide that cultural and educational immersive space to create and recreate soundscapes of small rural African villages or major metropolitan areas thousands of miles away from online users.

Unbound Sound: Sampling Digital Music and Culture, edited by Paul Miller (2008), speaks to the 21st century as an era where digital technologies invite us to hear the present through sonic snapshots of the past, when sampled and reminisced through music and spoken word archived in various media forms—film, television, radio and music. Sound is information, and provides context to our cultural histories. We interact physically with sounds continually; sound can be captured as physical and social expression through memory and media. In the later instance, sound provides a cultural memory, shaded with individual interpretation. Miller connects sound to urbanity; in such a way, sound is reshaped as the environment interacts with human culture.

R. Murray Schafer's 1977 *Tuning of the World* brought together sociologists, environmentalists and music composers to explore a new field of study: *acoustic ecology*. Bells, foghorns, clock towers and other sonic icons historically and culturally define our soundscapes today, as they did in the past. Schafer led a team of composers to create the *Vancouver Project* in the 1970s, and in this way he directed attention toward noise encroachment in the Canadian waterways. The recordings were crafted into compositions, springing from natural soundscapes. He then duplicated this project two decades later. Schafer's book and his Vancouver recordings have inspired a number of recordists and composers, from anthropologist Steven Feld to German composer Hildegard Westerkamp to wildlife recordist Bernie Krause. Schafer was instrumental to the launch of the World Forum of Acoustic Ecology, an international association that represents sound recordists and composers. Schafer reconceptualized the soundscapes—human and natural—that surround us on a daily basis as part of the composition of life.

He understands communities form geographically, socially, politically and in varied ways; so why not "along acoustic lines" (Schafer, 1994, p. 215). Adding, he states, "A consideration of the acoustic community might also include an investigation of how vital information from outside the community reaches the ears of the inhabitants and affects their daily routine" (Schafer, 1994. pp. 215–216). For instance Schafer (1994), drawing upon the work of Marshall McLuhan, points out that rural Africans dwell in "a world of sound—world loaded with direct personal significance for the hearer" (p. 11). Soundscapes are often unique and defined by the people who reside there and their specific environments: "Many of the most unique keynote sounds are produced by the materials available in different geographical locales: bamboo, stone, metal or wood, and sources of energy such as water and coal" (p. 59). Schafer points out even the sound of lighting, from candles to electricity, define a soundscape. The transition into modernity brought a redefinition to sonic spaces, culturally and physically.

Francisco Lopez (2005) points out that we cannot separate our "intrusion" as human beings from that of nature (p. 87): "Our bodies and imaginations engage in sonic transportation and reproduction more than the machines that we have intended for these purposes." Lopez continues, "And not only do different people listen differently, but the very temporality of our presence in a place is a form of editing...Our idea of the sonic reality, even our fantasy about it, is the sonic reality each one of us possesses" (p. 85). Concluding, he adds (p. 85), "What I'm defending is the transcendental dimension of the sound matter itself" (pp. 85–86.).

Emily Thompson (2002, pp. 1–2) in her historical study of sound during the industrialization of Europe indicates how daily soundscapes were reshaped through the sound of factories. Twentieth century musicians like Luigi Russolo, Edgard Varèse, and John Cage (Cox & Warner, 2005) responded to sonic challenges with new conceptions of music, and proposed a more practical definition to composition as being the organization of sounds. Henry David Thoreau provoked such discussions in America during the mid-1800s (and subsequently contributed to similar discussions that had been on-going for centuries in Asia), when he wrote two chapters in his classic *Walden* entitled *Sound* and *Solitude*. Motivated by his spiritual and intellectual roots, he noted the cultural and physical impact of his sonic refuge. It is from Thoreau that one can begin to understand the role of sound in life, and begin to carve out a personal Walden. Japanese cultural theorist Keiko Torigoe (1994) gives us a definition of sound culture that not only includes the concept of conscious sound making or listening; it is also about our perception of what we cannot or actually do not hear: "Sounds of the past, sounds of the future, sounds in our memories and dreams—all these kinds of sounds should be included."

Likewise, Tadahiko Imada (1994) explores Japanese sound culture from a variety of perspectives, and ultimately states there are "as many ways of listening as there are cultures and ears." He points out that the sound of the bloom of a lotus flower is below the frequency range of human hearing, yet people gather to listen to it in the early summer—and perhaps even imagine that they have heard it: "It seems the ancient Japanese people considered various sounds as the total 'scenery.'" One can become unaware of such interruptions in our soundscapes, as we become accustomed to certain sounds that define daily life (i.e., traffic, birds). Shin-ichiro Iwamiya (1998) conducted a questionnaire survey on sounds among foreigners living in Fukoka, Japan. American and European respondents described a noisy Japanese soundscape, whereas Asian participants, in contrast, heard a "silent" acoustic environment. The differences among the listeners were mostly likely contextualized within their personal memories of conversations and experiences. Schafer (2005) calls attention to the difficulty of separating sound from personal and cultural meaning and physical surroundings.

Technology Shapes Sound Culture

Virtual spaces are redefining how we hear sound apart from the real world. We sit at our computer desks and listen to the sounds of music and voices that emanate from our speakers. Of course, it is easier to immerse yourself into Second Life if you plug in your headphones. Nevertheless we exist and experience layers of sound, those that surround us in real life and those that we choose to focus on inside our computers. There is both a desire to experiment with sound in virtual spaces, as well as a comfort to hearing familiar sounds imported from real life, such as ocean or bird sounds. Much of virtual space is filled with music, mostly streamed from services or personal collections. Some composers create original music and sounds for their regions, and others are asked to create soundscapes for exhibits or landscapes in Second Life. Dizzy Banjo is one of the most well-known composers in Second Life. He has crafted regions to be enjoyed and experienced immersively, with sound becoming increasingly a significant design component within virtual spaces due to his efforts. He is the founder of Metamusic, an SL group that brings builders, designers, scripters, and musicians together to experiment with virtual sound. Banjo is a sound designer and composer in both second and real life. With an established career in radio, advertising and video game sound, he entered into Second Life in 2005. Six months later, he noticed that it needed a soundtrack: "He likens this to living through the 'silent era' of virtual worlds" (Soundtracks, 2009). The live music venues had sound from musicians, but the world lacked ambience, he observed, especially when businesses and organizations increasingly came aboard during his first year:

> ...they tended to be quiet, un-intentionally contemplative spaces. He took it upon himself to convince organizations that immersive sound was a great way to leverage the emotional potential of shared virtual experiences. (Soundtracks, 2009)

To create an immersive virtual environment, music and sound are necessary design considerations. Music evokes an emotional connection between people, similar to that of an exchange of ideas during a conversation (Storr, 1992). Music is encompassed within our daily spheres of sound. It is omnipresent and, like memory; it is both personal and culturally specific. Gary Ferrington points out "sound is critical to our daily existence in that it provides us with an acoustic reference to events around us—many of which are often out-of-sight" (Ferrington, 1994). As a cultural phenomenon, sound allows for elaboration to self and societal identities. As defined by theorists Breinig and Lösch (2002, p. 19), we can envision a continuum of identity positioning, socially and politically within "pluri-affiliations."

In this sense, sound is one part of our identity, and it is perhaps the most fluid part of culture. The soundscape is similar to the concept of landscape, and Schafer breaks it down into various components to clarify how individuals process sound culturally and physically. The keynote is the undertone of the soundscape: the unconscious sounds that compose the human listening environment. Soundmarks should be heard as sonic lighthouses (landmarks) that help to define a region, like a unique sound of a town church bell. Sound signals are heard as acoustic warnings like sirens and horns or perhaps the hourly chimes of the town square clock. Such sounds are rooted in cultural practices. Sound culture is not only the study of the material culture (Attali, 1985), but it reaches back to the very essence of communication. The soundscape serves the listener in conceptualizing the cultural sonic thread that unifies societies. In Second Life, the music composed for a region has the potential to exhibit the cultural soundscape of a people. When members want to experience Mexico, Japan, Brazil or any number of cultural representations inside Second Life, soundscapes can define or enhance the impression with authentic compositions of music and ambience. Residents sometimes share their cultural heritage, hanging flags and on occasion streaming national anthems. The intermingling of residents from around the world allows for exhibition of a variety of musical genres and ambient soundscapes throughout Second Life.

Schafer, and echoed by Steven Feld (1994), refers to the separation of sound from its source as "schizophonia" (Schafer, 1977, p. 90). The soundscape adds to the moment in Second Life. The landscape without the soundscape fails to capture the human spirit in motion. But sound without contextualization is open for interpretation. Francisco Lopez's compositions are conceptualized around what he calls "blind, profound and transcendental listening" in which the very act of recording diminishes the significance of the sound's origination (Lopez, 2005, p. 82; also see Lopez, 2007). That separation, increasingly evident today, is what encouraged Schafer to study sound for its cultural interpretation, and advocate sound preservation as a means of preserving tradition and identity. Second Life, at its best, serves as a means of cultural preservation and transmission.

Sound inadvertently becomes a product of the technology upon which it is located. The message is shaped by the medium (McLuhan, 1964). In the case of virtual worlds, these new spaces are redefining what and how we hear, apart from real-life experiences. Sound is reinterpreted within technology. Mark Slouka (2005) leans on the words of Thoreau to demonstrate the shifting of soundscapes:

> 'I love a wide margin to my life,' Thoreau remarked, quaintly, referring to the space—the silence—requisite for contemplation, or, more quaintly, the forming of self. (p. 42)

Slouka (2005, p. 42) contrasts Thoreau's world to that of the 21st century: "A century and a half later, aural text covers the psychic page, spills over; the margin is gone." He elaborates:

> Walking to work, we pass over rumbling pipes and humming cables, between airplane flight corridors and satellite broadcasts, through radio and television transmissions whose sounds, reconstituted from binary code, mix and mingle, overlap and clash, and everywhere drifts the aural refuse of our age. (Slouka, 2005, p. 42)

Slouka authored the book *War of the Worlds: Cyberspace and the High Tech Assault on Reality* in 1995, a Neil Postman-styled critique that aimed to dispel utopian promises associated with technology. Sound is both captive to the electronic media, and defined uniquely apart from it. Its physical vibrations are set in motion when sound is generated from primary sources. A person might exist in a variety of acoustic communities that intersect among gender or ethnicity, and real and virtual spaces. Phil Macnaghten (1998) describes sound as giving meaning to objects, animals and a plethora of phenomena. Macnaghten points out that "[s]oundscapes are part of the domestic life of most households, and increasingly of various 'private' public spaces (such as bars, clubs and cafés)" (1998, p. 131). Sound is shaped through cultural activities, whether they emanate from the real world or virtual worlds.

Soundscapes in Second Life

Nearly one year ago, some Walden enthusiasts created Thoreau's retreat on an impressive piece of virtual land in Second Life. The plot is now silent, and rows of tree are scattered across the landscape and along the water. I discovered no trace of what happened over that year, for I stumbled across this virtual Walden at the time of its sale. Thoreau lived at his secluded Concord plot for 2 years, 2 months, 2 days. Perhaps the makers of the Second Life Walden had merely retreated in a virtual space to contemplate on life. One does not have to seek a lifetime of "utopia" to understand its benefits and consequences. Thoreau's New England soundscape was rich with animal and nature sounds and the occasional train that crossed at the horizon of his landscape hidden by the woods. Second Life is a virtual social network platform that allows its millions of residents to create alternate identities, drawing from real and idealized life. Individuals often form memberships within community groups of like interests, perhaps gathering at a virtual nightclub, café, office, and beach—or in this case a re-creation of Walden. More than 50 members of The Dead Poet Society of Cetus Gallery District meet monthly in Second Life to converse for "an evening of poetry and literature readings in live voice." Founder Ethan Westland draws upon Thoreau's words in his SL profile:

> I went into the woods because I wanted to live deliberately. I wanted to live deep and suck out all the marrow of life...to put to rout all that was not life; and not, when I came to die, discover that I had not lived—from Walden. (Thoreau, 1854)

Westland makes the connection between real and second life, being that the imaginations of residents fuel the activities in virtual spaces. Members seek idealized spaces upon which to live, play, and learn, and they rely on the past and present for inspiration.

Second Life presents members with bountiful landscapes rich with color and textures, from ancient ruins to skyscrapers to circus tents. Beaches are accompanied by ocean sounds and seagulls. The chirping of birds is common to most natural soundscapes in this virtual playground. There are some unique soundscapes in sims like Durrat AL-Ghawwa, which was constructed to represent North Africa. A "call to prayer" is embedded within the soundscape that helps to define the culture of the region. The sound of a chapel bell in Moondance establishes a sense of community in the village atmosphere, and exemplifies the cultural and historical value of certain sounds in our daily life, apart from Second Life. Westerkamp states, "Sound is about place. Locality. It surrounds us like water. We are inside sound waves, they are touching us all the time...Sounds tell important truths about communities. They are the voices of societies" (*Living sounds*, n.d.). Sound informs us about communities of cultural practice:

> Christians ring church bells to gather a congregation at a certain time. They're goal-oriented. In India, being present in the moment is the most important thing. Ask people when temple bells ring and there's no clear answer. Hindu worshipers enter their temples and ring bells to wake up the gods. (*Living sounds*, n.d.)

In Second Life, Natural State is a region rich with sounds of farm animals and rural ambience, and as we listen there we begin to appreciate real-life sounds often taken for granted. Animal Island features a sonic diversity of wildlife. In many regions, it is common to hear water in its various forms through fountains, rivers and oceans. A number of Second Life stores have surfaced that sell ambient and environmental sounds, besides stores that cater to streaming music. But most soundscapes in SL lack the acoustic continuity and exacting detail expressed in real life. Imagine sound composer Hildegard Westerkamp (2003) importing her recordings of India into Second Life. The soundscape would become the composition (Westerkamp, 2002). Too often in SL, the music does not relate to the ambient sounds or distracts from the environment, indicating a need to consider community and social identity in every aspect of sound design.

Some exceptions, such as Midsomer Isle, demonstrate how a soundscape can draw listeners into a landscape, entangling the musical and non musical into a composition. Tourists also create music at one site on this isle. A number of instruments are set out for play and music making. Soundscapes designed to reflect real and imagined spaces could help us to understand how listeners are impacted by their sound environments. Such spaces could be designed better to reflect how we hear, as in the shifting of sound spheres and the immersive nature of ambient sound (drawing upon the compositions of Brian Eno and John Cage) (Cox & Warner, 2005). The use of voice in SL and how it interacts and integrates into soundscapes is another consideration. Many acoustic ecologists consider the human voice as both an interruption and extension of the environment. Beyond the elaborate soundscapes that provide a backdrop to the powerful landscapes in Second Life, sound can be heard as an extension of material culture, as members gravitate toward performance and social spaces such as clubs and bars.

Virtual Sound as Material Culture

Sony/BMG debuts and showcases real-life artists on Media Island in Second Life, and other companies are moving in-world. The radio industry has been a dominant player in determining what popular music will reach the public. This exposure is invaluable to the music industry. To some listeners, the convenience of tuning into a radio station and learning about a new artist is a significant part of a filtering process that assists them in choices amidst family and work priorities. When the radio industry launched the Jack FM format in 2000, it was based on the rise of the download culture. MP3 listeners had become accustomed to listening to their favorite songs randomly, and did not seem to mind when their favorite country song played after a classic metal tune. This sort of listening defies the programming logic long held dear to the radio industry. Jack FM offered a mix of music that tapped into the MP3 way of listening and attempted to make it a viable format. The concept developed, in part, as a result of an American Internet radio station created by Bob Perry, a radio station manager, who relocated to Connecticut to live near his wife's aging parents. The positioning statement for Jack FM sprung from the theme "playing what we want" and the format (or anti-format) was introduced to the listening public as "You Don't Know Jack" (*Big Sticks*, 2007). Some media headlines, like *Variety*, exclaimed that "radio's future sounds a lot like the past" (*Radio's Future*, 2007). Second Life is a digital culture that competes increasingly with real-life media and society and challenges the way we participate in media making and all forms of mediated entertainment. For the most part, Second Life provides an alternate space of communication and interaction within a mediated environment, one that nearly mirrors the real world in almost every way.

Second Life Radio

A promotional machinima opens with an African-American woman avatar introducing the streamed station Blacksoulrhythms.com. She is the station owner—Marjorie Dibou, an extremely articulate woman with a deep strong voice who deejays neo soul and rhythm & blues on Tuesday nights online and in-world. The film takes the viewer through the weekday lineup of on-air personalities and featured music during the week. The station looks and sounds professional—and the only difference is that the station personalities are also avatars. The online station has reached toward a new market—listeners inside Second Life. The station, originally known as Black Beats Radio, streams online and station personalities make regular appearances inside Second Life. The station plays a mix of jazz, urban adult contemporary, soul, and gospel, and is formatted with certain genres showcased on certain days. The station has made good use of Second Life, and has drawn its online listeners into virtual dance clubs and communities. Virtual listeners who experienced the station in-world now can take their favorite music into real-world homes and offices. Affiliated with the station is the SugarHill DJ School, which trains dj avatars through a three-part curriculum held in Second Life dealing with how to play music in virtual clubs and broadcast online.

In Second Life, traditional radio can be heard on the home receiver or online, as well in the car. Streamed stations, for the most part, are received through the computer. Listeners can download station podcasts, or create their own personal stations by downloading favorites onto MP3 players. A big part of the Second Life community is the use of radio and streaming of "live" music that is performed on a daily basis. Nearly every day, live music is performed in SL at a variety of venues, and many of these performers have developed their own fan bases. Representatives from RL and SL indie labels, as well as from major record labels, work from inside and organize events, anywhere from occasionally to routinely. *SL Live Radio* is one station devoted to the virtual indie musician, and it demonstrates the breadth and depth of music genres and artists available in-world. Some musicians double as nightclub disc jockeys; when they are not singing, they are spinning tunes. *SL Live Radio* was designed to create a home for these SL artists. *SL Live Radio* plays the music of SL artists exclusively, 24/7, and the station is available freely as a URL on an avatar's property or as a Web stream.

The owner and programmer is Radio Cher (Cher Harrington) who entered Second Life in July 2005. The station has its headquarters inside Second Life at the Zurich Opera House. She books musicians for SL Dublin and SL San Diego, and she uses her stream as a source for her own dj shows through SL. She posts an SL live music event calendar on her Web site, streamed out of the United States. The SL Live Radio (2010) site states that the station has 8,000 unique listeners per month, representing 80 countries. Furthermore, it states that 230 artists were represented on her station as of June 2009. The artists have agreed to share their music under the Creative Commons License. Since then, other stations have begun to specialize in formats exclusively airing Second Life musicians. Indie Spectrum Radio (2009) is a Second Life station committed to highlighting the original works of indie musicians at http://www.indiespectrum.com. The station was created by Second Life resident Fox Reinsch and made its debut November 2007. Reinsch, at one point, boasted of 120 SL artists and a playlist of 1,000 original songs on his site. As of 2010, the station continues to increase its artist base and audience.

Well-known SL radio personalities Trinity Serpentine and Nala Galatea had broadcast their radio show TriNala for five years, and that came to a close late August 2009. They had traveled across the grid to broadcast at various locations. Serpentine co-owns Radio Radio, an in-world radio station. Its founder, Madame Maracas, remains on-air at the station. Serpentine began SL at a time that allowed her to witness the early days of streaming in SL. She met the creators of Radio SLive, and she thought, "Oh my God, that would be a perfect fit for me because I love music and music is in my blood and my father was a dj on a radio station" (Fairchild, 2009). Galatea was already on-air at SLive in 2004, having teamed up with djs Cori Sunshine and Phinz Phaeton after being on SL for only 2 weeks. Serpentine continued, "I thought this would be a way for me to shine in SL—this would be my niche" (Fairchild, 2009).

Her incessant begging landed her a radio gig four months later. She rose quickly in popularity. She would also conduct the first live audio interview with Philip Linden. Soon after she met Galatea, they would become co-hosts and RL/SL partners, and eventually co-owners of Radio Radio. In the Radio Radio's Web personality profiles, Galatea is described as the "brains behind the board and the Howard Stern to Trin's Robin Quiver" (*Radio Radio*, 2009). Serpentine in an interview with Phaylen Fairchild explained how their show started getting more and more listeners, and how people brought newbies to the sim from where they would broadcast live.

The duo did live radio remotes and dj marathons that made headlines across the Metaverse. Radio Radio did the very first Relay for Life fundraiser in Second Life. Their station Radio Radio is one of the longest running in SL. Fairchild (2009) applauded Serpentine's accomplishments in SL, with regards to her career and long-standing relationship with her co-host, commenting specifically on the "transformative" nature of the virtual world, and observing that media does not sufficiently "focus on the good things that do happen." Galatea's station profile adds, "In-world she shares a home in Tehama with her wife Trinity. In her RL she is also partnered with Trinity, living happily with their two cats in a beachside town of San Diego" (*Radio, Radio*, 2009). The women have managed to create a radio audience in Second Life, and successfully operate a full-time radio station, complete with a full roster of radio personalities. Perhaps there are some lessons here for Internet broadcasters seeking new opportunities or audiences. Kurt Hanson (2007), in his column for *RAIN: Radio and Internet Newsletter*, pointed out Internet radio stations must consider the best way to use the Web that is unique from traditional AM/FM and satellite broadcasters:

> Webcasters who take advantage of the characteristics of the new medium—e.g., LAUNCHcast, Pandora, etc.—are, I believe, going to be the ones that see the greatest success in this medium...the Internet efforts of traditional radio broadcasters (AM/FM broadcast groups, satellite radio companies, etc.) are not playing in that game. (Hanson, 2007)

Second Life certainly fits the call for unique broadcast platforms. The Radio Ink Convergence conference has become one way to bring traditional and new media broadcasters into the same venue to discuss the future of radio, as it relates to streaming, blogging, podcasting, social networking, mobilecasting and more familiar forms of transmission (*Radio Ink*, 2007). Second Life has tapped into a virtual audience which transitions in and out of the real world.

Live Music Venues

In Second Life, several pubs and beer gardens attract 10 to 40 members to hang around and listen to live music on any night, particularly mid-week and weekends. Some musicians attract larger audiences than others, similar to the real world. Second Life has countless live music venues and dance clubs. Some members are loyal to certain venues, and others are groupies following around their favorite musicians throughout Second Life. The ambience varies among the pubs, and some have more charm and local color than others. Many spaces are designed as outdoor beer gardens, so avatars can pop in and out of the venue. Some members dance the evening away with significant others. Bars offer virtual alcohol drinks, from martinis to beer. Some venues are designed elegantly, while others are rustic. Ambient sound, noises, music, and voice interplay within virtual landscapes to convey emotions that draw upon what Jonathan Sterne would refer to as our audible past (Sterne, 2003). Birds can often be heard tweeting away in the background when music dips, and lapping sounds are common to venues near waterways.

Musicians are streamed from their personal residences into Second Life, and they interact with audiences in avatar form, such as follows:

> [12:32] Fellatione Aabye: when the living is easy
> [12:32] Spam Burger: it's getting warm now !
> [12:32] Sue Cisse: awww sooo nice Josie
> [12:32] Glitz Greybeard: love this song
> [12:32] Fellatione Aabye: awesome !!!!
> [12:34] Glitz Greybeard: Bravo (SPAM's Club, 2009).

Among her live music performances, Josie Anderton sings on Tuesdays at SPAM's Club at the Cajun Riviera. The text chat above is from her public performance on July 7, 2009, noon Pacific Standard Time (SL Time). SPAM's is a quaint, rustic venue that seems to attract a "good" crowd. The owner is Spam Burger. No doubt, he is a fan of Josie's. Anderton could be described as a torch singer. Her specialty is romantic ballads, and her voice is well suited for the sultry selections she sings. The audience responds sometimes by singing along:

> [12:40] Fellatione Aabye: rollin on the river, rollin on the river, rollin on the river

> [12:41] Spam Burger: mighty Mississippi, very good josie
> [12:42] Fellatione Aabye: Welcome Mattchoo to SPAM'S Club at Cajun Riviera!
> [Portcia Hynes bobs her head].
> [12:42] Spam Burger: hi matt, welcome to the tuesday party. (Anderton, 2009)

Slender, tall and curvaceous, her avatar stage presence is striking. Her long brunette hair definitely adds to her charm. Her speaking voice, with an alluring British accent, is as smooth as her singing. But off stage, she is humble about her talent. "I never thought I could sing," she admits (Anderton, 2009). Her singing roots can be traced back to her dabbling in amateur dramatics, engaging in "some acting, some singing in a company, singing on stage but in the back where no one would notice me, you know. But that was a few years ago" and that was in real life, she notes (Anderton, 2009). She had no intention of singing on stage, but that all changed when she entered Second Life:

> I came into SL and I got to know someone called BubbaC John. You have to go see him if you get the chance. He does Elvis...he's so much fun (laughs). His show is very very popular. I got to be friends with Bubba, and there's somebody else in SL, Kev Tyson, who I call my SL brother. And he's very good friends with Bubba as well. Kev has a habit of sending me songs that he sung, and so one day, I was messing around and said hey Kev I sang "Fever." I will send you one. So Kev went and sent it to Bubba. And next thing, Bubba's got me up on stage, his show...He kept going on with me, "I ought to sing, I ought to sing," and I kept going no, no, no. I can't sing. But then he got me to do a couple of duets with him. (Anderton, 2009)

She continued, "I do a couple of Ann Margaret songs with Bubba, which is great fun. We do them in the show sometimes if I'm there. So Bubba is always encouraging me saying, 'you should sing'" (Anderton, 2009). When she met Raven Kondor, another singer in SL, he heard her duets in SL and wanted her to perform a duet with him, 'You Don't Bring Me Flowers.' "And I did that, and it was really lovely, and even I thought wow that's really nice you know. So then I started looking into it, like perhaps I could do this, really," she explained (Anderton, 2009). "I just put a song list together, and practiced a bit. And Kandi Cornell at Blue Orchid Live asked me to sing regularly there, and that's how I started off really" (Anderton, 2009).

Like most SL artists, she had some streaming problems, "lag" on her stream. Finding a professional stream is one of the challenges that many novice in-world singers experience when performing live at various venues. Actually streaming problems haunt the long-timers as well, especially when crowds max out in a venue. Their stream must not only sound good to them, but to the crowd that shows up to hear them. Anderton recalls, in jest, "I did go through a stage, a habit of emptying clubs...I'd get there and I'd start. And all the people would just poof away. I couldn't figure out why" (Anderton, 2009). One day when she recorded her performance, she realized that her stream sounded "awful," she notes: "I didn't realize it was happening. I couldn't figure out why people were just leaving when I started. I had a really bad night one night when I had this gig in this club and it was packed when I got there. And I thought this was gonna be good and they were all gone within the first 10 minutes (laugh). So there you go" (Anderton, 2009).

For many of the more than 100 musicians performing regularly in Second Life, there is always the question of how well am I doing, am I performing in a way that appeals to my audience. Anderton (2009) admits, "I'm still not too sure about me singing but people seem to like it. People keep booking me. So I will keep doing it; that's how I get my money here at the minute." Singers in SL can earn on the average 3,500 Lindens and upward to several thousand for an hour long engagement. Some performers pack the venues, and earn top dollar.

Anderton loves watching the audience, and for her, that is what it is all about. She notes people's reactions through text chat. Voice chat is forbidden at most live performances. The text chat sometimes reflects the mood of the audience or the style of the performer. For Anderton, she enjoys a healthy chat among the attendees:

> Oh I love it. It's nice, you see people coming in. I've got my scanner going so I can see people come, and I say hi to them. And I like it when there's some chat going and people are having fun and trying to put you off and stuff like that, nicely...The problem is you can see the chat coming up on the screen. People are having fun and joke between themselves, especially if it's friends. So you're reading this chat that's coming on and then you forget where you are in the song. So I call it a Josie oops moment. (laugh)...I think people get quite used to that though. (Anderton, 2009).

As in real life, the spontaneity at live concerts is what energizes the audience and performers. Typical to Second Life live events, she interacts with the crowd through voice, and it is really this sort of interaction that motivates her to perform in-world. Listeners send her instant messages for requests, as with most SL performers: "People ask for songs for their boyfriend or their girlfriend, and so I have quite a lot of romantic songs; so that goes down quite well" (Anderton, 2009). The idea of real-world fame seems not as important to SL performers, as just connecting with an audience, "It's just fun. You're not going to find me out there on Pop Idol or whatever you know. No way," Anderton (2009) explains, laughing:

> ...I have a full-time real-life job so I've no aspirations about becoming a diva or anything like that. No I'm just happy to do a few gigs here in Second Life. It earns me enough Lindens to keep going...I have not really pushed for it. It's just something I do because I enjoy it. Same as my photographs; I like to take pictures. But I just do them for fun because I enjoy them.

Second Life, she explains, provides a "good platform for people to get some exposure. I think we are sort of encompassed in our little world." Anderton's photography in Second Life is evidence that her talent extends beyond her singing. Indeed she enjoys the artistic community of Second Life, bringing together photographers, artists, musicians, machinima makers and others into a small world of creativity. She has dabbled in all those areas, and Second Life has been the vehicle to let her do so:

> We forget our real world outside sometimes. But what goes on in Second Life does reach out into real life like the music streams and everything. So I suppose if an artist is really serious, they can get a lot of exposure here. So I think it can only be good. But you gotta put the work in it; it's a lot of work, there's a lot of organization and software is not cheap. I use streaming, and I needed a little bit of equipment, and then there's the music. And I mean, I don't play musical instruments. I've been to some concerts where people accompany themselves on guitar or whatever. I just use karaoke backing tracks. (Anderton, 2009)

Second Life is also a "great platform for listening to live music. I just love it. In an evening, I can see or listen to rock, classical music, or country, singers of anything; there's anything here, and there's some really talented people with really good music," she explains. "It's not all singing. There's somebody called Joquinn who plays beautiful guitar. It's just awesome. I've seen some amazing performers here in Second Life. The live music I just love it" (Anderton, 2009). Like many other non SL listeners, Anderton's parents can hear her play on Shoutcast. She explains, "I've got a Shoutcast stream, and my parents listen in on it sometimes...they will listen to me so they can hear me singing in Second Life. And I forget they are listening, and they ring me up afterwards, saying that sounded really good—and I will think 'God' I was just singing (laugh)" (Anderton, 2009).

Josie Anderton's experiences are comparable to most SL performers. Second Life has created a space for a collective of musicians to perform and support one another. They attend each other's performances and share the stage, inviting other singers to sing or play along with them. The crowds go wild when their favorite performers come together on stage. There is something unique about the music community in Second Life. Anderton (2009) concurs, by saying, "Friends and musicians I got to know in Second Life have been instrumental in helping me get settled technically...It's the people that I've gotten to know, the friends that I have gotten to know, that I have made in SL, that have helped me get started." That spirit of encouragement is common among Second Life performers. Anderton (2009) concludes, "I'd be willing to help anyone if anybody else wanted to start singing in SL. I'd just do what I can do to help them because I have had so much help. That's the sort of person I am anyway. I think we should, that's what we're here for to help each other. The place is big enough for all of us."

Streamed Radio in Second Life

In Second Life, as in the real world, "Internet Radio breaks down geographic boundaries and lowers the barrier for audio broadcasting. The listener now has access to a huge growing number of radio stations" (Krishnan & Chang, 2000). Joseph Catone (2006) notes, "By 2020, *eMarketer* estimates that Internet radio will have 180 million listeners and generate $19.7 billion in ad revenue." Although localization did not surface as a significant factor in the success of Internet radio, listeners gravitate toward programs that connect them to their towns or regions. The idea of geographic identity is becoming important to the image of a radio stream. Listeners sometimes seek geographic commonalities with stations located in places they live, once lived or visited. International members are attracted to clubs that symbolize urban areas in America. Boystown and I-Party are two popular Internet radio stations based out of Chicago. Both these stations are fairly popular in Second Life.

I-Party proudly exclaims its city of origin at the top of the hour and through drop-in sweepers. The stations appeal to those who have lived in Chicago, live there now, or perhaps are fascinated with being part of city life. Streamed stations are claiming geographic identities, and others form personalities based on themes. The virtual nightclub Chicagoland in Second Life draws hundreds of visitors per week. Two of the main streams are Boystown and I-Party. Image liners periodically announce the station's programming originates from Chicago. The manager arranges for live musicians to come and sing at the club. Otherwise, avatars dance to club music provided by streamed radio stations.

A juke box in the club initially was the "radio" station server for about 20 stations. Now, an electronic radio board, similar to a scoreboard, replaces that jukebox. A variety of stations can be played at a moment's notice, with digital readouts of artists and song titles displayed. Throughout the day, you might find 20 to 30 avatars from Australia, England, Canada, United States, Japan, Brazil, or anywhere else, connected into SL, dropping by to listen and dance, depending on what is going on at the club.

Martini in the Morning

A popular streamed program is Martini in the Morning, and actually it is part of a larger Web station that repackages oldies, or standards, by recreating the mood of an era gone by. The announcer is smooth in his delivery, and is in tune with his listeners' passion for this genre of music, which is becoming difficult to find across terrestrial airwaves. Brad Chambers is the host of the 5-hour radio program. The streamed station is syndicated by Standard Media Corporation, and was "developed primarily as an HD Radio side channel option for large market stations" (Stark, 2009). Chambers, company founder, notes that the idea was to broadcast the morning show on both coasts with "live personalities throughout the day [in] what he describes as 'a huge national marketing campaign.'" Chambers is heard regularly at Second Life venues across his in-world stream, and makes guest appearances at all the "rat pack" clubs, the Frank Sinatra-type of virtual nightclubs. The format is comprised of original standards and covers, featuring *Witchcraft* from Sinatra to a version by Robert Palmer, and maybe some Steve and Eydie and Marvin Gaye are added into the mix (Stark, 2009). Chambers explains, "conventional wisdom suggests that adult standards is a format that traditionally appeals to 65-plus listeners" (Stark, 2009). The music, however, "appeals to the full spectrum of baby boomers and younger listeners thanks to some hip, edgier artists who are rediscovering and popularizing this music" (Stark, 2009). The music at times can draw 30 to 40 people into a Second Life club, when Chambers hosts a live show in-world. Clubs in SL often become "laggy" when they exceed that number.

SL radio stations play the popular icons and newly rising stars on streamed stations that play in-world and on the Web. In SL, there is growing audience for movies, TV programs and music that is either produced in-world, or is broadcast in this virtual space. Some enjoy experiencing these mediated activities with their SL friends, partners, and colleagues. There is this sense of engagement with others and one's avatar, as one watches her "virtual double" view in-world televised programs or movies. SL newspapers report on the art, music, and media entertainment. Music in Second Life generates media content and publicity, from interview shows to live performances recorded for playback.

Conclusion

We interpret certain sounds and soundscapes within virtual spaces, as we would in real life. Sound is interwoven into the textual and visual messages created in Second Life. McLuhan (2005, p. 68) posits, "There are no boundaries to sound. We hear from all directions at once. But the balance between inner and outer experience can be precise." McLuhan wrote that passage in the late 1970s, before hearing was extended into virtual space. The inner space of Second Life can be an import of reality, or a new sound culture can be exported into real life. Digital media represents a new threshold and challenge for the study of sound as a marker in expressing cultural identity. Schafer, for instance, would likely call attention to those cultural practices and natural spaces under threat of extinction in real life. Might Second Life and other virtual spaces archive the real world? Aurality contributes a powerful emotive when drawing upon our memories and surroundings, and how we define what we hear is a product of our social and physical environment—and increasingly virtual environment.

References

Anderton, J. (2009, July 7). Interview, personal communication with author. Second Life.

Attali, J. (1985). *Noise. The political economy of music*, Minneapolis: University of Minnesota Press.

Big Sticks Broadcasting. (2007, December 1). Web site. Accessed April 8, 2009, from http://www.bigsticksbroadcasting.com/press.htm/

Breinig, H., & Lösch, K. (2002). Introduction: Difference and transdifference. In H. Breinig, J. Gebhardt, & K. Lösch, (Eds.), Multiculturalism in contemporary societies. *Perspectives on difference and transdifference* (pp. 11–36). Erlangen: Universitätsbund.

Catone, J. (2006, August 17). Update on the state of the internet radio. Read Write Web. Accessed April 8, 2009, from http://www.readwriteweb.com/archives/update_on_the_state_ of_net_radio.php/

Cox, C., & Warner, D. (Eds.) (2005). *Audio culture. Readings in modern music.* New York: Continuum.

Fairchild, P. (2009, March 17). Grabbing with Robustus Hax and Trinity Serpentine. Interview. Podcast. Second Life: Phaylen Fairchild Productions. Accessed August 18, 2009, from http://phaylen.com/?p=56/

Feld, S. (1994). From schizophrenia to schismogenesis: On the discourses and commodification practices of 'world music' and 'world beat.' In C. Keil & S. Feld (Eds.), *Music grooves: Essays and dialogues* (pp. 257–289). Chicago: University of Chicago Press.

Ferrington, G. (1994). Kids, noise and orchestrating the soundscape. *Techtrends*, *39*(1). Accessed April 25, 2005, from http://interact.uoregon.edu/medialit/openear/ readings/ferrington/kidsnoise.html/

Hanson, K. (2007, December 12). Oft-ignored fad: Internet radio is a different medium. Kurt's Blog, *RAIN*; *Radio Audio Internet Newsletter*. Accessed April 8, 2009, from http://textpattern.kurthanson.com/kurtsblog/130/often-ignored-fact-internet-radio-is-a-different-medium.

Indie Spectrum Radio. (2009). Web site. Accessed April 6, 2009; March 29, 2010, from http://www.indiespectrum.com.

Imada, T. (1994). The Japanese sound culture. *The Soundscape Newsletter*, *9* (September). Eugene, Oregon: World Forum for Acoustic Ecology, University of Oregon.

Iwamiya, S. (1998, June 26). Features of Japanese soundscape recognized by foreigners: A questionnaire survey on sounds for the foreigners living in Fukuoka. Acoustical Society of America, ICA/ASA Lay Language Papers, Seattle, Washington.

James, V. (2009, July). Performer showcase: Maxmillion Kleene. *Rez Libris*. Accessed July 8, 2009, from http://rezlibris.com/

Krishnan, V., & Chang, S. G. (2000). Customized internet radio. Hewlett-Packard Laboratories. Presented at the 9th International World Wide Web Conference, Ninth International World Web Conference, WWW9, www9, Amsterdam, May 15–19, 2000. Accessed April 8, 2009, from http://www9.org/w9cdrom/353/353.html/

Living Sounds. (n.d.). Interview with Hildegard Westerkamp. The Paula Gordon Show. Accessed June 6, 2007, from http://paulagordon.com/shows/westerkamp/

Lopez, F. (2005). Profound listening and environmental sound matter. In C. Cox & D. Warner (Eds.), *Audio culture. Readings in modern music* (pp. 82–87). New York: Continuum.

——. 2007). Web site. Accessed November 15, 2007, from http://www.franciscolopez.net/

Macnaghten, P. (1998). *Contested natures*. Beverly Hills, CA: Sage.

McLuhan, M. (1964). *Understanding media: The extensions of man*. Cambridge, MA: MIT Press.

—— (2005). Visual and acoustic space. In C. Cox & D. Warner, (Eds), *Audio culture. Readings in modern music* (pp. 67–72). New York: Continuum.

Miller, P. (Ed.) (2008). *Unbound sound: Sampling digital music and culture*. Cambridge, MA: MIT Press.

Postman, N. (1986). *Amusing ourselves to death*. New York: Viking Penguin.

Radio Ink. (2007). Convergence '08 Conference, San Jose, CA. Accessed December 20, 2007, from http://www.radioink.com/convergence.

Radio Radio (2009). Web site. Accessed August 20, 2009, from http://radioradiosl.com/

Radio's future sounds a lot like the past. (2005, August 14). *Variety*. Accessed April 8, 2009, from http://www.bigsticksbroadcasting.com/press.htm/

Schafer, R. M. (2005). The music of the environment. In C. Cox & D. Warner (Eds.), *Audio culture: Readings in modern music* (pp. 29–39). New York: Continuum.

——. (1977). *The tuning of the world*. Toronto: McClelland & Stewart. Reprinted 1994, Destiny Books.

——. (1994). *Our sonic environment and the soundscape. The tuning of the world*. Rochester, NY: Destiny.

SL Live Radio. (2010). Web site. Accessed March 29, 2010, from http://www.myspace.com/radiocher; http://www.slliveradio.com/; http://www.readwriteweb.com/archives/update_on_the_state_ of_net_radio.php/

Slouka, M. (2005). Listening for silence: Notes on the aural Life. In C. Cox & D. Warner, (Eds), *Audio culture. Readings in modern music* (pp. 40–46). New York: Continuum.

SPAM'S Club. (2009, July 7). Text chat. Cajun Riviera, Second Life.

Soundtracks to our virtual lives. Showcase Blog: Music. Linden Lab. Accessed June 29, 2009, from http://secondlife.com/showcase/blog.php?blog_category=5/

Stark, P. (2009). Martinis for breakfast? New HD format targets boomers with 'contemporary standards.' Accessed April 8, 2009, from http://www.radio-info.com/

Sterne, J. (2003). *The audible past. Cultural origins of sound reproduction*. Durham, NC: Duke University Press.

Storr, A. (1992). *Music and the mind*. London: Harper Collins.

Thompson, E. (2002). *The soundscape of modernity. Architectural acoustics and the culture of listening in America, 1900–1933*. Cambridge, MA: Massachusetts Institute of Technology Press.

Thoreau, H. D. (1854). *Thoreau reader*. Electronic version. Accessed May 30, 2005 from http://eserver.org/thoreau/walden00.html (publ. *Walden*, 1854).

Torigoe, K. (1994). Nerima silent places. *The Soundscape Newsletter*, No. 9, September. Eugene, Oregon: World Forum for Acoustic Ecology, University of Oregon.

Westerkamp, H. (2003). *Into India. Sound Path*. (independently released).

——. (2002). Linking soundscape composition and acoustic ecology. *Organised Sound, an International Journal of Music and Technology*, 7(1). Accessed December 21, from http://www.sfu.ca/~westerka/writings.html

CHAPTER NINE

My Avatar Is Watching Television: Media Makers and Audiences

> Virtual Filmmaking makes many leaps and bounds over real-life filmmaking...It doesn't usually require large crews, manual labor, insurance, permits, equipment, vehicles, craft services, or other headaches that tend to be production obstacles. The world is at one's fingertips...The art of storytelling has never been so accessible.
>
> —Ariella Languish (2008)

Carlobodia Popstar kicks back in his recliner, and clicks on his high-definition 60-inch wall television to catch his favorite comedy show weekly on the Treet TV network. He sinks deeply into his soft brushed leather chair, dims the environmental settings, and laughs at the in-world antics of the host on tonight's show. His virtual service features comedy, fashion, politics, and a variety of themed programs that air inside Second Life throughout the day in avatars' apartments, condos and homes. Television is popular in Second Life, as it is in real life. Dancing and music is relevant to the interests of residents, for socializing is one of the primary goals of SL residents. But television serves as a private getaway, to fill downtime in SL, to share what is going on across the grid, and to allow friends to watch similar shows together.

In essence, avatars are watching television programs on their virtual wide screens, and even subscribe to in-world cable services with original programming. It sounds a bit odd, to say the least, but many SL residents enjoy watching television in avatar form, either as a solitary or social activity. For other avatars, a Friday night of visual entertainment might be hanging out with some friends at any one of the several virtual drive-ins or movie theaters on Second Life to catch some classic or fairly new motion picture releases. In 2007, Bruce Willis' summer release of *Live Free Die Hard* was promoted inside Second Life at the Silverscreens region. Stuck in traffic, he was late for his virtual appointment, but all went well when he showed online and was greeted by a sim full of avatar fans:

> Everyone cheered and shouted as the original John McClaine joined us in the virtual flesh and by telephone. An exciting preview...was broadcast on several of Silverscreens' huge theater screens. Bruce Willis' avatar looked great as the questions about his movie and his thoughts of Second Life started rolling in. (Neal, 2007)

Cable and network television, Hollywood movie makers, and the video rental industry are making the connection between real and virtual spaces, increasingly, as an effort to market their content and expand their audience base, with Home Box Office (HBO) and CBS networks taking the lead in airing programming that crosses over between worlds. What is intriguing, as well, is the new breed of media makers that are creating original programs or films in SL. Treet TV, which as of summer 2009 encompasses Second Life Cable Network (SLCN), broadcasts within Second Life a variety of topical shows, from fashion to music to architecture. Other filmmakers can be located among The Second Life Machinima Artist Guild, whose members' works offer a rare look inside the virtual life of an avatar.

Virtual vs. Traditional TV Viewership

Virtual television is an extension of mainstream television broadcasting in many aspects, but its content is shaped less by network programming and more by an interest in creating locally originated content. Some Second Life programming has included virtual renditions of *Big Brother* and reality-based shows that have been popular on mainstream television. But these have been independent efforts at bringing reality TV into a virtual world. The shows created a lot of initial buzz, particularly among contestants, but overall they have not evolved into regular offerings on SL TV. Inadvertently, Second Life media producers entice residents to carry their RL viewing habits into the virtual spaces. One begins to note that Second Life residents are engaged with watching television in their digital homes and other landings inside this imagined living space, while sitting in front of their LCD computer monitors in real life (perhaps with a nearby HDTV television turned on in the background). The consumer is always within the confines of a larger corporate structure of the Linden Lab, yet the programming seems to be thriving with few restrictions, if any.

Second Life's television offerings, network and independent, have increased substantially over the last few years. The in-world group Second Life Television (SLTV) has nearly 70 members who are engaged in TV production and programming. By the time that the virtual world celebrated its 4th year anniversary, Australia's ABC and UK's SkyNews had increased their SL schedules, as have a number of U.S. programmers since then. Second Life is advertised on-line as "a 3D online digital world imagined and created by its residents." SL users, internationally, are becoming notable media makers, and HBO featured the first documentary produced inside this digital community in 2008. HBO purchased a documentary that was filmed by a real Hollywood producer, Douglas Gayeton; in fact his entire series *Molotov Alva and His Search for the Creator* was produced in-world as machinima. The show was broadcast on cable, and is available online via Cinemax's Web site. As a side note, its producers, talent, and overall team appear to be mainly comprised of men, after a review of the credits. In Second Life, however, women producers are as common as male media makers. Regardless of gender, relevant content that taps into the experiences of virtual viewers determines in-world success among media makers and their audiences.

CBS's *CSI: New York* brought TV viewers in-world on Wednesday, October 24, 2007, to help solve a crime by encouraging them to log onto its SL virtual forensics lab and to the crime scene in a mock build of New York City. The show *Down the Rabbit Hole* would end with a cliff-hanger, inviting its audience to figure "who did it" by solving the mystery in Second Life. Throughout the show, Second Life avatars (70–80% more females than males) engaged in the process of crime-solving while watching the show. A few days later on October 27, 2007, NBC's *The Office* featured Second Life through the antics of one of its characters who explored the virtual world.

News networks are increasingly represented within Second Life, and they compete with independent news organizations that exist only within this digital landscape. However, that will be discussed in another chapter dedicated to in-world news media. In this chapter, emerging digital media makers are presented within the context of a virtual media landscape that originates from many of their experiences as producers and consumers of traditional broadcast media. In contrast to mainstream network programming in RL, much of the SL programming is locally originated. In contrast, mainstream television programs or movies can be purchased through in-world video stores or watched through YouTube television sets inside SL homes. YouTube has a growing archive of out-of-circulation television shows as well as relatively new ones that can be streamed into one's TV set. Second Life viewers represent a world-wide audience, but much of the content is presented from a Eurocentric perspective.

Birth of Treet TV

The Second Life Cable Network emerged in 1997, created by Wiz Nordberg, and gradually began to offer an increased fare of in-world programming to Second Life residents with televisions. The programming was a mix of entertainment, business and public affairs genres, with the main thrust to keep residents tapped into the local virtual world scene. Many of the programs are studio-based interview shows, with some location shoots for specials or events. In July 2009, SLCN launched Treet TV that promises higher quality in production quality and content. Its Web site reads, "Treet is the world's first virtual TV network, bringing virtual world residents entertaining shows *like*

Tonight Live with Paisley Beebe, *Metanomics*, *Global Online Hockey* and *Giant Snail Races*" (Treet TV, 2009). The network also produces a broad spectrum of programs like "*Best Practices in Education Series*, and even press events for the *Transformers* and *Die Hard* film launches" (Treet TV, 2009). Programs are taped live, and then posted on the Web, and published as podcasts on iTunes. Programming is available in-world and on the Internet. Newer Second Life televisions are set up to easily play You Tube programming as well. Free TVs are provided by Treet, and several SL vendors have made cable programming available on their television sets. For those with television sets, they simply add the media URL, http://streams.treet.tv/live.mov. That site will showcase the programs that are taped live and played through on a daily basis.

Treet TV network, as did SLCN, offers several channels as well that focus on shopping, music, business, lifestyle, sports, community, and a TV guide. Two educational streams are also included: Metanomics and The International Society of Technology in Education (ISTE). As for individual programs, the list is expanding quite rapidly. One of them is aptly appropriate to SL, given that when residents buy land they often begin with a blank slate onto which they must create their builds. One such show that focuses on the building aspect of SL is *Designing Worlds: Better World*, highlighting in-world designs, from skyscrapers and estates to tropical islands. Of course, fashion is big in Second Life, and making a fashion statement seems a priority for both consumers and designers so as to fit into various social cliques. *Fabulous Fashion* offers a peek into some of the latest designs and designers. One week this show featured "some of the cutest darn skulls & blood dress you can imagine" (Treet TV, 2009). Another show featured the fashion and lifestyle magazine, *SXY2ND*, and a show was dedicated to Japanese and Asian designers. Another program offered a challenge among 35 fashion designers. Musicians in Second Life provide significant content for broadcast programs in-world. *Music Art on the Isle* features art, video and live music performance. Another show that features live music performances and interviews in SL is *Pop Vox*. *Music Academy* features background notes on performances in-world from the standpoint of the composers. Other programs spotlight authors, with *Media Ecology*, for example, directed at a specific scholarly community. One show featured Dr. Robert K. Logan, media ecologist and author of *Understanding New Media: Extensions of Marshall McLuhan*. Another one of its episodes revolved around an interview with Eric McLuhan, media ecologist and author, who brought insight into his father's early work in media studies. *Intel Tech Talk* is one of the computer program offerings, and it specifically deals with philosophy and practice in computer technology. *Cisco TechChat* is a program looking at security, environmental and broader issues related to computers in the virtual and real world.

Interestingly, sports have become a significant component of SL entertainment, and some cable programs along that line are popular among enthusiasts: *Dirtfield Races*, *Giant Snail Races*, *GOHA Hockey*, *TIM Cup Soccer*, and *SLSB Simboarding*. Another series aired on Treet TV has been *On Location*, which is much broader in scope and features interviews with journalists and movers and shakers of virtual worlds. *On Location* has dealt with discussions on SL and RL issues in medicine, politics and virtual economies, and actually links the worlds together with intelligent dialogue among the experts. One program that has been acclaimed in Second Life (and RL) is *The 1st Question*, a quiz show written, produced and hosted by Pooky Amsterdam of Pooky Media. It is taped in front of a live audience, and is the premiere game show featured on SL television. Machinima, which will be discussed later, is the art of filmmaking in virtual worlds. Most of these films are under 5 minutes, and many are featured on Blip.TV or at machinima screenings and award ceremonies. Typically, they are screened as SL/RL exhibitions or uploaded to various Web services for public viewing.

Mediated Discussion in Second Spaces

Given the demographics of SL users, it is not surprising that a number of women have found their way into virtual spaces as media writers and producers. Many women appear to be involved in the print media, writing for the local virtual newspapers. Many Treet producers actually have a larger purpose in mind than the production of weekly programs, and their shows typically support their SL agenda or mission. Cybergrrl Oh's Treet TV/SLCN program *Real Biz*, for example, has grown into a community for its viewers. Two of the notable producers/hosts are Cybergrrl and Paisley Beebe, and both women are worthy of in-depth discussion. It appears that women have quite a strong role in SL TV production, in terms of traditional content. From the outset, SLCN served as a creative venue for women as guests and hosts; its content mainly featured fashion, music, charitable causes, education, and entertainment.

Athena Isle: Cybergrrl Oh's Real Biz Community

A significant amount of media content is devoted to gossip and entertainment in SL, but that is not always the case; one site offers airtime to non-profit groups and businesses within SL, and connects women professionally and personally to one another. Consider the case of Athena Isle—"a Second Life community for writers, entrepreneurs, community builders, artists, women and moms. We hold weekly discussions with experts and authors and monthly gallery openings, parties and dances. We feature women's art in Athena Gallery and women's creations in Athena Wares" (Cybergrrl, 2008). This media group extends its reach to RL, with a blog outside of the virtual world connecting both realities. Even when you are not inside SL, you can catch the latest business buzz from Cybergrrl Oh, a self-described "seasoned business reporter in both her First Life and Second Life" (Cybergrrl, 2008): "I'm the host of REAL BIZ in SL. In real life, I'm a writer, blogger, and a freelance radio and TV producer. In Second Life, I can fly."

Cybergrrl is producer and host of *Real Biz* on Treet TV. The live weekly program spotlights companies and non-profit organizations, with a screen hit of more than 10,000. One can view the show live on the Web, but it is also archived and available in SL and on iTunes. Among the more popular programming choices is *New Biz*, especially among women; it has featured in-world businesses and non-profit events or organizations, such as Virtual Activism's awareness campaign to elevate focus on global issues and NGOs (non-governmental organizations) and groups like the South Texas Celtic Music Association that aids children in Northern Ireland. Another topic involved a tour around the Dell islands in SL with an interview from a company representative. Her shows have spotlighted the Green Data Center of IBM, The Gibson Island, The SL University of Cincinnati and the SL Fashion Research Institute, among others.

One gets a sense of the show's range of content from the blog, *Real Biz* (2008), which is an extension of the Cybergrrl site of Athena Isle. On the blog, you will see reminders for upcoming shows as well: "Stop by Athena Isle to attend a screening of the live...show REAL BIZ in SL with Cybergrrl Oh. This week's guest is World Bank. Athena Isle screening hosted by KrisBott Gears." More impressive is the fact that several other women have created a media collective on Athena Isle in SL: "Cybergrrl co-owns Athena Isle with 7 other women. She manages Athena Isle HQ where she hosts weekly roundtable discussions with authors and experts on Tuesdays at 12pm SLT (PST). She also [interviews] book authors and writing and publishing experts for Story Mountain, a writers retreat on Athena Isle" (Cybergrrl, 2008). Cybergrrl Oh's efforts are targeted toward professional women, who might also be moms. She has tapped into a connection beyond the professional to the personal. The team warmly welcomes all RL moms, inviting tips and advice to its blog readers and its isle visitors. Amusing comments by Cybergrrl Oh (2008) include the following excerpt from her blog post:

> ...in real life, I have a very active (translation: exhausting) 16-month old baby girl. But in SL, I'm child-free and actually want to keep it that way!...What motivates women to make their avis pregnant anyway? They must not have kids in RL.

She writes, jesting, "Or they are those supermommies who love being mommies all the time and were basically put on this earth to be mothers. That, I hate to admit, is not me. Do I go to SL to escape my RL? Not really" (Cybergrrl, 2008). She adds, "The things I do in SL are extensions of what I do in RL, at least in terms of work. And the friendships I'm making in-world are as good, if not better, than the ones I make on Twitter and other online venues." Concluding, she notes, "So I'm not really looking for a life in SL that is wildly different from my own..." (Cybergrrl, 2008).

Cybergrrl has made a connection to professional women, working women, and those moms who need diversion from real life. All gather for various reasons on the Isle, and follow along with the commentary on the various blogs that have sprung off from the main Cybergrrl blog. On Saturday afternoon, November 3, 2007, blog readers and SLers were invited in-world to meet Cybergrrl Oh (Aliza Sherman) who "has been helping empower moms, daughters and women entrepreneurs since the dawn of the Web." To take a look at the blog, simply link to http://athenaislewomen.blogspot.com/. Athena Isle (2009) has gone through some transitions and development, one of which was a name change, having been formerly called the SL Women's Club. Now the mom's club and women's club events are threaded together as part of Athena Isle.

Other Leading Ladies of Treet-TV

Angie Mornington of *Fabulous Fashion* made her show debut October 13, 2008, on SLCN. The program was created by Paisley Beebe, owner of Perfect World Productions and host of the weekly interview/entertainment program *Tonight Live*. Beebe's May 31, 2009, episode of *Tonight Live* focused on how math and art have merged, featured live music, and then offered information and support for dementia from an expert interviewed in-world in his avatar form. *Tonight Live* shows often include a segment that sheds light on a non-profit group with an in-world presence. Beebe is a real-life singer, and brings her talent inside SL, while also providing airtime to other performers. Moreover, she features various places and people in SL on her *Tonight Live*, which was Second Life's first weekly talk show taped live in front of a studio audience. Her supporting blog links her RL and SL careers for her viewers. The show has been very popular, and has drawn a sizeable audience of "more than 20,000 viewers" (Vanmoer, 2008) to her studios during taping. Like Cybergrrl, she has a MySpace page as her social networking platform. Her topics are varied within a particular episode, and run the gamut from informational to entertainment themes, with always a live music element included.

From her Web site (Paisley Beebe, 2008): "Paisley Beebe is the alter ego on Second Life of Leonie Smith, an Australian Jazz Vocalist, and Radio Host." She has sung professionally for 15 years, and has released two albums, *Sweet Jazz* and *Never The Less*. A review of the Perfect World Production staff, as shown on Beebe's blog, indicates that she has involved women in the production of her shows. For example in 2009, the *Tonight Live* crew was listed as Producer and Host Paisley Beebe, Producer Delinda Dyrssen, and Director Yxes Delacroix. *Fabulous Fashion*'s crew was comprised of Host Angie Mornington, Assistant Producer Autumn Foxx Sutherland, and Show Host and Paisley's Assistant Ember Farina. Beebe, Mornington, and RL/SL journalist Persia Bravin, host of *PopVox*, have been widely recognized as leading women of Tweet TV, and the list of notable female producers and presenters continues to grow in Second Life.

Metaverse TV

Treet TV is a leading programmer provider in Second Life. Metaverse TV (2009) offers an alternative service, and is building its base of programming quickly. Metaverse TV presents a slick commercial look, complete with a Web site that showcases several original in-world programs. It is intended to present an alternative to Treet and RL television among SL residents. It had also competed directly with SLCN, and perhaps that is one of the reasons why Treet TV was born. Metaverse TV is programmed closely to how it happens at a network television station that follows a commercial industry model. Music, news and game programs appear to be take-offs of real television shows.

One show, SL's *Hollywood Cubes,* was structured like *Hollywood Squares*. The 9 celebrities, well-known avatars in SL, filled the cubes, and 2 avatars competed with each other in a game of Tic Tac Toe. *Adventures in Dating* followed the trials and tribulations of two sisters on a journey to find romance over one year. Avatars compete for virtual stardom in *I Wanna Be a Celebrity*. The logo line is "stars are not born, they're re created." *The Late Show*, having had at least two hosts since its inception, is programmed with interviews, comedy, and music similar to shows on network and cable television. *MBC Weekly News* features anchor Dousa Dragonash as well as others; and Dragonash also hosts *Out and About*, an interview show on issues and places in Second Life. *Life On Line* is hosted by Steve Cropper about work, play, and life in Second Life. In the long run, how well Treet and Metaverse will be received by virtual audiences is dependent on RL viewing habits and time spent in Second Life, as well as how they want to spend their time in a virtual world, watching TV or experiencing SL for themselves.

For media makers, Second Life offers a training ground for real life, allows them to experiment with a new genre of media production and be one of the first to gain media experience in virtual worlds. It is an opportunity to chronicle human life in virtual spaces, for some believe we are moving toward the world illustrated in the Hollywood blockbuster motion picture *The Matrix*. At the very least, audiences and media makers appear to enjoy an immersive and interactive space that blurs the line between humanity and technology. Machinima makers, particularly, give us a glimpse into the power of storytelling in virtual worlds. Treet and Metaverse are establishing the groundwork for programming services that extend beyond Second Life, and are serving now as the lead content providers across the Metaverse.

The Art and Practice of Machinima

In Second Life, videos produced for TV are in actuality created as machinima. In simple terms, machinima means machine cinema. It was originally spelled machinema. This type of movie-making moves beyond traditional 3D animation to capture motion in real-time interactive environments of game worlds, single or multi-player. Machinima has grown from short movie clips of the early action shooter games to an art form that has found its way onto mainstream television and movies. It relies on the engine of the virtual game for capture of images and motion. Machinima is often defined by the virtual world in which the filmmaker resides, with the idea to create drama and comedy inside that space. Machinima is uniquely expressive of a virtual environment, such as Second Life. Some of the limitations, of course, are those with dealing with animating characters in general; for instance, how does one create continuity among the actors and events. In Second Life, the range of facial expressions and movements are only as good as the in-world animations.

However, machinima makers have overcome many of these obstacles with creative use of scripted objects or movements, as programmers have advanced the animations used for game play at an amazing rate over the past two years. For example, the dance animations in Second Life are very fluid and project a sense of realism. The characters in Second Life have become increasingly realistic, with skin, shape, facial features, clothing, and lighting adding to the illusion. Although facial expressions and body movements are somewhat limited in machinima, post production can enhance the scenes with special effects.

The backdrop to machinima is its discovery in the 1980s among game hackers who began to tap into the less sophisticated game engines of the time to record game action. In a sense, it became similar to making home movies or chronicling game plays. In the 1990s, players began to use the graphic engines from shooter games, like *Quake*, to capture speed runs, namely when a player advances through a level. Players would swap videos of speed runs, and the practice became common about game enthusiasts. Soon, *Quake* movies were created complete with fictitious storylines set within the game (Fall, 2009). The producers were typically avid game players. In October 1996, a *Quake* film, *Diary of a Camper*, a 100-second demo file, was distributed among the gaming community. The short run actually had a storyline beyond the typical game footage. Other filmmakers began to take an interest in machinima, and increasingly so when it inspired television programming and commercial advertising.

Through the 1990s, a number of advances in game technologies involving improvements in camera adjustments and character customization began to allow for improved media making. Companies began to crack down on movie making practices that relied on the game's internal engine. In 2000, Hugh Hancock created a machinima community to expand the art of in-game filming beyond *Quake* to other platforms. The genre would no longer rely on any specific game engine, and video files were the means for distribution and exhibition. His Website, machinima.com, became the information hub for those wanting tips on filmmaking techniques or reviews on technologies. Hancock founded the Strange Company, and is credited with creating the term machinima. One year later, Showtime featured a machinima film, *Hardly Workin'*, that won best experimental and best in SHO awards in the 2001 Alternative Media Festival. Steven Speilberg used machinima to experiment with special techniques for his motion picture *Artificial Intelligence: A.I.* Machinima themes sway toward science fiction, historical periods, and to a lesser extent social and political issues.

Hancock was among the founders of The Academy of Machinima Arts & Sciences (AMAS) which was instituted to elevate machinima to a legitimate film genre on an international level, and this has been facilitated more recently in part by its hosting of annual festivals. He remains active on its board of directors. According to AMAS Executive Director Paul Marino, machinima might be thought of as "visual narratives," filmmaking that documents events and performance, "artistically created characters moved over time (animation) within an adjustable virtual environment (3D game technology platform or engine)" (Marino, cited in Lowood, 2005, p. 10). Meaning is derived by the interaction between the player and the environment, particularly through the context of the activity as the performer is immersed in virtual role-play (Salen & Zimmerman, 2004). It is the situational play that conveys meaning in machinima, when all elements emerge to craft a storyline.

Machinima provides an example of where media is headed, in the sense that it encourages performer participation. Game platforms like Second Life depend on the interactivity provided by participants, and participation becomes commoditized as well through the process. Machinima becomes the voice and image of SL at times, and perhaps an enticement for others to join the game.

Henry Jenkins (2005), the Provost's Professor of Communication, Journalism and Cinematic Arts for the University of Southern California, and the former director of the Comparative Media Studies Program at the Massachusetts Institute of Technology, posits, "[W]e should document the interactions that occur amongst media consumers, between media consumers and media texts, and between media consumers and media producers." He continues, "It would be naive to assume that powerful conglomerates will not protect their own interests as they enter this new media marketplace, but at the same time, audiences are gaining greater power and autonomy as they enter into the new knowledge culture." He adds, "The interactive audience is more than a marketing concept and less than 'semiotic democracy.'" The marketability of machinima to mainstream audiences is undeniable, and platforms like Second Life provide accessibility to new audiences interested in creating their own stories. YouTube and other online services make these new media forms available to general audiences, beyond game players.

Machinima has found its way on to the mainstream and satellite networks, including the BBC, MTV, and HBO, the first network to air a full-length machinima film from a virtual world. The documentary *Molotov Alva and His Search for the Creator: A Second Life Odyssey* was shot and produced in Second Life. The premise of the documentary follows "a man named Molotov Alva [who] disappeared from his California home in [January 2007], just as a series of video dispatches by a traveler with the same name began to appear inside Second Life" (*Molotov*, 2009). Comedy skits, drama, and commercial productions are common genres of machinima that cross-over to the mainstream. Some games such as *Halo 3* have included software to help players create machinima. The biggest issue is the use of digital assets within the game. Machinima artists typically shoot their films completely in-world relying on game technology and capture ware. Second Life has allowed machinima producers to retain the intellectual copyright for their films, but that is not always the case with other game companies.

Henry Lowood, a profilic writer on game culture, states, "In the last decade or so, game players have used computer games as platforms for creating their own games, narratives, texts, and performances. They have reshaped the context of computer play" (Lowood, 2005, p. 10). He adds that they have done so, "not simply by creating personal artifacts equivalent to a home movie, doodle, or diary, but by fully exploiting games as a new medium for performance and artistic expression." The result has been an evolution in "storytelling technologies" available to the media maker, with machinima having become popularized in recent years. The actors, as performers and artists, have become a significant part of the game culture. To get an idea of how expansive the genre has become in recent years, Machinima.com is a commercial Web site that features original videos from a variety of popular games, from World of Warcraft, Sims 2, Halo, as well as others. Trailers, montages, music videos, game runs, and "original machinima series and movies" are part of programming fare on the site (Machinima.com, 2009).

The first full-length machinima series based on the motion picture *Terminator Salvation* was released May 2009 through iTunes, Xbox Live, Sony Playstation, and Amazon.com. It was produced by the film's director and Machinima Inc., distributed by Warner Brothers and developed and produced through Halcyon Games. It is a 6-part series that relies on the engine of the game *Terminator Salvation*. Its plot begins two and a half years before the motion picture's storyline (*Terminator*, 2009). "Machinima is the next generation of storytelling," posits Diane Nelson, president of Warner Premiere (*Terminator*, 2009). Cos Lazouras, president of Halcyon Games, explained to *Business Wire* (Terminator, 2009), "Re-purposing our game to produce the very first dramatic series in this medium is a fantastic innovation and will become the norm for game makers in the future."

Second Life Machinima

SL machinima groups include the Professional Machinima Artist Guild (Pro MAG) and Second Life Machinima Artist Guild (MAG) founded by Lowe Runo, Advanced Machinima founded by Frankie Rockett, Second Life Film Society founded by Reuben Linden, and Machinimatographers founded by Buhbuhcah Fairchild. The MaMachinima International Festival (MMIF), the brainchild of Chantal Harvey, is a member-driven organization that hosts an annual RL/SL screening, live from Amsterdam bringing together many of the SL machinima filmmakers and others working on various virtual platforms. Some of these groups are open to anyone interested in learning about machinima, especially in SL. MAG hosts an annual machinima contest every year, with winners earning top cash prizes and being honored at a formal awards ceremony. The works of the winners are screened at a large SL gathering of their peers, and a special newcomer category is also presented at the event. The Machinima Institute & Café founded by HVX Silverstar is an informational site with "do-it-yourself" instructions on machinima, and provides video on basic techniques. SL Film Society had been toying with ways of streaming live video from SL to the Internet and SLTV. On July 18, 2009, the Machinima Artist Guild was instrumental in the launch of Aview Television, creating a 24-hour broadcast network for machinima. LaPiscean Liberty is the founder and CEO of Aview, which streams a variety of genres from a mix of virtual-world filmmakers, as well as eclectic programming from MAG and the annual MMIF.

Like many SL filmmakers, machinamatopher Ariella Languish is a member of many of these groups and also has several years of video production and editing experience. In a 2008 interview, she called attention to the origination of machinima; "in short term [it] is making videos from game engines. It combines three elements: filmmaking, animation, and game play" (Languish, 2009). "The graphics are pre-rendered, although certain exceptions apply (such as Second Life), where users can create their own content. Machinima is capturing that content and editing it in an engaging way to tell a story," Languish (2009) explains. She began experimenting when she wanted to produce a documentary in college about a female Amazon tribe in a virtual world, and to present it to a real-life audience (Languish, 2009). She recalls, "At first, my intention was not to make machinima. It was merely to bring the game to people who aren't in the game" (Languish, 2009).

In 2008, she established ALM Productions—Ariella Languish—Machinima Productions. Languish (2009) explains, "Little did I know, what I was doing is a popular filmmaking genre that whole communities are enthused about, and as the visual effects guy from *The Matrix* says, 'Virtual cinema is inevitable.'" Languish (2009) adds, "Machinima helps bridge gaps between Second Life and those who are not yet familiar with virtual reality...I'd like it to become more mainstream, so there are greater means to creating a machinima for certain real-life products in commercials or music videos." Languish (2009) states she believes "the more people are used to this kind of animation in visual storytelling, the most they will expect it, and the more accepted it will become."

Linden Lab is aware of the benefits of showcasing Second Life through machinima. The filmmakers capture the beauty, originality, and potential of the human imagination on the Second Life canvas. These films are showcased on the Second Life home page, intriguing visitors to explore the virtual world and perhaps create their own story or identity as members. Second Life is a community rich with professional and amateur artists and media makers. The whole canvas of Second Life is open to one's imagination. Eric Call, known in Second Life as Eric Linden, was the senior artist for Linden Lab when he produced a western machinima based on an anonymous poem about two gunslingers. The poem "**Silver Bells and Golden Spurs**" provided the title and plot for the film. The piece was narrated and filmed completely in Second Life and made its debut in November 2005. As for the final outcome, Linden stated, "I wanted to use raw footage and let it stand on its own, using only simple dissolves and titles—which are common in most bundled software on off-the-shelf computer systems."

In this way, he continues, "I wanted to show would-be movie makers that anyone can create compelling stories and show interesting visuals if they approach their projects with creativity and thoughtfulness. That's really all Bells and Spurs is: a collection of sequential, cohesive images—put together in a thoughtful, creative and compelling way" (Linden, 2005). The film's narrative structure followed along with the poem that told of Dandy, the main gunslinger known for a chain on his watch that had a dozen silver bells hanging from it—each representing a man who had died from his gun.

Among its screenings were South By Southwest 2006 in Austin, TX, Paris (France) Cinema Festival, Bradford (UK) Animation Festival 2006, SIGGRAPH 2006 (Boston, MA) and the 2006 California International Animation Festival (CalAniFest, Modesto). The film is impressive when you consider that avatars and costumes had to be made and sets had to be constructed, among others things like directing a huge cast of avatar actors in the saloon and finding suitable animations for them to move somewhat credibly.

Second Life Machinima Artist Guild

Eric Linden made that film in 2005. Today, if you are looking for the go-to person in Second Life who can direct you to producers of machinima, that would be a man by the avatar name Lowe Runo. He is the point person for the leading group in Second Life that engages in creative film production. Runo has been involved in SL since December 29, 2006. Nearly three years later, he launched a full-service machinima network featuring in-world work across a variety of genres, from comedy to drama to documentary. He heard about machinima in the mainstream news and became curious, "found the web page and installed the software to take a look and the rest is history. Through the course, he "made a lot of friends who are no longer here (in SL) and many who now have become famous in the Metaverse in their own right."

Among the guild's membership is a cast of many actors, producers and creative types involved in capturing life in virtual worlds through machinima. The guild is comprised of more than 100 members. Many of their works can be seen on YouTube, and some are featured on Second Life's home site, serving as an example of daily virtual life and artistic possibilities in-world. The guild offers a quick rundown on a mix of photographers and filmmakers producing and performing in the art of machinima. Runo organized the Second Life Machinima Artist Guild in August 2008. Its organizational mission is to provide a network among Second Life machinima producers, actors, directors and technicians so that they might collaborate and share experiences. This collection of machinima artists represents only one group in Second Life, but it is the most visible in terms of showcasing the majority of filmmakers associated with SL. Many of these artists collaborate and showcase their works online, at RL festivals, and within the game world.

The guild's Web site offers a glimpse into their work, and provides opportunities for critique among members. The guild as founded by Runo was established to serve as a forum for in-world producers to exhibit and critique work. The majority of the machinima members see themselves as artists, but some create corporate videos for additional income. Some artists' works become showcased on mainstream media venues. Comedy, drama, romance, historical pieces and music videos are among the plethora of categories featured by the guild's machinima artists. Other media makers like Four Yip (2009) from the Netherlands create machinima using their photography and art. Yip is a professional advertising illustrator in real life; she uses Second Life as a canvas for the creation of fashion and media creation that she exhibits in-world and online.

United Kingdom's Toxic Menges is another one of the SL Machinima Artist Guild members. Her background in online community management, discussed earlier, laid the foundation for understanding virtual worlds and the people residing within them. So her love inside Second Life, as she states it, is "well mainly machinima." She has been involved in the planning and organization of large virtual world events such as SL6B, and has enjoyed dealing with virtual community events. Other than that, she has been involved in the music scene. In her words, she is into "machinima, shopping and the odd bit of sim management." In fact, she continues,

> I manage a sim, and I enjoy that, and dressing that for things like machinima because you have a place that's just a blank canvas that you can make into anything you want to. I enjoy creating I guess immersive themes. You can create something extremely outrageous with Windlight and create something that I would never be able to do in real life. I am not the slightest bit interested in filming anything in real life, and don't even have a video camera in real life because it is very, very limiting. I enjoy taking a blank canvas and making something you could never have in real life or creating something you could just kinda have like for your life. I suppose it is taking a blank canvas and making something out of it and see what is possible for us to do in here and seeing how far we can push that. I enjoy that a lot. (Menges, 2009)

Menges appears to be drawn to the fantasy landscapes and stories that can be told in Second Life:

> There was one which was called *The Secret* where there's obviously a girl who sat there, not much going on in her life. She sat there daydreaming in a forest and then suddenly she's off to sleep. And then she has become a wood elf. That's her dream...and in the pretty surroundings and all that, and then all of sudden she wakes up. But at the end, was that a dream, or actually did you do that, you just don't know. (Menges, 2009)

She is in the planning stages of creating machinima parodies, pointing out that Second Life provides the perfect place for that because it is such a strange mirror: "It is one of those mirrors in a carnival that distorts everything." Her idea is to use the television show *24* as an example for her machinima series:

> I'm in the very early stages of doing that, a parody of *24* in SL, where obviously the days are only 4 hours long. So it is going to be called *4*. And just to complete the parody, it's not terrorism the heroine will be fighting; she is fighting her way around the lucky chairs and the terrible fashionista scene of SL because that is where all the high drama and warfare take place in SL I think. (Menges, 2009)

Menges, like other guild members, have bonded as a community of media makers. They view and critique each other's work in a professional and caring way. The members exhibit a high level of professionalism in their pieces showcased on the guild Web site. Menges (2009) acknowledges that the machinima community has advanced considerably in a short amount of time, and anticipates the community will grow professionally and mature as a place of exhibition and networking:

> The machinima community in Second Life has come along in leaps and bounds in the last year. And they really are a friendly bunch...and if there is something they can do to help you they will. And everyone is very welcoming and people want to hear what people have done. And the thing about SL is if there is one thing you should do in SL it is to create things if you feel you should do it because we are in a place where you can't help but create. There is an acceptance of what people have made is what they have made. So I think go and do it and go and watch lots and lots of things. Show your work and get into the circle so you can talk to people and learn...I think everyone in SL should have a space lot anyway because it completely changes the way you use SL. Really play around, because there is a lot of things under the hood of SL that you don't really know about until you try and it is very very difficult to break SL. Unless you start going into the advanced settings, the Windlight settings, the day settings and things, you're missing out on seeing all these amazing things you can do because you just haven't looked. It really is a case of pushing all the buttons and seeing what things do...it is an exciting time. And we are all learning at the same time I think.

The Virtual Storyteller

Lowe Runo is a long-time real-life photographer who applies his professional skills to the incredible landscapes that SL provides. His machinima projects blur across genres to tell human stories set in virtual landscapes that resemble real places and real times, now and the past. In personal correspondence with Runo he states, "The Second Life Machinima Artist Guild…has prospered way beyond what I had envisioned. It exists in all major media platforms such as YouTube, Vimeo, Dailymotion, and Facebook to name a few." He continues, "Machinima will be THE storybook/novel/news of tomorrow in SL and RL, for everyone especially the very young." For machinima to work effectively, length is a significant factor, and most films are no longer than 5 minutes. Runo pointed out that "some of the longer ones can be tedious if they do not pique your interest at least every 2 minutes, like a documentary for instance."

To Runo, machinima benefits the producer when it is understood as "an outlet to express yourself and be creative," and in doing so conveys "really a super feeling" among the artists and the viewers. The storyline is critical, and Runo explains, "Start with what you have and worry more about telling a good story than a lot of special FX." Runo indicated that the tools used in producing media in his professional work as photographer are "not that far apart" from virtual media making…All rules of composition remain the same. Photoshop skills are also invaluable. Oddly enough all my video/film editing skills were perfected in SL," adding that SL "is a great training ground. The media is not changing so much as the AWARENESS of its usefulness has improved vastly." After nearly 3 years in Second Life, Runo's experiences may lead him to "related work outside the Metaverse in the future." "I cannot say in what form, but my time may be spent in another environment," he adds, referencing virtual opportunities on the horizon that may offer direct competition with Second Life's artistic community.

Machinima presents the voice of the game culture that has emerged over the past 30 years. Some producers, however, have commented on the copyright contentions that arise around the use of digital assets and music in machinima, and others feel that some virtual worlds are less secure than others when attempting to maintain proprietary control over films. Some producers are concerned about unauthorized early release or theft of machinima content. In essence, machinima is an art that began by a group of computer hackers, who capitalized on their skills to tap into game engines to make films on their game play. It is becoming more difficult than previously was the case to protect content in such an environment. The irony of the situation is that machinima relies on in-game content for its creation.

In retrospect, machinima artists may very well be considered the storytellers for the virtual generation, who are comfortable living between and in two worlds—virtual and physical, not unlike those literary spokespersons from a previous era. Steinbeck, Orwell, Hemingway, Clemens, and Bradbury were the American storytellers of the print generation. Author and Mix Artist Paul Miller (a.k.a. DJ Spooky) calls attention to the idea of "collective memory" on which the sampling culture is based, and Eric Davis (2009) refers to this new world order as "remixing the matrix." Machinima makers exist within the matrix to produce their art based on realities present in-world for them and their audiences. For example, Runo crafts his pieces to create a fluid storyline, using animation poses, special effects and editing. His film, *Memories of Le Village*, tells the story of a WWI pilot who crashes outside a French village, where he meets a woman who nurses him back to health, and they fall in love. The set design is authentic of the time period, and the storyline is set in 1918. From the initial crash of his plane, as the film begins in black and white, to the romantic dance between the couple, the story unfolds to capture the emotions behind the history.

Angels, another Runo machinima film, is rich in animation effects and costume, and presents the eternal conflict between dark and good over man's soul. It made use of Second Life places, namely Lost World Svarga and Dark Realm, to create the battleground scenes. In both of these films, dance is included as one way to connect the main characters. Runo explains, "Each project has its unique hurdles. Angels was one of my first to tell a complete story and involve other avatars. Typically "found" sims are the easiest to use as sets. I often hire someone better at building than myself, for this helps the speed of production greatly." Runo points toward the importance of human interaction, the personalities behind the avatars, when he states, "Creativity for me can be sparked by discovering a new unique animation or by a special relationship with another." Although, admittedly, creativity is "hard to define really."

In the 1940s, cinematographer Maya Deren, one of the first producers to film the Voudon dances of Haiti, captured cultural expression through dance. Miller (2001) explains, "In the lens of the camera the dance became a way of making time expand and become a ritual reflection of reality itself. Film became total. Became time itself—a mnemonic, a memory palace made of the gestures captured on the infinitely blank screen." In a sense, dance has become a ritual of expression in SL, in which the avatar form is symbolic of the human soul. Machinima allows for human expression through virtual interpretation. Animations simulate reality for the avatar. When a dance animation is well scripted, the participants, as avatars, appear to transcend into the virtual spaces. Couple dance animations create an interaction between the two avatars and those they represent. You might call them puppeteers, and their puppets are the avatars. At a certain point, the authenticity of the experience is determined by the interaction among the people behind their avatars.

The viewer appreciates the beauty of the dance, and taps into personal memories to fill in digital gaps. In media, there has been always a sense of voyeuristic immersion into the plot or song, where meaning is layered within one's experiences and the situational context provided by the viewer or producer. Machinima is a form of cinematic expression that documents life within virtual spaces, and draws connections between virtuality and reality. Eric Linden (2005) defines machinima as the "art of making real movies in virtual worlds." The relevance of machinima to some is that it conveys underlying emotions and motivation for participants in these virtual environments to live, love and create art in the Metaverse. A good film storyline taps into the human soul, and machinima is not different in that respect.

How well machinima will fare in the coming years due to intellectual copyright issues that sometimes limit creativity will likely be determined by larger questions of content ownership. Conceptions and definitions of creativity and originality will likely be addressed given the increasing interactivity and fluidity that has surfaced amidst a mashed up, mixed mediated culture, globally. Machinima makers collaborate on projects within SL and at times other virtual worlds, and the result is productions that bring together artists transnationally beyond physical restrictions. In December 2009, Stretch Mayo produced *Red Lashes of Mars*, a machinima based on the compositional work of Cypress Rosewood and sim creator and visual artist/designer Kolor Falls. The images from the film intentionally blended into the virtual terrain. The machinima and landscape merged into a larger composition, bringing artists across the world together to collaborate and elaborate on the meaning of art in virtual worlds to a global audience.

SL Machinima Artist Guild at SL 6th Anniversary

Second Life's 6th Anniversary comprised weeklong activities in 2009 preceding its official launch date, June 28th. The SL Machinima Artist Guild was invited to create an exhibit for the event, and was actually among a number of organizations and residents allowed to showcase its works. The Guild exhibited approximately 20 machinima films on several wall screens. On Saturday, June 27, 2009, a panel with members Rysan Fall and Cisko Vandeverre presenting and guild founder Lowe Runo and project manager Josie Anderton moderating related some key historical moments in the accomplishments of machinima makers and insight into the future of the genre. What is obvious is that the limitations of using game engines to create machinima will be overcome in the near future, and in the meantime producers see those limitations as part of the creativity necessary to produce in the genre. Members of the guild were on hand to answer questions and offer support to those interested in learning about machinima. Guild member Rysan Fall started off the series that afternoon with an overview on the history of machinima. He presented in voice, while guild members and others responded via text in the public chat. At one point, Fall commented that Comedy Central's *South Park* episode "Make Love, Not Warcraft" was significant because the television show was shot with many of its scenes as machinima. The plot took a satirical look at the multiplayer online role-playing game World of Warcraft.

SL television host Pooky Amsterdam asked whether the *Molotov Alva* film affected the genre. Amsterdam is host of *The 1st Question,* a quiz show which airs weekly on Treet TV and began on SLCN. Most guild members appeared to believe that the film's hype called attention to machinima, but did not feel it significantly impacted the overall genre. LaPiscean Liberty noted, "I'm not a machinima maker at all but I love to watch them and if I do, so would many others." Rosco Teardrop added, "SL can be good for some kinds of films—music, comedy, landscapes, but just hasn't the engine for deep drama." To which Liberty added, "If the content is good then the show will be watched." Runo echoed, "If the story is good, the machinima will be good." Liberty summarized, saying, "Machinima is the low-cost mechanism by which this content is created." Fall finished his presentation by adding, "I think we are in the forefront."

The next presenter was Cisko Vandeverre, an award-winning machinima filmmaker from Berlin, Germany. He presented completely in text through public chat. Vandeverre attempted to answer one of the more challenging questions of the day, "Is there a future for machinima?" He responded, weaving in and out of comments from other guild members,

> The future can be not so passive. I mean sitting in front of a screen is not very interactive. To make films and tell stories is one thing, but to have interactivity is the next step. So the viewers have the chance to be involved, but the meaning of watching will evolve in an 3d environment. So it will become real time action…No second medium. The first interaction I have seen already. Well—we all believe that the virtual world and the 3d environment is coming—like we are in right now? No, we are in Second Life. LOL. The technical will go in the direction to interact with the story.

LaPiscean Liberty added, "and it's not what we put on the screen; it's what we are saying about ourselves that they listen to." Other members agreed content was the most significant element of machinima, as with other media. The chat via text continued (SL Machinima, 2009):

> Cisko Vandeverre: right, to tell a story is the most important thing.
> LaPiscean Liberty: right the content
> Cisko Vandeverre: but to be involved in the story is the next step.
> LaPiscean Liberty: Virtual Worlds in general cross platform
> Cisko Vandeverre: we will see that definitely in the future —is it 10 or 20 years?? to overcome the old consuming of passively watching...[it] has already started. I think that most of you already shut down the TV time in your lives since you are in Second Life.
> Pooky Amsterdam: yes, agrees with Cisko. Why watch TV when you can star in your own cartoon movie every night?
> Cisko Vandeverre: so we are on the way.
> Cisko Vandeverre: ...I'm glad to [have] gotten to connect with so many people in the guild.
> Pooky Amsterdam: and the more the guild builds with other respected machinima organizations the stronger we all are.
> Cisko Vandeverre: to see what they are working on.
> Ariella Languish nods*
> Cisko Vandeverre: and share knowledge is also important.
> Pooky Amsterdam: but the bigger truth is we are all on the frontier...
> Cisko Vandeverre: I know we are all divas...We are definitely pioneers—all together.

In closing, Vandeverre reminded the guild, "the good thing about having a community is the sharing involved." Paisa Vella commented, "I have been extremely impressed with the knowledge sharing!" (SL Machinima, 2009).

Other Guild Members

As with any filmmaker, it is common for guild members to organize a crew, and to delegate responsibilities for sound, set design, costumes, shooting, producing, and editing. A significant site for those interested in learning more about machinima and its producers is The Ning website at http://slmachinimaarts.ning.com. Runo recommends it as "a good place to start to see the works of artists across a spectrum of genres." Often machinima makers do much of the design, shooting and editing themselves using what is available within Second Life. The landscapes and related builds in Second Life are natural sets, and seem to be waiting for a story to be told there. As avatars, SL residents typically visit these sites and create stories in their imagination or role-play with others. Some of the make-believe appears believable when you stay in-world over a period of time. Machinima artists merely capture these experiences and fantasies on film, and blur the lines between real and imaginary, as any good storyteller might accomplish using any other medium.

One prominent media artist in SL is AM Radio whose in-world installations and modeling have been crafted into machinima, and featured online in various forums including YouTube. His virtual builds are showcased through machinima makers like Nitwacket Machinima, who made a film of AM Radio's collective work. As one watches, photographs and moving images capture AM Radio's nostalgic and futuristic landscapes. Minimalistic but strongly powerful images create a machinima tribute to this artist's virtual modeling. In the machinima film, *The Far Away*, the viewer is invited to contemplate technology and its human artifacts. The University of Kentucky offered AM Radio space to create a piece at its SL site, and this work evolved into an immersive and interactive dreamscape (Au, 2008). Virtual media makers bring skills of photography, filmmaking, scripting, installation works and storytelling into play with one another to create Metaverse art and film. In Second Life, media is often a collaborative process, with filmmakers, photographers, builders, technicians, performers, and others working together to extend one another's work and ideas.

Carla Broek, another member of the SL Machinima Artist Guild, created a mixed reality machinima documentary that captured the social ills of the real world as played out also in virtual life. Called *Sorrow & Hope*, it made its debut online in May 2009 on Vimeo, with guild members providing positive feedback to her work. Another resource for beginning filmmakers is the Machinima Institute located in the Alliance Virtual Library information archipelago in Second Life. HVX Silverstar, a machinima maker, owns and manages the do-it-yourself in-world resource center. In real life, she is an academic librarian at the University of California Davis and works with faculty in Second Life in health infomatics and African-American studies, and documents the work of libraries in Second Life. Educators come into Second Life often with a desire to incorporate media into their virtual lessons and projects, but with few skills necessary to make it happen without assistance. Students who have grown up with laptops on their high chairs seem to gravitate toward media making, and machinima becomes merely an extension of everyday life.

Conclusion

In SL, there is a growing audience for movies, TV programs and music that are either produced in-world, or broadcast in this virtual space. Some enjoy experiencing these mediated activities with their SL friends, partners, and colleagues. There is this sense of engagement with others and one's avatar, as one watches her "virtual double" view in-world televised programs or movies. There is another sense of engagement among the media makers of Second Life, as they tell the stories within the virtual world. The SL Machinima Artist Guild membership appears to be balanced with as many women filmmakers as men, and the themes are diverse in content. One in-world company noted already is ALM Productions (Languish, 2009) which has produced a variety of features for SL that can be accessed on the Web.

A number of educators, like Angela Thomas, are involved in creative sophisticated builds, such as her virtual reenactments based on literature. She has been interviewed by TV host Paisley Beebe. Thomas is a prominent RL lecturer, author, and conference speaker on virtual worlds. Overall, women content providers for SL television appear to gravitate toward fashion and entertainment, yet increasingly women appear interested in making media that addresses SL business and finance sectors, as well as ways to bring RL education into alternate worlds. Educators are experimenting with media technologies in Second Life, even if they have not readily done so in their real classrooms.

In fact, women owners are major contributors to SL's virtual economy and education. SL runs on a virtual economy that can connect highly educated women with each other (in RL and SL) and mentor those females who would like an opportunity to have careers in SL (when it is not possible in RL due to family obligations or physical disabilities). Second Life allows women to fly beyond the glass ceiling of RL, and these moments are increasingly and dramatically captured by women making media in Second Life. In Second Life, media makers, regardless of gender, gather to collaborate on projects. They are the media pioneers of a new world.

References

Ariella Languish. (2009). Web site, Ariella Languish—machinima productions (ALM), available at http://www.alm-productions.net/

Au, W. J. (2008, November). Kentucky dreaming: AM radio's latest metaverse installation. *New World Notes*. Accessed March 22, 2009, from http://nwn.blogs.com/nwn/2008/11/kentucky-dreami.html/

Athena Isle. (2009). Accessed October 20, 2009, from http://athenaislewomen.blogspot.com/

Cybergrrl Oh. (2008) Blog sites. Accessed October 20, 2009 from http://athenaisleentrepreneurs. blogspot.com/

Davis, E. (2009). Remixing the matrix: An interview with Paul D. Miller, a.k.a. DJ Spooky. Accessed May 31, 2009, from http://www.djspooky.com/articles/erikdavis.php/

Fall, R. (2009, June 28). SL Machinima Artist Guild Presentation. Second Life.

Four Yip. (2009). Profile. Virtual art initiative. Accessed June 10, 2009, from http://www.virtual-art-initiative.org/Virtual_Art_Initiative/Artists/Pages/ four_Yip.html/

—. (2009). Rezzable. Discover the Virtual World. Accessed June 10, 2009, from http://rezzable.com/style/fashion-inspired-crimson-shadow/four-yip/

Jenkins, H. (2005, February 19). Interactive audiences? The collective intelligence of media fans. Accessed June 1, 2009, from http://web.mit.edu/cms/ People/henry3/collective%20intelligence.html/

Languish, A. (2009, January 18). Interview. ALM Productions. Venture SL Blog. Accessed June 3, 2009, from http://www.alm-productions.net/.

—. (2008, December 7). Will Second Life machinima be adopted by mainstream. *Rez Libris*. Accessed June 28, 2009, from http://rezlibris.com/

Linden, E. (2005, November) Silver bell and golden spurs. Background and film. Accessed June

1, 2009, from http://www.secondlife.com/

Lowood, H. (2006). High-performance play: The making of machinima. *Journal of Media Practice 7*(1), 25–42.

—(2005). Real-time performance: Machinima and game studies (PDF). *The International Digital Media & Arts Association Journal* 2(1), 10–17. Accessed May 31, 2009, from http://www.idmaa.org/journal/pdf/iDMAa_Journal_Vol_2_No_1_ screen.pdf/

Machinima.com. (2009). Web site. Accessed June 9, 2008, from http://www.machinima.com/

Marino, P. (2004). *3D game-based filmmaking: The art of machinima.* Scottsdale, AZ: Paraglyph.

Menges, T. (2009, July 15). Interview, personal communication with author. Second Life.

Metaverse TV. (2009). Web site. Accessed June 9, 2009, from http://www.metaverse-tv.com/

Miller, P. D. (2001). Material memories: Time and the cinematic image. Notes for the Oberhausen Film Festival 2001. Accessed June 4, 2009, from djspooky.com/articles/material_ memories_eng.php/

Molotov Alva and his search for the creator: A Second Life odyssey (2009). HBO documentary films. Accessed June 9, 2009, from http://www.hbo.com/docs/programs/molotovalva/index.html/

Neal, C. (2007, June 11), Bruce Willis joins Second Life. Associated Press. Accessed June 22, 2009, from http://www.associatedcontent.com/article/268580/bruce_willis_joins_ second_life.html?cat=19/

Paisley Beebe. (2008). Blog site. Accessed from November 2, 2008, from http://tonightlivewithpaisleybeebe.com/

Real Biz. (2008). Blog site. Accessed from November 2, 2009, from http://realbizinsl.blogspot.com/

Runo, L. (2009, July 13). Interview, personal communication with author. Second Life.

Salen, K., & Zimmerman, E. (2004). *Rules of play: Game design fundamentals.* Cambridge, MA: MIT Press.

SL Machinima Artist Guild. (2009, June 28). Chat text transcript. Presentation. Second Life.

Terminator Salvation: The machinima series explodes online as the first long form dramatic machinima production (May 19, 2009). *Business Wire.* Accessed June 9, 2009, from http://www.pr-inside.com/terminator-salvation-the-machinima-series-r1262277.htm/

Treet TV (2009). Web site. Accessed June 7, 2008, from http://www.treettv.com/

Vanmoer, D. (2008, October 13). Fabulous fashion: New show to air on SLCN. *SL-Newspaper.* Accessed October 20, 2008, from http://www.sl-newspaper.com/

CHAPTER TEN

News Media across the Metaverse: Reporting Live from a Virtual World Near You

> About 6 million people worldwide are regular visitors to the Metaverse, being registered members of one or more virtual worlds. Some...virtual worlds...have their own news source, whether blogs, forums, or magazines [and] some titles that examine what is happening in virtual worlds from a national point of view...
>
> —*Metaverse*, 2008

In October 2007, Second Life Cable Network aired "Covering a Virtual World," a documentary that followed the experiences of three RL journalists as they reported on SL events: They "explained how essential in-world news is for residents to access what's going on in-world without actually having to log on to Second Life. This can be quite beneficial for those...when at work or due to a firewall" (Waldschmidt, 2007). The journalists pointed out that "finding sources and stories in the virtual world can be quite challenging because it relies heavily on word of mouth, which means that an in-world journalist must continuously build a large network of friends" (Waldschmidt, 2007). "An in-world journalist can virtually contact and speak to a source that is across the earth in just a matter of seconds," and in one instance a journalist had "talked to an Iranian student about his first-hand experience during the Iraq vs. Iran war" (Waldschmidt, 2007).

Second Life, for many members, is not an escape from the real world, but an extension of it, particularly when it comes to responding to news reports of world conflict. For example, SL Israeli members became overwhelmed when virtual pro-Palestinian activists came to their region in Second Life to protest, subsequent to the real world violence in Gaza that flared up in early 2009. The sim had to be closed down for awhile to address the influx of incoming protestors (Lawinski, 2009). Ron Kutus of the pro-Israel organization Stand With Us, pointed out, "It's very hard for people to distinguish between emotional commentary about the conflict and factual journalism about the conflict...you have an open forum and people who are not educated about the conflict are being told misinformation all the time" (Lawinski, 2009). Tempers flare, and people takes those emotions in-world.

During the 2008 USA Presidential campaign, video games tapped into the interest and excitement surrounding the upcoming elections. The BBC (2008) reported, "Obama takes lead in virtual world." The game was called Super Obama World, designed as "a satirical look at US Politics, with Obama collecting flags and dodging lipstick-wearing pit bulls, lobbyists and Sarah Palin" (BBC, 2008). In Second Life, Barack Obama and John McCain supporters created virtual campaign offices that attracted many people from both camps to drop in out of curiosity for dialogue, debate or information. On Election Night, supporters filled campaign sims, cheering on their candidate and jeering the opponent from their respective headquarters. They wore virtual T-shirts and waved banners, as they watched the events unfold on mainstream media in the real world (Associated Press, 2008).

This chapter explores the role of news media in Second Life, as either an extension of mainstream news agencies in the real world or as a unique offshoot of community media tapping into the needs and interests of a virtual audience base. Now a decade into the 21st century, print media in the real world have for the most part acknowledged the necessity of maintaining an Internet news and information portal for its readership. Second Life newspapers and magazines typically are Web-based, with some distributing hard copies of their print publications in-world. *Avenue Magazine* created a special print edition to distribute to attendees of the 2009 Second Life Community Convention in San Francisco. *Avenue* made its debut in SL on October 1, 2008, covering lifestyle, fashion, architecture, and business news for an in-world readership.

Inside SL, there is something comforting to virtual residents about having a tangible (although virtual) product, newspaper or magazine, one that opens similar to a PDF document. Readers can pick up a copy of their favorite SL magazine through a kiosk at various high-traffic sites. Readers, in many instances, become subscribers. In either case, the magazine is delivered to their inventory. When they want to read the magazine, they simply drag it from their inventory, and set it on a table, or the ground, or whatever. At that point, they can turn the pages of the publication, as they would in real life. In Second Life, this is done by clicking on a page. One such magazine that does this well, from creation to distribution, is *The Best of Second Life Magazine*.

The BOSL Publishing Empire

Fashion fuels much of the Second Life economy. At the heart of the fashion scene is the Best of Second Life Fashion District. Top designers are strategically located along and around Couture Boulevard in this high-rent district. And at the heart of the BOSL district is *The Best of Second Life Magazine*. *BOSL*

Magazine is the brainchild of one man—Frolic Mills—who rules this fashion empire with compassion for newcomers to Second Life and a child-like wonder regarding the amazing creative opportunities afforded through virtual worlds. His desire has been to document virtual life in this parallel universe. But again, this is not an ordinary man, although he humbly perceives himself to be just that—an avatar that got a break along the way from some nice people he met during his previous virtual lives before settling on his present avatar.

Mills' private hideaway is located in a Second Life treehouse—a treehouse skybox to be precise. Decorated with paintings rich with color, texture, and culture, the owner of this space surrounds himself with virtual beauty. He was dressed in a tuxedo for the interview, and his silvery ash coiffure added to his distinguished appearance. He looked like he belonged in this room, both Mills and the space emanating world-class charm. During this interview we sat on large, roomy red leather sofa chairs. Colors popped about the room, a mix that normally might have clashed but actually worked in harmony here. The furnishings include some eccentric items, such as a floor to ceiling aquarium and a koala bear strategically placed on the sofa.

His avatar profile mentions his real and Second Life love of writing, poetry, music, theatre, and exploring. The room reflected the rich personality of a businessman and creative artist who enjoys life, especially his second one. On the coffee table in front of us, it seemed fitting to see a DVD copy of *The Devil Wears Prada*—a fashion-themed movie classic featuring Meryl Streep and Anne Hathaway. The DVD was positioned on the corner of the table, vertically. Near it, the July edition of *The Best of Second Life Magazine* rested on the first page of a feature interview with Philip Linden. Linden was interviewed by the owner of this office, Frolic Mills, the CEO and publisher of *The Best of Second Life Magazine.*

You might say that Second Life was a fateful decision for both Linden and Mills. Both were chosen to be virtual-world entrepreneurs on their own respective paths. Mills (2009b) explains, "I don't think anyone really 'chooses' SL—I actually believe it's the other way around. The learning curve in Second Life can be steep, so I am convinced that the ones who do stay are those who were treated right by someone, somewhere." Linden created Second Life, and Mills, well, he makes sure that all its beauty, creativity, and special moments are preserved in photos and print.

Mills' corporate office, for the most part, fits with the image of a publishing executive—clean lines, silver and black decor set against a light wooden panel floor. Chrome-framed magazine covers showcase the various editions of *BOSL* on the walls. Black leather chairs are intentionally positioned around a large circle rug. One can only imagine how many discussions have taken place in his office headquarters. *BOSL Magazine* is available throughout SL as well as via the Internet and is definitely among the top print publications in Second Life. Its images are captivating, and its presentation is professional. Stories vary from issue to issue, but SL fashion and lifestyle news probably best define the magazine. If you want to know what is happening in-world among the movers and shakers, from designers to entrepreneurs, *BOSL Magazine* is the publication to read.

Mills had no idea that he would one day be the founder of such a renowned magazine in Second Life, in terms of visibility and circulation. He began, like we all did, as a simple avatar in 2007. As he explains: "Well, on my third day in SL I saw a notice in a Latin disco that they were hiring DJs, and I jumped on that and was hired immediately! That was fun, and many, many things happened after" (Mills, 2009b). He says he owes his success to the friends he made when he began Second Life: "But you are absolutely right, I was treated very very nicely. Most people don't know this, but Frolic Mills is my third avatar, the first two never made it, and I forgot their password (laughs). I do suppose third time is a charm" (Mills, 2009b).

It might be absurd to outsiders of SL to think that a successful real-life businessman would turn to moonlighting in a virtual world. Mills is an economist in his real life, with a banking and marketing background, and resides in Venezuela. Second Life has provided him with a new career path in another world, and a new identity: "Mr. Mills is a monster of my own imagination," he laughs (Mills, 2009b). He elaborates on the winding road that led to the creation of *BOSL Magazine* and his related fashion empire that he operates alongside of 37 writers, photographers, and editors:

> Like I said at the beginning of this conversation, Second Life had chosen me (in a way), and not the other way around...the only decision made at the beginning of this game was to become a DJ...and I did! Then one day Mr. Kirk Claymore invited me as a model to his agency, and that got me on my way to modeling, from model to fashion and then to my magazine. My magazine was supposed to be my own personal diary of great and fantastic places I had seen, that for some reason nobody spoke about. I was only able to find discos and sex clubs at the beginning of my Second Life, so I decided to write about the beautiful things I saw every day in SL—and then a friend of mine offered to buy advertisement (which I didn't know I could do), and that's how *The Best of SL Magazine* was born. (Mills, 2009b)

Mills (2009b) adds, "Perhaps this is one of the nicest things about SL, as it is in RL; SL can take any turn any day. And this opens the door to discovery, which perhaps is the reason I am always interested in opening the Second Life platform." Mills' mission has "not varied from the original intent, which was to inform others about great things created every day in Second Life" (Mills, 2009b). He explained his frustration at the beginning of his SL existence, to "only find mediocre clubs" when there were so many incredibly talented artists out there. "And now, almost 2 years later," Mills (2009b) adds, "we take the same pleasure in discovering these amazing people and letting others know...*BOSL* is just a guide to share our discoveries in this virtual medium. I am the luckiest man on earth...My staff means all to me!!"

The magazine has thousands of kiosks across Second Life. Mills teleported me to a region that he set up to keep track of his kiosks, and the numbers were easily into the thousands. The magazine is circulated through these vendors as well as in-world groups and outside subscription networks. Monthly circulation is estimated at over 100,000, including the hits to his website at http://www.thebosl.com.

Mills has a broad perspective of in-world media and taps into its pulse through his network for virtual-world communicators. He founded Associated SL Press, which brings together members of television networks, radio stations, print media as well as bloggers, and it has nearly 80 members. Mills meets with other publishers in SL in addition to his readers on a regular basis. He has listened to the good and bad about SL media, and is in a position to speculate on opportunities ahead for virtual world media. Mills (2009b) has thoughtfully considered the content role of *BOSL Magazine* and other web-based media for the near future: "It is my experience that the trend in any Internet-based print media (SL or RL news on Internet) is that we must focus on interesting graphics. People are not too willing to read long stories online. They are reading to get the info from a good picture. But I honestly believe this is true of all media news based on the Internet."

Along this line, he sees *BOSL Magazine* to be a visual medium, beautifully laid out with photographs and, increasingly, video coverage, such as the accompanying website's addition of professionally produced machinima featuring fashions from top designers. In 2009, several video features were produced professionally to highlight several fashion shows that took place during the BOSL Fashion Week in August.

Mills applauds his staff for its coverage of BOSL FASHION WEEK 2009, as exhibited on the BOSL website, which he posits as "a perfect example of how it should be done (in my opinion)...short paragraphs and to the point and then GREAT pictures to go with it. The site is located at http://www.thebosl.com. Mills sees *BOSL* expanding to other platforms outside SL to be inclusive of other virtual worlds: "In fact, bestvirtualworlds.com is mine, and we intend to use it very very soon! I have a feeling that many companies will follow in Philip Rosedale's vision, and there will come a time when we will have many platforms out there" to choose from (Mills, 2009b). Bestvirtualworlds.com "would do the same as *BOSL* does but on a wider scale.

We would inform about the great works in all Metaverses! I find this quite exciting! It would include a reference to compare and contrast virtual worlds, for example: Second Life to Blue Mars, etc." (Mills, 2009b). In essence, Best-VirtualWorlds.com would serve as a comprehensive information hub, reporting on life across other worlds in the larger Metaverse.

Mills (2009b) asked the author, "Did you see the interview I did with Phil? He was quite righteous in that SL was a world to discover, and that it was the nature of its unpredictability that made it great...I couldn't agree more." In that interview, Linden explained to Mills (2009a, p. 100): "If I wasn't constantly surprised and excited by things people do and build in SL, I'd know that something had gone wrong." He continued, "I always felt that the unpredictable nature of developments in the world would be one of the key indicators that we were doing things right—that same magical threshold of possibility had been reached." Linden added, "What excites me more is the possibility that SL can make the real world better and safer by connecting different cultures and people more quickly than otherwise might have happened" (Mills, 2009a, p. 100). In that interview with Mills, Linden contemplated the context upon which Second Life exists, an era of possibility and exploration:

> Second Life and virtual worlds are still very early and very complex to make work, which, I think, is why there isn't as much competition as you might expect...[M]any people...(like me) who have been dreaming about these worlds for so long are often surprised by this." (Mills, 2009a, p. 99)

It's within this era of unpredictability that Mills and his staff attempt to report on the virtual world of Second Life and its counterparts. Some of these worlds have come and gone over the past several years, indicating the trial-and-error process and evolutionary nature of the Metaverse. But one thing appears certain—Frolic Mills has gotten it right with *BOSL*.

Overview of SL News Media

Obviously some credible journalism programs at major universities see value in Second Life, at the very least, as a means to teach reporting skills. In April 2008, The London School of Journalism offered a series of free lectures within Second Life. SL members were invited to attend lectures presented by journalism professionals. The virtual campus already had up to 1,000 visitors per day to its online site, and organizers had hoped to use SL to experiment with journalistic techniques among its students. Other programs presented at universities, such as in the case of The Edward R. Murrow College of Communication in Washington State University (WSU), have been the result of partnerships with foundations and an intention to stimulate dialogue on new media technologies for news gathering. In February 2009, WSU educators invited technology executives and journalists into a forum to discuss journalism in an era of virtual worlds, and the role of commercial and citizen reporting.

Increasingly, with the rise of virtual worlds becoming more comparable to and competitive with Second Life, questions on how to cover these "games" is significant for a couple of reasons. For one, when thousands to millions of people gather together from across the world, the historical phenomena of such occurrences, particularly when on a regular basis, becomes newsworthy. Secondly, when people begin to substitute mainstream media choices for virtual ones, well RL media companies take note, even if they merely stand on the sidelines to observe these trends. Several print media groups report on Second Life activities, with some leaning more toward news and others toward entertainment.

As Second Life grows in membership, the media companies have begun to form alliances among each other. Broadcast media were discussed in an earlier chapter covering television and machinima. This chapter concentrates on the print media, and somewhat the crossover into the broadcast media among some news organizations.

Second Life Herald

One of the earliest newspapers was the *Second Life Herald*, which was launched on October 23, 2003, by philosophy professor Peter Ludlow. As it exists today, the newspaper is more or less a tabloid blog, and its history is documented in Ludlow's MIT Press book *The Second Life Herald* published in 2007. Ludlow had the idea to document virtual life, as it evolved first on The Sims and other MMOGs. The tabloid was first known as the *Alphaville Herald*, and garnered attention for its controversial investigation into the seedier sides of cyber-life, such as gambling and prostitution. It would challenge Linden Lab's policies and practices in its coverage of the Metaverse. Its coverage was hard-hitting, yet sensational. As it evolved into the *Second Life Herald,* it covered primarily SL. The overall *Herald* staff reveals a mix of men and women on its editorial staff. The content mainly gravitates toward SL news and entertainment, leaning strongly toward the sensational and lauding what it believes to be its muckraking role in the Metaverse. It also covers news regarding other MMOGs and virtual worlds. The *Herald* remains a tabloid, and is available online at http://www.secondlifeherald.com. It is no longer the only news enterprise in SL, and competes with several other print media—including those affiliated with real-life mainstream media organizations.

The Rise of Competition

Other newspapers and magazines have surfaced, some having only short runs, since the *Herald*'s debut. One SL newspaper, *The AV star*, a strong advocate for Linden Lab, closed down in 2008, following SL Reuters news service's departure from Second Life. Adam Reuters was the primary SL reporter for the online news service that connected its SL viewers to its RL Web site. The Reuters news agency reported minimal traffic at its in-world site, as the reason for pulling out of SL. Meanwhile, CNN has expanded its role in Second Life, with its goal to tap into a virtual-world audience for story ideas, as a way to keep tabs on happenings across the Metaverse and to learn a little more about how those in virtual worlds acquire their news.

In 2008, CNN created a citizen journalism program for SL residents that would encourage wanna-be reporters to post photos, text, audio and video to iReport. CNN's Lila Kind, a senior producer for interactive storytelling, elaborated on the network's rationale, "You get an amazing integration of what's actually happening on a hyperlocal level, block by block, by individuals living the experience" (Wagner, 2008). CNN began its citizen reporting program in 2006, tapping into eye-witness coverage by RL viewers, and by 2008, the idea to test the program on a virtual world became a reality. Similarly, NPR's Science Friday has developed a live audience for its show in SL, and in this way it can get instant feedback from attendees.

The Metaverse Messenger

Another newspaper with longevity is *The Metaverse Messenger*, a weekly newspaper. Some of its featured stories have included headlines like *Commercial sim premiers*, *Interview with an SL vampire*, *Second Citizen rises from the grave*, *Resident of the Week*, and *Sim of the Week*. The newspaper is fairly serious in content and presentation, and models itself after conventional newspapers. It was created by Katt Kongo and Phoenix Psaltery in August 2005. It is published as an online PDF at www.metaversemessenger.com, and reports a readership of more than 100,000 on its Web site: "The newspaper has been featured in publications such as *De Nieuwe Reporter*, *Metro Times*, www.channel4.com, *The International Herald Tribune*, *The Guardian*, *Adweek*, *AAJA Voice*, *Austin-American Statesman*, *The Phoenix*, *Business Week*, *Clickable Culture*, and many others" (Zimmer, 2006). Kongo taps into the sense of community created within Second Life's various constituencies, who still, however, belong to the same worlds—real and virtual: "I feel that there are certain aspects needed for a community to exist, and one such aspect is a way to spread news, whether it's a newspaper or word of mouth. The larger a community grows, the more efficient its means of sharing news should be" (Zimmer, 2006).

Kongo illustrates, stating, "I look for stories that would educate and inform readers, and even occasionally entertain them, like the recent article on the group of residents whose religion dictates the worship of (SL founder) Philip Linden. Generally speaking, if an article would interest me, it would also interest the M2 readership" (Zimmer, 2006). Moreover, she points out, "A newspaper helps residents function by providing a tool which they can then use to make decisions with—where to buy the best clothing, what to do on a Friday night, how to use new SL features, and more" (Zimmer, 2006).

A hard copy of the newspaper is typically published for the annual Second Life Community Convention. Kongo is an RL experienced journalist; and she has set up training programs to assist in teaching journalism within SL. Her methods have real-world applications. Initially, she opened the "center to give [her] staff members, and any interested SL residents, a basic education in journalism, basically what would amount to an Associate's Degree" (Zimmer, 2006). She stresses the importance of maintaining in-world credibility, and explains that the company motto, "A real newspaper for a virtual world," encapsulates the organizational mission: "[W]e strive to be as like a meatworld (real world) newspaper as possible. A print format, even though it's electronic, is part of that. And print is here to stay. People just need to find new ways to use it...And yes, we do have plans to add other news formats" (Zimmer, 2006).

The SL-Newspaper

SL-Newspaper is among the growing print media, with its third-year anniversary celebrated in November 2009. This newspaper can clearly boast to a strong balance of men and women on its staff, with a number of women reporting on fashion, entertainment, business and finance. A few of the reporters are also RL journalists or work in media. *SL-Newspaper* covers SL business, art, fashion, music, and entertainment news, and keeps track of trends in SL. The newspaper is online, available both in SL and RL. Alesia Schumann is a real-life reporter and moonlights in-world for *SL-Newspaper*:

> As you could guess, my first days as an SL user were filled with questions as to how this virtual world works and what I could really do around here. After a couple of days of teleporting to different kinds of places and events to find something interesting to do or visit, I thought it would only be natural to turn to what I do in real life, at least to get started. (Schumann, 2009)

Schumann also operates a photo studio in Second Life. Initially, however, Schumann sought out a writing position at "a media outlet that needed help" and that was the *SL Enquirer*, a virtual newspaper that mostly reports on entertainment, not really about general news or business. Schumann (2009) explained, "That way, I could define a part of my use of Second Life. This is a big deal because when you discover SL, you want to find a purpose. Otherwise, you may doubt how useful it is to be around here outside of buying clothes and partying at clubs." Schumann (2009) continues, "So I did a fair bit of reporting at the *SL Enquirer*, but in the end, I thought this publication was not as serious as I wanted, so I quit. At a social event, I met the day-to-day manager of the *SL-Newspaper*...This virtual newspaper is a better fit for me since it actually does news and allows me to handle more commentary."

Schumann's interest in covering the financial sector of Second Life has led to an in-world business expertise. She states, "Business is overly important in SL and it is one of my fields of interest. I feel that it is only normal to do some of that" (Schumann, 2009). She provides commentary generally on "the topic of running a business in SL. I still believe that this place hasn't yet got out of the 'entrepreneur period' that characterizes a world which is in its infancy. This is still a world of early adopters, not yet a world which is popular with mainstream media or the general public" (Schumann, 2009). She adds, "In its own way, SL is still a startup and business conditions are an important issue. SL needs to have great business conditions to grow and reach a much larger public to become mainstream" (Schumann, 2009).

She has provided well-researched commentary on the economics behind the fashion industry, for instance, questioning the impact of real-world companies on SL businesses. In one of her columns, she wrote:

> The Second Life News Network raised a most interesting question recently about the rise of Armidi and their ability to suck the grid's talent pool of clothing and hair designers...The risks of an Armidi monopoly would be homogenized fashion and a lack of personal style in new clothing. While this and other usual problems related to monopolies are genuine questions, there might be a case to favor a bigger Armidi stranglehold on SL fashion. (Schumann, 2008a)

Second Life has provided her an opportunity to establish herself as a respected columnist with a growing expertise in virtual world business. Elaborating, she goes on to say,

> I am not exactly looking for SL to benefit RL, so to speak, rather to complement RL by doing things that I like but which would take too much time to handle. It would be fun, in RL, to do commentary. This, however, would add an incredible workload to an already busy schedule in general, if only to research topics. Since I like to spend some of my free time in SL, this research and fact-gathering is done as I am around. So, I can write my commentary rather quickly when I have an idea for a column. (Schumann, 2009)

Schumann (2009), from her coverage of SL and her real-life journalism experience, has developed a professional and personal perspective regarding the role of virtual media:

> I see the mission of SL media as more of a niche than in RL. I do not think that the media here will reach the same mass media status that they do in RL, reaching almost everyone everywhere. In RL, whether you watch TV, read the papers or listen to radio, it is hard to avoid the news. In SL, newspapers are probably the only formal type of media that exist and you have to see a vendor somewhere on a sim or actually seek them through the search functions. I can understand why newspapers are more of a niche thing than in RL. People get enough news in RL; they may not be looking for that in SL.

Schumann adds that she personally would be surprised to see a whole lot of media companies coming in-world to report on virtual worlds: "Since SL media are not that big of a deal; there are very little gains to make from it. And let's face it: the media are in one difficult economic position these days in North America." Schumann (2009) does not perceive SL as having a valid advertising model to support a strong news media, particularly anything of the level to interest mainstream media outlets.

Schumann sees "no real competition" from mainstream media in Second Life, pointing out, "This really is a fringe phenomenon. For instance, Reuters was the only real business-oriented news media in SL." Schumann (2009) expressed concern with what she thought were more relevant issues, stating,

> My problem with the media around here is consistency. We all spend the time we can spend around here, which means that on a busy day, we may not be around to cover an interesting story. This means that if you are a reader, you will look at SL media and realize that they do not bring a large coverage of news and events, day in and day out. The only way to fix this is to have a broader base of reporters, but recruiting and keeping them has been a rather difficult task for newspaper owners.

Schumann (2009) interestingly believes that "negative press is extremely dangerous for the Lindens. Back in 2007, when grid outages were common, the noise around SL's lack of reliability turned SL, which was a promising idea for the mainstream media, to this 'virtual world that doesn't work.'" She pointed out, merely reviewing archives one will note, that the *Economist*, which had been mentioning Second Life "frequently a couple of years ago" had subsequently reported "almost nothing" on it in recent years. Schumann says, "To get here (to SL), you have to hear about it." In the past, Schumann (2008b) has also criticized Linden Lab, for example, when the SL grid had created a considerable amount of downtime for its residents, impacting in-world businesses. However, the Lindens, she observes, "do need good PR from SL newspapers," in order to mature and sustain their virtual-world economy (Schumann, 2009).

That is a point that not all news media entrepreneurs and journalists in SL agree with, with some seeing SL news media as a check and balance for Linden Lab, and some also see the possibility of virtual media expanding coverage into RL while based in-world. In the near to distant future, as SL media expand their reporting toward covering issues pertaining in and across other virtual worlds, now being developed, attention may be somewhat diverted from the Lindens to other virtual world moguls.

Metaverse Broadcasting Company (MBC) News

Robustus Hax is owner of Metaverse Broadcasting Company (MBC). Metaverse Television, part of MBC, is one of two television broadcast networks in SL. His media operation covers in-world news and entertainment as well as creates original content for its television station. *Metaverse Messenger*, the weekly newspaper mentioned earlier, is not affiliated with Hax's media operation. Hax wears many hats in his company, including being the co-producer of MBC's reality show *I Wanna Be a Celebrity*, hosted by Trinity Serpentine, one of the original founders of Radio Radio and once co-host to the show TriNala, one of the longest-running radio programs in Second Life. The celebrity reality show that she hosts is produced by Phaylen Fairchild, along with Hax. Fairchild (2009) said, that she and Hax knew from the start that "the celebrity format would be a wonderful format and also an entertaining format to sort of introduce ourselves to [the SL] creative community...It's like if we can't get out there to them, let's create an avenue to get them to us." Hax explained that there is not a lot of training "to prepare you to film a live reality show. I mean I've filmed live before, a live broadcast where you just sit and record everything" (Fairchild, 2009). There is that human side to it all, and he added "when you have to follow cast members around, you want to catch every little word they say 'cause even their movements, their avatars' movements can be funny." Overall, he points out, "You don't want to miss anything. It's high intensity. It's high intensity...and the emotional part of it too. I didn't expect that at all. You're sitting there watching this go down and there's feelings involved, people's friendships" (Fairchild, 2009).

Hax questioned himself initially whether reality television could really work in Second Life. He acknowledges that emotions are real in Second Life, pointing out that "you can just tell" even though you can't really see an avatar's expressions (Fairchild, 2009). Other reality shows in SL have included RL television take-offs like *Big Brother*, along with shows such as *Celebrity Survivor* produced in Italy for Second Life. Fairchild notes that those programs did not see the success that MBC's reality show has experienced during its on-air run. She credits much of the success of the show to Hax's long in-world history of "creating media in SL," beginning with his first show, *The News: SL4B*, which originated after the idea of Metaverse TV was conceived, yet before "we had live capabilities and we could broadcast people" (Fairchild, 2009). Hax elaborates:

> It was pretty much at that point I decided people would need to be broadcasting these events 'cause they would send out a message to 30,000 people online to come check out Philip Linden speak at a sim that can hold 80 people max. (Fairchild, 2009)

He recalls, laughing, "I got into the sim and filmed myself sitting there. Philip couldn't get on 'cause the sim was packed. I'm assuming someone in that Linden office just decided at random to get a couple of avatars off" (Fairchild, 2009). By this Hax is referring to the ejection of SL members from a sim to make room for the then Linden Lab CEO, Philip Linden.

Hax's Second Life adventure began when he was bored at work one day, browsing online, and came across a *Business Week* article in late 2006 featuring Anshe Chung, Second Life's major entrepreneur at the time, and the story "intrigued" him: "I'm a pretty big nerd. I've been around since the bulletin board days before the Internet—so any type of geekiness intrigued me—a virtual world with land and you could build whatever you want" (Fairchild, 2009). When he first joined Second Life, he did some building and made some attempts at marketing, but it was the people he met along the way that would make the difference in his virtual path: "I just got immersed in this endless sea; I was on the mainland, and I would fly for a day just looking at stuff. It was amazing" (Fairchild, 2009). His first project was a skyscraper on a small plot of virtual land before he had even been on Second Life for 2 months. When his prims ran out, he moved on to other ideas. He was making T-shirts and building things, but what he was doing in actuality was developing a network of friends: "We all had ambitious plans" (Fairchild, 2009). For Hax, it was how television might be used through virtual worlds that interested him, beginning with a personal goal of just being able to "watch regular TV with my cousin who was across the country in SL…So I just began looking up what I needed to do a stream into SL. It was born through that I guess" (Fairchild, 2009)

Hax looks much too young to be a media entrepreneur. At the time of our interview in August 2009, he was about to turn 29. By then, he had been in SL for nearly 3 years. Second life has allowed him to express his creativity "in a way not possible in real life," Hax (2009) recalls, explaining:

> I'm very much into "creating," writing books, reading books, dreaming big, SL has allowed for me to take that creativity to a new level…I am not in media in the real- life sense nor have a background in it; everything I've done I've learned myself sort of feeling out the waters to where I am now.

He mentioned that he was working on a science fiction novel. His strategy, in his own words, is "stick my nose in everything," Hax (2009) says, smiling. Ambitious, curious, and driven to change the way news is reported on virtual worlds like Second Life, the newspaper *The Metaverse Tribune* might be the vehicle to connect RL to SL, and to connect all the dots between virtual worlds. The Metaverse Broadcasting Company has the capacity to cover events in broadcast and print media with the launch of *The Metaverse Tribune* in August 2009. Through this paper, Hax "seeks to go further and look at the virtual worlds as a whole, as an online level of human society" (*Metaverse*, 2008). Moreover, to be competitive and relevant within the virtual television industry, especially if he intends to nurture real world connections with his audience, Hax knew that he would have to shift to more storytelling from less talking heads to engage his viewers.

Hax (2009) elaborated, it is difficult to establish a sense of community in virtual worlds, for "the medium in which information is passed is fragmented," especially given the state of journalism and communication inside Second Life. He explains, "It is hard to keep track of news and find what's going on...I wanted to create a medium where people could stay connected whether it's from their parcel, the web, their mobile phone, etc., but at least a place they could 'stay in the know'" (Hax, 2009). "I think what I'm doing right now is just really breaking the iceberg to what's possible with media and virtual worlds," he adds.

To Hax, "the virtual world is a real place; events happen here and real people are here. It's only natural a television station or broadcasting company would follow. Right now we are mainly Second Life, but we do work in the other virtual worlds and would like to expand more on our coverage of other virtual worlds." In 2009, his plans included the "launch of a new sim, built by Lumiere Noir, one of the more renowned builders in SL." Indeed, he completed that project soon after our interview and relocated his operation. That sim is dedicated to the MBC enterprise, broadcast and print. Hax is making his mark on how virtual news is presented and content is created to serve in-world audiences. His volunteer staff works alongside him, redefining news and entertainment content for audiences comfortable living in both real and virtual spaces, and perhaps increasingly virtually:

> Mostly the inner circle of people that work with me do so out of their own passion for Second Life and media...We're not a big business at this point so I don't have paid staff quite yet, but will be enlisting for people to work on our new sim in the future. I work with people all over the globe so it's pretty amazing. (Hax, 2009)

"Some of them are RL media people, but they won't tell me who they really are," he says, seemingly amused at the concept (Hax, 2009). The distinction between real-world and virtual-world journalism is becoming less clear, with Hax realizing that his audience increasingly demands information that impacts every aspect of their life. In many aspects, Metaverse Broadcasting Company caters to an audience with a world view, given that the composition of SL's membership is international (Hax, 2009):

> We actually did a breaking news story last year when there was an earthquake in the UK. [MBC News Anchor] Dousa was able to report about it live, we got it on YouTube and it was a huge hit. People were shocked at how quickly we were able to break the story. I would love one day to be able to broadcast on cable television using machinima to create the content. It's probably the most cost effective way to create programming.

Dousa Dragonash is the lead anchor of MBC Weekly News, which is streamed in-world on SL televisions and online across the Web. It is the longest running virtual world news program. Hax speculates on the future of media, stating:

> As the technology gets better and more people are brought in I do see the big media companies eventually trying to set up shop here…but I do see live video as a major piece to the puzzle. Once bandwidth increases and computing power gets better, we will see a large growth in that area. Right now there are only two broadcasting companies sending live video into Second Life, I'm one of them, and the reason it's so narrow is because of those limitations; streaming live costs a lot of money and SL limits to QuickTime right now, which is another obstacle. (Hax, 2009)

As far as the balance between RL and SL content reported on by Metaverse's news operation, Hax admits,"Dousa and I argue over that all the time." But all that philosophical banter is good between the two, for they have accomplished much together. He continues,

> Right now I believe we're focused on virtual worlds. If we are doing real-life news topics I'd like for it to relate in somehow to Second Life, or hear a person in Second Life speak on the RL news topic, where we would be contributing our own content to the context of the RL News. (Hax, 2009)

Hax (2009) points out, "I think right now people don't get their mainstream news through virtual worlds yet." Elaborating on the increasingly significant role of Web news media, Hax (2009) states, "It's hard to take RL TV News seriously anymore. I get most of my RL news off a site like Digg. It's a social news site; basically users 'dig' the most relevant news and it goes to the front page." He foresees media playing an important role in-world, as it should in the real world. Hax (2009) says, adamantly, in the spirit of a true journalist, "Linden doesn't have any say about what news we report or if we are critical of them which we usually are. I think being critical of them is good because it could help spur change."

Conclusion

Publications come and go in Second Life, and some have expanded their coverage to all the virtual worlds across the Metaverse. A number of specialty magazines exist within SL, some of which are only online. The *SLentrepreneur Magazine* made its debut January 2008, with niche coverage of business in Second Life. Visiting a magazine stand in Milan (SL), I came across a variety of kiosks featuring high-quality glossy magazine publications, among them *ICON Lifestyle Magazine*. I first came across that magazine on the coffee table of Frolic Mills, CEO of *BOSL Magazine*. It was on the same table as his July edition of *BOSL*, featuring his interview with Philip Linden. Print media flourishes within Second Life, and the hard (prim) publications are as real as any real-life publication.

Among the publications at the Milan magazine stand were those that covered fashion and lifestyle in Second Life: *Second Style* (fashion), *BeStyle: The Best of Italian Style*, *Avenue Magazine*, *Essence*, *Vain Inc*, *Captured (Deutsch)*, *Les Tresors Mode*, *Retropolitan*, *DMI The Magazine*, and *X-Factor*. Other magazines appeared to explore the fantasy culture within virtual worlds, with titles such as *Role Play*, *Inner World*, and *Uncover*; the latter publication states in its mission its vision is to uncover beautiful people, places, events and creations in SL. This chapter also explored the main newspapers in SL, but certain groups have their own "village" press that report on group activities and common interests. *The Metaverse Journal*, founded in November 2006, is a blog that exemplifies how some SL journals successfully target certain populations. *The Journal* is professional in presentation and content, and is dedicated to the Australian perspective in virtual worlds. As in RL, some publications are intended to reach national audiences and others cater to local communities or constituencies; all are valid when they serve their particular readerships. On the local level, for instance, *Avalonian* is a newsletter for the residents of Avalon Town. It captures the local spirit of the community, and provides updates to happenings in the region. A section in the small press is called *Colleen's Corner*, authored by Avalon Estate owner and founder Colleen Kesey. In the November 2009 issue, Kesey (2009) writes on the significance of American Thanksgiving as one that should remind us to "not forget those who need our help because they are alone, or hungry or afraid. Volunteer somewhere to help others or invite someone to share in your abundance. Be a friend." She continues, "Let us give thanks for each other and for this life, full of struggles, fun and adventure. I wish for each of you life's full promise, both here and in real life" (Kesey, 2009). Residents within virtual worlds thrive on communication, with some demanding more information than others. For many readers, it is the connection among residents that is critical.

Mainstream media would have a difficult time understanding the relevance of in-world events. But the reporters, photographers and editors within SL are also residents of virtual words. They belong to the community that they report on, be it a daily, weekly or monthly basis. They have a stake in the success of their virtual life. For most publishers in SL, they take their virtual jobs seriously and execute their mission with integrity. For all the occupations in SL and virtual worlds, being a reporter (or even a publisher) is not the easiest path toward accumulating wealth. SL escorts often earn more than journalists, who many times work for free. Most reporters feel their work is a service to the world they live in, even if they have to log into it with a password.

References

Associated Press. (2008, October 23). McCain, Obama supporters rally in Second Life virtual world. *FoxNews.com*. Accessed June 14, 2009, from http://www.foxnews.com/story/ 0,2933, 443777,00.html/

BBC. (2008, November 12). Obama takes lead in virtual world. Accessed April 1, 2010, from http://news.bbc.co.uk/2/hi/technology/7722721.stm

Fairchild, P. (2009, March 17). Gabbing with Robustus Hax and Trinity Serpentine. Interview. Podcast. Second Life: Phaylen Fairchild Productions. Accessed August 18, 2009, from http://phaylen.com/?p=56/

Hax, R. (2009, August 16). Interview, personal communication with author. Second Life.

Kesey, C. (2009, November). *Colleen's Corner*. *Avalonian Newspaper*. Second Life.

Lawinski, J. (2009, January 9). Gaza conflict moves to virtual world. *FoxNews.com*. Accessed July 21, 2009, from http://www.foxnews.com/story/ 0,2933,478626,00.html/

Ludlow, P., & Wallace, M. (2007). *The Second Life Herald: The virtual tabloid that witnessed the dawn of the metaverse*. Cambridge, MA: MIT Press.

Metaverse Tribune launches. (2008, August 1). *SL Pulse*. Accessed August 20, 2009, from http://www.slpulse.com/content/view/417/2/

Mills, F. (2009b, August 17). Interview, personal communication with the author. Second Life.

—.(2009a, July) A conversation with Philip Linden: *Best of SL* exclusive interview with the chairman of the board and founder of Second Life! *Best of Second Life Magazine*. Accessed July 13, 2009, from http://www.thebosl.com/

Schumann, A. (2009, August 12). Interview, personal communication with author. Second Life.

—.(2008a, May 27). Is an Armidi fashion monopoly a bad thing? *SL-Newspaper*. Accessed August 11, 2009, from http://15timez.blogspot.com/2008/03/is-armidi-fashion-monopoly-bad-thing.html/

——. (2008b, May 10). Second Life has to grow into adulthood. *SLNewspaper*. Accessed August 11, 2009, from http://15timez.blogspot.com/2008/05/second-life-has-to-grow-into-adulthood.html/

Wagner, M. (2008, March 24). CNN creates citizen journalism channels on web, in Second Life. *InformationWeek.com*. Accessed August 13, 2009, from http://www.informationweek.com/ blog/main/archives/2008/03/cnn_creates_cit.html/

Waldschmidt, S. (2007, October 7). Into In-World News. Accessed July 21, 2009, from http://ehub.journalism.ku.edu/j201/second_life/Second Life/

Zimmer, L. (2006). Real journalism in a virtual world: Interview with Second Life's *Metaverse Messenger* publisher Katt Kongo. *Business communicators of Second Life*. Accessed August 19, 2009, from http://freshtakes.typepad.com/sl_communicators/2006/09/real_journalism.html/

BBC. (2008, November 12). Obama takes lead in virtual world. Accessed April 1, 2010, from http://news.bbc.co.uk/2/hi/technology/7722721.stm

SECTION 3

The Good and Bad of a Virtual Society

CHAPTER ELEVEN

The Fringe of Second Life: Sex, Violence and Crime

> "She bent over this guy and all of a sudden, the casket just explodes with light, and the lid pops open and the guy jumps out. He is no longer a person; he is now a full-blown demon in a very well-made skin of a demon. I mean, he was a demon. He was reborn under Satan to be their protector to have a major role, to become a major player in the clan."
>
> —Landis Desidero, SL vampire victim

Tatum followed the dark, worn asphalt street, cautiously. Neon signs were plastered above entrance ways to gray concrete buildings. The moon and the signs radiated above her, giving her just enough light to see a few yards ahead. A man in a tattered black jacket and faded jeans stood at the entrance of one of the alleys. She scurried past him, but he said nothing to her. Her fears aroused by what she could not see and what she heard: sounds of the looped downbeat of industrial techno vibrating from one of the buildings. She hurried past a store window sign, *Dark Delights*, an enterprise that catered obviously to the resident vampires that she had not yet encountered. A flashing light caught her eye. The building seemed empty, like it had once been a nightclub. She ducked into the building to regroup her thoughts; her imagination now going wild, not sure if she feared the streets or what might be inside the buildings. The entrance was long, as she passed through the door. Small white lights lined railings along the walls down the long corridor path. The music transitioned to an urban mix of hip-hop with sensual and forceful lyrics. She followed the path until she was at the entrance of a run-down strip joint.An intense blue light made the place seem cold. But she noted several people within the place. A middle-aged woman in red sequined top and slick black shorts caught her eye, as she watched her dance against a steel pole on top of an old wooden round table. The pole extended to the ceiling. One man sat on a chair, half watching the dancer and half attending to his drink on the table. He occasionally looked toward the men gathered around the bar. They stood there, quiet, perhaps conversing to each privately. But what they said was hidden within the lyrics of the music. Then, a man with long dark hair, wearing a black leather long jacket and dark pants approached Tatum from behind, extending greetings. In awe of his magnificent wings, she remained silent. He greeted her again, and with a warm smile, added, "So you are new to

Second Life?" This was her first real encounter with the underworld of Second Life, having arrived only a couple of weeks ago. Her profile was a dead give-away: she was a noob, way out of her element. Easy prey.

This scene illustrates part of the dark side of Second Life: seedy alleys spotted with sex pose balls, random shootings on street corners, unsuspecting tourists as prey for vampire lairs, and glimpses of dystopian communities of the future. The chapter begins with a look into the dark fantasy cultures of Gorean and Vampire, as well as provides a glimpse into sex, violence, crime and consequences in Second Life.

Dark Communities

Second Life is filled with hundreds of islands and builds that are reminiscent of science fiction and horror movies. Some of the sets are perhaps more realistic than one would find in a Hollywood movie. For some, Second Life provides them with an opportunity to role-play within various contexts. The performers become the movie stars to a plot that twists and turns better than a Stephen King novel because it is the interaction, often spontaneous, between the people within these settings that defines the storyline. Textures are created to provide a realistic feel to the places. Light sources are carefully crafted and placed. Some mock avatars are set up in various poses to enhance the sense of mystery and realism. Who is that stranger over by the alley? Am I in danger—is that a real avatar or is it a prop? Layers and layers of a semblance of reality add to the virtual experience.

For many residents, the dark side of Second Life appeals to their curiosity and their willingness to explore those fantasies often considered socially unacceptable in real life. For some, it is like walking into a movie or a novel, but they are the actors. Their interactions with props and other people compose the experience. A number of Gorean communities are present within Second Life, and much effort is spent on recreating that time period. One community's set of rules warn, "No observers." For this group, they want people who are willing to immerse themselves into the game, and its rules. And for many of these communities, the rules are many. In Gorean role-play, typically women have a choice of being a slave or free woman. On a member's first visit, if she chooses to be a free woman, she is advised to expose minimal flesh or she might be taken captive. On one occasion, my guide for the day, a slave woman, served a master whom she had to approach in a certain way with submissive text. He seemed fairly considerate of her, but the situation appears odd to anyone like me not persuaded of the benefits of submission. As a free woman, I could roam about, and did so, until there was a warning of a raid on the horizon. Being only my first day there, and without any weapons or knowledge of how to use them if I had them, I simply teleported to my safe Second Life home, zillions of teleport beams away. That would be considered cheating to most members of the Gorean community. The day of my visit, from what I experienced, was uneventful and I didn't have the time or energy so late at night to wait for the raid. I was warned that free women could be taken captive and claimed. Although that is obviously impossible unless one is willing (for one can leave the game), I departed to surroundings more in line with my real life. Themes within the Gorean community vary from pirates to medieval times to vampire fantasy. Undeniably, sex and violence are major currents within the Gorean culture. Yet, friendships and lasting bonds are made among some of the membership, and many players have no problems separating their real life from their role-play. Second Life provides them an opportunity to explore a world that is completely alien to their daily life.

Role-Play and Fantasy in Vampire Culture

In Second Life, fantasy role-play attracts certain members. For some, it is purely theatrical; for others, it is an emotionally expressive outlet that they cannot fully tap into in real life. Vampire communities are somewhat popular in Second Life among some membership. Occasionally, outside a dance club, a notice will state, "No biting allowed." Most clubs refrain from drama, and sometimes that means banning vampires, or at least any attempts at biting patrons, whether given permission or not from the intended victim. Landis Desidero had the opportunity to get a glimpse of the darker side of Second Life. The author interviewed him about his experiences within a vampire village, and agreed to use a pseudonym for his avatar name. Desidero's perspective is one of an outsider, and his narrative on his introduction to the vampire culture provides an interesting peek into the larger dark fantasy culture within the shadows of Second Life.

He begins his tale, by reflecting on how a vampire woman approached him at one of the alternative dance clubs in Second Life:

> I was at the Alt.7, my favorite club to just hang out and listen to good music and dance. Some stranger, an oddly dressed woman came up to me. She started talking to me. She was really open and friendly. I didn't think much about it at the time. And then she asked me in IM (instant message), writing, "Is it okay, if I bite you? Amused I said, "What do you mean, if you bite me?" Well, she says, "I'm a vampire. I'm just playing a game. If I bite you, it's just part of the game." And I talked for about 5 minutes before I even would think about it, about her biting and all that. And she began to explain to me about the game and how it's played all over Second Life. I was really curious because I hadn't heard anything about this before. (Desidero, 2009)

The vampire game, Bloodlines, has a Web site that lists its members. He would agree to let her bite him. Even though he never bit anyone himself, he is listed on the site as part vampire—with his genealogy being a small percentage of the bloodline:

> After a few minutes, I realized she was pretty nice and sincere. I said, "okay," and I agreed, and when I did, a window opened up asking my permission to activate an animation that would allow her to bite me. So I clicked yes and accepted the bite. And she like immediately popped up, jumped on my neck, and bit me, and left two bite marks on my neck. It was really freaky. Actually the animation was so good; it just made me even more curious—accepting the animation also means you accept a gift. The gift is that you get to keep those bite fangs that are on your neck. So we began to talk more about the game called Bloodlines. As we talked about it, she said, "Well in order to play the game, you have to have the HUD—in order to operate and to play in the game." So I said, "Just show me where the HUD is." I wasn't sure if I wanted to get into it that seriously. She took me back to her clan. Apparently, of Bloodline, there are different clans of vampires. They don't compete or anything like that. It's just that all these different clans have one head. It's kind of like each one has a family and one head vampire. Everyone operates, like under a pyramid, under this one person. So we went to the village of this one clan. She started introducing me to some people, and they all seemed nice, friendly and wanted to talk about it. It looked like any other village in Second Life, kinda old world European village. I was meeting people and she showed me where the HUD was and I went ahead and just got the HUD so I could check into it. I thought, it just didn't seem part of my identity. But I was still curious enough so instead I sent an alt back to purchase the HUD with the idea for him to become a vampire. And that's kind of what I did later that afternoon. (Desidero, 2009)

Desidero went back that afternoon with an alternative avatar that "looked an awful lot like me, and people just assumed it was me." He said yeah, "It is me, it's just my alt." He actually used the excuse that his wife wouldn't approve of him being a vampire. He said he did mention it to his wife, saying, "Honey I will come back and bite you and show you what this is all about." To which, she of course sternly said, "No way in Hell," mused Desidero. When he returned as an alt to purchase the HUD, he met some different people. The woman who initially brought him there "wasn't around but her best friend was so I started hanging out with her and some of her friends. In fact, I met a guy friend—he was a pretty nice guy." Desidero added, "I met the head vampire. Really strange. She looked like something that stepped right out of a very well-made movie set. She was attractive but in a very dark way." He described her as a tall sinister-looking woman, with long hair and reddish eyes, "but very nice. And she even talked to me in IM, reassuring me, this is all totally cool."

Desidero had come prepared. He had changed his clothing to match the village setting. He wore a black cloak and leather pants and his jet black hair skimmed the top of his neck, shimmering against his dark olive complexion. He noted his surroundings, and met up with the woman he had seen earlier that afternoon:

> Walking around the village, the place, I found, they have a lot of vampire products, and everything fairly much associated with clothes. I found a movie theater, and I found playrooms, a lot of sexual devices, things to tie people up, to chain people up, and things like that. So you can tell sex was a big part; they had a place for that in this little society, in this village. I came later that evening, took a break for a few hours, and I met up with the girl who I had met earlier that day. When I saw her—the first thing I noticed was there was something different, I noticed she was crying. She had real tears pouring out of her eyes. I asked, "What happened?" She said, "Well my best friend died." I thought this is really strange and the way she talked, she was really mourning over her friend dying. (Desidero, 2009)

He continued, remembering how he was caught off guard by the events that unfolded over the next few hours:

> She was crying and she asked me to hang out with her because she was telling me the story of her friend dying and she was trying to get in her "mourning mode." She was crying real tears, and I thought she was serious, like it had happened in real life. She said, "Yeah the funeral will be tonight at the church." I said, "Oh, okay." I spent about 45 minutes with her and I said, "I gotta go." It was all very strange and very depressing. And I remember I came back even later, about 9, 10 o'clock at night. I came back to the village; it was night. It was quite eerie; there was a mist everywhere. I happened to notice by a church, light. I went by this old beat-up church with the classic graveyard, dark trees moving around and I noticed all the vampires were gathered in there. And they were sitting inside the church. And this girl actually comes out of the church and welcomes me and says, "The funeral is about to start. It's an open casket, would you like to come?" "I was a little shocked, so this is a Second Life funeral." I went in, and sat down with her and a lot of strange spooky characters in this place. They tried really hard to look as sinister and as evil, as dark and disturbing as they could—men and women. Very graphic designs of horror and vampires and there were demons of all kinds. As I walked by the casket, I camed over and looked; there was a guy I had met earlier that day. He's in the casket laying there dead with an open casket. As I'm sitting there in the pew, people are going up giving eulogies about this guy. I didn't know what to think. I thought, man, they're really being serious about this. (Desidero, 2009)

The church filled with vampires and demons provided juxtaposition to his decoding of the funeral ceremony, by all means a sobering event. He went on with his story:

> Then the head vampire, the head of the clan, begins to go up and do her eulogy and yahda yah. Then she starts to pray, and begins to pray to Satan, and call upon Satan's grace and dahdahda and carrying on. People are cheering her on. I was already uncomfortable when I came in there and now I'm really uncomfortable because this is a bit more of a role-play game than I wanted to get into—these people are serious about their satanic worshipping, or so it seemed and so forth. She bent over this guy and all of a sudden, the casket just explodes with light, and the lid pops open and the guy jumps out. He is no longer a person; he is now a full-blown demon in a very well-made skin of a demon. I mean, he was a demon. He was reborn under Satan to be their protector to have a major role, to become a major player in the clan. I guess this

> was a promotion on his part. And I'm just watching in total unbelief cause it was—they worked so hard and so well to make it—so real. And they were so into the role-play; it freaked me out so much that when I left there (laughs) I didn't come back. I didn't have anything to do with anybody. I disconnected that HUD really fast. That was as far, I didn't ever get to bite anybody, didn't want to, and I went as far as I could just to check it out. And I knew for sure it definitely wasn't for me. (Desidero, 2009)

Fantasy role-play is served well within Second Life. The interaction between people, props and settings invites the unfolding of a storyline. Members within the various role-play communities contribute to the events that happen along the way. There is a basic understanding of what is occurring, but how it will play out depends on the interaction of those involved, and sometimes those observing. Each community has its own set of rules that guide the role-play. Sexual fantasy is an individual choice, not a requirement. Members invest what they can of themselves into the game, and for some it might seem too much of an identity shift. Some members have left these communities reporting they had become addicted to such role-play. Others are convinced it is merely a game within a game, and a creative pastime. Bloodlines is definitely a social networking type of game, if you consider the connections and interactions made between members within its large community of vampires. Bloodlines is a culture that thrives on interaction among people who might be normal in everyday life, but within the game they abide in a community grounded with twisted notions of life, death, and sex that might appear odd to outsiders—outside of their SL community, and to those in real life who are timid about exploring this lifestyle. Some people in SL belong to RL vampire communities, for example.

The Sex Fantasy Industry

People fall in love in Second Life, and have romantic encounters that can be somewhat assisted through animation. Some encounters progress to the real world and marriage. Others seek out relationships that challenge conventional mindsets, even their own in real life. It's just a game, some say. Housewives, school teachers and even lawyers have set up alternate identities to explore their sexual fantasies. Some of this can be expressed in Gorean and Vampire communities. But for others, their role-play is sexually-driven. The Linden Lab has instituted new policies that limit adult content to certain red-light districts of Second Life, and designated a continent dedicated to it (Wagner, 2009). The change in policy was in response to many members, particularly educators, who wanted a safe and predictable experience for students (Wagner, 2009). With an increasing number of companies, colleges and universities establishing a presence in-world, Linden Lab decided to carve out a small part of the virtual world for extreme adult content, defined as representations of explicit conduct or genitalia, intense violence, photo-realistic nudity, and sexually-themed areas. Wagner (2009) debunked the myth that Second Life was "all about sex," indicating cybersex comprises less than 5% of mainland content." SL user hours increased nearly 25%, and in-world transactions (user-to-user) have risen 30%, but only a small percentage is adult content (Wagner, 2009).

Philip Linden (Rosedale) has stated publicly that sex is not necessarily a negative part of a virtual world. Sharing his perspective, he said, "In a lot of ways, the presence of sex as an aspect of creative expression and playful behavior in a place like this is healthy, because it indicates we're doing something right" (Wagner, 2007). Sex, in these terms, becomes the outgrowth of people making connections with one another in ways familiar to them in real life (Wagner, 2007). In May 2007, *InformationWeek* published an investigative piece on "Sex in Second Life," mainly consisting of a series of interviews with people, in their avatar representations, involved in the sex industry in Second Life. One prominent sex industry business woman pointed out, "One learns a lot about the truth of human nature from charging guys to pay for cartoon sex, and then watching them flock to it. 99% of people will tell you that they are against pornography, and yet it's 40% of online activity" (Wagner, 2007).

Another woman interviewed was in a long-term virtual relationship, spanning several months, but in real life, she said she was a housewife and her husband was well aware of her activities: "It's a 3D chat room and it in no way infringes on our lives." Her husband, she states, "thinks it's a riot that I am a domme...before sl my major computer interface was solitaire, then i came here, and im running clubs, i have slave girls, i have loves and adventures and it's all a fun adventure to him and me" (Wagner, 2007). Red flags are typically raised by SL members and those looking in from the outside when residents role-play as children: "Some of that so-called 'ageplay' is innocent, with the simulated children playing on jungle gyms, singing songs, and doing other things that real-life children do. But some of the ageplay is sexual. The ratio of innocent to sexual ageplay is about 50-50" (Wagner, 2007). In an editorial by *AskMen.com*, a question was offered to readers to consider whether certain acts deemed illegal in real life but committed virtually by members of Second Life, such as those involved in the "pimping of virtual child prostitutes," should be prosecuted by real-world standards (given that all the members are legal adults) (*Second Life Sex*, 2007).

The extreme cases involve children "being bound, whipped" (Wagner, 2007). That type of activity is banned by Linden Lab, and no official reports of that kind have made headlines since 2007. Some of the activity may have gone far underground, with certain people becoming less open about their activities—making any kind of enforcement difficult for any corporation trying to oversee an operation comprised of millions of avatars. Sex work seems to attract stay-at-home moms trying to make some extra change for laundry or a loaf of bread. In that sense, sex workers, primarily women, making only a few dollars an hour can be perceived as being exploited. However, a number of in-world sex workers are professionals (other than sex industry) in real life, making high incomes (Wagner, 2007). The real risk is when emotional connections are made in unhealthy situations.

On the contrary, explains Rosedale, "A lot of the sex relationships in Second Life are driven more by lengthy, meaningful discussions...People have sex in Second Life because they have incredibly deep relationships, not just because they want to have sex" (Wagner, 2007). Moreover, people should not consider Second Life as "an anonymous environment. It's really no more or less anonymous than the real world. If you want to travel to a faraway city where no one knows you and go into a strip club, that's anonymous too" (Rosedale, cited in Wagner, 2007). Second Life can create the feeling that you are "really talking to another person across a table...And sometimes when people are talking across a table, that leads to sex. In real life and in Second Life, too" (Wagner, 2007).

The Illinois Institute for Addiction Recovery is the nation's only Internet treatment program. Most of its treatment goes to those addicted to online gambling, but at times online social networks and virtual reality sites have contributed to situations where patients could no longer separate reality from game play. In extreme cases, the virtual person becomes real to them (Michels, 2008). In a high-profile case that made national headlines, Kimberly Jernigan, 33, was arrested for allegedly attempting to abduct her virtual ex-boyfriend that she met in Second Life. Thomas Montgomery, 48, in another case, was sentenced to prison for 20 years for killing a coworker who had been "involved virtually" with a woman that both met online in Second Life (Michels, 2008). Montgomery "reportedly posed online as an 18-year-old Marine and started an Internet relationship with a middle-aged woman from West Virginia, who was, herself, posing as an 18-year-old student" (Michels, 2008). In an editorial in *The Christian Science Monitor*, Jim Sollisch (2007), regarding punishment for virtual crimes, wrote that lines become blurred between reality and fantasy because "digital worlds such as SL have made us all creators and suspenders simultaneously. And that changes everything by creating a fictional world with two key characteristics of the real world." The first characteristic is randomness, in the sense that we cannot "control everything that happens to our character. And the other is time" (Sollisch, 2007). For instance, most fiction has an ending, where the story ends: "But the digital fictional world of SL, like real life, is 24/7. Maybe if you suspend your disbelief for too long, it's difficult to return to disbelief" (Sollisch, 2007).

Game Media Violence

Gentile & Anderson (2003; 2006) suggest that violent games may have a greater negative impact on children and adolescents than violent television, namely because players identify with their characters. In Second Life, the avatar is the character. Second Life has a special teen grid, in addition to the adult grid. Although research on the impact of game media violence is concerned with underage populations, one wonders how we all might be affected by games that simulate real life in many ways. It is necessary, for the time being, to look toward the research conducted on minor age populations. Researchers concluded in 2007, "[T]here is ample scientific evidence demonstrating that exposure to media violence increases the risk of aggressive behavior...However, the media industries profit from it, and parents and policymakers receive mixed messages about the effects despite the fact that...the effect is real and sufficiently large to warrant action" (Gentile, Saleem, & Anderson, 2007, p. 53). Their report added, "[T]he effects are likely to become greater over time, as different media converge, become more interactive, become more global, and colonize more spaces in our lives" (Gentile, Saleem, & Anderson, 2007, p. 53). Consider that video game profits have outpaced those of the movie industry since the early 2000s (Markoff, 2002) and the significance of this research becomes evident. Exposure to media violence is a likely factor in aggression, by tapping into emotions of empathy and hostility (Bartholow, Sestir & Davis, 2005; Bartholow, Bushman, & Sestir, 2006). A high level of violent game play was more likely to be associated with lower levels of empathy (Funk et al. 2004). Fantasy violence, rather than realistic violence, is more likely to lead to "acceptance" of behavior among participants in real-life situations (Kirsch, 2006, p. 224).

In a *New York Times* online article, reporter Seth Schiesel (2007) reviewed several cases where federal courts had blocked state and local laws on video game violence. He summarized his report, stating "As video games have surged in popularity in recent years, politicians around the country have tried to outlaw the sale of some violent games to children. So far all such efforts have failed." The first major game case in 2001 involved an Indianapolis ordinance that attempted to regulate public game arcades. Overall, attempts to regulate video game content have been met with legislative debate over media influence on social behavior (Duranske, 2007; Funk et al. 2004). How much impact do media have on viewers, and particularly in this case how much does playing games impact real-life decisions and actions? Judge Richard A. Posner of the United States Court of Appeals for the Seventh Circuit posited that "exposure to imaginary violence—whether in 'The Odyssey,' 'War and Peace' or Ultimate Mortal Kombat 3—can play an important role in the development of a child's moral, social and political outlook." He stated, "Violence has always been and remains a central interest of humankind and a recurrent, even obsessive theme of culture both high and low" (Schiesel, 2007).

Continuing, he explained, "It engages the interest of children from an early age, as anyone familiar with the classic fairy tales collected by Grimm, Andersen, and Perrault are aware" (Schiesel, 2007). He continues, "To shield children right up to the age of 18 from exposure to violent descriptions and images would not only be quixotic, but deforming; it would leave them unequipped to cope with the world as we know it" (Schiesel, 2007). In contrast, there are quite a few examples of games being used to create positive experiences and used for anti-violence training. One real-life group CeaseFire went inside Second Life to conduct training for outreach workers and others working on ways to stop inner-city violence. The first island was designed "to develop an environment that replicated the look and feel of the Chicago neighborhoods," complete with litter and graffiti and boarded-up buildings. The second island, CeaseFire Isla, situated nearby, "is adjacent to CeaseFire Island and is largely Latino in look and feel" (Cofsky, 2008).

Virtual Crime

John Quain (2007), reporting for *PC Magazine*, discussed how Second Life was attempting to "address an expanding array of problems, including theft, assault, attacks by gangs, and rape. And what often starts out as a prank (called 'griefing' by enthusiasts) can turn into a violent rampage, such as the virtual shooting outside an American Apparel store." American Apparel was one of the first name-brand clothing stores in Second Life. Quain (2007) noted that virtual crime and violence "could…detract from the many commercial and corporate environments in Second Life." In 2007, the *Los Angeles Times* covered the story, and added that "the virtual American Apparel store had closed, and other advertisers [were] having second thoughts about Second Life" (Quain, 2007).

Second Life has spent a considerable amount of time since then addressing issues of crime and violence, and more recently (as mentioned earlier in this chapter) establishing policies regarding blatant and extreme adult content present in-world. As in real life, Second Life has had its share of crime. Bringing millions of people together into any world, there will be conflict and crime. The Second Life Community Report lists regularly recent disciplinary actions as determined by the Second Life Governance Team using Linden Lab's Community Standards as the guide. Most of the incidents involved assaults with script objects, spamming, and disturbing the peace, which resulted in warnings to suspension from the game up to 2 weeks. A few cases dealt with sexual harassment, verbal abuse cases and indecency incidents with suspension for multiple days being the most extreme punishment (*Incident report*, 2009). Some of the more violent types of crime reported in 2007 seem to have diminished.

There is the rare case in virtual worlds where people carry their crimes of deceit and passion from the virtual to real life, and that might mean real or virtual violence or murder. When real people interact in the virtual, anything is possible and often beyond the control of Linden Lab and similar companies. In another game called Maple Story, a woman murdered her avatar husband when he divorced her online. She retaliated by hacking into his character and eliminating it. Virtual crimes as well as their consequences and punishments are becoming challenges in-world as well as in real life, as courts attempt to sort through issues of property rights.

Moreover, there is a sensational side of virtual worlds that captures the attention of news media and its audience. Is reality mirroring virtual life, or vice versa? Murder, mystery, and romance are intriguing topics in real life and Second Life. On February 2008, *CSI: NY* led its television audience inside Second Life to solve the murder of an avatar crowned the Paris Hilton of Second Life. The killer had assumed the victim's avatar and the chase was on to find the person behind the SL mask. Media has always used a bit of reality to hook viewers into a plot, fiction being often inspired from life experiences. In 2006, with in-world casinos then operating in Second Life, a virtual mafia don, Marscellus Wallace, moved his operations from the game Sims Online to SL. He set up his organization to handle all types of Second Life problems, from disparaging reputations to scripting assaults (*New Crimes*, 2006). In 2005, another group waged a series of attacks on Second Life's servers, bringing the world down. The difficulty of punishment is that some banished members can return through alternate avatars.

In January 2006, Linden Lab tested some experimental methods of "rehabilitating offenders" (*New Crimes*, 2006). For example, "Second Life resident Nimrod Yaffle reverse-engineered some computer code to help him steal another player's virtual property. He was reported and became the first resident to be sent to a new area of the game, The Cornfield—a kind of virtual prison" (*New Crimes*, 2006). The Cornfield is located on a section of Orientation Island 1. Its name was inspired by the *Twilight Zone* episode "It's a Good Life." Whenever Yaffle would log into the game "all he could do was ride a virtual tractor and watch an educational film about a boy who drifts into a life of crime" (*New Crimes*, 2006). Another report in *Clickable Culture*, by Tony Walsh (2006), confirmed the existence of the prison at that time. Au (2008) reported that it still remained two years later. Many a good avatar have attempted to teleport into it. For now, the legend of The Cornfield continues, whether it is in operation or not. The story does make one ponder how virtual crimes will be dealt with in the future, particularly if the lines between real and virtual increasingly blur into one lifescape.

In November 2006, residents gathered to listen to Rosedale, who addressed complaints over incidents of crime inside Second Life. Some clamored for an official system of law and order, and since then Linden Lab has established stronger community standards of conduct. At that time, however, the virtual West was fairly wild while Linden Lab was exploring regulatory options that worked globally and allowed for freedom of creative expression, while reigning in the bad guys. *Business Week* reporter Catherine Holahan (2006) explained:

> Many wanted to know what Second Life's creators planned to do about a new program, nicknamed CopyBot, that enables users to quickly copy characters, objects, and buildings, potentially eroding the value of people's virtual property. Others wanted to know about viruses with the alleged potential to steal members' identifying information.

The report continued, "Still others were worried about the growing menace of mafias and gangs that are forcing members out of public areas," citing an example where certain groups had taken over a nightclub and chased off avatars (Holahan, 2006).

When a resident reports criminal activity, if they have been directly impacted, they will receive notification from the Linden Lab that the incident report was handled and a ruling was made. Otherwise, little is discussed about crime in Second Life among membership, aside from rantings time to time about the occasional griefer. The griefer is a Second Life member who is intentionally hostile to a community. Church services have been disrupted when griefers with machine guns have shot at the congregation. Some griefers point guns at residents, attempting to rob or rape them. In most cases, the residents can teleport out of harm. If a person is caged, they can shut down their computer, if they cannot escape the situation due to a scripting virus. Continual harassment of a person or a community, however, can become tiresome for members. A person who has encountered violence in real life might find it harder to ignore similar activities in Second Life. Second Life is not a perfect world, and its residents represent the imperfection of real life. In that members can gender play, it would be difficult to profile the typical griefer. From personal experience, my encounters and conversations with the occasional griefer have indicated many to be college-aged male perpetrators.

A Safer Virtual World?

In Second Life, some advertisements promoting the sale of weapons have depicted images of scantily clad women holding high-powered machine guns. Firing ranges are set up in private places by residents in Second Life. There are also publicly designated firing ranges. For some, these activities are simply stress relievers or skill-based, and they cause no harm to any other residents. Just about any type of weapon is available in Second Life, but for the most part weapons are restricted to only designated areas. The blatant violence from the SL gang warfare of 2007 seems to have subsided.

You might find an occasional "illegal drug" store, more like a cove in the alley, in some of the regions of Second Life designed to be "seedier" reflections of real life. These regions, however, are typically well designed and textured, and are very realistic and intentionally modeled after the dangerous zones of large cities. Such stores sell these so-called goods to curious residents, in their representative forms, with the drugs simulating the effects of various illegal drugs on their avatars. Sometimes a member is approached by someone role-playing as a drug dealer. Some of these sites also carry urban fashions, and use the dark motif to promote a rebellious attitude as part of their image when selling clothes. Other regions are simply crafted as dystopian tourist sites, depicting the worst areas of urban crime and life.

Yahoo! video game columnist Mike Smith (2009) reviewed the safety of some of the top virtual worlds, pointing out some of the dangers of this 20–30 million audience around the world: "From addiction to theft to divorce, careless behavior in virtual worlds can lead to real consequences." Smith (2009) points out that "when obsessed players put virtual rewards over real jobs, relationships, and chores, lives get ruined. World of Warcraft, merely by virtue of being the biggest and most successful virtual world to date, is the chief culprit" (Smith, 2009). Researcher Sven Rollenhagen, on behalf of Sweden's Youth Care Foundation, reported, "There is not a single case of game addiction that we have worked with in which World of Warcraft has not played a part." He continued, "It is the crack cocaine of the computer gaming world. Some people are literally unable to drag themselves away and will play it till they drop." The report was endorsed by the Swedish National Institute of Public Health, which indicated that computer game addiction was "becoming more widespread in Sweden and across the world" (*World of Warcraft*, 2009). The report was preceded by the hospitalization of a 15-year old boy in Sweden who had collapsed in "an epileptic-type seizure brought on by sleep deprivation, lack of food, and too long a stretch of concentrated game playing" (*World of Warcraft*, 2009). World of Warcraft players establish relationships with one another as part of working out battle strategies.

For Second Life, relationships in-world can appear "as convincing and satisfying as real-life friends" (Smith, 2009). The intensity of virtual worlds is fueled by the emotions of those involved; some people invest money, time and emotional resources into these games. The adrenalin rushes from sex and violence can become highly addictive to certain players. Second Life has been blamed for breaking up marriages and relationships in real life (Smith, 2009). The "reality" of Second Life becomes evident when new relationships are formed and others are torn apart. The emotions and actions are real in Second Life—and their powerful impact on people in both lives—real and virtual—may be a testament to the human investment—positive and negative—made by members into games of these kinds. If crimes of passion in Second Life and other virtual worlds continue to make headlines in mainstream press, the emotional role that Second Life provides its participants will likely receive greater attention and study.

Conclusion

After several years of operation, Second Life, for the most part, is a much better place with stronger enforcement of community standards, especially among business owners. Indeed, the real power rests not with gangs and weapons, but those with money and influence in Second Life. Power in Second Life is achieved through networking, and those in power often determine opportunities for other members as in real life. So in some ways, the frontier days of Second Life are over, and being replaced with modern-day savvy politics among the influential members behind Second Life's economy. Second Life careers, marriages and hopes and dreams can be achieved or shattered, like in the real world. Second Life sometimes takes its toll on residents when the game is played for what is considered serious stakes—sex, money and power. Second Life is redefining safe and fair play among virtual worlds.

References

Au, W. J. (2008, June 13). Alicia finds the cornfield. *New World Notes*. Accessed October 6, 2008, from http://nwn.blogs.com/nwn/2008/06/alicia-finds-th.html/

Bartholow, B., Bushman, B. J., & Sestir, M. A. (2006). Chronic violent video game exposure and desensitization to violence: Behavioral and event-related brain potential data. *Journal of Experimental and Social Psychology*, *42*, 532–539.

Bartholow, B., Sestir, M. A., & Davis, E. B. (2005). Correlates and consequences of exposure to video game violence: Hostile personality, empathy, and aggressive behavior. Accessed July 29, 2009, from http://web.missouri.edu/~bartholowb/pdfs/BSD-VGviol-PSPB-2005.pdf/

Cofsky, A. (2008, December 16). More on Second Life from Candice Kane of CeaseFire. *RWJF*. Accessed July 27, 2009, from http://rwjfblogs.typepad.com/pioneer/2008/12/ more-from-candice-kane-of-ceasefire.html/

Desidero, L. (2009, July 28). Interview, personal communication with author. Second Life.

Duranske, B. (2007, August 22). *NY Times* covers rejection of game violence laws; Psychiatrist says games could reduce violence; Violent game sales up, Violent crime down. *Virtually Blind*. Accessed July 27, 2009, from http://virtuallyblind.com/2007/08/22/schiesel-video-game-violence/August 22nd, 2007.

Funk, J. B., Bechtoldt-Baldacci, H., Pasold, T., & Baumgardner, J. (2004). Violence exposure in real-life, video games, television, movies, and the internet: Is there desensitization? *Journal of Adolescence*, *27*, 23–39.

Gentile, D. A., & Anderson, C. A. (2006). Violent video games: Effects on youth and public policy implications. In N. Dowd, D. G. Singer, & R. F. Wilson (Eds.), *Handbook of children, culture, and violence* (pp. 225–246). Thousand Oaks, CA: Sage.

——. (2003). Violent video games: The newest media violence hazard. In D. A. Gentile (Ed.) *Media violence and children*. Westport, CT: Praeger.

Gentile, D. A., Saleem, M., & Anderson, C. A. (2007). Public policy and the effects of media violence on children. *Social Issues and Policy Review, 1*, 15–61. Accessed December 26, 2009, from http://www.drdouglas.org/drdpdfs/GSA_SIPR(2007).pdf

Holahan, C. (2006, November). The dark side of Second Life. *Business Week.com* Accessed July 27, 2009, from http://www.businessweek.com/technology/content/nov2006/tc20061121_ 727243.htm

Incident Report. (2009, July). Community. Second Life. Accessed July 25, 2009, from http://secondlife.com/support/incidentreport.php/

Kirsch, S. J. (2006). *Children, adolescents, and media violence: A critical look at the research.* Thousand Oaks, CA: Sage Publications.

Markoff, J. (2002, May 24). Recession? Don't tell the video game industry. *The New York Times*, p. 4.

Michels, S. (2008, August 26). Virtual relationship leads to criminal charges. *ABC News*. Accessed July 26, 2009, from http://abcnews.go.com/ TheLaw/story?id=5650591&page=1/

New crimes, new punishments. (2006, May 19). *The Second Life Herald*. Accessed July 29, 2009, from http://www.secondlifeherald.com/ slh/2006/05/new_crimes_new_.html/

Quain, J. R. (2007, August 29). As a crime wave sweeps Second Life, adherents are looking for answers. *PC Magazine.com*. Accessed July 29, 2009, from www.pcmag.com/article2/ 0,1759,2177593,00.asp/

Schiesel, S. (2007). Courts block laws on video game violence. *New York Times.com*. Accessed July 27, 2009, from http://www.nytimes.com/2007/08/21/arts/television/ 21vide.html?ex=1345348800&en=7d9c05d547e4012d&ei=5088&partner=rssnyt&emc=rss

Second Life sex crimes. (2007, May 11). *AskMen.com*. Accessed July 28, 2009, from http://www.askmen.com/daily/blogs/technology/second-life-sex-crimes.html/

Smith, M. (2009.). Virtually safe: Five real life pitfalls of online worlds. Videogames. Yahoo.com. Accessed August 1, 2009, from http://videogames.yahoo.com/ events/plugged-in/virtually-safe-five-real-life-pitfalls-of-online-worlds-and-some-safer-alternatives/1333240/

Sollisch, J. (2007, June 18). In Second Life, no jail time for fictional crime. *The Christian Science Monitor*. Accessed July 26, 2009, from the June 18, 2007 edition, http://www.csmonitor.com/2007/0618/p09s02-coop.html/

Wagner, M. (2009). Second Life putting a leash on sex, violence. *InformationWeek*. Accessed July 28, 2009, from http://www.informationweek.com/news/ personal_tech/virtualworlds/

——. (2007). Sex in Second Life. *InformationWeek*. Accessed July 27, 2009, from http://www.informationweek.com/news/software/hosted/showArticle.jhtml?articleID=199701944/

Walsh, T. (2006, January 1). Hidden virtual-world prison revealed. *Clickable Culture*. Accessed October 5, 2009, from http://www.secretlair.com/index.php?/clickableculture/

World of Warcraft more addictive than cocaine. (2009, February 27). *Telegraph.co.uk*. Accessed July 23, 2009, from http://www.telegraph.co.uk/technology/4863325/World-of-Warcraft-more-addictive-than-cocaine.html/

CHAPTER TWELVE

Diversity in Second Life: Virtual Expression through Culture and Gender

> At one time, there wasn't that great variety of things in here. Everything kind of looked the same, you know (laughs), from one place to the next. But now it is more diverse than ever before. Look at us, we have stores that sell Egyptian clothing, and stores that focus on saries, and things that you would wear if you were from India or Pakistan. So I really love seeing that.
>
> —Journey McLaglen, *Prism owner and fashion designer*

For people of racial and ethnic cultural backgrounds, SL fashion designers particularly specializing in African or Asian skin and hair have been difficult to find in-world until more recently. Whereas some members want to experiment with their identity, many do so within the confines of their real race or ethnicity. Gender play is much more popular than experimenting with skin color, unless one is interested in a non-human color, like blue. An influx of shops featuring African, Latino or Asian skins appeared in late 2008 in Second Life. Communities of people based around culture and language are surfacing across SL, and many of these regions have become cultural centers, complete with shopping malls that cater to residents and visitors seeking destinations outside the Euro-centric perspective.

One of my graduate students joined Second Life as part of a class exercise. For this particular student, she appeared to be one of a few African-Americans when she entered the virtual landscape. Even her attempt to create herself as a person of color was met with challenges; a general search did not produce leads on groups or stores that were culturally specific. By reviewing profiles at some dance clubs that seemed to cater to a diverse mix of avatars, she was able to locate a sphere of cultural relevance that matched her interests and racial and ethnic background. This process involved a few weeks of concentrated investigation into groups listed on avatar profiles. She began to locate other members and groups from members' profiles. Asking members' questions helped her find stores and sites off the beaten path in Second Life. The process was time consuming and for the average newcomer it might prove to be too challenging of a task.

A number of Asian communities have created malls and venues that showcase cultural builds and live entertainment and make available to residents specialty skins, hairs, and clothing designs. For the most part, until more recently, white skin and bodies have dominated the marketplace. Female bodies tend to be full-figure as the norm. Men tend to be bulky and muscular to the point of extreme. When someone first enters Second Life, they are often more willing to experiment with hair color and appearance, than when they become assimilated within the mainstream virtual culture.

Virtual worlds conjure up visions of utopian societies connected through cyberspace. By examining a virtual world within a larger Metaverse of virtual worlds, we can consider how concepts of tolerance, respect, peace and understanding function outside of real life. In a sense, members develop respect and understanding for other virtual residents through the process of adjusting to the newness of the cyberworld. It is a respect for the differences that help to make Second Life a diverse and creative community, and it might potentially translate into improved listening and working together toward global solutions in real life, as naïve as that sounds. A number of non-profit groups are celebrated and supported in-world, and are met with encouragement and support by SL residents.

Second Life members can be anything they want, but what if they want to merely extend who they are in real life? How much of yourself and cultural identity can you bring into Second Life? Needless to say, some of those hoping for a cyberutopia have a gut realization that a virtual world can only be as "good" as its residents. Humanity—in all its weakness, strength and diversity—is reflected online and inside Second Life. Second Life, however, does allow communities of similar interests based on language, location, and indoctrination to come together in unique ways. For one, people who join Second Life have the commonality of an interest in online communication, and that is already a step toward openness and curiosity. Second Life, now several years old, has established strong communities of interest based on race, ethnicity and gender, as well as brought together members of the disability population in real life into a universe where possibilities abound.

This chapter examines such possibilities within Second Life, exploring concepts of race, ethnicity, gender and physical challenges in one virtual world. What are the experiences of African-Americans, for example, when entering what appears to be a very white cyberworld? In terms of gender representation, 10 percent of the female avatars are actually men in real life.
SL filmmaker Toxic Menges (2009), who has played other multiplayer online games, does not see gender as an obstacle for her inside Second Life; and it is

because one can cloak identity that it becomes less relevant and perhaps helps to level the playing field:

> It is more egalitarian in SL. In SL, there are more things you can actually do where you are not going to have as much barriers in your way. If you are a man or woman, it doesn't really make any difference. You're judged on your art, on what you do, and it's that way because most people don't really care what sex you are despite what avatar you have and what you look like. I don't think it makes a difference very much in the machinima and photography field. You are judged on what you have done on the last thing you've done. And I think that is really good. I have never had personally any backlash from being a woman and attempting to do this. Imagine you were to do it on World of Warcraft or something; you might come across something like that. But I think it is pretty egalitarian really; it is really fair. I haven't heard anything [negative] actually. You've got to be a very strong person anyway to do [machinima] because it is quite time consuming, and you certainly need a certain level of experience. And if you don't have that, it shows up very quickly, but that can apply to either sex. I think we are lucky in SL, because we have the freeing persona of the avatar and people frequently are not the sex they are on their avatars. And people are treated quite equally to a certain extent. I haven't heard anything, but I am quite strong so I don't think I would.

When people come into Second Life, are they seeking personas similar to themselves or communities similar to their needs and interests in real life; or, rather are they seeking to redefine their communities and expand their identities by exploring gender, race, and ethnicity? Disabled populations have become active members in a variety of communities, but for many of them it is important to remain connected with others who also identify with their real-life needs and issues.

The Identity Project

In the summer of 2008, I taught a graduate course entitled The Virtual Community: Social Trends, Theories and Application inside Second Life. The course brought graduate level students in-world to examine social issues within Second Life, and allowed them to build, experiment, and interact with structures and people. The students were challenged to consider social, political, and economic issues relevant to virtual communities, particularly looking through the lens of their avatars in Second Life. For the Identity Project, students were asked to create an avatar, an avatar profile, and a social networking account, as well as to maintain a journal of their experiences interacting with others in various settings. The mix of gender, race and ethnicity among the students provided for cross-cultural discussions on potential benefits and pitfalls about socializing and media making within a virtual environment. Students were introduced to a variety of issues through in-world guest speakers (with credentials verified by the instructor). Guest speakers were invited to speak on topics that ranged from religion to law to design considerations, all within the framework of socializing in a virtual space.

Field trips helped students to explore concepts and spaces which they might not otherwise have had the opportunity to do. Most of all, students had an opportunity to explore their individual and social perspectives in this brave new world. When students entered Second Life, they seemed to gravitate toward anywhere they might find people, and particularly help of every kind to find their way around this strange, but vaguely similar, world. Second Life, in many aspects, resembles real life, with its buildings, dance clubs, houses, stores, and familiar RL icons. Yet, it is quite a chore to learn how to maneuver through this world. Within a few days, some students searched through Second Life to locate communities that they identified with based on race and ethnicity. Many of them had unique and contrasting experiences, depending on perceptions they brought within Second Life from their real life.

One African-American woman felt that other members were ignoring her, and she was having a difficult time making connections with others. One of her classmates, a white Caucasian male graduate student, said he had similar experiences. They agreed that they felt like "outcasts" because they were new to the game, owing to their very noob appearance. Some people ignore new members because they are perceived as needy, whereas others try to mentor them. One Asian student located a brown paper bag with a smiley face to cover her avatar's head. She said she felt comfortable with that image for the time being.

The International Population

Contrary to belief, from first look, Second Life is comprised of a diverse population of residents, drawing from Europe, Asia, Australia, and North America. Japan, Brazil, South Korea, China, France, England, Ireland, Canada, Mexico, and the United States have a strong presence in Second Life. Many of those involved are connected to Second Life because of their affiliations with educational institutions and corporations that have an in-world presence. Others who reside in Second Life have a range of expertise in art, graphic design, making fashion, marketing and public relations, writing and producing media, and so forth. Most are comfortable with online communication and creativity, and have experience with chat rooms and instant messaging. Culture is expressed at dance clubs and through fashion, and malls are often centers of activity for certain communities. From a fashion design perspective, Second Life showcases a diversity of styles from around the world. From hair to shoes, avatars can achieve any look they want. Those unfamiliar with the English language can be easily equipped with on-body translators, and more and more clubs and businesses have staff members that wear them, for in Second Life businesses have to cater to an international clientele.

Japanese fashions are becoming popular in SL, with notable designers like Mirai Jun, owner of Ce Cubic Effect, among the in-world leaders. Stores featuring Oriental furniture, clothing and houses, as well as social hot spots like dance clubs and romantic parks are attracting members from other countries aside from those in Asia. Japanese companies have found creative ways to connect SL to RL, especially with regards to marketing and branding of technology products. One of the nation's leading mobile phone companies did a talent search for SL avatars with the look and personality to become potentially "virtual idols," as part of a marketing plan to promote music, movies, and other media (Au, 2009).

The Japanese community has made a strong presence in the social and educational infrastructure of Second Life. Fashion is only one aspect. Overall, Japanese communities understand the potential of Second Life; although new to the game, they bring with them experience from their own virtual worlds in their country. Add to that, the nation is far more technologically advanced than many countries in the world. Their citizens have a framework already for appreciating anime and game play: "Although business and institutional uses of virtual worlds have attracted attention, the social potentials of SL for communication are not yet well recognized in Japan"—but perhaps more so than other countries. The Kira Institute was established to help Japan make the transition from a national virtual economy into a global model for the world. Kira Japan, as a branch of the Kira Institute, was set in place to illustrate how virtual worlds enhance cultural life and "potentially bridge the gap between Japanese and English language users" (Kira, 2009).

The Kira Institute began in the late 1990s, as an attempt to explore possibilities for the future, from both the vantage points of scientists and social scientists. The institute made its debut in SL Japan in October 2008 when its organizers made a "presentation at a bar called 'Bar Tube' in [SL] Tokyo to a large crowd of heavy SL users, IT journalists, and metaverse planners" (Kira, 2009). The Kira Café was established, and weekly bar talks became a featured addition to the institute, albeit attendance was less than a dozen. The attendees, even though sometimes small in number, were influential in their respective fields; each with an interest in seeking what is to come in the future and having some say in how it might be accomplished via virtual worlds. Kira Institute members initiated discussions with "key players in the Japanese language SL, and [conducted] visits to various labs such as the National Institute for Informatics, a group of scientists devoted to the development of virtual communications, and Uchida Yoko, a company that specializes in promoting educational uses of virtual worlds" (Kira, 2009).

African-Americans in Second Life

In searching for African-American groups on Second Life, the author came across more than two dozen. Groups ranged from clubs, cafés, and book companies, to discussion groups. At the time of this search, The Soul Lounge & Café had 547 members, The Baobab Academy & Culture Center had 91 members, The Tribal Drum Group had 88 members, and Afro-Atlantic World had 49 members. Other groups were associated with dance clubs representing various music genres, from rhythm & blues, reggae, and jazz to hip-hop. With nearly 20 members, Souljah Sotry claimed to be the first and only African-American help service. The Soul Vibes Nightclub is a popular club, and its population draws international members and many people of color. Soul Vibes features a variety of music, from classic oldies to romantic, as well as soul, funk, rhythm & blues and jazz. The music streams to its patrons 24/7, with live deejays occasionally popping into the club. Stores and a beach area are featured as well.

Pennelope Bellic joined SL in June 2008 as a first-year graduate student of media. Her particular study investigated the identity of African Americans in virtual communities, with her focus on Second Life. In her research project, she proposed three questions: "What are the main characteristics of the African American virtual community? What actions in the African American virtual community are influenced by real life? What possible role do virtual communities play in the lives of the African American participants in general?" (Johnson & Davis, 2008). Bellic initially found that it was a challenge locating African Americans on SL, and shares her experiences in the passage below:

> In the beginning I met some in "typical" places where African Americans would hang out. These places included hip hop clubs, strip clubs, and ghettos. They were the most populated by African Americans. Later, I found that there were African Americans who were fashion designers, real estate managers, club owners, and etc., so I visited these respective places. Learning this showed me that the main characteristics of African Americans in SL are the same as in RL. Which are, hard working, diligent, polite, reliable and we have many careers, yet are not all from the same place. We want to be able to connect with other African Americans and Africans from all over the world and discuss social issues, politics, history, spirituality and any other significant topics. In the end, we just want to have fun. (Johnson & Davis, 2008)

She also discovered the strength of Second Life is rooted in its ability to bring people together to explore and discuss issues. Various communities can share philosophies and viewpoints safely among each other: "I found that SL is a site of discussion that can give voice to issues of belonging, power and racial difference in any culture, as participants engage in a dialogue online. African Americans use the virtual communities to meet one another 'face to face' and exchange words and ideas through text" (Johnson & Davis, 2008). Within Second Life, face to face exchanges are interpreted through one's choice of avatar representation. Bellic points out that some of these personal interactions are "influenced" by "everyone else's definition of beautiful:"

> They create avatars related to what they think is "acceptable." For instance, blonde is more acceptable in RL versus darker hair, and thin is in versus a more voluptuous body. I didn't create my avatar like that. I created her in a unique image, as an individual, and to stand out (besides her skin color). She has curves, different hair, and wears unique clothing. While observing Second Life I saw people argue, perform acts of commerce, exchange knowledge, share emotional support, make plans, brainstorm, and some found love and friends; this all happens in RL. The difference is here it is done with words on a computer screen. (Johnson & Davis, 2008)

In Second Life, the bodies selected are typically more full-figured and taller than one would imagine for a virtual world. Many residents choose female avatars with curvaceous bodies. In real life, the Western image of women is tall and slender (although increasingly slender body types are becoming popular among SL members). In SL, women are often represented as strong and tall. Men are tall and muscular. Fashions cater to these bulkier bodies. Attractive avatars receive more attention in social circles than those that are not. Bellic feels confident that being a woman of color is a decisive choice, with meaningful consequences in Second Life. Her identity in SL is an extension of her real-life experiences and goals:

> Virtual communities reveal much about the construction and maintenance of African American identities, as well as the everyday realities of their lives. These social environments are driven by preexisting information in real life of the African American community; and thus as participants interact in these social environments, they manage their information in a variety of ways. As an African American participant who chooses to stay African American online, your online identity is separate from everyone else's, further articulating how you are different. I believe one's identity online is a fusion of his or her real-life image and the image they would like to obtain. This is because people are cautious about the amount and type of information they offer about themselves and it's difficult to manage personal information in this kind of environment, in that most people want to be truthful but not give away too many details. Many SL users have shared their stories about their personal lives, relationships, or work with me. (Johnson & Davis, 2008)

She concluded, "I found that researching virtual communities proved to be enlightening when studying identity formation and construction within the African American culture. It was especially informative when examining how these social networks affect the meanings of African American identity, but also how they share in an experience of 'blackness' that exceeds national." Elaborating, she adds, "While on SL I've met people from different parts of the world, and this changed my picture of the cyberworld. And because of that, SL is slowly becoming a resource of knowledge, producing a collection of information that I can search and access" (Johnson & Davis, 2008).

Black Pioneers of Second Life

Fatima Ochl is the publisher of *Ochl's Guide*, which is an entertainment guide to SL clubs. She reviews music clubs and locations for *SL Review* and is actively writing about SL. On her Web site, she has provided commentary and compiled some interesting perspectives on the black experience in SL from some pioneer black avatars. Her site is called *Fatima's Black Board: Reflections on the Black Experience in Second Life* and her journey into exploring blackness on SL began soon after she joined: "[L]ast fall I stumbled across the rez day party of Nubiian Craven, the owner of 519 deSignz and a regular at Irie Vibes. Nubiian was being teased about her age, which of course prompted me to click her profile. She had been in SL since 2004!" (Ochl, 2009). She adds, "I realized she must have been one of the early residents." Ochl (2009) became "curious about how many other black people were in that early group." She began "randomly clicking on people [she] knew or was introduced to and was surprised to learn that there were actually more than a few that came in at that time. And there was even one black avatar who was a beta tester in 2003!!" (Ochl, 2009).

In essence, for Ochl, armed with that revelation, "the seeds for this story were sown. We, as black and brown avatars, are still complaining about how hard it is to find skins and about how isolating the early months in SL can be" (Ochl, 2009). Contemplating on the experiences of those black pioneers, she mused, "I couldn't imagine what those early avatars of color experienced. I set off to investigate" (Ochl, 2009). Through the process, she became aware of the diversity within various black communities, observing "we are all molded by the values and experiences of our families, our neighborhoods and...bring a unique individualistic part of us to the table. What might be essential to my concept of blackness can be completely irrelevant to other avatars' sense of blackness." She adds, "...yet we are all still firmly rooted in the black experience" (Ochl, 2009). Some of the comments from the early pioneers included the following, as compiled and edited from Ochl's Web site:

> I knew there had to be other people of color and nationalities in SL, but it was impossible to know who really is a person of color when the game allows individuals to be whoever and whatever they desire. We need to realize that our experience here is no different than anyone else's. We are not persecuted here or physically maligned.

> We have the same access to resources as our white counterparts and the same ability to create. Here, the future is truly ours to realize. Someone once told me that I was brave for appearing in my ads for my clothing business as a black avatar because they were afraid to do so for fear of not attracting a broad customer base. But I am who I am and I'm quite proud of it...One thing I am quite proud of in SL is the church, River of Life. It's not a role-play but an actual church with actual services. It has become a large part of the black community for worship on Sunday mornings.

Sunrise Mansion and Art Gallery

Second Life African-American artist Indea Vaher exhibits her art in Second Life. The crossover into a virtual canvas seemed a natural fit for an artist and creator who thrived on brilliant color and the excitement generated by working across media. Communication has been historically encoded as cultural expression through various media. In her work, Vaher draws attention to codes used within cultural media platforms (drums, quilts) among enslaved Africans in the U.S. The Sunrise Mansion and Art Gallery made its SL debut in 2009. Her biography explains that her mansion was inspired by

> ...Marie Therese Coincoin a former slave who became a wealthy business woman and established Melrose Plantation in the late 18th century. It later became an artist colony and Melrose spawned the artistic achievements of Clementine Hunter, one of the South's foremost primitive artists among others. (Sunrise Mansion, 2009)

The statement goes on to point out that Vaher expresses "that tradition in SL with Sunrise Mansion and Gallery as a vehicle to encourage emerging artists and to display her artwork featuring the history of the people it represents." It continues, "Indea's paintings focus on two areas of African American history and culture, the Gullah Culture of the Sea Islands and the Black Creole culture of the Cane River valley." The Sunrise Mansion and Gallery also features the works of other SL artists, as well as "artifacts and items unique to these cultures, such as indigo and rice cultivation, dyed clothing, sweetgrass baskets, quilting and features food and music of the culture" (Sunrise Mansion, 2009). When Vaher opened the Sunrise Mansion in Second Life, she wanted it to be both a gallery and a museum:

> I didn't want it to focus solely on my own art. I wanted other artists from the Diaspora to come out in Second Life and to show their work and to share their work. Not just African-American artists, for I focus on any artist who would want to work with me. So it is doing really well and I met some really great people. Recently I had an aboriginal Australian do a show here and it was wonderful. (Vaher, 2009)

For her grand opening in late winter 2009, Vaher brought her RL art into Second Life, focusing on the Gullah Culture. A note card given to all attendees documented a bit about the historical significance of her art:

> Time has stood still for more than a century on this rural island off the Atlantic Ocean. Dirt roads lead to houses where Gullah families live in clusters the way their ancestors did in Africa. Women wearing head wraps and aprons weave baskets from sea grass and sell them to tourists on their way to the affluent outlying islands. The Gullah people have been able to preserve so much of their African cultural heritage because of geography, climate, and patterns of importation of enslaved Africans. (Gullah Culture, 2009)

Her other focus is on the Creole culture, "a celebration of the blending of French, African, Spanish and Native American cultures" (Sunrise Mansion, 2009). Vaher captures significant components of the Gullah and Creole culture within her work: "Pieces created by Indea Vaher represent the landscape, customs, and heritage of the coastal areas of both the Sea Islands and Louisiana as characterized by marshes, bayous, open and natural sun and moonlight, and pastoral homes, schoolhouses, and churches" (Sunrise Mansion, 2009). Vaher's work has been recognized internationally "as a genuine illustration of the history and traditions of African American southern culture...She is well known for her brilliant coloring, intricate human and landscape forms, and themes that represent life in the Sea Islands region and the bayous of Louisiana" (Sunrise Mansion, 2009).

For Vaher, her journey into a virtual world began in 2008 when a friend already within Second Life invited her to take a workshop on Kabbalah. "She kept telling me to come in and check it out and get an avatar. At that time, we were on a kind of spiritual quest, you could say, exploring different things." She continues, "I was never interested in the Kabbalah, but she told me to come in and take a look. Once I got my avatar and came in, I saw that there was much more than a workshop here, I started to explore Second Life" (Vaher, 2009). Love at first sight, you might say, for Vaher, when she immediately recognized the creative potential of working in a 3D environment, rich with color—and indeed color has defined her work throughout her artistic career. Second Life presented the perfect opportunity for Vaher to extend her creativity into a virtual platform:

> As an artist, Second Life actually opened a new avenue of creativity for me. What happened to me was this; I'd lived most of my life as an artist. I was pretty productive and fairly successful in my real-life career but suddenly because of health issues, I was not in a position to be as active as I was before, especially with traveling exhibitions and doing a lot of the projects that I have been accustomed to doing for many, many years in real life. So I was bored and depressed, which is the reason a friend suggested that I come check out Second Life. The Kabbalah classes were to help me with the depression. However I started to see the creative possibilities everywhere! I had never heard of Second Life, and I wasn't much into television, or *CSI*, as other people had found out about SL. So I was transfixed by this virtual feast for senses. One of the things that impressed me was everything was art, from the avatar, to the Sims, the

> plants, the sky, the colors used. It was like a 3D canvas. Wow I thought this has all kind of potential including music, which is another one of my favorite mediums. (Vaher, 2009)

The process for Vaher was optimistically cautious as she began to perceive the new world she was now immersed within as a tourist, but through the lens of an artist. As she explored Second Life, taking in her surroundings and making friends, she knew this was a space into which she could culturally express herself with and to people across the world:

> At first I was fairly timid about coming out with my art because I had not seen anything quite like it in Second Life. I was in Second Life for about 6 months before I decided to show. My interest is in Southern African-American history and culture. As far as I could see, there was somewhat of a lack of representation in that particular area of history in Second Life. I thought that it might be interesting to see if I could bring over from my real life some of the projects that I have done in the past to see how they would be received and just for the pure pleasure of seeing if I could recreate it in a 3D format/environment. (Vaher, 2009)

Vaher describes her work as reflecting her ancestry. She began studying her genealogy two decades ago, when she became intrigued with the history of African-American culture:

> My mother was Creole. My father was African American Choctaw, both were from Louisiana with a long linage and deep roots there. When I began to study my genealogy I was living in The Sea Islands at the time which is off the coast of South Carolina-Georgia. On these barrier islands history has been somewhat preserved. On the particular island I was living, bridges weren't built until the 1940s. So a lot of the African culture that was brought over during slavery was preserved. It is called the Gullah culture. In the Gullah culture, a lot of the West African mores, language, rituals and way of life had been preserved there. It was very interesting to see the similarities to the Louisiana culture, so I began to do paintings that focused on this aspect. A lot of inspiration for my work came from my mother and grandmother, based on the stories they had told me, and what I had experienced growing up under their influences. I took the stories I'd heard from Louisiana black culture—New Orleans and the northern Louisiana Cane River valley area, and compared them to the Gullah culture. I found a lot of similarities there. So my primary focus became the African Creole and Gullah Culture connection. (Vaher, 2009)

In 2009, she made calls for artists along the themes of African American medicine and African folklore. She also has increasingly featured works relating to the Middle Passage, and created an installation with a slave ship with an exhibit in the bow and an auction block. The installation was featured on the SL television series "Designing Worlds." In early 2010, she created an art and quilt exhibition in SL featuring the "Codes of the Underground Railroad," with the idea behind the theme illustrating how those codes were "hidden in plain sight and aided in many escapes." Vaher works with textures in real life, and brings them into Second Life as art. Vaher (2009) explains, the codes were in everything, in music, blacksmithing, even in the iron work. The blacksmiths used coded messages in doing their work; instead of the drum, it was "the banging of the anvil." She adds, "One of the things I do with the exhibits is always have music. I try to find something themed, if possible, to go with the exhibit. I love music, and I play a little bit of guitar. I come from a family with some pretty talented musicians" (Vaher, 2009). Second Life provides Vaher opportunities to bring various media into her exhibits and create interactive spaces within a 3D virtual environment, where she meets people across the world. Albeit all are avatars, the art and the artists behind the avatars are real.

Disabled Communities in SL

For most members, flying is an amazing feat even if only in a virtual world. For those disabled in real life, Second Life allows some of them opportunities to simply walk down a street or to dance in a club. Some real-life groups are making the crossover from real life to Second Life. The Disabled American Veterans (DAV) group in Second Life has been established as a social networking tool to provide members "with a new avenue of outreach, social interaction and advocacy." Its goal has been to reach a "younger generation since it supports a networking structure with which they are familiar. More importantly, it will provide an opportunity for physically disabled members to get involved using a virtual environment to interact and collaborate." The point of its presence in Second Life has been to increase participation among members who might not be able to physically attend chapter meetings. DAV also uses Second Life for presentations and training, making use of the graphic capabilities within Second Life.

Deeley (2008) discussed how a group of adults with cerebral palsy, assisted by their nurse, in a day care program in the United States, share one avatar named Wilde Cunningham. In real life, most of the members use wheel chairs and need people to help them with their daily needs. The members using this one avatar "have built their own houses, have pets, gardens, even a baseball field. They also have many close friends and a large social network" (Deeley, 2008). Some members enjoy the freedom from their disability and for others, they see Second Life as a platform to make "disabled people visible" (Deeley, 2008).

In another instance cited by Deeley (2008), a man by the avatar name of Simon Walsh said he is "smoother, sexier; [with] no beer gut" in Second Life. He explains, "In real life I'm very active but speech can be a problem; I wear a helmet because my balance isn't great; I wear bibs and nappies and I need assistance with most everyday things so, as Walsh, social and romantic relationships are much easier." Some have moved their real businesses inside Second Life, when their health waned in real life, becoming fashion designers, event planners, business consultants, builders, club owners, and musicians. Friendships become strong in Second Life, with disabled members forming social and support networks for each other during hard times, such as when someone goes through difficult medical treatments in real life.

The Linden Lab has worked ambitiously to facilitate the needs of the disabled communities within Second Life, going as far as setting up a private island to "accommodate a group of people with Asperger's syndrome, a less severe form of autism" (Deeley, 2008). The group was comprised of members of a chat site that Academic Program Director John Lester "had developed for people with neurological disorders" including characteristics of social isolation and awkwardness and eccentric behavior (Deeley, 2008). The island was established to encourage members of the group to socialize among each other and to prepare them to enter other areas of Second Life. In other instances, Second Life had allowed members with severe paralysis to experience new opportunities, so their lives would no longer be defined by their restrictions (*Disabled*, 2007). Some experiments have shown how technology is providing a means for even those with the most extreme disabilities to participate in Second Life, from shopping to running a business.

In a CNN report, Steve Mollman (2007) introduces Simon Stevens, who lives in England, as the man who can throw a party for your business to market your product or service: "He'll take care of the logistics. He'll provide a DJ and live musicians. He'll take care of the security, too, discouraging obnoxious types from ruining the event." The reporter continues, "Never mind that Steven has cerebral palsy, and uses a wheelchair. This might be a concern in the real world, but in Second Life, where the 33-year-old works, his disability is not a disadvantage." And not only does he experience new freedom, but he generates a fairly good income that converts well into real money. He stated that he earned approximately $10,000 in real world income, and earns it by "helping a large car manufacturer set up its presence in Second Life, and that he earns thousands more on other projects. And his commute? It's a few seconds from his bedroom to his home office. Once he's at his computer, there are no disadvantages in the virtual world" (Mollman, 2007).

In Second Life, it is not uncommon for managers and staff at clubs to have disabilities that might prohibit them from participating in real-life occupations. From 19 to 80 years of age, many have found a new way to define themselves through virtual occupations or accomplishments. Some dance and fall in love for the first time in Second Life. Some use virtual wheelchairs as a symbolic tool to remind those in SL to respect those in real life with disabilities. For some, Second Life allows for a much fuller real life than the reality that sometimes imprisons them in daily life.

Choice in Virtual Gender

Over the past decade, a number of scholars have discussed how radio and television have shaped the image of the queer community (Fejes & Petrich, 1993; Gross, 1983; Hoy, 1991; Johnson & Keith, 2001; Johnson, 2008; Kielwasser & Wolf, 1992; Moritz, 1992). Johnson and Keith (2001) attempted to chronicle the annals of queer radio and television, and their extension to the Internet in their book *Queer Airwaves*, relying on station records and interviews with many of the leading lesbian/gay/bi-sexual/transgender (LGBT) producers in America. A newly arising question, however, concerns how the concept of gender is being transformed within the context of new media reality games. One would be hard pressed to find an equivalent literature base devoted to new media, with some notable exceptions like Tom Boellstorff's (2008) *The Coming of Age in Second Life*.

Second Life is a virtual social network platform that allows its millions of members to create alternate identities. A growing transgendered community is apparent in Second Life, with groups established such as Transgender Denmark, Femme by Choice, TG Unlimited, Transchristians, Transgender Suicide Memorial, Othersexed in SL, Omnisexual Beings and so forth. Three groups, in particular, provide outreach to transgender populations on SL: Transarcadia (2009) ("a group for those participating in extended transgender [sexual] role-play in Transarcadia"); Transformations (2009) ("a self help group for transgender people in SL to get together and help each other become the gorgeous [sic] girls they want to be"; and the Transgender Resource Center (TRC) (2009) (a group that "fosters the development of a positive, helpful, and diverse community providing peer support to those facing the unique challenges that confront transgender individuals and to promote the acceptance of transgender individuals within Second Life and society at large"). In fact, TRC adds the following in their group mission statement: "If you are transgender, transsexual, gender queer or questioning, or have a genuine and serious interest in issues related to gender identity, please visit us at our cozy digs for an open and honest chat by the fireside." Second Life allows for identity expression in a safe environment that provides for nondisclosure and experimentation, but in an altered state of reality. The boundaries between a real and second life are self-determined. The 1st Annual Second Life Transgender Day of Remembrance was held on November 20, 2007, "in memory of victims of violence directed against the transgendered" (*Transgender*, 2007). During the service, SL residents and supporters shared "personal stories and memories of friends, loved ones, and members of the community who were victims of hate crimes or who committed suicide…" (*Transgender*, 2007). The memorial was held at Elysium Gardens:

> …Second Life's first full region (simulator) devoted to providing Second Life's expansive transgender community with a location devoted to its specific needs…[M]ost other transgender focused locations in Second Life…tend toward overt expressions of sexuality. (*Transgender*, 2007)

Elysium Gardens, on the other hand, was created to serve as a "mature and respectful alternative" to other community spaces within Second Life (*Transgender*, 2007). Second Life offers a diverse space for residents to create homes, meeting spaces, and their own avatars (and often multiple avatars), while extending identities beyond limitations of gender. Elysium Gardens is a romantic island that attracts people from all over the world to its beautifully designed surroundings to enjoy its island grasses, sandy beaches, waterfalls, mountaintop dance floors, cave hideaways, and varied spaces to explore and converse.

In Second Life, gender is a choice. From the moment one creates an avatar, the decision to become a man or woman avatar is made. However, once a gender is selected, members can change gender by altering their bodies, skin and clothing quite readily. The avatar's name stays the same, but all else is fair game. In Second Life, a small percentage of the in-world population is transgendered, allowing those who would have to undergo costly surgery in real life to experience life as a different gender, or perhaps as a representation somewhere along the continuum of gender. Truly, the Second Life gay community is diverse within itself, with more than 2 dozen sites to visit and socialize in with others. *Gay World* offers music, dancing, and shopping. Other places offer intimate spaces for couples. Some sims are presented as gay resorts. The bottom line is many of these sites encourage social networking and a way to mentor newcomers. *Gay Wired* reporter Bryan Ochalla (2007) reported on how Second Life gave its players "complete control over their virtual experience. They can walk, run or fly around the game's locales, some of which are based on real-world counterparts such as Provincetown or entertainment fantasy lands such as *The L Word's* West Hollywood," where they can "meet and socialise with other residents." Part of that socialization process might involve coming in and out into a virtual world to connect to other queer people.

In the early days of Second Life, Georgetown University grad student Donald Jones was introduced to Second Life by one of his professors; he began to look toward Second Life to further his understanding on the construction of identity and space online: "As a gay man who grew up during the computer age, I learned a lot about what it is to be gay online" (Ochella, 2007). He explained, "The Internet is where I first met other gay people after I came out in the mid 90s...As years have gone on, I've continued to use the Internet to connect with and meet other gay people" (Ochella, 2007). Jones (2007) explored how LGBT individuals and groups used space in-world and created their bodies inside Second Life as part of his thesis *Queered Virtuality: The Claiming and Making of Queer Spaces and Bodies in the User-Constructed Synthetic World of Second Life*. He surveyed more than 300 people for his survey, and interviewed 20 people inside Second Life. He found that some people use Second Life as a means to express gay feelings that they cannot share in real life, perhaps due to social pressures or real-life commitments such as marriage. Other men simply feel comfortable as women inside Second Life. Jones explained an instance where that was the case for one person he had interviewed:

> [I]t was a profound experience to see himself as a woman and to interact with other people within Second Life as a woman...I also encountered plenty of gay people within Second Life who were just there to play around...there were plenty of straight people "playing" gay as well. (Ochella, 2007)

Jones' research indicated that 20% of the LGBT residents he interviewed had "experienced some form of homophobia within Second Life; overall he believes the virtual world is a welcoming place" (Ochella, 2007). Feeling welcomed can create emotional connections to those seeking safe spaces to explore their identity—in-world and in the real world. Edward Castronova (2005, p. 121) in *Synthetic Worlds: The Business and Culture of Online Games* posits, the "emotional effects" produced by synthetic worlds "affect" life on Earth. It is not possible to separate the emotions, for they are real in both worlds. Jones (2007) begins his thesis by illustrating one of those significant connections sometimes made inside Second Life: "One evening in 2005, I was hanging out in the 'glbt zoned' sim of Provincetown in the virtual world of *Second Life* when I came upon a 'newbie' sitting on a couch near the entrance. I sat down and said hello" (Jones, 2007, p. 1). As the conversation continued, he discovered that the man was an 18-year-old "from the Pacific Northwest who lived with his parents and worked in a heavy labor industry. He had known he was gay for some time now, but his living and work situation prevented him from exploring his sexuality or from being 'out'" (Jones, 2007, p. 1).A sense of space, place and home are key concepts, according to Jones,"in the formation of community and individual identity within...[u]ser-constructed virtual/synthetic worlds, in which users can construct alternative/idealized/fetishized/fantasized digital bodies and spaces" and these constructions "provide a new frontier for community building and meaning making for individuals and groups, particularly for those who may be excluded from the larger public sphere in their particular locality" (Jones, 2007, p. 2). In his thesis, Jones (2007, p. 87), expounds, "queer bodies interacting and creating within queer spaces build new queer lifeworlds that transcend space and time in the actual and provide for new configurations of queerness and community in the virtual." Second Life thus becomes a world of possibilities that allows one to experiment with "sexual ideation and gender multiplicities" and queer spaces in the virtual begin to create links between "the actual and the virtual" allowing for exploration among "those in transitional and questioning positions." Add to that, Jones (2007, p. 87) points out the "potentialities of *Second Life* for future political activity."

Citing examples, Jones (2007, p. 89) states that meeting places like dance clubs or sims such as Provincetown or Fire Island have real-world meaning, and these icons bridge "physical world time and space allowing diasporic queer peoples to connect within transgeographical space that point to larger queer lifeworlds." For transgendered residents, Second Life allows for an expansive view of gender and political activism. As Jones points out, "In other words, *Second Life* can function as a meeting place for queer people who can then engage within their local communities in the physical world...In June 2007, for example, the largest Pride event in *Second Life* to date was organized" (2007, p. 90)."

In Second Life, the LGBT festival Second Pride is "a week long celebration of love, diversity & unity" comprised of several sims (land areas) that host live music and theater performances, a museum acknowledging gay and lesbian historical figures, stores and informational booths that are set up, along with amusement park rides—all as part of the festivities (Jones, 2007, p. 90). Fundraising typically supports humanitarian organizations and efforts, but the connections made between worlds raises questions and possibilities for the role of platforms like Second Life in the future. While SL attendees may not be as numerous as the crowds who turn out for New York's City Pride events, there is a shared responsibility among all participants, springing from one's real-world commitments and increasingly extending to their virtual memberships:

> ...the visual playground of *Second Life* allows the construction of utopic instances of political action and visibility. While the scope of such activities is limited for now, what possibilities will arise when a virtual pride *can* support thousands of people celebrating in one place? (Jones, 2007, pp. 89-90)

Jones (2007, p. 91) continues, "What potentials for unified action could such virtual spaces have as participation within them becomes more ubiquitous? Is there power in the construction of virtual museums or homonormative spaces that virtually concretize particular dreams of a more visible and accepted global queer community?"

Brokeback Mountain: A Global Queer Community

Brokeback Mountain (known also as Brokeback Babylon) is a beautiful beach island along a virtual waterfront in Second Life. The sandy shores are inviting, and causal seating allows people to sit along the beach to chill or converse with others. In the distance, waves crash against the tall rocks that separate the swimming areas from the high seas. Country music is streamed across the beach area. It is a great place to make friends, and provides a respite for those who have traveled SL far and wide, looking for friendly spaces and faces to be themselves.

At one end of the beach area, there is a magnificent white cathedral—where inside, icons of real paintings, rich in color, are etched on large stained glass windows. The art embodies the spirit of Brokeback, reminding its viewers that bonds of love are both spiritual and genderless. An art gallery resides on a docked cruise ship. On the upper deck, one can see the sands below, as well as the waves rebounding off the high rock cliffs in the distance. The shimmery cross on the cathedral gently glows against the night sky and stars. Draghan Marksman showcases his original art work on the ship, where he captures passion and romance on canvas in his portraits of couples and images of men. Of course, the point of Brokeback is to be who you want to be, man, woman, or somewhere along the gender continuum. It is a safe place, where love and friendship are simply expressed between adults through art, music, dance, dialogue, and sometimes a deepening of relationships.

Marksman concurred with the author's observations that in Second Life gender might be thought of as continuum, in a world where people can express themselves individually and uniquely regardless of how one looks in real life. Particularly, this is important to transgendered members: "Second Life allows them to be what they want to be sooner than in real life; it is a great help to them" (Marksman, 2009). Marksman continues, "When a man says he is a woman, well in his head, he is. People can relate as they want to relate in Second Life." For Marksman, his story on how he would become involved in Second Life would occur much earlier: "It started on the forum; Second Life came a while after" (Marksman, 2009). The forum he refers to is the one he came across after the motion picture *Brokeback Mountain* had been released in 2005. The movie was a romantic drama between two cowboys. He explains:

> I was looking for a place to meet people who had been fascinated by the movie. I discovered a forum that was just about to open. I soon became very involved in it and made friends. I soon became part of the moderation team and because I suppose I have a certain charisma I became very popular among members and was named co-administrator. Eventually, the person who had opened the forum left and I was left at the head of it. The forum became a tremendous success: 375,000 messages. So I

> started to find ways to make it more interactive and SL came as a way to chat and meet. (Marksman, 2009)

Second Life provided the perfect opportunity to expand the forum and connect people in a more interactive way than through posting, and the sim—Brokeback Babylon—would become increasingly important and grow with Second Life. Brokeback began in 2005, under the leadership of Marksman (2009): "I have a gift for making acquaintances and friends so at the end I knew everybody in the community. Well at first I had no idea how SL worked so I started with half an open space, and then a full open space (what we call homestead now) and then half a full sim—and finally a full sim." The membership grew as the dedicated land increased. Basically, the Brokeback community resides on a massive island, and has brought people together from across the world: "The idea came when I saw it was a means for people living everywhere in the world to interact as in an RL meeting. We have members from Canada, France, England, Germany, etc. They can share a moment here, enjoy the venue and be with friends" (Marksman, 2009).

For fans of *Brokeback Mountain*, it might be natural to seek out anything related to the movie in the SL search engine. Many members have created spaces that replicate real-life icons of some sort—cities, clubs, stores, and movie settings. In fact, some of the members found out about the group through entering search terms related to the movie. Some did a search on the word "gay." Other terms that might bring up Brokeback in the search results are gay wedding, gay rights, and even the name Draghan Marksman. Brokeback is designed to create a community atmosphere with a church, club venue, beach hangout, and even stores: "To some people it is very important. There are some people who are here all the time because it is like a family. Some I have met in RL too" (Marksman, 2009). Wedding ceremonies in the cathedral vary from public to private: "Some people want to get married all by themselves in private ceremonies. I do not see them all. Some want a full party. It's good to say you are committed to someone; it's a token of love" (Marksman, 2009).

Second Life has been a success in terms of Marksman's goals, in that the forum and the sim have also served as a place "we could use to promote gay rights; it's not just a community. We organize events for the annual International Day against Homophobia every May 17th and also work with the Aids awareness center" (Marksman, 2009). Regarding how the day was executed and received in-world, "Last year was a huge success. We have exhibitions, live singers, and even sometimes conferences. We managed to get 21 partners/sims last year," recalls Marksman (2009). That is no small feat given the coordination issues among various sim communities across Second Life, especially given the time zone differences and just trying to coordinate events among people across the world.

In late 2009, an Olympic-like sports multi-day event was held to collect funds for the International Day against Homophobia, which has been a key part of the Brokeback mission. The sports event, according to Marksman (2009), is "quite a lot like the Olympics" in terms of the variety of sports represented, with fencing, ice skating, horse racing, wrestling, archery, swimming, soccer, and other activities as examples. Ultimately, Marksman (2009) acknowledges his larger goal of getting "straight and gay people together, having them come for an event so they can meet, talk and get to understand one another. What I want for the future is getting more straight sims to take part. I never ask money from anyone, rather I ask them to support us and spread the word."

Beyond the discussion inspired by the movie forum, there was a second forum added in 2009 to the Brokeback group, one that focuses on Second Life photos and allows for comments on various images posted. The photos are not specifically gay related, and not exclusive to Brokeback, but they feature landscapes, art and fashion, for example, within Second Life. The online site was created by one of the members, photographer Marry Hobble. Moreover, photos taken of the art within the St. Josh Gay Cathedral are showcased on this addendum forum at http://slphotos.forumactif.net/.

Conclusion

Journey McLaglen, fashion designer and business entrepreneur, points out that appearance is the first layer that people notice in Second Life. However, it is the personality that ultimately becomes visible to those around them, and that is likely to determine one's circle of friends:

> When you strip away all the exterior of things that make us judge one another, we're suddenly left with just our personalities. And the personalities are what come through, is who you are on the inside. Even though we all may have beautiful avatars, and there tends to be this movement toward perfection, probably because of the influences we have in real life. I would say that I have noticed it is sometimes harder for people who choose to look different in Second Life to actually make friends as easily as people who choose to define themselves by what we would see in a magazine, so to speak. For example, I have a friend who only wears blue hair, so people think of him as a noob even though he has been here a long time. And he's never changed his skin. If you look at Philip Linden, it's the same thing—he's got his original shape and skin. You really can't judge anything here by what you see. It's what we've managed to strip away when one looks at one another and they recognize that this is the façade that we've built for ourselves. But what really matters is what comes through when we talk, when we type, when we communicate. The distinction now, I would say, changes for everyone as they grow in Second Life. When I say grow, you go through a series of

phases. First, is where you just want to be social. The very first stage is curiosity. People are curious about everything when they first come in here. It's fairly easy to see when you go into a sim; you see a lot of people new, and they attach sexual organs outside their clothes, walk around naked, and do these crazy things that they would never dream of doing in real life. That doesn't last very long. Once they realize it is okay, they tend to gravitate toward the thing that interests them the most; maybe it is role-play for some people like vampires and things like that. Then they find a family or a clan, and they begin to feel comfortable in this social framework. (McLaglen, 2009)

Second Life is merely another way for people to interact with others, who can present themselves as they wish to be seen and perceived, and it allows for the personality of the individual to take precedence over appearance (after a certain skill level is achieved). Members' individual and cultural perceptions from their real-life influence their interactions within Second Life, but often people begin to look toward this virtual space as a place to redefine themselves—physically and socially. At the very least, Second Life does encourage people to reflect on their identity in real life, and allows them opportunities to extend or alter their personalities. No longer is their world solely defined by their immediate RL families, friends and social circles, but they might begin to see how they fit in globally with others on a larger cultural continuum of expression.

References

Au, W. J. (2009, July 23). Second Life avatars sold as cellphone "Idoru" on major Japanese mobile carrier. *New World Notes*. Accessed August 14, 2009, from http://nwn.blogs.com/nwn/2009/07/second-life-idoru.html/

Boellstorff, T. (2008). *The coming of age in Second Life: An anthropologist explores the virtual human*. Trenton, NJ: Princeton University Press.

Castronova, E. (2005). *Synthetic worlds: The business and culture of online games*. Chicago: University of Chicago Press.

Deeley, L. (2008, March 24). Is this a real life, is this just fantasy? *The Times*. Accessed February 24, 2009, from http://women.timesonline.co.uk/tol/life_and_style/women/body_and_soul/article1557980.ece.

Disabled American Veterans (DAV). Group profile. Second Life.

Disabled could enjoy life in Second Life. (2007, November 28). *The Sydney Morning Herald*. Accessed June 6, 2009, from http://www.smh.com.au/news/World/Disabled-could-enjoy-life-in-Second-Life/2007/11/28/1196036950371.html/

Fejes, F., & Petrich, K. (1993). Invisibility, homophobia and heterosexism: Lesbians, gays, and the media. *Critical Studies in Mass Communication 10*(4), 395–422.

Gross, L. (1983). The cultivation of intolerance: Television, blacks, and gays. In G. Melischek, K. E. Rosenagren, & J. Strappers (Eds.), *Cultural indicators: An international symposium*. Vienna: Austrian Academy of Science.

Gullah Culture (2009, February 9). Exhibition notecard. Second Life.

Hoy, C. T. (1991). An historical look at male homosexual characters on network entertainment programs. Master's thesis. Carbondale, IL: Southern Illinois University.

Johnson, P., & Davis, B. G. (2008). The virtual educator & student: Understanding the real world through second spaces and identities. Virtual Worlds Conference. East Carolina University, NC. Online Conference held in SL, November 10.

Johnson, P. (2008, May). The howl not silenced: The rise of queer radio. Competitive Paper. International Communication Association. Montreal, Quebec, Canada.

Johnson, P., & Keith, M. (2001). *Queer airwaves: The story of gay and lesbian broadcasting in the electronic media.* Armonk, NY: M. E. Sharpe Publishing.

Jones, D. (2007, November 6). *Queered virtuality: The claiming and making of queer spaces and bodies in the user-constructed synthetic world of Second Life.* Master's Thesis. Georgetown University. Accessed June 23, 2009, from http://hdl.handle.net/1961/4293/

Kielwasser, A. P., & Wolf, M. C. (1992). Mainstream television, adolescent homosexuality and significant silence. *Critical Studies in Mass Communication* 9(4), 350–374.

Kira Japan. (2009). Web Site. The Kira Institute. Accessed August 1, 2009, from http://www.kira.org/

Marksman, D. (2009, August 14). Interview, personal communication with author. Second Life.

McLaglen, J. (2009, August 7). Interview, personal communication with author. Second Life.

Menges, T. (2009, July 15). Interview, personal communication with author. Second Life.

Mollman, S. (2007, July 10). Online, a virtual business option for disabled. CNN.com. Accessed July 12, 2009, from http://edition.cnn.com/ /2007/BUSINESS/07/10/virtual.disabled/index.html/

Moritz, M. J. (1992). The fall of our discontent: The battle over gays on TV. In D. Shimkin, H. Stolerman, & H. O'Connor (Eds.), *State of the art: Issues in contemporary mass communication* (pp. 262–267). New York: St. Martin's Press.

Ochalla, B. (2007). Gay gaming: Special edition. *GayWired.com*. Accessed July 19, 2009, from http://www.gaysports.com/page.cfm?Sectionid=14&typeofsite=storydetail&ID=1164&storyset=yes

Ochl, F. (2009, May 3). Pioneer Black avatars: Early days in SL. Fatima's Black Board: Reflections on the Black experience in SL. Accessed July 19, 2009, from http://www.fatimaochl.net/

Sunrise Mansion & Gallery (2009, February 9). Exhibition notecard. Second Life.

Transarcadia. (2009). Group charter. Second Life.

Transformations. (2009). Group charter. Second Life.

Transgender day of remembrance observed in Second Life. (2007, November 18). Press Release. *SL Pulse*. Accessed July 18, 2009, from http://www.slpulse.com/content/view/116/

Transgender Resource Center (TRC). (2009). Group charter. Second Life.

Vaher, I. (2009, August 3). Interview, personal communication with author. Second Life.

CHAPTER THIRTEEN

Religion in Second Life: Virtual Gods, Spirituality and Fellowship

> In Second Life, the online virtual universe that is attracting 3.7 million users, you can light virtual candles for Shabbat, teleport to a Buddhist temple or consult the oracle for some divine guidance.
>
> —Shona Crabtree, *Finding Religion in Second Life's Virtual World*

The approximately 20 or so wooden lawn chairs encircle a campfire along the sandy beach of Eternal Creations. On some nights, under the virtual stars, residents kick back to talk about eternal life, happiness and their real and virtual lives. One summer night in 2008, some of the members shared family photos from real life, in between music and fellowship. Eternal Creations is a community of more than 1,500 members, comprised of residential and business isles connected to the main island. Boating races, balloon rides, dancing to Christian music, Bible studies, playing and building on sandboxes, and just hanging out with friends make up some of the community activities. Club Eternal at one point was the main Christian dance club, boasting of more than 500 members. Owned and operated by a real-life couple, Shuffield Philbin and Terri Latte, the club had been the most successful, longest-running Christian dance venue in Second Life, bringing together people to dance to streamed music, live musicians and deejays and offering monetary contest prizes. On certain nights, other Christians gathered on Hope Springs Eternal, part of the larger Eternal Creations community to pray and worship together.

This chapter examines the concept of spirituality in Second Life, particularly seeking out those engaged with in-world prayer and evangelism in a significant and meaningful way. Nearly every religion is represented in Second Life, from Mormons, to Wiccan, to Buddhists to Pentecostals. Certain regions have become designated as religious sites by residents, and draw members into activities and fellowships. Some regions are hostile to outside religious communities, and some religious communities have to contend with hostility toward them on an occasional to regular basis. This chapter examines prayer and ceremony in Second Life, and their impact on the possibilities of interfaith activities and tolerance among the religions represented in Second Life. Two case situations are examined in this chapter, looking at particularly Buddhism and Christianity in Second Life due to their fairly large and active membership bases.

The Electronic Church

New media columnist and author Julian Dibbell aligns virtual reality in some ways as "an essentially spiritual experience" (Grossman, 2007). He has been a consultant to Linden Lab. He states, "You see signs and signals but you give them meaning...by what is happening in the mind and soul of the believer" (Grossman, 2007). The Emergent Church, in its electronic form, is a response to a global awakening of artistic and technological expression (Sample, 1998; White, 1994). Spirituality within silence, spoken word, and song has become imbedded within soul and machine (Wilson, 2002). One might suggest that flames of revival were fanned by radio evangelist Aimee Semple McPherson, who arrived in Los Angeles in 1918 with a passion and talent for God and theatrics. By summer 1923, she had more than one half million followers, and opened the 5,300-seat Angelus Temple in Los Angeles. She established more than 400 branch churches and 178 mission stations in the world. It was radio that made McPherson a household word in the 1920s and 1930s.

The electronic church through radio had emerged within the United States. McPherson brought together Hollywood celebrities, musicians and pastors into the same venue. Her radio show popularized gospel, jazz, and rhythm and blues and fueled a hunger for soul music on the West Coast. Since then, radio and television have served as informational tools for certain denominations, both traditional and off mainstream in delivering their messages (Stacey & Shupe, 1982; Hadden 1988). The amount of influence they have on the spirituality of a people is a less known consideration than merely the fact that they remain a part of broadcast programming choices and formats. Saying that point, however, virtual communities might be perceived as the next step along the way in the transmission of such rituals and beliefs.

One of the leaders of the post-modern church is Fulbright Scholar Thomas Hohstadt, author of *Dying to Live*. He calls for a new artistic vision in the future church. It is a church that embraces the diversity throughout the world. In the U.S and Europe, coffee houses, galleries, house parties, and sometimes church buildings have become sites of alternate worship. Jones (2004) initiated The Boaz Project to inspire a vision of a new "non-linear, multisensory and art-driven" worship service "emerging from...the global alternative Christian subculture" (Jones, 2004). The Boaz Project was a two-year effort that began in 2000 by the Baptist General Convention of Texas to identify new ways of engaging young people into ministry (Foster, 2001). Jones (2004) illustrates how poetry, light, and motion interplay to create a worship environment and experience.

The virtual church is an extension of that vision. In the late 1990s, Ralph Schroeder, Noel Heather, and Raymond M. Lee (1998) suggested "some implications of the potential spread of virtual religion for religion in the world-at-large. The question that can be posed is: will the spread of virtual religion have a corrosive or an invigorating effect on religion in contemporary society? People bring their energy into the sacred." The authors concluded, "participants feel that they are co-present, they do coordinate their 'voices' and their gestures (their attentiveness at the keyboard, for example." In this way, they continue, "A prayer meeting in the virtual world may not provide the same type of religious experience as a conventional church service, but it certainly reproduces some of the essential features of the latter—albeit in novel ways." In the final analysis, "the E-Church world, for all that is said about the ephemeral nature of virtual reality or virtual worlds, perpetuates—even if it also transforms—this role of the sacred in society" (Schroeder, Heather & Lee, 1998).

Interestingly enough, those words were written more than a decade ago. The same questions exist and offer little more than speculation about the future of religion in a mediated world, real or virtual. Edward Lee Lamoreux (2007), in his article about online religious practice on the Internet, sheds light on how technology is enhancing spiritual practice through virtual worlds like Second Life. People connect one with another in rituals and expressive worship, and the immersion into such practice allows for transformative opportunities not previously possible through computer-mediated environments.

Religion in Second Life: An Overview

In 2008, the BBC reported on a trial version of Muxlim Pal, a virtual community targeted to Muslims: "Muxlim Pal is the newest facet of web network Muxlim.com, which describes itself as 'enhancing the Muslim lifestyle'" (Peckham, 2008). Its mission is to make connections among Muslim communities. Similar to Second Life, members connect with one another in a variety of social venues, from shopping malls to office spaces to music venues. Its goal is to provide connections "specifically aimed at Muslims living in Western nations" and those interested in learning more about the culture (Peckham, 2008). Similarly Christian communities have been experimenting over the past few years with games devoted exclusively to Christian themes. Visions, for example, is a game focused on the beginnings of Christianity. Second Life likewise can be used to educate residents through building replicas of religious icons or allowing for role-play to recreate a historical event or period. More than other virtual worlds or games, Second Life has provided an interactive virtual forum for spiritual participation and discussion, particularly directing attention to and raising curiosity on what religious practices might look like in the future.

In 2008, the Future of Religions conference was held in Second Life, and speakers came together to discuss new virtual movements online and inside virtual communities. The event was held in Extropia, an SL futuristic community. The keynote address was given by William Sims Bainbridge on "Immortality of Avatars: Deciding between the Paths of Science or Religion." The presentation investigated virtual communities within Second Life and World of Warcraft, and explored the conflict between science and religion, such as threats to traditional views from artificial intelligence and cyberimmortality. Anthropologist Tom Boellstorff, author of *Coming of Age in Second Life*, explored the ideals of place and identity in Second life, and how these become represented and actualized in virtual worlds. Another presenter, Helen Farley, pointed out how Second Life provided unprecedented opportunities for religious communities to engage with one another.

Second Life has stimulated quite a few conference themes and panel topics over the past five years, and religion has become one of the major threads of discussion within virtual conferences. In July 2007, University of California at Berkeley students held a panel inside Second Life that was broadcast to real life. "The Faces of Faith in Second Life Showcase and Conversation" was the last in a series of panel discussions themed "God, Sex and Family," and aired live through SLCN, the Second Life Cable Network. Don Lattin, religion writer, moderated the panel of Second Life spiritual leaders, scholars, and worshipers. In Lattin's opening remarks, he explained the series focused on "choices about marriage, dating, the building of community, family and faith…'God, Sex, Family' projects are being streamed (video, audio, content) into different tents created to look and feel like a church revival" (Andrade, 2007). The panel investigated "religion on the Internet, and more specifically, religion in Second Life," especially "looking at how people experience spirituality in Second Life—things like prayer, evangelism/proselytizing and congregational life [and how it] is different in Second Life and Real Life. Or is it?" (Andrade, 2007). The panel raised some interesting questions that probably raised more questions than provided for answers: "Does the anonymity of Second Life foster or impede the spiritual connection between people of faith and between people and God? Do some religions work better than others in Second Life and the Internet?" Other questions posed included, "Does the 'anything goes' philosophy of Second Life get in the way of authoritative religious teachings? Can groups with a history on animosity—like Muslims and

Jews—find common ground in Second Life?" (Andrade, 2007). Among the faiths represented were Islam, Hare Krishna, Quakers, and Jewish.

Boellstorff was on hand to contribute to the discussions from his in-world anthropologist perspective based on his SL experiences and observations documented in his book *Coming of Age in Second Life*. Beth Odets (Beth Brown, RL) was the virtual resident expert representing the Jewish faith on the panel. She would also present at the Second Life Community Convention (SLCC) in August 2009 in San Francisco regarding her in-world faith experiences. In August 2006, she had built the first SL Synagogue Temple Beit Israel, which evolved into a virtual Jewish community. She has been featured on mainstream news media, such as NPR, Fox News, CNN, and *Jerusalem Post* as well as SL media. Her panel concerned provoking conversation around several issues; for instance how real-life spiritual values were expressed within Second Life, and whether "potentially volatile situations surrounding real-life controversies/wars involving Jewish and Palestinian relations" might be moderated through virtual dialogue" (SLCC, 2009). Other discussions centered on "bringing people closer to their real-life faith through Second Life, the development of an active spiritual community, and the crossing from second life to real-life media as being the representative in Second Life for the Jewish faith" (SLCC, 2009).

In May 2007, The NBC Nightly News featured a segment on religion online in Second Life (*Religion online*, 2007). The anchor began, "Just as in real life, good and evil exist in Second Life, and religion is finding a way there too. But is virtual religion real religion?" The segment transitions into a man casually dressed, sitting behind his computer desk. The man states, "I can just get up in my pjs, turn on the computer, and I'm right there." The segment then cuts to Don Teague, NBC Correspondent, reporting from Oklahoma. He reports, "This strange world where humans can fly is also a new religious frontier where real-life churches, synagogues, and mosques are trying to gain a foot hold." The story transitions to Craig Groeschel, senior pastor of LifeChurch.TV, who says, "When Jesus told us to go into the world, we took him very literally."

Teague continues, "LifeChurch, an evangelical mega church, has invested thousands of real dollars to build a presence in Second Life…LifeChurch is basically the same church whether it is in the real world or the virtual world; the big difference in Second Life is the people." Teague adds, "In Second Life, our virtual selves can be male or female, human or not. This man [a clip of a cheetah avatar] came to church as a cheetah wearing shorts, and told me he only feels accepted here where he can be whatever he wants." The man said,

"I've been to many churches in real life and none of them give me the satisfaction as a virtual church."

In Second Life, your identity is often expressed in your profile, particularly in the listing of the groups you have joined along the way. The largest religious groups include LifeChurch.com with 841 members. Other large groups report memberships as follows: IslamOnline (781), Buddhists of SL (786), Christian Church of Second Life (742), The Islamic society (431), and Jews of Second Life (272). A few Satanist groups exist; among them is Diabolus Templum with 52 members. The Academy of Pagan Learning has 179 members, as of 2009. Eloise Pasteur (2007) points out, "Doctrines which may be more minority in the western world in real life do well." Many residents do not join groups, although they may participate in some of the activities. There is a limit of 25 groups per avatar. So group membership is only one indicator of residents' involvement in spiritual practices. Large membership does not necessarily translate into an actively engaged religious community. Noting religious group affiliations in one's profile is sometimes no more than a symbolic act for some members.

USA Today reporter Cathy Lynn Grossman went to Second Life to explore the "holy season for the world's Christians and Jews—on Earth and the parallel cyberuniverse, Second Life." She observed SL avatars worshipping online according to their own rituals and forms of worship: "Wherever the human imagination goes, so goes the spirit. Second Life is now also opening windows on religious and spiritual expression. Theologians and philosophers may debate the authenticity of religious life online, but out on the Internet faith frontier, believers are too busy to listen" (Grossman, 2007).

One of the larger Christian ministries in Second Life is Abundant Living Ministries, and members attend its ALM Cyber Church. According to its founder Ben Faust, "Worship is always between you and God, wherever you are" (Grossman, 2007). Faust, in his mid 30s, resides in the USA, but his congregation is comprised of people from around the world, of varying ages: "a growing number are traditional, if virtual, places of prayer, study, support and counseling. Faust, an ordained evangelical minister, had no desire to pastor a real-world church or give up his day job programming websites" (Grossman, 2007). Instead, he purchased a parcel of virtual land upon which he built his non-denominational evangelical church that looks "like a contemporary church, complete with a drum set, Bible studies, a concert hall and a recreation center." In real life, he is a member of Potter's House Worship Center, "where he works with the children's ministry and the food pantry—programs that can't be replicated in Second Life, where children age 12 and younger can't be members and there are no hungry avatars" (Grossman, 2007).

Some worship centers have animated poses for pray and worship to assist avatars in kneeling, or raising their arms in praise. Animated poses for religious practices are increasingly becoming popular within virtual worlds. Grossman (2007) interviewed one of the officer's of Second Life's Islamic Society, who prays in a "replica of a 10th-century mosque in Cordoba, Spain...bigger than the one in his small hometown two hours from Stockholm." Sten Muhammed Yussif Widhe, in his mid 60s, states, "I put my avatar in praying position and I pray at the same time. My prayer in my room is valid and my prayer online is symbolic" (Grossman, 2007). Religious practice within Second Life is less, however, about attending church, and more about connecting spiritually to others. The group IslamOnline Islands in SL provides Muslims, as well as non-Muslims, a way to experience beliefs and practices and provides training and education. There is a sense of fellowship among believers. Less than 10% of SL members attend denominational religion, with a fraction of residents regularly attending services or ceremonies within churches, synagogues, or mosques (Grossman, 2007). For some, churches and temples provide opportunities to reconstruct the architectural past.The Latter Day Saints Church is represented inside Second Life with "probably hundreds or thousands of Church members who participate in Second Life" (Idswebguy, 2007). One group of approximately 50 members from around the world coordinates much of the online activities and literature. On the island, there is a visitor center, chapel and a residential community: "Over 100 people a day wander through the buildings on a self-guided tour, complete with pictures, quotes, and other information about the Church" (Idswebguy, 2007). The site's informational links connect in-world members to the Web church.

The crossover from one's second to real life is evidenced through baptism, when a real person makes a deep spiritual connection in a virtual environment. Antonio Spadaro, in the Italian Jesuit journal *La Civilta Cattolica*, explains that virtual worlds like Second Life should be considered an extension of missionary work: "Deep down, the digital world can be considered, in its way, mission territory...Second Life is somewhere where the opportunity to meet people and to grow should not be missed, therefore, any initiative that can inspire the residents in a positive way should be considered opportune" (Greene, 2007).

Hope Springs Eternal

Hope Springs Eternal is an outgrowth of Eternal Creations, and is owned by Sher Salmson. As a Second Life resident, she has counseled many Second Lifers who discuss their real or Second Life problems, ranging from marriage and family issues to financial difficulties, along with of course spiritual questions. She is assisted by other residents in uplifting people through prayer and worship. Hope Springs Eternal has become a popular place for secular and Christian audiences to gather. Some of the artists and bands that play in Second Life also perform worship music at her concert venues. Hope Springs embodies the spiritual hunger present in Second Life.

Escorts, strippers, demon wannabees and a cast of characters sometimes show up at venue activities, prayer meetings or the larger Eternal Creations community. If they are coming to cause trouble, they typically find themselves getting prayed over, and many come back to visit again, making friends there. Hope Springs is about people loving people in avatar form. There is no church per se on Eternal Creations. In fact, that is counter to the mission. The people comprise the church in all its diversity.

The foundation is Christianity for many of the residents who live among the Eternal Islands. But others are welcome to live, play and pray there. On the day that I interviewed Salmson, she had a weeklong line-up of singers planned. One of her favorite singers, among the many, is AcousticEnergy Nitely. He is one of the most popular secular singers in Second Life, but he seems to consider Salmson, her venue and her mission as a special place to perform his other music, Christian. It is not the beautifully landscaped venue that attracts visitors. It is not the ocean view. It's not even the overall ambience and worship music. It is the heart of one woman in love with Jesus, with a sincere desire to love others. Hope Springs Eternal is her church, in a way. Biblically, it could be easily argued this fellowship is how communing through God was intended—through loving one another. At concert events, devout followers use pose balls to raise their arms toward the virtual heavens, swaying to the worship music. Others dance in any way they see fit, letting the music move them.

Sher Salmson, founder of Hope Springs Eternal, with her long wavy platinum hair and piercing baby blue eyes, is an avatar. She spends long days in a virtual world, connecting real people to each other and God in Second Life. The person behind the avatar is a warm, compassionate counselor with one foot in the real world helping others on a daily basis on problems of domestic violence. Her other foot is immersed in Second Life, where she counsels and prays with others, who sometimes carry real-life baggage in-world. Some perceive SL as an opportunity to escape from reality, connect with others, or completely start their life over in a virtual world. Many members are invited into Second Life through friends, or they see a news clip on television and become curious. Others stumble across Second Life by accident as they explore the Internet. For Salmson (2009), it was a friend who told her about

Second Life "and I had not one clue as to what it was. And I found it rather hilarious as a newbie. But I had never even been in a chat room before. So I was totally unprepared for the interaction that people can have on the Internet." She adds," And to take it further and come into a virtual world where there are actually representations of the people that you talk to, it's really been an experience. But I was very much unprepared. I thought it was a game" (Salmson, 2009).

It soon became obvious to her how real people were impacted by other people and decisions through Second Life experiences. Salmson (2009) points out, "A lot of people still think it is a game. And that certainly affects your mindset when you come in. I found out real fast it is not just a game and that some people make it a game. But there are real people behind each avatar."

"So when I came in," she explains, "I will not say the things that happened to me in the beginning, but I will say those very things almost made me run screaming into the night, rather than staying." Two weeks into Second Life, in what she might call a divine appointment, she met Eternal Creations Founder Sonic Rang and Founder of Morning Star ministries OneWayUp Wise:

> I met Sonic and OneWay and they have an awesome ministry at Eternal Creations and I believed in their ministry. And I noticed that there might be a gap of prayer...I had noticed so many good things going on, but as far as people coming together to pray I personally had not seen that yet. So Sonic took a chance on me. He didn't know me. But again he is a man of faith. He gave me a free place to open a prayer ministry. I got really excited about that. I had never considered myself a prayer warrior. As a matter of fact, I'd rather be in the background than in the thick of things. But I find myself in the thick of things many times. So we began the prayer ministry. (Salmson, 2009)

Very shortly, thereafter, Eternal Creations made a big move to the islands that now serve as its community. She purchased a piece of property there and the prayer ministry was established on a residential island. In the beginning, the prayer circle was near her house, which provided a comfortable space for talking to, praying with, and counseling people. Eventually, she took down the house and moved the prayer circle underground. The land above was picturesque, and designed for worship. Underground, distractions were few for those in prayer. Above ground, the space was used for live worship and fellowship. For many seeking answers in life, or just needing some caring advice, Hope Springs Eternal became as close to utopia as possible in Second Life, an oasis for spiritual counsel and connections with others:

> What I found is there are a lot of people who had lost hope. Not just Second Life, but in real life. In fact, some people had lost hope in real life and had come to Second Life seeking. And again these people come seeking one thing, but many times God

> finds them right here in Second Life. So I was talking to the Lord about it, about how people had lost faith, had lost hope. And without hope we just don't do well. And he said very clearly, in my heart, not audibly: Hope Springs Eternal. That is the name he gave me for the ministry where I operate. Well Hope Springs Eternal has been on for about 2 years now, very close to 2 years. I began with one prayer circle. One day a week, where people would come together and pray for each other or the lost, or ministry, to give thanks, to give praise reports, and since then God has prospered that ministry. It isn't me—It's Him. (Salmson, 2009)

At least 2 days a week there is a prayer circle, attended by approximately 25 people; "that is a lot of people who come to pray...because they need prayer. One night a week, we have Bible study." On October 2008, Hope Springs Eternal became the first all-Christian live music venue in Second Life. Whereas other venues play a mix of Christian and secular music, and churches play Christian music, Hope Springs Eternal presents live worship and praise within the style of other contemporary music venues in Second Life. Since that first venue, she has built a second praise and worship venue, also located at Hope Springs Eternal: "It's in the sky and it's called Christ the Solid Rock. And we have praise and worship minimum once a week live. A couple of weeks it's two and three times a week that's scheduled and then we also have impromptu praise and worship. So that is kind of the gist of Hope Springs Eternal" (Salmson, 2009).

Salmson works alongside others who have helped her with the various components of the ministry over the past two years, one of which has been SavannahGrace Constantine, who typically leads the Monday night prayer meeting. The meeting runs for at least 2 hours, and people openly share real- and Second Life issues and concerns and work through them with prayer. Salmson (2009) adds, "But another aspect of the ministry there is simply walking in God's love. It's based on biblical teachings in] 1 Corinthians, Chapter 13. And we reach out to people; we listen and we love, and we don't condemn." Hope Springs Eternal is designed to provide in-world encouragement to Christians and those seeking answers to life issues:

> We try to encourage people or encourage Christians to step out to ministry. There have been many people who have come to Eternal Creations and they have renewed their dedication to God. They have rededicated their life and there have been people saved who have actually just turned their life over to the Lord. So God is alive and well in Second Life and His eye is on Second Life and every person in it. (Salmson, 2009)

Salmson is a director of a domestic violence unit for a prosecutor's office in real life, elaborating, she has found that many people, in fact almost the majority of people that she has encountered through her ministry have been abused in their life, particularly "many from childhood and many from adulthood in domestic violence relationships. So that's another thing that God has used as far as ministering to those that are hurt or broken" (Salmson, 2009). She explains, "There are many victims of domestic abuse in Second Life. I have personally worked with them." Continuing, Salmson (2009) adds, "and again, being a woman of faith and knowing that there is no coincidence, you would be very surprised how many people I have encountered and it turned out that is exactly what the purpose was to help them right now in a real-life situation where they were in danger or just to even acknowledge that what happened to them was wrong and to offer them hope and encouragement and resources." Salmson's ministry serves as a safety net for people who might get lost along the way in their real and Second Life, and sees the reality behind Second Life:

> I think that probably 99.9% of the people are caught off guard. Second Life mirrors real life. There's not a whole lot you can't do in real life that you cannot do in Second Life. But the thing is of course what we have to depend upon are our caricatures that we build of ourselves and mostly we use type. So the way it has turned out in Second Life apparently is that there is a concentration of emotions. So emotions are very volatile in Second Life. And from that, there are lots of healthy and unhealthy relationships that are formed in Second Life. That is one of the things I believe that the Lord has used as far as the Christian community is concerned in Second Life—is that when people are broken and hurt they end up—many—finding a place where they can be safe and they can be loved in a healthy way and encouraged. (Salmson, 2009)

She states, acknowledging that many scoff at "a thing called the divine appointment," that "anyone who works in ministry in Second Life who is in tune finds there are many of those to be had in Second Life. Second Life, if you will come in at it from the aspect of ministry, is a huge virtual mission field. So it's just an awesome opportunity to be able to work on the field in Second Life. Of course, I'm going to tell you straight up again I'm human—I'm a Christian—but I'm a sinner saved by grace. So it is not that I'm special. It's that He is special" (Salmson, 2009).

People who have grown up with video games might not think of Second Life as anything beyond a game, knowing that for instance gamers shoot at one another or drive cars fast without real consequences. "And they look at this, like it is a video game," she cautions, elaborating, "So therefore there are people who come into Second Life that don't realize that there's great potential for other people to be hurt...There are people who come into Second Life who are challenged physically, some emotionally and some mentally. So again there are quite a number of people in Second Life who do not realize the impact that they can have on another human being. And I'm talking about a serious impact" (Salmson, 2009).

Salmson has had her share of reality in Second Life; she has "talked with people who were threatening suicide. I'm not talking playing a game. I'm talking life and death." In other cases, she has worked "with victims of domestic abuse who are currently in domestic violence situations and left those situations because they were in danger." Salmson (2009) states:

> I have worked with people who have lost loved ones and are totally depressed and feeling abandoned. Anything that you would encounter in real life as far as hurting people I think that they're just concentrated in Second Life. Again, it mirrors real life. So I guess what it boils down to is this, in a nutshell, when I came to Second Life, I didn't come for ministry. But I'm a woman of faith. And I saw it; I saw the field that was ripe for harvest. And I couldn't step away. There has been recently a friend of mine in real life who told me that I needed to leave Second Life, that it was an unhealthy environment for Christians, that you are supposed to flee evil. But I guess what I say is when I even entertain that, God brings someone in my path just like yesterday, just brings someone right there and gives that divine appointment; and I wonder if every Christian left Second Life, who is going to be there, who is going to be there to speak to that person and share the hope that we have within us. So even though there are scoffers and doubters and people who do not believe in God at all, I have even seen people who feel that way who have come into His presence in Second Life...Just don't look at us when we mess up, because I mess up, don't look at us, look at Him. I guess that is the bottom line.

As in real life, people have to deal with personal struggles, temptations, and all the things that happen in Second Life. "But if you come in," she explains, you can begin to understand how God can "take this very medium that is meant perhaps for some things that aren't very good," and use this very medium...to reach out and touch the ones that come in here and have no idea that He would find them here" (Salmson, 2009). Beyond that, Salmson knows how to access resources to help those with real problems, such as domestic abuse victims: "It's just a matter of accessing the Internet and getting good information because I believe knowledge is power. So that is another aspect of the ministry that the Lord has actually given me, the opportunity and privilege to do in Second Life" (Salmson, 2009).

Buddhism in the Virtual

Resting Thor is a respected Buddhist teacher and practitioner in real and Second Life, where spiritual forces that steer his life have an opportunity to flourish in unique ways touching others within and beyond his computer screen. Thor says he was never a gamer, stating "Second Life doesn't seem to be a conventional game anyway, right?" Like others, when he entered Second Life, the potential of virtual worlds was speculative and untapped. His journey began as an exploration, springing from his professional experience and interests:

> I guess a couple of things led me to investigate Second Life. First off, I do a lot of computer work professionally and in virtual reality. It had some professional lure to me because my business does a lot of 3-D virtual modeling kinds of things for engineering companies...And then I spent the last 10 years focused on a fairly rigorous spiritual education program in Buddhism. (Thor, 2009)

Thor travels extensively throughout the year for business "at least a third of the time, sometimes half time, so this was a way to connect up to people whom I had been doing previously with voice. This was nice to have an opportunity to connect to people more, a kind of pseudo physical connection I guess" (Thor, 2009). He added, "You can see, you can gesture, you can create environments that are great visual aids and teaching aids." Second Life provided a means to connect him with others online spiritually as well as to provide training and education in-world:

> The reason spiritually I got into it was one to connect up to people that I couldn't connect up with easily with travel except through some kind of computer technology. Second Life was intriguing because I could work on some of the graphic visualization aids or models that are useful when we do visualizations and meditations. Some of them are complex, the meditations that is. I have created some models in Second Life of different meditational objects so that has been helpful too. Also, in our tradition, we like to identify with different spiritual representations of ourselves with different deities and so I have been able to walk around in this reality in different forms and shapes. That has been helpful in creating an alternative self-identity. (Thor, 2009)

Thor, like others, has discovered Second Life is a tool for facilitating alterations to one's form. Distantly similar to what some might call role-play, Buddhists through Second Life have been provided the means to explore identity as a powerful training and communicative tool.

Second Life, although seemingly a massive community on the surface, is a way for members to connect within small groups, which work well in-world. As Thor (2009) explains,

> Second Life seems to be really helpful one-on-one, when talking to spiritual practitioners. It is a nice venue for just chatting about questions that come up or details about practice or concerns, personal issues that people have you know kind of ministering or counseling, or one-on-one education that works really well.

Second Life also "works really well for teaching venues, like we're doing Tibetan. We're learning a language so you can practice the Tibetan language and that has worked out really well" (Thor, 2009). A significant amount of energy is devoted to mediation inside Second Life among the Buddhist communities. Thor, for example, typically conducts worship and practice activities in-world four times out of the week, mainly because of different demands on his schedule. Within Second Life, Thor has a place to meditate with another practitioner:

> We meet and meditate in real life while our avatars are sitting in a place that, we think, is conducive to that. We each have our own individual meditation practice that we are doing in real life. So it's really useful as a kind of training buddy, or maybe a worship buddy where we're practicing together at the same time. We will meet because we are expecting each other to be there. So we'll get out of bed and we'll get up earlier to get there to practice our meditation than when we might often not if it were just the one of us. So it is like [having] a virtual training partner or in this case a practice buddy or a practice partner that makes me more consistent. (Thor, 2009)

For most Buddhist Second Lifers, it is not a matter of having to advertise activities necessarily but word of mouth inside the community of people there that has contributed to increased membership. It is difficult to persuade the real-life Buddhist community to make the virtual crossover. Thor (2009) states, "In my particular Buddhist community we have maybe 3,000 people or so scattered around the U.S and the world. And I have advertised to that community."

"There's a lot of interest in what I'm doing in, but not a lot of participation" in Second Life on that regard. He continues, "It seems that people are either Second Life users or not. It's hard to pull a lot of people into Second Life. For some reason, they don't gravitate to it. But if they like Second Life, it works really well" (Thor, 2009). Those 3-D gamers, power computer users and those with backgrounds in graphic design are more likely to come into Second Life: "But in general I haven't had a lot of luck bringing in—I haven't pushed it extensively—people from outside of Second Life." Other than that, the Buddhist community is fairly active within Second Life:

> And we have some good participation in different Buddhist discussions and teachings and meditation settings...There's probably five active places within Second Life where there is at least one or more daily meditations that you can attend and that doesn't count like your yoga or other religions. So any way there's a lot going on in Second Life within Buddhism, and that community is active, and those people are comfortable in Second Life obviously. (Thor, 2009)

As for the total Buddhists in Second Life, Thor (2009) estimates 4,000 to 5,000 members. Within the larger global community, information is distributed through email, Web sites and blogs within groups, with email as the primary communication tool. One SL group has set up a forum on a Web site. For the rest, administrators send out notices from their Second Life groups "and that's the main way people communicate in Second Life with those notices that go out to the groups saying we have a meditation session starting in 15 minutes at the Zen retreat or that kind of place—a lot of those notices every day" (Thor, 2009).

Thor's group has nurtured strong bonds among members, and these relationships have shaped lives in significant ways beyond Second Life. Thor shared a case where at least three people "have started going regularly to real-life Buddhist temples and have gotten a lot more personal real-life training as well." He points out,

> Second Life seems to be a great place for people to explore and branch out and meet people. One lady I know now is hooked up with several real-life groups that do similar things to what she was interested in Second Life. So she left her job she had on the East Coast and is going through a kind of spiritual discovery practicing with a group in Scottsdale, Arizona. (Thor, 2009)

Thor went on to say,

> People meet other people and they make a real connection with people, a real connection with different communities, churches and temples. And so it changes their real life. It's not just limited to what happens inside Second Life...The stories you typically hear in Second Life are people that meet in like matchmaking or dating or something similar. In here, though, the people who come to the Buddhist groups, they are not there for a dating connection or anything. A lot them are trying to deepen their spiritual insights or spiritual education or have different issues with pain or suffering in their life. (Thor, 2009)

For instance, Thor (2009) shares, "One of the members was caring for her husband over the course of a chronic, degenerative nerve condition. She obviously took a lot of comfort in meeting every night and talking to the community she had." He continued,

> She had a lot of friends in here she communicated with and then when he passed there was a support group here that I think provided quite a bit of support for her. And she is one of several people I have met in the Buddhist group that have been caring for elderly or chronically ill people. Second Life seems like a very convenient way for people who have those kinds of responsibilities to easily participate in a community and yet not have to leave the bedside for any real length of time. So for any other caregivers this is a nice opportunity for people to stay connected. (Thor, 2009)

In his profile, Thor refers to himself as a Buddhist practitioner and event organizer. Essentially what he does is try to find ways to connect Second Life to real life at least from the Buddhist perspective. Some of those ways that happen include offering classes and teachings:

> In Second Life, I try to make people aware of what's going on in real life. In real life, I teach Buddhist classes in Houston, Texas, and I have been a fairly devoted practitioner for the last 10 years. I practice the Tibetan and Indian lineages of Buddhism...Frankly when I'm in Second Life, it's a small Buddhist group, maybe one person chatting or maybe a 20-person discussion or a public meditation session. (Thor, 2009)

Four or five fairly large sims or builds in Second Life are Buddhist oriented. One place of worship and teachings is called Bodhi Island, "a large kind of Buddhaland or enlightened land. So there's some big Zen kind of places, where people meet" (Thor, 2009). However, he adds,

> The Japanese Zen tradition type of places seems to have the most interest and activity going on. I think at a universal level, Buddhists seem to like the Zen Japanese look and feel about things. There are, however, a number of places where individuals have created meditation places. For example in the morning, I meditated in a small meditation room which one of my friends had built...I also have a single 512 parcel...[on which] I have a room where I have some cushions there so I can meditate. (Thor, 2009)

Thor is convinced that virtual reality will help define religious practice in the future: "I think the virtual reality aspect of Second Life is really compelling for a certain percentage of our population. I think it is going to be more common place over time, right?" (Thor, 2009). Indeed, he speculates, "Eventually we will all be plugged" into virtual worlds. At least, he explains, "those of us who want to be will be plugged into this kind of alternative or maybe even augmented second reality...It is definitely an opportunity for sharing ideas, communicating or meeting with other religious practitioners" (Thor, 2009). He continues:

> There's no doubt that there will be thousands if not millions of people that practice different religious traditions in these kinds of communities in the future. It is just very convenient and very useful. It's not the same as being there, but if you had real-life events, like if you had real-life temples that had connections to Second Life, that did teachings inside Second Life, that had Second Life avatars from around the world participating..." (Thor, 2009)

Perhaps such activities would help to solidify the real to virtual world connections for some people. Presently, text messaging is used as a primary means to communicate within Second Life, and Thor sees that as "an inherently inefficient way to communicate." He explains,

> I think the voice is the future of Second Life, and a lot more efficient way to communicate than 5 or 6 words at a time. That's my own opinion. I think you are going to see virtual Sanghas (groups of religious practitioners) that have—like you have television based Sanghas, I say "Sanghas"—[I mean] churches. So you have churches that are essentially television based. Everybody is watching the services and doing whatever they do or just passively watching it. I think you are going to have more active participation—that kind of media-enabled thing, and that will become more and more popular. (Thor, 2009)

Second Life is merely the beginning, he suggests, pointing out that there might be something else on the horizon other than Second Life, perhaps in the short run a Wii or an Xbox modified to appease a consumer market interested in extending their spiritual life through virtuality (Thor, 2009).

Is Second Life a Game?

Some see Second Life as a mirror of reality; others see it as a game. Some people try to sort out their religious beliefs and convictions online, and one of the ways that happens is through dialogue exemplified below. The following transcript conveys a conversation held among members of an open enrollment SL Christian group. The avatar names have been changed and the transcript has been edited for clarity. The conversation begins when a member announces that he got married in SL. The chat gains the attention of others, who also join into the discussion. Questions arise on the meaning of partnership in Second Life. For some, partnership is equivalent to marriage. For others, it is a statement of wanting to be with another person in Second Life. The dialogue ensued around Second Life choices in forming identities, creating alternate selves, and merely wanting to test waters on what it means to be a Christian in Second Life.

[19:00] Bradley Eunice: i just got married on here!!!!
[19:00] Kat Winz: YAY111
[19:00] Marina Fledge: oh wow.
[19:00] Kat Winz: Awesome!
[19:00] Ande Nightfire: Congratulations.
[19:00] Lydia Finkle: Congratulations.
[19:00] Kelly Kaegle: Congrats!
[19:01] Mindy Tazzle: Congratulations!
[19:01] Eloise Whitlock: someone needs to explain *getting married on here* to me
[19:02] Lisa Smide: I would like to know that too???
[19:02] Ande Nightfire: I'm pretty sure it's been done before.
[19:02] Eloise Whitlock: are you married in RL? If so, is your RL wife the one you just got married to here in SL?
[19:02] Bradley Eunice: no im not married in rl.
[19:02] Eloise Whitlock: so then you are role-playing?
[19:02] Bradley Eunice: NO!
[19:03] Eloise Whitlock: well how do you *marry* on SL if not in RL?
[19:03] Kat Winz: some people take it a step further and actually have an SL wedding too.
[19:03] Lindsey Shipley: Marriage in SL is the partnership option.
[19:03] Bradley Eunice: yes.
[19:03] Eloise Whitlock: I know what it is, LOL I am partnered in SL to my RL husband.
[19:03] Lindsey Shipley: usually it is with RL boyfriends/girlfriends or husbands/wives. If not then, I don't know why.
[19:03] Kat Winz: I went to an SL wedding last Saturday, and they are married in RL.
[19:04] Eloise Whitlock: can't see how you can be married any other way without RL first, unless you are role-playing. RL marriage, resulting in SL partnership...that I can see.
[19:04] Bradley Eunice: that is it.
[19:05] Eloise Whitlock: ok so next ? Is it right to partner in SL when you are not married

in RL?

[19:05] Kat Winz: and sometimes people meet people in SL, grow a relationship, meet in RL, and then get married in RL and SL.

[19:05] Bradley Eunice: yes

[19:05] Lindsey Shipley: No, it is not right.

[19:05] Eloise Whitlock: well good luck to that.

[19:05] Lindsey Shipley: SL is not a matchmaking service, it is a game.

[19:05] Lindsey Shipley: :)

[19:05] Eloise Whitlock: but I find the majority do not work.

[19:06] Kat Winz: it can be similar to match.com, eharmony, etc...

[19:06] Eloise Whitlock: SL is not a matchmaking service, or shouldn't be, moreover it turns out to be a means of leading us away from the Lord's will...which is to wait on him for a partner/spouse in RL.

[19:06] Oklmada Tunnel: Dating in SL can work...but there's a difference between dating and "marriage."

[19:07] Kat Winz: yes there sure is.

[19:07] Eloise Whitlock: it is not a game, it involves your mind and decision making, which here for the most part are not biblically based, such as SL partnering/marriage.

[19:07] Vron Pantle: I don't consider SL a game. Consider that Lindens are real money, people have businesses on here, many colleges and universities have a presence here. You can find many different companies throughout SL. To me it is an extension of RL.

[19:07] Kat Winz: who is to say that the Lord's work of introducing two people together cannot be on SL. It is not a game. RL and SL mesh so much.

[19:08] Oklmada Tunnel: And dating in SL should only be with the intent of finding out if you want to meet and take it further in RL.

[19:08] Kat Winz: a big difference. Yes, we are the humans and the emotions BEHIND the avatars. If we remember that then, good choices CAN and WILL be made, according to God's will.

[19:09] Lindsey Shipley: RL and SL do not mesh at all together. I see to it that it doesn't.

[19:09] Kat Winz: oh i respectfully DO NOT agree.

[19:09] Eloise Whitlock: if it is they'll be marrying in RL first.

[19:09] Kat Winz: you cannot be two people.

[19:09] Eloise Whitlock: not playing house in SL first.

[19:09] Marina Fledge: let's not argue.

[19:09] Eloise Whitlock: you cannot separate yourself in SL and RL, you are one person...God sees all we do, even in SL.

[19:09] Lindsey Shipley: so to me this is a game.

[19:10] Kat Winz: dialoging.

[19:10] Lindsey Shipley: the character is not me :)

[19:10] Kat Winz: not arguing.

[19:10] Lindsey Shipley: i just happen to control it.

[19:10] Eloise Whitlock: the character IS you, it's what's lurking in your heart.

[19:11] Cyndee Clydno: avi's are a visual representation of your spirit self image...what u do here does matter.

[19:11] Marina Fledge: I'm more me on SL than I am in RL.

[19:11] Eloise Whitlock: but if what we do in SL doesn't honor the Lord, we should not be doing it...pretty simple...you cannot separate SL just because you want to call it a

game...God sees all we do and He's not into games.
[19:11] Lindsey Shipley: so your inner self can be multiple people? I have all sorts of virtual people.
[19:11] Cyndee Clydno: facets of u yeah.
[19:12] Lindsey Shipley: so...playing Warcraft 3 is a facet of me?
[19:12] Kat Winz: hmmm.
[19:12] Lindsey Shipley: or playing an alien on Halo 2?
[19:12] Lisa Smide: Since when do we tell God what he is or isn't doing??
[19:13] Kat Winz: for His greater good?
[19:13] Cyndee Clydno: maybe not the actual thing, but HOW you play it...that's you.
[19:13] Lindsey Shipley: most if not all people on SL make up characters much like any 3D shooter for the fun of it.
[19:13] Kat Winz: many do that.
[19:13] Eloise Whitlock: I pray these two *UNmarry* and consider the Lord first here in SL AND in RL...must go, God bless all.
[19:13] Cyndee Clydno: we weren't talking about looks here...we were talking about actions.
[19:13] Oklmada Tunnel: What is the point of marriage in SL if it's not a mirror of an actual marriage?
[19:13] Kat Winz: and being a hypocrite there?
[19:13] Lisa Smide: There are games here to play, just as in RL. But what you do here is no different than what you dwell on in your mind. If it is not good, then don't dwell on it.
[19:13] Kat Winz: how about going to church on Sunday?
[19:14] Eloise Whitlock: I will leave you with a thought though, if you were married and your spouse had another wife in SL...would that be ok? I think not...think about what you are doing please!
[19:14] Lindsey Shipley: linden labs makes excuses to make money so they try to mirror reality.
[19:14] Kat Winz: that is not okay, to have diff SL and RL marriages.
[19:14] Lindsey Shipley: real life doesn't have access lines we bounce off of and if it mirrors reality so much, then what is all these red access lines?
[19:15] Kat Winz: no.
[19:18] Autor Fierce: SL is not essential and we can experiment diversity.
[19:24] Oklmada Tunnel: SL is an incredible opportunity and resource. It is a game—when done in role-play, or when playing little games. It is informational, we can learn much. It can help us grow spiritually as we connect with one another. It can help the lonely, though not replace the necessary in-person relationships. It can be a harmless distraction. It can also be a place to fall into sin if you're not careful, to learn more than you want or should of "counter" cultures, to get your heart broken, to lose your way. It's very complicated, and I think keeping grounded and accountable in Christian areas is necessary to staying on the right track here.
[19:25] Kat Winz: YES! CHOICES.
[19:25] Autor Fierce: right!
[19:25] Kat Winz: That is life—choices :)
[19:26] Autor Fierce: Lord is calling everyone of us to make a most pure life and to choose HIS Love, not the love by the world.
[19:26] Kat Winz: Be in the world and not of the world—yes. SL or RL.

From the conversation above, many Christians construct SL as an opportunity to extend their faith online. Role-playing is not widely accepted among SL Christian communities, particularly if it parts from biblical principles. Second Life is a dynamic space that offers challenges to the meaning of life—first and second life, regardless of one's views before they sign up as a member. The question of whether Second Life is a game or not was clearly debated but remained unsolved.

Conclusion

Interfaith opportunities occasionally arise in Second Life, but mainly most groups work within their faith in planning activities and counseling members. Religions for the most part simply co-exist within Second Life, responding to the needs of their members and those seeking answers of a spiritual nature. Spirituality is a component of Second Life that cannot be taken lightly or considered exclusively within a group or individual, merely if one considers the potentiality of one's actions transcending virtuality and residing within thoughts and actions of people in real life. Residents bring real emotions, issues and expectations to Second Life. Second Life thrives on creating community, building relationships across communities, and catering to the sense of exploration possible in a virtual world—an exploration of mind, emotions, and physicality. René Descartes, a French philosopher and scientist, considered the mind and spirit as one entity. The mind thrives on the creativity within Second Life, and an inherent spirituality springs forth—internal or eternal, depending on one's beliefs. What people believe to be real becomes real, and they cannot necessarily separate their emotions from their actions—and real life blurs into Second Life, and vice versa.

References

Andrade, K. (2007, August 2). This revolution will be televised from Second Life: UC Berkeley students broadcast live from virtual world of Second Life to Real Life. Accessed July 25, from http://newsinitiative.org/story/2007/07/31/ this_revolution_will_be_televised/

Boellstorff, T. (2008) *Coming of Age in Second Life*. Trenton, NJ: Princeton University Press.

Crabtree, S. (2007, June 15). Finding religion in Second Life's virtual world. *Washington Post*. Accessed July 13, 2009, from http://www.washingtonpost.com/wp-dyn/content/article/2007/06/15/AR2007061501902.html/

Faces of faith in Second Life showcase and conversation. (2007, July). God, sex and family. Seminar series, sponsored by University of California, Berkeley & SLCN, Second Life Cable Network.

Foster, F. (2001, April 4). Boaz project builds bridges between modern and postmodern; Baptist General Convention of Texas NEWS. *Texas Baptist Communications*. Accessed at http://www.bgct.org/communications/article-4-4a-01.htm/

Future of religions conference. (2008, June 4 & 5). Second Life.

Greene, M. (2007, July 29). Jesuits see the potential of Second Life Jesuits. Kotaku.com. Accessed July 25, 2009, from http://kotaku.com/283622/jesuits-see-the-potential-of-second-lifeJesuits See the Potential of Second Life/

Grossman, C. L. (2007, April 1). Faithful build a Second Life for religion online. *USA Today.com*. Accessed July 13, 2009, from http://www.usatoday.com/ tech/gaming/2007-04-01-second-life-religion_N.htm/

Hadden, J. (1988). *Televangelism, power and politics on God's frontier*. New York: Holt.

Hohstadt, T. (1999). *Dying to live*: The 21st century church. Odessa, TX: Damah Media.

Idswebguy. (2007, May 11). Mormons active in Second Life. Access July 25, from http://www.ldswebguy.com/2007/05/11/mormons-active-in-second-life/

Jones, A. (2004). Accessed July 25, from http://tallskinnykiwi.typepad.com/tallskinnykiwi/

Lamoureux, E. L. (2007, November). Online religious practice through the looking glass: Spirituality and the netweb. *Journal of Communication and Religion*, 30 (2), 340–375.

Pasteur, E. (2007, April 6). Where now for Second Religion? *Second Life Insider*. Accessed July 10, 2009, from http://www.secondlifeinsider.com/ 2007/04/06/ where-now-for-second-religion/

Peckham, M. (2008, December 11). Second Life for Muslims launches online. Accessed July 25, 2009, from http://muslimmedianetwork.com/mmn/?p=3349/

Religion online in Second Life. (2007, May 22). NBC Nightly News. Accessed July 22, 2009, from http://www.youtube.com/watch?v=1-BGQKaKi18/

Salmson, S. (2009, July 22). Interview, personal communication with author. Second Life.

Sample, T. (1998). *The spectacle of worship in a wired world: Electronic culture and the gathered people of God*. Nashville: Abingdon Press.

Schroeder, R., Heather, N., & Lee, R. M. (1998). The sacred and the virtual: Religion in multi-user virtual reality. *Journal of Computer-Mediated Communication* 4(2). Accessed July 21, 2009, from http://jcmc.indiana.edu/vol4/issue2/schroeder.html/

SLCC. (2009). Real life religion within Second Life panel. Second Life Community Convention, August 12–16, 2009. Accessed July 23, 2009, from http://www.slconvention.org/ convention-tracks-and-topics/real-life-religion-within-second-life-panel-communities-2009//

Stacey, W., & Shupe, A. (1982). Correlates of support for the electronic church. *Journal for the Scientific Study of Religion 21*(4), 291–303.

Thor, R. (2009, July 21). Interview, personal communication with author. Second Life.

White, S. J. (1994). *Christian worship and technological change*. Nashville: Abingdon Press.

Wilson, L., & Moore, J. (2002). *Digital storytellers: The art of communicating the gospel in worship*. Nashville: Abingdon Press.

CHAPTER FOURTEEN

Conclusion: A Second Look at Virtual Worlds: Is the Future Now?

> The goal is let a person create a digital alter-ego that can travel to many virtual worlds, keeping the same name, look and even digital currency…Think of it as passports for avatars. So that pink-headed cutie you made for Second Life can also take up residence in There.com…for example.
>
> —Steve Lohr, *Free the Avatars, NY Times.com*

It has begun! Travel between virtual worlds, although you should expect a few bumps on the super highway between worlds. Traffic might be a bit congested at times. That is expressed as lag in the virtual world. But the idea is to allow people to hop between worlds, as if they were traveling to other continents or maybe even planets. You can visit your friend across the Metaverse or get some cute knickers on Virtual Planet X. Is this a *Star Wars* movie in the making? The point is, the more that people "can communicate, inform and entertain each other freely on a network, the more valuable it is" to us as a society (Lohr, 2007). In Edward Castronova's book *Exodus to the Virtual World*, one begins to see a world unfold where various forms of communication (open chat, voice, and instant messaging) overlap and inform members on multiple levels of understanding. Linear communication sometimes loses its accuracy when it is not contextualized, and Second Life provides a meaning to text and communication.

No longer are words left flat on the computer screen. Perception is affirmed through multiple channels of communication facilitated through virtual platforms like Second Life and other emerging worlds that also connect with one another, and will do so increasingly in the near to distant future. Mark Deuze (2007) states, reminding us of what futurist Alvin Toffler predicted nearly 30 years ago, "This invisibility of making and using media simultaneously can be set against the increasing invisibility of media in everyday life." Millions of people are engaged in virtual worlds, as tourists, entrepreneurs, educators, and artists. In fact, the SL economy is booming, you might say, having "enjoyed the sixth consecutive quarter of record growth and activity in the in-world economy" (Linden, 2009). "At nearly USD 50M per month user-to-user transactions, the Second Life economy is now on an annual run rate north of half a billion US dollars, making Second Life the largest virtual economy in the industry," stated Linden Lab in a report released in August 2009. Some of the highlights of the Second Quarter for 2009 included record sales for SL's Xstreet online merchandise, as well as:

> –144 million US dollars in total user-to-user transaction (increasing 94% from the same quarter in 2008)
> –3.2 billion of "voice" minutes (increasing 48% from the same quarter in 2008)
> –Residential land purchases increased 11% from 2008 (Linden, 2009)

Apparently, what did slow was the growth in the total user hours, but that was explained away by Linden Lab's new policy of "limiting the use of automated, scripted avatars (BOTS)" (Linden, 2009). Overall, in one year, the SL economy has "nearly doubled, which is a testament to the creativity, dynamism and energy of Second Life Residents," continued the Linden (2009) report that gave accolades to SL users. The controversial finding in the report centered around the monthly statistics for June 2009, which indicated that 90% of "all in-world activity" in SL was driven by a core of approximately 130,000 users (Au, 2009). Wagner James Au (2009), of *New World Notes*, a blog that follows SL trends, reported:

> On the very high end, that's 22K people who are in-world 300 hours or more per month—i.e., on average, *ten-plus hours a day*. But the low end is what concerns me far more: 401K unique users are not even staying in Second Life more than three hours total...

To this Au (2009) responds, "At this point, less than 350K Second Life users are logging in long enough to be a regular part of the in-world economy and the community."

As noted already, Linden Lab explained the dip in user hours based on their revised corporate policy. But, even if those statistics indicate that only a core base of members are regularly plugged into SL for extended periods of time, doesn't the question become, at that point, realistically how many hours should a person dedicate to a virtual world, particularly if they have an active real life—family and job? Do we really want the millions of members to immerse themselves totally into Second Life and other games? Are we ready for a complete transition from real life to the virtual? For many, their second life is as important as their real life, if not more important in some aspects. It is not so much a case of addiction for these members, as one of having established friendships that are as meaningful as ones that have been made in real life. On the other hand, how do you sustain an economy in SL without growing the core users? Time will tell. In 2009, Linden Lab began to take that issue seriously, and started considering incentives to keep people logged on longer than they would have been otherwise. Again, what are the social ramifications of such incentives on the users?

Students are sometimes introduced to Second Life through their classes on virtual campuses. They make connections to their teachers and other students, and these experiences are real. It is not always how long they stay online, but the quality of their experience. As long as people are communicating to one another, what is read and said is valid—and meaningful. The words leave an impression on us. As humans, we respond to the words and the visuals. In a 3D environment, our senses may be even more alert than in RL because our attention is often focused within the confined virtual world. Corporations and educators are using SL as a tool to mentor and train people for real world activities. Media makers in real life are now bringing their skills in-world to report on virtual worlds, and at the same time they are making crossovers back to real-life media. The bulletin boards of the early days before the Internet made a significant contribution to people's lives and how they communicated to each other. Now, decades later, virtual worlds have extended our communication abilities. The disabled can walk, run, work and dance inside these virtual communities. For someone who feels trapped in bed or the wheelchair, a virtual world allows them an opportunity to connect with other people from all over the world.

Perhaps, it is the purpose of virtual worlds that must be more definitively established than has been the case so far. Corporations and education institutions contribute greatly to the SL economy, and that also spurs membership. In another sense, I have made wonderful contacts in SL that I now occasionally Skype, rather than IM in Second Life. I have contacted many people I met in SL through other social network services like Facebook. I have met them at conferences. I watch SL activities on YouTube and read SL newspapers and magazines when I cannot log inside Second Life for whatever reason (or just want to watch television as I browse SL media on the Internet). Those indirect instances were not calculated in the report. Furthermore, with the introduction of Xstreet and other like merchant services, members can buy SL fashions, furniture, land or whatever online, without even going in-world. Xstreet is popular among SL users, but such online services might reduce the number of hours one spends inside SL to find and purchase a certain product. I like the old fashioned method of wandering around SL malls and looking at the in-world classifieds.

The Lindens own Second Life, and they do have to be concerned about the bottom line in terms of sustaining a strong economy. But the same may be said of any government or economy across the world. Second Life is a world filled with artists, builders, communicators, engineers, computer programmers, scientists, educators, and others who might be searching for their place in Second Life as well as real life. It is a world that is made by persons who live there, and there is a gentile spirit of collaboration, for the most part, that runs through this alternate life stream into each resident.

Closing Thoughts

The future of Second Life is uncertain in the sense that technology continues to expand at a rapid pace. Linden Lab is on the forefront of this technological expansion as it works to make it easier for avatars to travel to other virtual worlds. None of them appear as impressive, at the writing of this book, as Second Life, if measured solely in terms of the sophistication of relationships developed thus far among content creators of the media. Many members have invested several years of their life into the game, which has become arguably a major part of their real life. Some have taken their real businesses into Second Life, and alternately Second Life businesses into real life. What is really significant to consider is how virtual worlds will define in the years ahead the lives of children and teens, who are already linked into the Internet for entertainment, news, and communicating with their friends—some of whom they have met in worlds like Second Life's teen world:

> In America, nearly 10m children and teenagers visit virtual worlds regularly, estimates eMarketer, a market researcher—a number the firm expects to increase to 15m by 2013. As of January, there were 112 virtual worlds designed for under-18s with another 81 in development, according to Engage Digital Media, a market research firm. (*Online playgrounds*, 2009)

Virtual worlds are comprised of media, and they are indeed media. The convergence of media happens in-world, where television, radio, print, and the Internet collaborate to create an experience based in communication and message delivery. Philip Linden once had a dream of traveling in space, and he did—the space that surrounds our daily lives. It is a world that we can travel from within our homes, and this inner space is cause for reflection on who we are and what we mean to each other in our real life and second life communities. The world is at our fingertips—as for which world, you decide. And again, how long you work and play in a virtual world will be dependent on how much it relates to your real-life needs, wants and dreams–for now, anyway, I suppose.

References

Au, W. J. (2009, August 13). Stat shock: Just 133K Second Life users responsible for nearly 90% total monthly SL user hours! *New World Notes*. Accessed August 15, 2009, from http://nwn.blogs.com/nwn/2009/08/sl-has-133k-hardcore-users.html/

Castronova, E. (2008). *Exodus to the virtual world: How online fun is changing reality*. NY: Palgrave Macmillan.

Deuze, M. (2007). *Media work: Digital media & society*. Cambridge, England: Polity.

Linden, T. (2009, August 12). Linden Chief Product Officer. The Second Life economy—second quarter 2009 in detail. Second Life Blog. Accessed August 15, 2009, from https://blogs.secondlife.com/community/features/blog/2009/08/12/the-second-life-economy--second-quarter-2009-in-detail/

Lohr, S. (2007, October 10). Free the avatars. *NY Times.com*. Accessed July 10, 2009, from http://bits.blogs.nytimes.com/tag/linden-lab/

Online playgrounds: Virtual worlds for children. There is life in virtual reality after all. (2009, July 23). *The Economist*. Accessed August 15, 2009, from http://www.economist.com/businessfinance/displaystory.cfm?story_id=14098380/

EPILOGUE

The Rebaking of Second Life: Creating Virtual Worlds That People Inhabit

Wagner James Au is the noted author of *The Making of Second Life* (2008) and his blog *Notes from the New World* continues his documentation and critique of the high-tech culture of Second Life and other emerging worlds. Linden Lab hired him as an embedded journalist for Second Life in 2003, and as such he was given access to the making and evolution of SL and its creators. Consequently, he broke new ground in reporting on a virtual world. His professional experience has included game development, freelance reporting, and consulting on the technical and economical aspects of virtual worlds. His perspective is an invaluable one to understanding where Second Life began, and where it might be headed. It seems appropriate that Au would offer some closing comments, given that he was there in the beginning to report on Second Life.

Au spoke to me about how virtual worlds, notably Second Life, have changed since he began tracking them. Second Life has been an interesting virtual world to follow, particularly because it offers its users the ability to create content far more than other games. However, there might be drawbacks to such a model, which may offer limitations toward keeping the base of active users to a consistently high level. Some new virtual worlds have entered the market that have attempted to challenge Second Life's user content model, and have leaned toward creating worlds where residents can simply enjoy ready-made environments. In this case, the idea of building community has less to do with object construction and more toward creating networking opportunities among virtual residents. Au reflects on Second Life's evolution over the years, and looks toward the future. Virtual worlds are making their mark on the lives of many, but only about 8% of the United States, for example, is actively participating in virtual worlds. Countries like Japan provide a view to the future, with many people embracing virtual worlds to a significantly higher degree than the U.S. or Europe.

Sitting down on a stool on a wooden platform on my SL beachfront property, Hamlet Au, as he is known in-world, shared his perspective on how Second Life must respond to remain socially and economically relevant among the growing number of virtual worlds. As I sat on my stool, I listened to this interesting-looking avatar dressed in a white suit and white shoes, sporting black framed glasses that matched his black hair, mustache and well-trimmed goatee. As previously noted, he was originally hired to observe Second Life, by Linden Lab as part journalist and part ethnographer. He would go on to write about his experiences in a book about the making of Second Life. In this interview, he proposes that Second Life may have run its course, although it has significantly made an impact on how other virtual-world designers are creating their games. As Second Life works hard to make itself more user friendly not only to its members, but to those who might be interested in participating, its competition is growing and maturing as well. A 3D immersive world provides many opportunities to create events, experiences and structures, compared to 2D Web-based games like Metaplace and YoVille. The latter suggests a less interactive environment in terms of technical and social applications, but it still allows for social networking among participants. And that seems to be the bottom line for many players, the ability to connect with others easily in creative, usable environments.

Interview with Wagner James Au

Q: What is the state of Second Life, as far as its future in the game business of virtual worlds?

WJA: Second Life has gone through a lot of changes since I started writing about it in 2003. Really kind of the early growth phase went all the way up to I would say late 2005. At that point, we got more and more interest from media. There has always been a lot of media coverage, but it's just started getting more and more intense. In late 2005, early 2006, that's really when the very first hype wave started with *Business Week* having its cover story [on Second Life] in March 2006. Like I write about in my book, *The Making of Second Life*, a lot of the similar patterns we saw with the dot.com boom in 1998, 1999, when all these companies said "oh we got to get into Second Life, it's going to be the next big thing." So we had millions of dollars spent on creating advertising sites on Second Life—that's really when the outside SL interests began. But really from the beginning, there has been a large diversity of user-created content. What's more interesting to me though, there's a diversity of community—communities and sub communities of SL that are using it for all kinds of aspects from role-play to game development. You have business applications, science and education applications, and etc. Right now, though, Second Life is in sort of a do-or-die period. It's already proven to be successful on a user aspect. You have about 750,000 [monthly] users. But if you read my blog from a week ago (August 13, 2009), I noted that by Linden Lab's own statistics, most of that activity is from 133,000 users, which is quite small for an online world.

Most of the activity is from a small segment of the Second Life user community. So the big challenge now for Linden Lab as a company and Second Life as an online community is whether it can grow its hard-core user base. There were a lot of initiatives at SLCC [Second Life Community Convention]—a greatly improved viewer interface that looks more intuitive and user friendly and a much more enhanced Web site, which will include even social networking features. So I think it is going to be the big challenge now—if Second Life improves on all these basic aspects that have helped other online role-playing games grow, will Second Life grow as well? The big question to me is still whether the whole concept of a user-created virtual world can go mass market. I hope it can. Most of the big virtual worlds have at least some aspect of user-created content. But with Second Life, you are talking about the whole thing being user created. The challenge with user-created content like you see on YouTube and other user-created content sites is to create enough search tools so you can find cool stuff fairly quickly. Most YouTube videos are crap, and it's like 90% people blathering, old movies or whatever. But there's enough search tools and links and so on, so you can find fairly good stuff within a few minutes. With Second Life, it takes hours and hours. So that is going to be one of the big challenges. So really it is in this do-or-die phase. It's got to grow. That is where everything is riding in my opinion.

Q: What are some examples of successful communities in Second Life?

WJA: I will give you three examples; one is the Japanese-language community. It is gigantic. We are not even fully grasping how large the Japanese community of Second Life is. I think numerically it is about 100,000 or so. The guy who runs Second Life's largest Japanese portal told me that it gets about 15 million page views a month. They are more like Second Life blogs. The Japanese community is very active and if you look at the content, it is really awesome. If you go to Japanese sims, fashion-themed community areas, it is really incredible. With the Asian market in general, online worlds are really huge. So the Japanese are already getting into it. I suggest if they grow, that can make it grow across the rest of Asia.

The education community is really gigantic. I'm really impressed, especially if you go to SLCC, there's people involved in education on all kinds of aspects: people using it to teach or to come up with new teaching tools. So that is another example.

Another one is the role-playing community in Second Life. One of the largest communities in Second Life is around a vampire game called Bloodlines, which by one of the developers' estimate has 28,000 regular users who log into Second Life for this role-playing game. That has caused some controversy because people are so active there—it is like you have to spread the disease of vampirism by biting people.

Q: What are some of the virtual worlds to watch in the near future?

WJA: There are a lot of virtual worlds to watch for all kinds of reasons. Will they be important for Linden Lab and Second Life users to watch? Of course, one of the big ones coming now is Blue Mars. It's made by a company called Avatar Reality. It has a lot of Second Life aspects, including user-created content, but the graphic package is a lot better. It uses what is called the CryEngine which is like the top game engine right now. It doesn't allow dynamic user-created content. Your avatar can't stick its hand out, and make a cube. You have to put it into a developer queue and it must be approved by the company. They have some deals with some large content creators, like there's Syd Mead who did the production design for *Blade Runner* and some other great sci-fi classics. That's an interesting version of Second Life. They are definitely aiming for immediately useable by the average consumer. And I think they intended that most of the people who go on are not going to create content; they are going to go on to enjoy the content. It is sort of going opposite of Second Life's user-created content toward consumer-usable content. Most active users on Second Life are content creators on some level or another. Blue Mars is going the other way around.

Others to watch are virtual words that are connected to social games, like there's one called YoVille. You have to log into Facebook or MySpace to even play it. It's a very simple rudimentary graphic virtual world, but it does have internal e-commerce user-creator content. It's huge—it has nearly 17 million regular players. So it is actually bigger than World of Warcraft.

Another one would be Metaplace. Metaplace is pretty much Second Life, but it is all based on the Web by a really smart game developer named Raph Koster. He's learned a lot from his background as a game developer and he's creating a sort of Second Life-type virtual world. That is also an interesting one to keep an eye on.

Q: How much participation might we anticipate for virtual worlds in the near future?

WJA: As for the whole concept of virtual worlds, we are still in a very early period…I did an analysis of virtual worlds, and it looks like about 1 in 12 people in the U.S. are in a virtual world of some kind which is a good start. It's going to be awhile before any particular virtual world becomes really large and mass market. MMOs like YoVille are bringing in people to virtual worlds who weren't even in virtual worlds until the time they play something like YoVille. I think that is going to expand the market. So that is one to watch.

Wagner James Au's blog *New World Notes* covers issues and events happening in Second Life on a daily basis at http://nwn.blogs.com.

References

Au, W. J. (2009, August 24). Interview, personal communication with author, August 24, 2009.

Au, W. J. (2009, August 13). Stat shock: Just 133K Second Life users responsible for nearly 90% total monthly SL user hours! *New World Notes*. Accessed August 15, 2009, from http://nwn.blogs.com/nwn/2009/08/sl-has-133k-hardcore-users.html/

SECONDARY REFERENCES

Active Worlds. Wikipedia. Accessed June 12, 2009, from http://en.wikipedia.org/wiki/Active_Worlds.

Ahuja, M. K., & Galvin, J. E. (2003). Socialization in virtual groups. *Journal of Management, 29*, 161–185.

Attali, J. (1985). *Noise. The political economy of music.* Minneapolis: University of Minnesota Press.

BBC. (2006, November 6). Big Brother enters virtual world. BBC News. Accessed December 4, 2008, from http://news.bbc.co.uk/2/hi/entertainment/6122140.stm

Breinig, H., & Lösch, K. (2002). Introduction. Difference and transdifference. In H. Breinig, Jürgen Gebhardt & K. Lösch (Eds.), *Multiculturalism in contemporary societies. Perspectives on difference and transdifference* (pp. 11–36), Erlangen: Universitätsbund.

Cage, J. (2005). The future of music: Credo. In C. Cox & D. Warner (Eds.), *Audio culture: Readings in modern music* (pp. 25–28). New York: Continuum. Reprint 1961.

Cassell, J., & Jenkins, H. (1998). *From Barbie to Mortal Kombat: Gender and computer games.* Cambridge, MA: MIT Press.

Castells, M. (2001). *The Internet galaxy: Reflections on the internet, business, and society.* New York: Oxford University Press.

—.(2004). *The network society: A cross-cultural perspective.* Cheltenham, UK: Edward Elgar Publishing.

Current list of universities in second life. (2007, July 25). Second Life Research. Accessed December 15, 2008, from http://www.secondlife.com

Eno, B. (2005). Generating and organizing variety in the arts. In C. Cox & D. Warner (Eds.), *Audio culture. Readings in modern music* (pp. 226-233). New York: Continuum.

Fessenden, H. (1940). *Fessenden, builder of tomorrows.* New York: Coward-McCann.

Filipponio, F. (2006, October 23). Pontiac buying property in Second Life. Accessed from June 12, 2009, from http://www.autoblog.com/2006/10/23/pontiac-buying-property-in-second-life/

Foucault, M., Hurley, R., Faubion, J. D., & Rabinow, P. (2001). Power: Essential works of Foucault, 1954–1984, *Volume III*. New York: New Press.

Gotved, S. (2006). The construction of cybersocial reality. In D. Silver & A. Massanari (Eds.) *Critical Cyberculture Studies* (pp.168–178). New York & London: New York University Press.

Guest, T. (2008). Second Lives: A journey through virtual worlds. New York: Random House.

Habermas, J. (1989/1962). *The structural transformation of the public sphere.* Boston: MA: Beacon Press.

Hall, S. (1996). Introduction: Who needs identity? In S. Hall & P. du Gay (Eds.). *Questions of cultural identity* (pp. 1–17). London: Sage Publications.

Haythornthwaite, C., & Wellman, B. (2002). The Internet in everyday life. NY: Blackwell.

Herman, E.S., & McChesney, R. W. (1997). *The global media: The new missionaries of corporate capitalism.* London, England; Washington, DC: Cassell.

Hlebec, V., Manfreda, K. L., & Vehovar, V. (2006). The social support networks of Internet users. *New Media & Society, 8*, 9–32.

Huffhines, A. (2008, April 1). Philip Linden testifies before Congress. SLNN.com. Accessed December 12, 2008, from http://www.slnn.com/index.php?SCREEN=article &about=philip-linden-before-congress&page=2/

Jenkins, T. L. (1997). Black futurists in the information age. In A. Teich (Ed.) (2002), *Technology and the future*, 9th ed. Belmont, CA: Thomson Wadsworth. Reprint.

Johnson, P. (2006). Hearing transdifference: Sound, strife and sonic processes of cultural negotiation. *Journal for the Study of British Culture 13*(2), 173-185,

Kendall, D. (2000). Social problems in a diverse society. New York: Allyn & Bacon.

Kilbourne, J. (2000). *Can't buy me love: How advertising changes the way we think and feel.*New York: Free Press.

Langman, L. (2005). From virtual public spheres to global justice: A critical theory of Internetworked social movements. *Sociological Theory 23*(1), 42–72.

Levinson, P. (1999). *Digital McLuhan: A guide to the information millennium*. New York: Routledge.

Linden Lab. Corporate Site. Accessed December 26, 2008, from http://lindenlab.com.

Linden Lab. Wikipedia. Accessed December 28, 2008, from http://en.wikipedia.org/wiki/Linden_Lab.

live365. (2009). Accessed June 1, 2009, from http://www.live365.com/

Lopez, F. (2005). Profound listening and environmental sound matter. In C. Cox & D. Warner (Eds.), *Audio culture. Readings in modern music* (pp. 82–87). New York: Continuum.

Marvin, C. (1998) Thinking *about electric communication in the late 19th century*. Oxford: Oxford University Press.

Machinima. Wikipedia. Accessed June 12, 2009, from en.wikipedia.org/wiki/Machinima.

Macnaghten, P. (1998). *Contested natures*. Beverly Hills, CA: Sage.

McLuhan, M. (1962). *The Gutenberg galaxy. The making of typographic man*. New York: New American Library.

——. (1951). The mechanical bride: Folklore of industrial man. New York: Vanguard Press. Reissued by Gingko Press, 2002.

——. (2005)Visual and acoustic space. In C. Cox & D. Warner (Eds.) *Audio culture: Readings in modern music* (pp. 67–72). New York: Continuum. Reprint 1989.

Mesa, A. (2009). Brand avatar: Translating virtual world branding into real world success. New York: Palgrave Macmillan.

Miller, P. D. (2005). Algorithms, Erasures and the art of memory. In C. Cox & D. Warner (Eds.), *Audio culture: Readings in modern music* (pp. 348–354). New York: Continuum.

Online playgrounds: Virtual worlds for children. There is life in virtual reality after all. (2009, July 23). *The Economist*. Accessed August 15, 2009, from http://www.economist.com/businessfinance/displaystory.cfm?story_id=14098380/

Park, S. B. (2005). *The mechanics of online social interaction: How cyberspace and physical territory interplay in Korean computer-mediated communication environments*. An unpublished dissertation, Philadelphia: PA.

Philip Rosedale. Wikipedia. Accessed June 12, 2009, from http://en.wikipedia.org/wiki/Philip_Rosedale.

Radio. Wikipedia. Accessed June 10, 2009, from http://en.wikipedia.org/wiki/Radio

Reuters, A. (2008, March 14). Exclusive—Rosedale to step down as Linden Lab CEO. Accessed March 14, 2008, from http://secondlife.reuters.com/stories/2008/03/14/exclusive-rosedale-to-step-down-as-linden-lab/ceo/.

Reuters, A. (2006, November 6). Virtual reality TV: Big Brother to launch in SL. *Reuters*. Accessed December 3, 2008, from http:// secondlife.reuters.com/stories/2006/11/06/virtual-reality-tv-big-brother-to-launch-in-sl/

Reynolds, I. (2007, November 27). Disabled could think their way around second life. *Reuters*. Access June 2, 2009, from http://www.reuters.com/article/internetNews/idUST29565020071127?feedType=RSS&feedName=internetNews

Rheingold, H. (2002). *Smart mobs: The next social revolution*, Cambridge, MA: Perseus Publishing.

Rosen, C. (2004). The age of egocasting. *The New Atlantis, A Journal of Technology & Society, 7* (Fall 2004/Winter 2005). Accessed September 19, 2007, from http://www.thenewatlantis.com/archive/7/rosenprint.htm/

Rymaszewski, M., & Au, W. J., et al. (2008). *Second Life: The official guide*, 2nd ed. Indianapolis, Indiana: Wiley Publishing, Inc.

Sardar, Z. (1999). Western colonization of the future. In A. Teich, (Ed.) (2002), *Technology and the future*, 9th edition. Belmont, CA: Thomson/Wadsworth. Reprint.

Schafer, R. M. (1977). *Soundscape: Our sonic environment and the tuning of the world*. New York: Knopf.

Schifrin, M. (2007, December 24). Rocking the virtual world. Special Report. *Forbes.com*. Accessed July 19, 2009, from http://www.forbes.com/forbes/2007/1224/103.html

Schwoch, J. (1990). *The American radio industry and its Latin American activities, 1990–1939*. Champaign: University of Illinois Press.

Second Life. Wikipedia. Accessed December 28, 2008, from http://en.wikipedia.org/wiki/Second_Life.

Secondlife.com. Corporate Site. Accessed December 28, 2008, from secondlife.com.

Shoutcast. Web site. Accessed December 21, 2009 from http://www.shoutcast.com/

Small, B. (2004). Online personals and narratives of the self: Australia's RSVP. *Convergence: The Journal of Research into New Media Technologies 10* (1), 93–107.

Slouka, M. (2005). Listening for silence: Notes on the aural life. In C. Cox & Daniel Warner (Eds.) *Audio culture: Readings in modern music* (pp. 40–46). New York: Continuum. Reprint.

Social Network Service. Accessed March 10, 2009, from http://en.wikipedia.org/ wiki/Social_network_service

Sugden, J. (2008, August 13). Universities running in second life. *Times Online*. Accessed December 15, 2008, from http://www.timesonline.co.uk/tol/life_and_style/education/student/article4523668.ece

Tapscott, D. (1998). *Growing up digital: The rise of the net generation*. New York: The McGraw-Hill Companies: http://www.netlibrary.com/

Taylor, T. L. (2006) Play between worlds: Exploring online game culture. Cambridge, MA: The MIT Press.

Terdiman, D. (2004, May 8). Fun in following the money. *Wired Magazine*. Accessed December 15, 2008, from http://en.wikipedia.org/wiki/ Philip_Rosedale#cite_ ref-wiredmagazine-fun-in-following-the-money_2-0.

Terkel, S. (1997). *Working: People talk about what they do all day and how they feel about what they do*. New York: New Press.

Thompson, E. A. (2002). *The soundscape of modernity: Architectural acoustics and the culture of listening in America, 1900–1933*. Boston: MIT Press.

Tubella, I. (2004). Television, the Internet, and the construction of identity. In M. Castells (Ed.), *The network society: A cross-cultural perspective* (pp. 385–401). Cheltenham, UK: Edward Elgar Publishing.

Turkle, S. (2005). The second self: Computers and the human spirit. 20th anniversary edition. Cambridge, MA: MIT Press.

Valdes-Dapena, P. (2006b). Second Life cars: Virtual world has its own economy and its own wheels. CNNMoney.com. Accessed June 21, 2009, from http://money.cnn.com/popups/2006/autos/second_life/index.html.

Varèse, E. (2005). The liberation of sound. In C. Cox & D. Warner (Eds.) *Audio culture: Readings in modern music* (pp. 17–21). New York: Continuum.

Virtual Reality. Wikipedia. Accessed June 12, 2009, from http://en.wikipedia.org/wiki/Virtual_reality.

Wajcman, J. (1991). Feminist perspectives on technology. In A. Teich (Ed.) (2002), *Technology and the future*, 9th edition. Belmont, CA: Thompson/Wadswoth. Reprint.

Walker, J. (2001). *Rebels on the air: An alternative history of radio in America*. New York: New York University Press.

Walsh, T. (2007, October 26). CSI: NY meets "Second Life." *Clickable Culture*. Accessed June 9, 2009, from http://www.secretlair.com/index.php?/clickableculture

Wellman, B. & Gulia M. (1999). Net surfers don't ride alone: Virtual community as community. In B. Wellman (Ed.) *Networks in the global village* (pp. 331–367). Boulder, CO: Westview.

White, B. A. (2007). *Second Life: A guide to your virtual world*. Indianapolis, IN: Que.

Whitty, M. T., & Carr, A. N. (2006). *Cyberspace romance: The psychology of online relationships*. New York: Palgrave Macmillan.

ZiZi, P. (2002). The virtual sphere: The Internet as a public sphere. *New Media & Society*, 4(1, March), 9–27.

Interviews and Personal Communication

Trinidad Anatine. Interview, personal communication with author, July 15, 2009.
Josie Anderton. Interview, personal communication with author, July 7, 2009.
Wagner James Au. Interview, personal communication with author, August 24, 2009.
Jerod Bagley. Interview, personal communication with Nanci Burke. July 24, 2009.
Landis Desidero. Interview, personal communication with author, July 28, 2009.
Robustus Hax. Interview, personal communication with author, August 16, 2009
Faith Hema. Interview, personal communication with author, July 9, 2009.
Draghan Marksman. Interview, personal communication with author, August 14, 2009.
Journey McLaglen. Interview, personal communication with author, August 5, 2009.
Toxic Menges. Interview, personal communication with author, July 15, 2009.
Frolic Mills. Interview, personal communication with author, August 17, 2009
Brody Muircastle. Interview, personal communication with author, July 15, 2009.
Lowe Runo. Interview, personal communication with author, June 13, 2009.
Sher Salmson. Interview, personal communication with author, July 22, 2009.
Alesia Schumann. Interview, personal communication with author, August 12, 2009.
Restless Thor. Interview, personal communication with author, July 21, 2009.
Indea Vaher. Interview, personal communication with author, August 3, 2009.
MyGoshYakan. Interview, person communication with author, July 30, 2009.

INDEX

A

B

C

D

E

F

Digital Formations

General Editor: **Steve Jones**

Digital Formations is an essential source for critical, high-quality books on digital technologies and modern life. Volumes in the series break new ground by emphasizing multiple methodological and theoretical approaches to deeply probe the formation and reformation of lived experience as it is refracted through digital interaction. **Digital Formations** pushes forward our understanding of the intersections—and corresponding implications—between the digital technologies and everyday life. The series emphasizes critical studies in the context of emergent and existing digital technologies.

Other recent titles include:

Felicia Wu Song
Virtual Communities: Bowling Alone, Online Together

Edited by Sharon Kleinman
The Culture of Efficiency: Technology in Everyday Life

Edward Lee Lamoureux, Steven L. Baron, & Claire Stewart
Intellectual Property Law and Interactive Media: Free for a Fee

Edited by Adrienne Russell & Nabil Echchaibi
International Blogging: Identity, Politics and Networked Publics

Edited by Don Heider
Living Virtually: Researching New Worlds

Edited by Judith Burnett, Peter Senker & Kathy Walker
The Myths of Technology: Innovation and Inequality

Edited by Knut Lundby
Digital Storytelling, Mediatized Stories: Self-representations in New Media

Theresa M. Senft
Camgirls: Celebrity and Community in the Age of Social Networks

Edited by Chris Paterson & David Domingo
Making Online News: The Ethnography of New Media Production